Social deviance
A substantive analysis

THE DORSEY SERIES IN SOCIOLOGY

Editor

Robin M. Williams, Jr. *Cornell University*

Social deviance
A substantive analysis

ROBERT R. BELL

Professor of Sociology
Temple University and
Latrobe University (Australia)

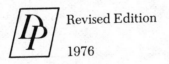 Revised Edition

1976

THE DORSEY PRESS Homewood, Illinois 60430
Irwin-Dorsey International London, England WC2H 9NJ
Irwin-Dorsey Limited Georgetown, Ontario L7G 4B3

Revised Edition

First Printing, January 1976

ISBN 0-256-01663-1
Library of Congress Catalog Card No. 75-22683
Printed in the United States of America

To my wife, PHYLLIS,
who is my partner in all that matters

Preface

During the five years since I wrote the First Edition many changes have occurred in American society. These changes have made some substantive areas treated in the first edition no longer of great relevance. This was true of three chapters, "Abortion," "Militant Students," and "The Hippie Movement," all of which have been dropped from this edition. I have added two new chapters: Chapter 8, "Suicide," and Chapter 10, "Venereal Disease." These seemed to be two substantive areas of social deviance worthy of analysis. In the remaining chapters I have updated and added some new interpretations. Some chapters have been greatly altered while others have been changed very little.

December 1975   ROBERT R. BELL

Contents

chapter one

The conceptual approach

A major interest of American sociology in its early days was the social problems of those days. The early American sociologists looked around in the rapidly developing urban areas and saw what they felt were many undesirable patterns of behavior. Often their interest was not in why the problems existed, but rather in attempts to eliminate the problems. It was common for many early sociologists actually to be involved in various types of social reform, frequently with little knowledge about what they wanted to reform.

Around the beginning of the 20th century, as American sociology developed, most sociologists came from rural backgrounds and were concerned with the new urban influences and the new patterns of urban social behavior. As Mills has pointed out, most of the social problems of that period arose because of the deterioration of certain traditional values in the urban environment. Those values could only flourish in a relatively homogeneous and primarily rural environment. Therefore, the early "problems" discussed typically concerned urban behavior, and even when rural problems were discussed they were seen as the result of urban encroachment. So the early sociologists quite often viewed the disorganizational characteristic of social problems as "merely the absence of that *type* of organization associated with the stuff of primary-group communities having Christian and Jeffersonian legitimations.[1] In general it may be said that the traditional idea of a social problem emerged initally as an attitude of middle-class reformers around the end of the 18th century and the beginning of the 19th century. This idea resulted not only from

---

[1] C. Wright Mills, "The Professional Ideology of Social Pathologists," in Mark Lefton, James K. Skipper, Jr., and Charles H. McCaghy, *Approaches to Deviance* (New York: Appleton-Century-Crofts, 1968), p. 15.

the stresses created by the new urban industrial order but also from a new scientific ideology and a growing humanitarianism.[2]

In the early part of the 20th century sociological interest started to shift away from social reform. More and more sociologists began to study social problems as sociological problems. This meant that the problems were studied with increasing objectivity and with lessening concern for directed social change.

During the 1930s the interest of sociologists shifted increasingly away from the study of social problems and social movements. This interest began to lie in a systematic approach to the analysis of social and cultural sources of deviant behavior. It was argued that "the sociological task was to explain variations in rates of deviant behavior, not its incidence, and functional theory emerged as a means of explanation."[3] Even where the interest in social problems continued over the years, not only did the approach change, but also the substantive areas that were considered to be social problems. Any substantive area can be seen as a social problem only when it is related to a given society at a given point in time. "A look through the textbooks in the field over so short a period as the last 25 or 30 years would be enough to demonstrate that there is no necessary continuation in any of the subjects covered. Several decades ago poverty was the dominant theme, and today it is discussed briefly or has disappeared altogether."[4] The above statement, written in 1963, itself shows how rapidly what is of interest as a social problem changes, because today poverty is once again a social problem area of importance to sociologists.

Often in the past no theoretical perspective was developed and used in the study of social problems. This was especially true in the writing of textbooks, in which the author would begin with an introductory chapter that defined social problems, their alleged causes and cures, their extent, and so forth. The rest of the text would be a series of distinct chapters dealing with social problems but not conceptually related to one another in any fashion. Whenever a theoretical approach was developed it tended to be related to a social disorganization model. The social disorganizational approach looked at the harmonious and inharmonious aspects of the structure of society. It looked at the ways in which basic activities in the organization of a society were either mutually reinforcing or mutually contradictory. "Social disorganization may then be conceptualized in terms of some conflicts among norms and values in a society. Social disorganization deals with ways in which activities which are in some

---

[2] Jessie Bernard, *Social Problems at Mid-Century* (New York: Dryden Press, 1957), pp. 90–91.

[3] Albert J. Reiss, "The Study of Deviant Behavior: Where the Action Is," in Lefton, Skipper and McCaghy, *Approaches to Deviance*, pp. 56–57.

[4] William Petersen and David Matza, *Social Controversy* (Belmont, Calif.: Wadsworth, 1963), p. 3.

sense the product of, and legitimized by, the social structure conflict with one another."[5]

One of the problems with the disorganizational approach is that when it is applied to deviant behavior it tends to overvalue conformity, implicitly if not explicitly. "There is a kind of halo around conformity and almost any kind of nonconformity tends to be viewed as a problem."[6] Of course, given certain values in a society, disorganization might be seen in a desirable goal. For social organization, as well as for social disorganization, stress may be generated. For example, the stress in social organization "may be exploitative, characterized by gross inequities that create the stresses of poverty and illness in a disenfranchised class."[7]

Whatever the theoretical explanation given to social problems, a social problem is in part the result of a discrepancy between the values of a society and the actual state of that society. Therefore, a primary motive for the study of social problems has been to look for ways to prevent, control, and ameliorate them. Basically social problems can be said to exist when they are defined as such by members of a society. Initially this may be done by intellectuals, social scientists, or policymakers, but eventually the definition must be accepted by at least one broad stratum of society. This clearly implies that underlying each social problem there is generally a difference of opinion or a clash of values.[8]

Jessie Bernard has suggested that three types of criteria were used in the past to determine whether or not a given stress situation was judged to be a social problem.[9] The three types were:

1. *Humanitarian-sentimental.* Does the situation cause pain or suffering? Suffering is intrinsically bad, and therefore anything which produces it should be changed, reformed, or done away with. However, the absence of suffering does not necessarily imply the absence of a social problem.

2. *Utilitarian.* A stress situation confronting some members of a society is a social problem because it imposes costs on the rest of the society, either official, in the form of taxes, or unofficial, in the form of voluntary contributions. Often in the past anything which was defined as interfering with business or disturbing the peace was viewed as a social problem. Within this context sickness would be considered a social problem, not because it causes pain or suffering, but because it slows down production or because it costs the taxpayer money.

3. *Dysfunctionality.* Anything that threatens a group, a nation, a

---

[5] Ralph H. Turner, "Value-Conflict in Social Disorganization," in Lefton, Skipper and McCaghy, *Approaches to Deviance*, p. 24.

[6] Bernard, *Social Problems*, p. 139.

[7] Ibid.

[8] Petersen and Matza, *Social Controversy*, p. 2.

[9] Bernard, *Social Problems*, pp. 105–6.

society, or a culture constitutes a social problem. The threat that constitutes the social problem exists within the group and is not something outside it.

It is clear that these types of criteria have a limited application to what might be defined as social problems today. They represent a simplified cause and effect view of social problems that often existed in the past.

By the 1950s the concern with social problems as traditionally studied had lost prestige and interest among most American sociologists. To a great extent this was due to the scientific view of sociology that emerged in the 1930s and reached its peak following the end of World War II. Jessie Bernard represents the approach of the scientific sociologist toward the traditional study of social problems. She writes that so long as those who studied social problems "substituted moralistic judgments for careful observations and interpretations, they could not be scientific. So long as they assumed answers instead of looking for them, they were not scientific. So long as their terminology reflected a condemnatory attitude toward people, they were not scientific."[10]

Clinard has suggested that prior to the 1950s American sociologists probably had comparatively little difficulty in dealing with the concept of deviance. Deviance was taken as given, in a way suggesting that everyone agreed that certain behavior was either abnormal or deviant. "Obviously everyone was agreed that 'deviance' was delinquency, *all* crimes (generally lower-class crime, however), prostitution, homosexual behavior, mental disorder, drunkenness and alcoholism, illegal drug usage, and suicide."[11]

Many of the areas that historically have been treated as social problems have come to represent a number of the important substantive areas of sociological specialization today—delinquency, criminology, minority groups, problem areas of the family, and so forth. In the broadest sense social problems came to be distinguished from other types of problems by their close connection with moral values and social institutions. Merton points out that "they are social in the sense that they pertain to human relationships and to the normative contexts in which all human relationships exist. They are problems in the sense that they represent interruptions in the expected or desired scheme of things; violations of the right or the proper as a society defines these qualities; dislocations in the social patterns and relationships that a society cherishes."[12] The modern argument has been that sociologists should study social problems in the same way that they study other forms of human behavior. "As a scientist,

---

[10] Ibid., p. 117.

[11] Marshall G. Clinard, *Sociology of Deviant Behavior*, 4th ed. (New York: Holt, Rinehart and Winston, 1974), p. 11.

[12] Robert K. Merton and Robert A. Nisbet, *Contemporary Social Problems* (New York: Harcourt, Brace and World, 1961), p. 4.

the sociologist has a professional responsibility to deal with such matters as crime, suicide, narcotics, and ethnic tensions" in the same way as he approaches the rest of society.[13]

The belief has also developed that social problems should be studied not only for what they shed in the way of insight on themselves, but also for what they may contribute to the better understanding of the rest of society. This belief is based on the assumption that social problems, even the worst of them, generally have a functional relationship to the rest of society. For example, many have suggested that even prostitution exists only as a reflection of the value that is placed on the monogamous family and the sanctity of marriage. In fact it may be argued that all social problems have some value to society even if it is nothing more than providing careers for those who deal with or attempt to eliminate the social problems. This suggests an irony in that those who supposedly work the hardest to eliminate a social problem often have the most to lose if they are successful. For example, what would happen to the Federal Narcotics Bureau if there were no more illegal narcotics users?

Ultimately any study of social problems can be understood only in light of what a society holds to be right and proper. "At bottom, social problems are problems of moral value; they are problems because the behavior involved in these breakdowns and deviations is widely regarded as immoral, illegal, or potentially destructive of some established institution."[14] But basically the social problem approach has lost its utility in sociology because it has not provided a theoretical framework for understanding what constitutes social deviance and what the interrelationships are between the areas of social deviance and the rest of society. Because of the drawbacks between the traditional social problems approach a new perspective has emerged since the 1950s—although its roots go much further back.

THE SOCIAL DEVIANCE APPROACH

In the 1950s and 1960s there developed in American sociology a rapidly increasing interest in the study of deviance.[15] To a great extent this new

---

[13] Ibid., p. 9.

[14] Ibid., p. 11.

[15] See: Howard S. Becker, *Outsiders: Studies in the Sociology of Deviance* (New York: Macmillan, 1963); Howard S. Becker, *The Other Side: Perspectives on Deviance* (New York: Free Press, 1964); Marshall B. Clinard, ed., *Anomie and Deviant Behavior* (New York: Free Press, 1964); Albert K. Cohen, *Deviance and Control* (Englewood Cliffs, N.J.: Prentice-Hall, 1966); Robert A. Dentler, and Kai T. Erikson, "The Functions of Deviance in Groups," *Social Problems*, 7 (Fall 1959), pp. 98–107; Kai T. Erikson, *Wayward Puritans: A Study in the Sociology of Deviance* (New York: Wiley, 1966); Jack P. Gibbs, "Conceptions of Deviant Behavior: The Old and the New," *Pacific Sociological Review*, Spring 1966; Edwin Lemert, Jr., *Human Deviance, Social Problems, and Social Control* (Englewood Cliffs, N.J.: Prentice-Hall, 1967); David Matza, *Delinquency and Drift*

interest was due to a dissatisfaction with the previous definitions of social problems and the previous attempts to explain deviant behavior. Social deviance has been defined as "behavior which violates institutionalized expectations, that is, expectations which are shared and recognized as legitimate within the social system."[16] This definition suggests that deviant behavior is a reflection of how persons perform and of the structure of the groups within which they perform. In other words deviance has both an individual and a group perspective, although the usual pattern for analysis is to look at the interaction of deviants within a social setting. A somewhat different way of defining deviance is to say that it refers to behavior by an individual to which the group responds with the feeling of danger, embarrassment, or irritation, bringing "special sanctions to bear against the person who exhibits it."[17] Erikson makes the important point that "deviance is not a property *inherent* in any particular kind of behavior, it is a property *conferred upon* that behavior by the people who come into direct contact with it."[18] For example, if one uses a narcotic he is not a deviant simply because he has taken the drug. If the drug is given to him in a hospital for medical treatment, taking the drug is not defined as deviance, but if the drug is given to him by an illegal "pusher" it is.

The notion of deviance is implicit in the very idea of society. This point was made many years ago by Durkheim and has been accepted by sociologists ever since. Durkheim wrote, "Imagine a society of saints, a perfect cloister of exemplary individuals. Crimes, properly so called, will there be unknown; but faults which appear venial to the layman will create there the same scandal that the ordinary offense does in the ordinary consciousness."[19] As David Matza points out, the moral improvement of a society will not in itself diminish deviation since the very fact of moral uplift will suggest new and more demanding standards of conduct.[20] For example, in Victorian England social morality reached new levels of "purity"—but that simply meant that one was defined as "impure" for doing much less than during an earlier or later period.

Sociology has made several major contributions to the study of deviance. One is that "persistent deviance typically is not an individual or group innovation, it has a history in particular locales."[21] This means that

---

(New York: Wiley, 1964); David Matza, *Becoming Deviant* (New York: Prentice-Hall, 1969); Hyman Rodman, "The Lower-Class Value Stretch," *Social Forces*, 42 (1960), pp. 205–15; Earl Rubington and Martin S. Weinberg, *Deviance: The Interactionist Perspective* (New York: Macmillan, 1968); and Leslie T. Wilkins, *Social Deviance* (Englewood Cliffs, N.J.: Prentice-Hall, 1964).

[16] Dentler and Erikson, "Functions of Deviance," p. 98.

[17] Erikson, *Wayward Puritans*, p. 6.

[18] Ibid.

[19] Emile Durkheim, *The Rules of Sociological Method* (Chicago: University of Chicago Press, 1938), pp. 68–69.

[20] Matza, *Becoming Deviant*, p. 13.

[21] Matza, *Delinquency and Drift*, p. 63.

many areas responsible for deviance have existed for some time and have contributed to a history and to certain systems of deviant behavior. The time factor is an important influence on social deviance because when deviance persists it often becomes patterned (although not all deviance is systematic, nor is all systematic deviance socially organized). There may be systematic individual deviance where there is no interaction among the participants. That is, many deviant patterns are practiced by solitary individuals. For example, transvestites follow similar patterns but do not usually interact with one another.

Another major contribution to the study of deviance by sociologists has been suggested by Howard Becker. He argues that the new approach to the study of deviance always involves an interactional process between at least two kinds of people: "those who commit (or are said to have committed) a deviant act and the rest of society, perhaps divided into several groups itself. The two groups are seen in complementary relationship. One cannot exist without the other; indeed, they are functions of one another in the strict mathematical sense."[22] This view clearly suggests the possible development of subcultures, a concept which will be discussed later in the chapter. The new approach differs from the earlier sociological concern with social pathology, where deviance was seen as direct evidence of social disorganization.

The new approach to deviance generally follows the model of the scientific approach, rather than that of the earlier value commitment or the commitment to directed social change. David Matza defines this approach in terms of neutrality. He writes that "neutrality, buttressed as it is by the philosophy of science, is the sentiment toward deviant phenomena commended by most contemporary sociologists. We are to empathize with neither the correctional enterprise nor its deviant subjects."[23]

The new approach to the study of deviance has several research implications. First, the researcher is dependent to a high degree on what members of deviant groups give him in the way of information and insight. Because the deviant is often engaged in an illegal activity he must be careful to protect himself. Therefore, the deviant's misleading of the researcher may be a real problem in the study of deviant phenomena. As Matza points out, since "authority may frequently intervene to counteract or arrest the deviant tendency, deviant persons must frequently be devious."[24] In other words deviousness is a part of the pattern of much deviance, and being devious in the presence of outsiders may be seen as a normal characteristic of persons participating in deviant phenomena. [25]

Second, the new stress on deviance means that at least some new

---

[22] Becker, *Outsiders*, p. 2.
[23] Matza, *Becoming Deviant*, p. 37.
[24] Ibid., p. 39.
[25] Ibid.

questions are being asked in research. In the past, whenever it was possible to identify the deviant individuals making up a social problem area the research tended to concentrate on the question of cause. For example, in the areas of criminal behavior the overwhelming concern in the past was to find out why some people become criminals while others do not. With attention "almost exclusively focused on the underlying forces pushing individuals into deviance there is relatively little consideration of just *what* the deviance itself is. Indeed, various specific forms of deviance are often viewed as being caused by the same underlying forces."[26] It will be seen in the presentation of most of the research in the chapters ahead that the focus of study in deviance has been much less concerned with *causes* and much more with the *consequences* of deviance for both deviants and the broader society.

In the discussion that follows much of what is said has been drawn from the thinking of those who represent the new approach to the study of deviance that has developed since the mid-1950s. Our interest will be in looking at the meaning of deviance, the relationships of deviance with the rest of society, some legal aspects of deviance, and the concept of deviant subcultures.

MEANINGS OF DEVIANCE

First of all, a distinction must be made between deviant behavior on the level of social interaction and deviant behavior of basically an individual or psychological nature. A person who believes he is being injured by the magical practices of his associates would be diagnosed as a psychotic and paranoiac if he lived in a university community. However, if he were a member of a group which believed in magical practices his belief in magic might be entirely expected and normal. In fact, if he did not share the general belief in magic he might be thought of as deviant by his associates.[27] The above illustrates the cultural relativity of social versus individual deviance. Of course, some forms of deviance are almost always deviant and almost always individual in all societies (for example, incest).

There may also be groupings of individual deviants who do not interact socially. For example, most transvestites share a particular sexual orientation and may have similar behavior patterns, but unless they interact socially in some symbolic ways they are not social group deviants. It does not appear to be common for transvestites to have any great influence on one another through social interaction. Therefore, they would most accurately be defined as individual deviants who make up a statistical category called transvestites.

[26] Edwin M. Schur, *Crimes without Victims: Deviant Behavior and Public Policy* (Englewood Cliffs, N.J.: Prentice-Hall, 1965), p. 2.

[27] Alfred R. Lindesmith and Anselm L. Strauss, *Social Psychology* (New York: Dryden Press, 1956), p. 665.

What does the term *deviance* imply? It probably suggests a number of different meanings, depending on the respondent. Possibly the simplest and most common definition of deviance is a statistical one, that is, anything that varies too far from the average in society, is defined as "deviant." Put another way, what is defined as "normal" is frequently what is statistically average. As Simmons points out, "This is the basis of most psychological tests. If you fall near the average you're okay; if you fall too far from it you're not."[28]

Thus, deviance implies some straying from certain patterns or norms. People may be classified as straying on the basis of a number of criteria. For example, "the clarity of the path, the distance from the path, the auspices under which the path is constructed or commended, whether one strays from the path in isolation or in company, the penalty, the motives, commonly imputed for straying and so forth."[29] Yet, given the complexities in defining paths of deviance when all is said and done, "we inevitably return to the wise observation that there are many kinds of deviance and that deviance is in some measure a matter of degree."[30]

As previously suggested, it is important to keep in mind that there is always some deviance in society. Complete deviance or complete conformity represent "ideal" types at either end of a continuum, and in no society is either extreme ever achieved. Somewhere between the extremes in a society is the range of tolerance acceptable to the society. This allows for some deviance being acceptable to society but sets up limits beyond which social and often legal punishments are the consequence of deviance. For example, the drinking of alcoholic beverages is acceptable to society so long as the drinking does not go beyond a certain point—a point seen as threatening in some way to society.

It might also be added that not only does society define some deviance as acceptable, but it may even take some satisfaction in the deviance it tolerates. Sagarin has suggested that in the United States there is often pride in tolerating nonconformity. Provided that the nonconformist "operates within certain socially stipulated limits, the nonconformist is almost glorified; however, when he goes outside these limits, he is pilloried."[31] Given this kind of acceptance, Sagarin suggests that when some kinds of deviance are glorified by society this may arouse in other deviants the hope that they too may become a part of the mainstream of society, "if not by becoming conformists themselves, then by forcing a redefinition of their deviant characteristics as acceptable conformity."[32]

Often the extent and the nature of society's reactions toward deviants

[28] J. L. Simmons, *Deviants* (Berkeley, Calif.: Glendessary Press, 1969), p. 21.

[29] Matza, *Becoming Deviant*, p. 10.

[30] Ibid.

[31] Edward Sagarin, *Odd Man In: Societies of Deviants in America* (Chicago: Quadrangle, 1969), p. 240.

[32] Ibid.

will be determined by how the deviant presents himself to society. That is, often among any given group of deviants there is a range of possibilities as to how a given deviant may present himself. This will be reflected in the particular patterns of behavior he follows in his deviance. For example, a homosexual male may live with one partner for several years, circulate with other discreet homosexuals in a circumscribed way, and not fit the stereotype of homosexual social "traits." By contrast another homosexual may center his life in the public places of homosexuality, aggressively seek out new sex partners, and make it known to the broader society that he is a homosexual. In these two cases it is how one presents his homosexual "self" to the broader society that determines how he will be seen. The amount of interaction and the number of others involved in a deviant activity is not simply a uniform function of a type of deviance. So in many types of deviance the individual has some choice in selecting behavior patterns that will determine the extent to which the broader society knows of his deviance.

Some deviants bring attention to their behavior by denouncing themselves to the broader society. The deviant usually does this by shouting out that he has sinned and wants to repent. This serves the important function of reaffirming the validity and "rightness" of the norms of society. For example, contrast the social reactions to two unmarried pregnant girls: one of them says that she has done wrong and is sorry she is pregnant; the other says that she is glad she is pregnant, will have her baby, and has no intention of getting married. In the first case the girl is saying that the social values are right and that she is wrong and regrets her action. The second girl is saying that the social values are not right for her and that she is not sorry for what she did. As another illustration, society can accept deviant acts that are seen as those of sick people because such acts leave the values and norms intact—the people who commit them are seen as not responsible for their actions, and the assumption is that if they were not sick they would abide by the values and norms. In general a society will accept deviance when deviance does not threaten the norms and values held to be important.

It would also appear that for many people some deviance has a mysterious quality—a quality of the unknown, the strange, and sometimes the exotic. For example, even though most Americans have been saturated by the mass media with the marijuana phenomenon they still know little about it factually, but rather respond within the context of the unknown and mysterious. This means that often a relatively few persons are functionally able to define what deviance is, and when the mass media go along with their definitions the few often become the unquestioned definers for the majority. It would appear that some forms of deviance become less defined as deviance as they get to be better known and understood in society. As a result such behavior or attitudes may shift from being defined as deviant to being defined as irregularity. "This is why premarital sex is no longer considered deviant in most quarters and why the acceptance of marijuana as a mild intoxicant is becoming widespread. But as long as something remains deviant most people will know little of it, and as long as people don't know, it is likely to remain deviant."[33]

Frequently what is defined as deviance, as well as the kinds of definitions that go with the behavior, is a result of social class or power differences in society. For example, it is often the welfare worker who defines for the poor, the physician who defines for the woman wanting an abortion, or the priest who defines for the woman seeking birth control help. Inherent in the thinking about many areas of deviance is the assumption that some persons are better able to decide for others than those other persons are able to decide for themselves. This is a kind of "playing God" syndrome which is very often based, not on fact but on subjective evaluation and the power to control or influence the deviant. This also helps to explain why the deviant is very often hostile to those in power—he is being treated like a child and told what would be better for him.

In American society it is difficult to clearly determine what deviance really is. In part this is due to the strength and influence of those who define behavior as deviant. Often those with strong moral beliefs are strongly committed to defining deviance as they see it. But morality is like deviance in that it is relative to time and place. "Moral meanings are constructed, negotiated, hammered out in an interactive process. Rather than being absolute, morality tends to be abstracted, situated, made to fit our everday experience."[34] Sometimes the moralist becomes an absolutist in defining deviance. The absolutist believes that, regardless of time and social context, some "high" values allow us to detect and define deviance. "The absolutist believes that he knows what really *is*, what people *should be* and what constitutes full and appropriate development. In the case of suicide, for example, he believes that life is obviously and almost always better than death."[35]

Because there is never universal agreement on what deviance is, there is always a potential for conflict. People look at the world from angles influenced by slightly different value systems, and often what becomes the prevailing view of what is right is determined not by any evaluation of "rightness," but rather by the power to impose rewards and punishments related to what one defines as right. Even when there is no conflict, people vary by different reference groups, and therefore the definition of

---

[33] Simmons, *Deviants.*, pp. 8–9.

[34] Clinard, *Deviant Behavior*, p. 14.

[35] John Lofland, *Deviance and Identity* (Englewood Cliffs, N.J.: Prentice-Hall, 1969), pp. 23–24.

deviance is generally relative and subjective. As a result different judges often react very differently to the same behavior. As Simmons points out, "Everyone, square or hip, straight or criminal, is outraged by something."[36]

Basically the ultimate measure of whether or not an act is deviant depends on how those who are socially significant in power and influence define the act. No act would be deviant in its social consequences if no elements of society reacted to it. And in any given society what the response to an act will be is always problematic. Those who commit deviance must do so in a social setting in which their behavior will be defined as such if there are to be real social consequences to that behavior.

It is clear that there is a high level of relativity to what will be defined as deviance and to the sanctions that will go with the definitions. It is always important to keep in mind that what will be defined as deviance will vary by time and place. One reason for differences in response to deviance over time is that a society will on some occasions direct its attention to some forms of deviance but not other forms. This is seen in the various attentions directed over time to gambling, drug use, homosexuality, and so forth. Differences in the responses to deviance may also be determined by who commits the act and who has been defined as being harmed. For example, the middle class often defines as juvenile delinquents lower-class boys but not middle-class boys, although the behavior of both groups may be the same. Still another variation in defining deviance may be due to the consequences of an act. A girl is generally not strongly condemned for having premarital sexual experiences; however, if she gets pregnant she may be subjected to strong punishment.

Clinard has suggested that deviance is a valuable sensitizing concept. The concept guides our examination of empirical cases in which norms have been violated and helps us to avoid taking universal positions about norms or making psychological assumptions using such terms as *abnormal* or *maladjusted.* Sensitizing concepts are quite consistent with a social order, such as present-day American society, which emphasizes fluidity, differences between the norms of groups, and the ability of the actor to reshape his environment.[37]

From the previous discussion it is clear that deviance is a "naming process." That is, regardless of the act the behavior must be defined as deviant by some important or significant elements of society. However, the person who is defined as a deviant may or may not define himself in the same way. The relationship between deviance and the broader society is a basic one. It has sometimes been assumed that if the broader society

---

[36] Simmons, *Deviants,* p. 19.
[37] Clinard, *Deviant Behavior,* p. 27.

defines persons as deviants then they are deviants. While this may be true for the broader society it is not necessarily true from the perspective of those defined as deviants. The deviants may not accept the definitions applied to them, or they may define themselves as deviant for different reasons.

The "naming process" has been incorporated into the attempt to explain deviance in terms of labeling theory. Essentially the labeling approach sees the individual as acting to fit the way in which he is defined. For example, the boy who hears himself defined as a delinquent acts according to that definition. The stress on labels means that the interest in deviance is not on how deviance comes about but rather on the consequences of being defined as deviant. The labeling point of view grew out of the widespread recognition that labels are not applied randomly throughout the population of those who break rules. To illustrate: not all juveniles who break rules are labeled delinquents—often the label is applied to rule breakers in the lower class but not in the middle class. Another problem with the labeling approach is that many people who commit deviant acts over a long period of time are never apprehended or labeled. "Certainly by far the majority of persons who are deviant are not labeled, whether their acts involve stealing, homosexual behavior, comarital relations, marijuana use, drunken driving, or crimes committed by businessmen or politicians."[38]

From the point of view of the broader society deviance is what that society defines as such and not something inherent in particular values and patterns. Erikson has pointed out that at any given time "the 'worse' people in the community are considered its criminals, the 'sickest' its patients, no matter how serious these conditions may appear according to some universal standard."[39] Therefore, it is not the forms of behavior per se that distinguish deviants from nondeviants: "it is the response of the conventional and conforming members of the society who identify and interpret behavior as deviant which sociologically transforms persons into deviants."[40] The deviant is one to whom that label has been applied successfully; deviant behavior is what people label as such.[41] Erikson writes:

> From a sociological standpoint, deviance can be defined as conduct which is generally thought to require the attention of social control agencies—that is, conduct about which "something should be done." Deviance is not a property *inherent* in certain forms of behavior; it is the property conferred upon these forms by the audiences which directly or indirectly witness them. Sociologically, then, the critical variable in the study of

[38] Ibid., p. 25.

[39] Erikson, *Wayward Puritans*, p. 26.

[40] John I. Kitsuse, "Societal Reaction to Deviant Behavior: Problems of Theory and Method," in Becker, *Other Side*, p. 88.

[41] Becker, *Outsiders*, p. 9.

deviance is the social audience rather than the individual person, since it is
the audience which eventually decides whether or not any given action or
actions will become a visible case of deviation.[42]

Closely related to the definitions of deviance, and often even implied
in the definitions, are the attempts to define its causes. In the Western
world the oldest and most common view of the causes of deviance has
been one of individual pathology. That is, the something wrong exists in
the deviant individual. In an early day the deviant was thought to be
possessed of devils, while later on he was believed to have genetic defects.
Because his "problem" was seen as inside him, it was generally believed
that little could be done for him. He was punished, destroyed, or
removed from the rest of society. Under the biological or genetic interpretation of deviance it was believed that something inherent in the deviant
set him apart from the nondeviant. For example, from Lombroso to the
present, criminals have been defined as biologically distinctive in one way
or another. However, in recent decades the explanations of the causes of
deviance have for the most part shifted from genetic explanations to
explanations based on illness. That is, the view of the deviant has moved
from seeing him as morally or biologically defective to seeing him as
having psychological incapacities. This has meant that often society has
shifted its views of how deviants should be dealt with from punishment
to treatment.

It would seem clear that deviance cannot be explained on any simple
cause and effect basis because it represents a diverse phenomenon with
complex causes. "Sometimes there is a biological anomaly, sometimes a
disrupted home, sometimes bad companions, sometimes too little legitimate opportunity, sometimes too much pressure, and so on."[43] In discussing the various areas of deviance in the chapters ahead an attempt
will be made to look at some of the casual suggestions, and in general it
will be seen that a number of causal explanations are given for some areas
of deviance.

Before leaving the discussion about causes of deviance it is necessary to
indicate the possible effects of the mass media. It seems clear that the
amount of exposure that the mass media, and especially television, give to
almost any activity influences how it will be viewed and the importance
that will be attached to it. For example, in recent years the hippies were
undoubtedly made to be socially "important" to a great extent by the
mass media. By 1967 every major magazine and newspaper in the United
States had devoted space to the hippie phenomenon. This was also true of
radio and television. The possible influences of mass media coverage on

---

[42] Kai T. Erikson, "Notes on the Sociology of Deviance," in Becker, *Other Side*,
pp. 10–11.

[43] Simmons, *Deviants*, p. 51.

the many different kinds of social deviance will be discussed in connection with our examination of some of the specific deviances.

Just as there are many theories attempting to explain the causes of social deviance, so too there are many attempts to suggest what might be done to cure social deviance. It is almost always the case that when cures are suggested the assumption has been made that a cure is needed. That is, one might assume that the first level of consideration would be to find out whether a cure in an area is needed—but this is rarely ever a serious consideration. Often the deviant also assumes without serious question that a "cure" is needed. When the deviant agrees to the cure recommended for him he is agreeing with the definer who has designated him as a deviant needing help. For example, when a homosexual seeks out psychiatric help to rid himself of his homosexuality he is in effect agreeing with those who have defined him as a deviant. "There is a consensus between the designator and the deviant; his dependence confirms the norm."[44]

As suggested earlier, most views of the causes of deviance are on the personal rather than the social level. Therefore, most suggestions for cures are aimed at individual alteration rather than at social change. As Wilkins points out, "If one takes the view that crime is identical with sin it is likely that one will restrict one's thinking to remedial measures affecting only the individual."[45] Therefore, most curative theories follow the lines of trying to affect the individual, through force, medical treatment, or education.

A common view of individual responsibility for deviance is that the deviant is willfully aggressive against the norms of society or is too weak to follow the norms that most people do. If the deviant is willfully aggressive, for example, commits criminal acts, his treatment will generally be punishment and imprisonment. On the other hand, if he is a drug addict, which often means that he is defined as a weak-willed individual, he will be treated in a repressive manner. He is therefore not allowed to have legal drugs, and he must then seek them out through illegal sources. Thus, one possible consequence of the "cure" of not allowing him to get legal drugs is to intensify his deviance. He is placed in a position where it will probably be necessary for him to resort to deceit and crime in order to support his drug habit. His drug behavior "is a consequence of the public reaction to the deviance rather than a consequence of the inherent qualities of the deviant act."[46]

It is often very hard for many Americans to accept the fact that for many social problems there are no real cures. This is in part due to the

---

[44] Joseph R. Gusfield, "On Legislation Morals: The Symbolic Process of Designating Deviance," *California Law Review*, January 1968, p. 60.

[45] Leslie T. Wilkins, *Social Deviance*, p. 73.

[46] Becker, *Outsiders*, pp, 34–35.

belief that American "know-how" can find a solution to almost anything. This belief explains why many Americans willingly turn to all sorts of "quacks"—many believe that those who say they have a solution must have one because these Americans believe that there "should be" a solution. People are often attracted to a simplistic view of how to resolve problems. This is reflected in such things as *Reader's Digest* articles, "Dear Abby" columns, and television commercials. People are constantly being told about new "miracle drugs" that never reach the market, to "stand firm and your children will respect you," or that all their dating problems can be solved by using a new deodorant. But cures to social problems may be nonexistent or very complex; rarely are they simple. It may also be that some cures work only for some people; for example, Alcoholics Anonymous works for some but not all alcoholics. In actual fact it may be that the passage of time "cures" more deviance than any psychological or social programs.

Generally the assumption is made that if a cure can be found, and can be applied successfully, then the problem will be solved. However, it sometimes happens that when one problem is alleviated or cured, that very success may contribute to the emergence of a new problem. For example, one problem in the United States has been the second-class status of the woman. As this has changed and she has achieved greater rights as a human being, the rights have not always been in areas she would define as desirable. That is, not only did she achieve opportunities for education and occupation closer to those of the man, but she also achieved greater opportunities to become a drug addict or an alcoholic. Clearly, one important question in looking at the cures of social problems or deviance is what the consequences of success are.

DEVIANCE AND THE COMMUNITY

It has been stressed that deviance is common to all societies, but that what is acceptable is not inherent in an activity but rather dependent on how society views that activity. Deviant behavior is therefore common and natural to a society and is a "normal and inevitable part of social life, as is its denunciation, regulation, and prohibition. Deviation is implicit in the moral character of society." Sartre wrote that "to give oneself laws and to create the possibility of disobeying them come to the same thing."[47] In deviance, then, there is always a relationship between individuals engaging in particular patterns of behavior and the community which defines that behavior. As pointed out, different societies may define the same thing in different ways. For example, norms about premarital chastity for the female may fall anywhere along a continuum

---

[47] Quoted in Matza, *Delinquincy and Draft*, p. 13.

from high permissiveness to high authoritarian control. As another illustration, Wilkins points out that a property-owning society will define deviance with respect to property-owning concepts, beyond which action will not be allowed. And if the deviance is carried out the action will be defined as illegitimate or illegal. By contrast a nomadic society will not have any such concept of property deviance.[48]

In most instances most people in society are socialized effectively to the approved values of society, and as a result they control their own behavior and don't have to have external sanctions brought to bear. Basically all social systems depend on a successful socialization system to insure conformity. But when self-control does not work, and the individual violates the rules, external sanctions are often used. So the prime mechanism for controlling behavior is the application of sanctions. "Rewarding proper and punishing improper behavior not only corrects the person's conduct at a given time but also acquaints him with what is expected and teaches him to direct his own behavior."[49]

In the past when the power of the community was directed at defining an activity as a social problem or as unacceptable deviance there was little that deviants could do about it in any organized or systematic way. However, this has been changing because of an increasing tendency for deviants to organize both defensively and offensively. A few years ago when deviants sought each other out it was usually for mutual support and protection. For example, male homosexuals would go to their own vacation spots to escape critical treatment from the broader society. But now some homosexuals are not attempting to escape but rather are taking the offensive and aggressively attacking the dominant society by insisting on their right to do what they want sexually. Many other persons who have been defined as deviants are being provided with advice and guidance on how to avoid moral and legal restrictions on their behavior. This would seem to be a logical extension of the old American tradition on how to avoid moral and legal restrictions. For many years there has been a great body of information on how to avoid paying income tax or how to pursue "sharp" business practices—some legal, some illegal, and some highly questionable.

It is also important to look at the deviant in relation to the broader society as well as at the broader society with reference to the deviant. One important question with regard to the deviant in society is how much choice he has in his deviance. Very often people become deviants because they have little or no control over the situation. A person may be a member of a deviant social group because he was socialized to it or because he was in a particular social setting at a given time. An illus-

---

[48] Wilkins, *Social Deviance*, p. 49.
[49] Ronald L. Akers, *Deviant Behavior: A Social Learning Approach* (Belmont, Calif.: Wadsworth, 1973), p. 6.

tration of the first might be a child growing up in the black lower class, and an illustration of the second a teenager as a part of an adolescent subculture. However, in most societies there are also people who "choose" a deviant career *because* they know it offends an important value of the broader society or because they have a need to challenge some dominant values. The rebellious or militant college student was in some cases an illustration of this type.

In the late 1960s it was common for persons to deliberately turn against some of the values of society and sometimes to deliberately become deviants. When they did they very often sought each other out and became part of deviant social groups, for example, the hippies, the draft resisters, the New Left, and so forth. In time the new deviant groups frequently spawned their own deviant subgroups; for example, splinter groups emerged from the New Left. Often in such situations the conflict between the subgroups becomes greater and more intense than that between the subgroups and the larger society. So in terms of values and behavior patterns there may be a number of different levels of social deviance, with each being deviant relative to the others.

It is obvious that most deviants encounter problems in filling their deviant role demands. For example, the woman engaged in extramarital "swinging" has to reconcile her new sexual role with the monogamous sex life role she was socialized to. It is also clear that certain kinds of deviants have a great deal of difficulty in maintaining their deviant roles. For many, the strain of fitting statuses, roles and selves together is too great or not worth the effort. As Rubington and Weinberg put it, "In the first case, certification seems unattainable, and the person experiences no interior peace, no real self-acceptance. In the second case, his certifi- cation is no blessing, but actually a curse."[50] These writers go on to point out that the neurotic homosexual is a good example of the first case and the drug addict an illustration of the second. "Failure or success in certification comes to the same end. The homosexual wishes to resolve his unconscious conflicts whereas the addict wants to give up his ad- diction."[51] The high strain for the individual practicing deviance is also often reflected in his steady practice of duplicity in trying to explain his behavior to the broader society. There are two possible consequences to such duplicity. "It may make it possible to knit together one's repertory of statuses, roles, and selves into a plausible whole, in which case the person comes to believe the story himself he has invented and told to other people. Or the strain of duplicity is so great that he must ultimately give it up."[52] Furthermore, the deviant is often caught in a position of filling unsupported statuses that are also sometimes illegal. Therefore, one

---

[50] Rubington and Weinberg, *Deviance* , p. 322.
[51] Ibid.
[52] Ibid., p. 319.

would generally expect that the deviant, in contrast with the nondeviant, would have more problems with his self-identity.

However, to point out that deviants often have role problems and confusion is not to say that all deviants are unhappy and would like to change their style of life. The idealogy of the broader society generally assumes this to be true, but the facts suggest otherwise. The deviant's degree of frustration or unhappiness will often be determined by the kind of deviance he is involved in. For example, as Lemert points out, persons who deviate because of such things as stuttering, systematic check forgery, alcoholism, and drug addition are marked by the almost total absence of any durable pleasure. "Instead their lot is one of gnawing anxiety, pain, unhappiness and despair, in some cases ending with deterioration or suicide."[53] But by contrast many other deviants appear, by any reliable measure, to be just as happy as the nondeviant population. Very often the deviant considers his behavior to be quite reasonable and rational, and from where he sits, with his needs and attitudes, what he does is quite logical. Many homosexuals are as happy as or happier than many heterosexuals. Deviance and happiness or role satisfaction is not an either/or proposition; that is, some deviants are unhappy and some are happy, as is the case of nondeviants. Yet, statistically there is probably more unhappiness and role frustration for deviants than for nondeviants.

It may be that most of the problems the deviant encounters in his deviant role are due to social reactions and definitions of his situation rather than to his personal problems and inadequacies. That is, personal disturbance is the result of society's reactions to the deviant. Simmons writes that "the free-floating paranoia and defensiveness so commonly seen among pot-smokers, homosexuals, Puerto Rican gangs, and other deviant groups are easily traceable to the ever present threat of retribution from the surrounding society, not to an earlier personality syndrome nor to anything in the deviant activity itself."[54]

Wilkins has made the important point that all societies reject many types of deviants. That is, "both saints and criminals have been excluded from the cultures into which they were born, and the majority of saints have suffered exactly similar fates to the deviant sinners."[55] Societies recognize deviance, but not the direction that the deviance takes. So what gets stigmatized in a society is not always easy to determine or anticipate. For example, Schur points out that because of the importance of sex to questions of personal identity, confirmed homosexuality (if recognized) appears to carry a built-in stigma. "But not all kinds of 'differentness' or deviating behavior are equally stigmatizable, nor is being easily stigmatizable the same as actually being stigmatized."[56]

---

[53] Lemert, *Human Deviance*, p. 55.
[54] Simmons, *Deviants*, p. 15.
[55] Wilkins, *Social Deviance*, p. 71.

Wilkins has also pointed out that it is usual to think of deviant behavior as almost automatically implying bad or undesirable behavior. However, there is deviant behavior that is "good" or functional for society. For example, the genius, the reformer, the religious leader, and many others are "deviant from the norms of society as much as is the criminal."[57] It is possible for an individual to be deviant by doing *more* than is expected. He may be more upstanding and more moral by going even further than usual in the socially approved direction. Instances might include the mother who is exceptionally committed to her family, the policeman who constantly risks danger, or the child who never gets into trouble. This type of deviation is more apt to be rewarded than punished. "Negative reactions, if any, are likely to be envy, jealousy, or backhanded compliments."[58] Therefore, deviance alone is not a sufficient condition for behavior to be seen as undesirable, but rather it must also be morally or legally defined as "bad" deviance. It is also true that a society does not always define conformity as desirable and that the person who unquestioningly conforms may be seen as a problem. This might be true of the child in school, though not of the enlisted man in the army. So one may think of deviance as falling on a continuum of human acts ranging from the most sinful to the most saintly. In reality there are very few social acts in our society which are regarded as extremely saintly or extremely valuable to it, and there are very few acts which are regarded as extremely sinful or seriously criminal.[59] Most activities, whether deviating or conforming, fall somewhere between the two extremes.

The discussion has centered on the defining of deviance as coming from the broader society. Actually the defining might range from high social agreement to agreement among relatively few individuals. But defining a behavior as deviant is not going to be very significant if the few who define it that way have no real influence on others or on the deviant. The same thing is also true in how people react to a particular deviance. If most people define something as deviant but irrelevant, then that deviance is not very important. However, even when most people respond to someone's deviance with tolerance, but a few do not, this may make the deviant somewhat wary. And if the few have any influence, then it doesn't take much in the way of negative reactions to create problems for the deviant. Even when the few do not seek to "expose" the deviant to the community they may still attempt to exert pressure on him. For example, they may attempt to reform him and bring him back into the fold.

The deviant often finds that even if he accepts the definition of his

[56] Schur, *Crimes without Victims*, p. 5.
[57] Wilkins, *Social Deviance*, p. 45.
[58] Akers, *Deviant Behavior*, p. 7.
[59] Ibid., pp. 46–47.

deviance and abandons his deviant role he doesn't always leave behind the stigma of his former deviance. For example, frequently when a person has been in prison or a mental institution his status as an inmate and patient may be reactivated in the community long after he has left the institution. Often when it is found out that a person was institutionalized this is given more weight in determining how one will respond to him than are face-to-face experiences. "Once he knows of the person's 'past,' the layman quite naturally withdraws the benefit of the doubt that he automatically accords to people in most ordinary social contacts."[60] There is sometimes a legal requirement that the person report his previous deviant status, for example, the ex-convict in applying for particular jobs. In certain attempts to treat various types of deviance the individual is constantly required to think of his past status. In fact in some cases his deviant status is regarded as permanent. This is true in Alcoholics Anonymous, where a man may not have had a drink in years but is constantly told that he is still an alcoholic. Also the past deviant status of an individual may go with him because it is seen as significant or as something that should be known about him.

Social reactions to deviance are often influenced by its being viewed within a medical context. This point will be examined and applied to the analysis of many of the substantive areas in later chapters. But at this point it may be suggested that while the pathological view of deviance so common at the turn of the century no longer prevails the idea of "sickness" is often applied. In this context deviance is often seen as something unhealthy. Furthermore, defining deviance as sickness generally strongly influences social views of deviance. When acts are seen as sick the persons committing them are not usually subject to the general norms of society. They are usually seen as not being personally responsible. "Hostile sentiments toward sick people are not legitimate. The sick person is not responsible for his acts. He is excused from the consequences which attend the healthy who act the same way."[61]

From the point of view of the larger society deviance sometimes performs a positive function. This may be true when the deviant violates rules which the larger society holds in high respect and thus brings the members of that society together to express their outrage over the offense, so that in bearing "witness against the offender, they develop a tighter bond of solidarity than existed earlier."[62] Therefore, deviance cannot always be treated as disruptive to the broader society but may actually contribute to preserving its stability. This helps to explain why on some occasions, but not on others, a pattern of behavior may be defined as

---

[60] Rubington and Weinberg, *Deviance*, p. 115.

[61] Joseph R. Gusfield, "Moral Passage: The Symbolic Process in Public Designations of Deviance," *Social Problems*, Fall 1967, p. 180.

[62] Erikson, *Wayward Puritans*, p. 4.

deviant. That is, the broader society defines the pattern as deviant and subject to social outrage because a scapegoat is needed to help bring the society's members together. Furthermore, it is known that deviant activities often appear to get support from the very agencies that have been developed to suppress them. One obvious explanation is that often the controlling agency needs the deviance to maintain its own existence. As suggested earlier, if there were no illicit drug trade there would be no need for the Federal Narcotics Bureau. But even beyond this, many institutions gather deviant types (and people marginal to the deviance) into tightly segregated groups and provide them with settings in which to teach one another the values and skills of a deviant career. As a result members of society often push individuals "into employing these skills and attitudes of a deviant career, and often provoke them into employing these skills by reinforcing their sense of alienation from the rest of the society."[63]

Erikson has pointed out that many cultures develop patterns that provide for the expression of deviance. First, there are societies which have special days or occasions for general license during which the members are allowed to violate the usual rules, for example, the Mardi Gras in New Orleans and similar pre-Lent activities in the Caribbean and some South American countries. Second, there are societies which see deviance as a natural form of behavior for some groups, for example, the special behavior tolerated among adolescents and young people. Third, there are societies in which special groups are allowed to deviate from the ordinary rules. An example would be a nudist colony in the United States.[64]

THE LAW AND DEVIANCE

It is necessary to say something about the function of laws with reference to deviance. The concept of law implies rules characterized by regularity. "A *law* may be defined as a rule of human conduct that the bulk of the members of a given political community recognize as binding upon all its members."[65] However, the extent to which a law is binding varies greatly, and the sanctions against deviance may range from none to very severe. It is important to keep in mind that a law is one kind of rule. A rule enacted into law has the police power of the state behind it, whereas unenacted rules are dependent on informal sanctions. So laws always imply a formal governmental context of power and authority, although the existence of power and authority doesn't necessarily mean

---

[63] Ibid., pp. 15–16.

[64] See ibid., p. 28.

[65] Julius Gould and William J. Kolb, eds., *A Dictionary of the Social Sciences* (New York: Free Press, 1964), p. 378.

that they will be used. A society may feel strongly about something and yet feel that social ends may be better met by having the controls remain informal and general rather than by having them enacted as formal laws with a more precise application. This is because many rules (such as the Ten Commandments) function primarily as ideals, "as positive models toward which the population should strive, in addition to being negative limits. By making the rules more realistic the institution would hence lower the ideal standard of 'good'"[66]

The law makes an important distinction in defining what is illegal. That is, in most cases what is illegal is not being something but rather possessing or doing something. For example, it is not illegal to be a drug addict, a homosexual, or an alcoholic. For the drug addict, what is illegal is "the illegal procurement, possession, or use of illegal drugs; for the homosexual . . ., it is homosexual acts of almost any nature and for the alcoholic it is public intoxication."[67]

There is no necessary relationship between the importance of an area of behavior and whether or not it will be controlled by law. For example, the use of marijuana is probably much less dangerous than the use of alcohol or cigarettes, but the laws about marijuana use are severe while the laws about alcohol use or cigarette smoking are few and weak. Often a society exaggerates the danger of the things it wants to control. Once again a good illustration is the overstated dangers of marijuana. It is quite possible that the exaggerated stereotypes about hazards arise from a universal bias. "Every society seems to grossly exaggerate the terror and risks of what is disapproved of and to minimize the risks of approval and encouraged behavior."[68]

The important point is that something doesn't have to be dangerous to society to be against the law. Some acts may be criminal or deviant not because they are dangerous, but because they are legally proscribed as such. In fact the law may be irrational in that the members of the society cannot explain it, but the law is real nevertheless. Or a law may be "arbitrary" because "it is imposed by a powerful minority and, as a consequence, lacks popular support and is actively opposed."[69] Therefore, laws may not reflect the dominant values of society, as was the case, for example, with the old "blue laws." And some laws may represent the consensus or perhaps a majority, yet be opposed by a large number of the population, for example, the gambling laws in many states. What often happens is that the enforcers of policies where there is high social disagreement become ambivalent in their enforcement because the public is

---

[66] Simmons, *Deviants*, p. 117.

[67] David Pittman, *Alcoholism* (New York: Harper and Row, 1967), p. 112.

[68] Simmons, *Deviants*, p. 70.

[69] Jack P. Gibbs, "Conceptions of Deviant Behavior: The Old and the New," in Lefton, Skipper, and McCaghy, *Approaches to Deviance*, pp. 46–47.

for the most part indifferent toward particular forms of deviance.[70] However, there are some who argue that even though a law does not prevent certain acts from occurring it is still effective. Schur says that while some laws may not deter they still have strong influence "through their influence on the social meanings read into various acts or behavior patterns, and through their role in structuring total problem situations."[71]

However, it seems clear that with a few possible exceptions the more intense the enforcement of laws the greater the effect the laws will have on deviance. Pittman points out that this can be seen in the treatment of drug addicts in America. Even though addicts may never encounter any law enforcement agency personally, they cannot help but be constantly aware of the law's presence. "The secret manner in which they must purchase drugs is the product of law enforcement. Many of their associates have had personal contact with the law. Finally, the high price and low quality of the black market drugs are a result of social policies. The stringent enforcement of narcotic laws produces secondary deviance among drug addicts. The addict must resort to illegal behavior to support his habit, usually petty larceny and prostitution."[72]

The processing and handling of the legally defined deviant have become the work of complex social agencies set up to perform these functions. Their control of deviance is performed within the context of an elaborate and often precise set of official rules. There may also be private agencies dealing with the deviant, but these differ in several important ways from the legal agencies.

> In power, in legitimacy, and in routine, public regulation and private regulation are at opposite poles. Generally, the power of the political state stands behind officals who take action against the deviant; they have the principle of legality supporting them, and their work with deviants is efficient and routine, i.e., carried out in accordance with a stock, offical plan. In the operation of private regulation power is frequently distributed equitably between the deviant and others, the rule of law is irrelevant when people may be strongly committed to opposing norms, and action against the deviant need not take place according to any plan at all.[73]

It seems possible that in the near future laws will be increasingly influenced by a new and emerging view about deviance. This view is that people should be legally punished only for acts that are socially dangerous, independent of their moral character. The new view makes a distinction between public and private morality, as well as between illegality and immorality. It would restrict the law to those acts which offend against public order and decency or subject the ordinary citizen to what

[70] Pittman, *Alcoholism*, p. 109.
[71] Schur, *Crimes without Victims*, p. 7.
[72] Pittman, *Alcoholism*, pp. 110–11.
[73] Rubington and Weinberg, *Deviance*, p. 109.

would be offensive or injurious. It argues that laws do not build character.[74] This view can be illustrated in the area of sexual behavior. Such sexual activities as rape, exhibitionism, solicitation, and so forth would continue to be against the law. However, private sexual activity between consenting adults would no longer be subject to legal control. There is some evidence that this kind of distinction is being made in the planning of new legislation in several states.

SUBCULTURES

The purpose of the last part of this chapter is to briefly discuss a more complex level of social deviance—that of subcultures. "The term *subcultures*, though not the concept, did not become common in social science literature until after the Second World War."[75] The variables used to distinguish subcultures have been many and varied. As a result there have been so-called subcultures of longshoremen, professional baseball players, university professors, hippies, prison inmates, Texas oilmen, delinquent and nondelinquent gangs, the worlds of fashion, musicians, behavioral scientists, homosexuals, and adolescents, and so forth. The term *subculture* has ranged in application from two persons in a family unit all the way to the suggestion that men and women each constitute a separate subculture. The term has frequently been used as an ad hoc concept when a writer wanted to emphasize normative aspects of behavior that were different from the general social norms.

However, the usage most valuable for our purposes concerns itself with groups in some conflict with the broader society. Within this usage the "norms" of a delinquent gang or the standards of an adolescent peer group have often been designated as subcultural.[76] It is useful to look more specifically at how the concept of subculture has been defined and particularly at how the definitions relate it to the "conflict" point of view.

It should be remembered that whenever the stress is on the subculture a close relationship, often both positive and negative, to the larger society is always implied. In this broad context, when the concept subculture is used it refers to a subdivision within society that forms a functioning unity of values and behavior patterns that have an integrated impact on the participating individuals. The concept of subculture implies that all groups in a society share many factors in common, but that the *areas of difference* peculiar to a given subculture are the focus of major interest at a given time. And the areas of difference may shift over time.

---

[74] Elmer H. Johnson, "Abortion: A Sociological Critique," in Jeffrey K. Hadden and Marie L. Borgatta, *Marriage and the Family* (Itasca, Ill.: F. E. Peacock, 1969), p. 333.

[75] Marvin E. Wolfgang and Franco Ferracuti, *The Subculture of Violence*, (London: Tavistock, 1967), p. 97.

[76] J. Melton Yinger, "Contraculture and Subculture," *American Sociological Review*, October 1960, p. 627.

A simple operational definition of culture and subculture has been provided by Sebald. He suggests that "since for sociological purposes *culture* refers to a blueprint for behavior of a total society, the largest human grouping, *subculture* refers to the blueprint for behavior of a smaller group within the society."[77] He goes on to point out that it is a "special blueprint of the society."[78] However, the formal definitions are only the starting point for analyzing a concept. One must move to the interrelated statuses, norms, and functions subsumed in the concept and also examine how the concept is related to other major social concepts.

In the discussion that follows it is assumed that *all* subcultures are deviant. This appears logical, given the "conflict" level in which the concept is to be used. To say that all subcultures are deviant is not necessarily to say that from the point of view of the larger society they are all "bad." The larger society may see the deviance as something it cannot control and must simply accept. For example, adolescent subcultures may be seen as acceptable deviant behavior resulting from "growing up" but still defined negatively with regard to the ideal values of the broader society. Actually, from the perspective of the broader society, many subcultures are seen as falling along a continuum of "badness," and what is regarded as "bad" varies over time. So while subculture implies deviance it does not follow that deviance necessarily implies "badness."

Subcultures often emerge as a response to a problem faced in common by a group of people. Many people who engage in certain kinds of deviant behavior feel that their beliefs are not shared by other members of the society. It is assumed that often the deviant person wants to share his deviance and will seek out others like himself. However, many deviants perform their deviant behavior in private and have no desire or opportunity to develop that behavior with others and therefore have no desire or opportunity to develop a subculture. An example, previously mentioned, would be many transvestites—they are individual deviants, but they do not constitute a subculture.

For a subculture to emerge, far more is needed than simply individuals who suffer a common fate. It is also necessary for such individuals to be in contact with one another and to find out through communication that they actually do have common values and interests. When subcultures develop they present "a common understanding and prescribed ways of thinking, feeling, and acting when in the company of one's own deviant peers and when dealing with representatives of the conventional world. Once these deviant subcultures come into being and flourish, they have consequences for their bearers and conventional outsiders as well."[79]

It is difficult to determine the amount of time which makes participa-

---

[77] Hans Sebald, *Adolescence: A Sociological Analysis* (New York: Appleton-Century-Crofts, 1968), p. 205.

[78] Ibid.

[79] Rubington and Weinberg, *Deviance*, p. 203.

tion in a subculture significant for the individual. What is more important, however, than the simple measure of time is the amount of "significant involvement." Take, for example, a homosexual who spends his workweek in contact with the broader heterosexual society and has no involvement with his homosexual subculture during that time but on the weekend becomes totally immersed in his homosexual subculture. While most of his life is spent in the heterosexual world, his "significant involvement" is with the homosexual subculture. In fact the workweek may be very insignificant to him, something he has to put up with, and many of his thoughts during the workweek may be directed at his way of life on the weekend.

There is one type of setting for a full-time deviant subculture. This has been defined by Goffman as a "total institution." The term refers to a place where people live and work with a large number of like-situated persons, where they are cut off from the broader society for significant periods of time, and where they lead an enclosed, formally administered life.[80] In a total institution all aspects of life are carried out in the same location under the same general authority. Each member's daily activities are performed in the close company of other members, all of whom are treated alike and required to do the same things together. All aspects of these daily activities are closely scheduled, and the whole sequence of activities is imposed from above through a system of explicit rules and a group of designated leaders. "The various enforced activities are brought together into a single rational plan purportedly designed to fulfill the official aims of the institution."[81]

Goffman suggests that total institutions in American society may be divided into five general groupings. First are those institutions set up for the care of persons felt to be both helpless and harmless, for example, the blind, the aged, and so forth. Second are those institutions set up to care for persons defined as both incapable of taking care of themselves, and as a threat to the community, even though the threat is defined as unintentional, for example, patients in TB sanitariums and mental hospitals. Third are institutions set up to protect the community against persons who are believed to represent intentional dangers. Here the primary interest is to remove the individuals; their welfare and rehabilitation are secondary. An illustration would be a jail or a penitentiary. Fourth are institutions purportedly set up to more effectively pursue some worklike task, for example, army barracks, ships, boarding schools, and work camps—such institutions—justify themselves on instrumental grounds. And finally are total institutions which are set up as retreats from the world while also serving as training stations for the religious, that is, abbeys, monasteries, convents, and so forth.[82]

---

[80] Erving Goffman, *Asylums* (New York: Anchor Books, 1961), p. xiii.

[81] Ibid., p. 6.

[82] Ibid., pp. 4–5.

For the person in a total instituion the subculture becomes in effect his entire life—he does not participate in any broader culture. Even persons who come in from the outside to work in total institutions have their behavior altered as a result. From the extreme of the persons in a total institution, persons with subcultural involvement taper off and increasingly participate in the broader culture. It seems reasonable to suggest that almost all Americans have some involvement with subcultures, at least at various stages of their life cycle, but that most of their involvement is in the broader culture.

There are also some people who engage in behavior that is not acceptable to the broader society or to a subculture they might be thought to belong to. A "marginal deviant" has been defined as one who has been excluded from the conventional world and at the same time has been denied admission and certification in a deviant subculture.[83] One example of a marginal deviant would be a "reformed drunk," a social type that is recognizable among certain types of alcoholics. The reformed drunk is both sober and intolerant of drinking and generally believes that his sobriety is due only to himself. "These attitudes are not shared by conventional people or by most alcoholics. He is out of both worlds. When he comes into contact with either of these worlds the signs and symbols he puts forth are not accepted."[84]

While some deviant subcultures may get their members through no real choice on the part of the members themselves, as, for example, do prisons and mental hospitals, other deviant subcultures may be entered by individual choice, as is true for the subcultures of homosexuals, sexual "swingers," marijuana users, and so forth. Persons who choose to become a part of a subculture usually believe that there is something for them to gain by doing so. For example, the homosexual does so to be with people of similar sexual interests, as well as for many other reasons. Sometimes, after joining the subculture the deviant may want to hide his subcultural involvement from the broader society. This often means that the deviant will present to the broader society signs and symbols that will give him a social identity quite distinct from his personal identity. Frequently, "secret homosexuals working in all-male groups find it necessary to join in conversations that ridicule or condemn homosexuality; in so doing, they obtain, at least in this group, a social identification as heterosexual."[85]

SOCIALIZATION TO SUBCULTURES

While we have pointed out that it is difficult to measure the significance of involvement in a subculture in terms of hours, there is another aspect of time which is important, and that is the continued involvement

---

[83] Rubington and Weinberg, *Deviance*, p. 320.
[84] Ibid.
[85] Ibid., p. 318.

in the subculture over a period of time. This suggests that individuals need varying amounts of time to become socialized to a subculture. And once an individual has been socialized he must actively participate so that the subculture will be maintained. Therefore, the emergence and maintenance of a subculture has something to do with the continuing nature of deviant behavior. However, a subculture will not necessarily emerge and continue simply because a deviance is ongoing. For example, the physician-addict is continuously addicted, yet he does not show subcultural involvement. It is not then merely the continuing nature of the deviant act that establishes the basis for a subculture but, again, the *need for continuous contact with like individuals in order to carry out the deviant act.*[86]

Basically it appears the *necessary condition* for the emergence of a subculture is the existence of a number of persons in a society who seek a solution to common problems and who are able to interact effectively with one another. "The *sufficient conditions* for the establishment of a subculture lie in the acceptance of common norms and values specifying the 'proper' and 'right' way of doing things."[87]

Once a subculture is in operation one of its important functions is the recruiting and socializing of new members. It sometimes happens that persons who want to be members of a subculture are not accepted—for example, the child who is too young to be accepted into the adolescent subculture, the delinquent who is seen as too dangerous to the delinquent gang, and so forth. Rubington and Weinberg suggest that subcultures, much like colleges, can be rated on how hard they are to get into and how hard they are to stay in.[88] Once the individual is admitted he may be put through a period of apprenticeship before he is fully accepted. "He must learn a stock of beliefs, values, norms, and ways of acting that will guarantee continued participation in the group and, at the same time, provide some of the gratifications for being deviant."[89] He may over time stay or leave, but whether or not "he becomes fully committed to the deviant way of life depends partly on the mode of entry, content, and instruction as well as the nature of the deviant acts practiced."[90] Rubington and Weinberg go on to point out that the deviant who wants to sustain his new identity must make the signs and symbols of the subculture his own. He must be able to present deviant behavior when it is required of him or when he wishes to. His actions must be certified first by the subculture and then by himself. "Put another way, if he fails to learn from his teachers he is in jeopardy of being called inauthentic."[91]

---

[86] Schur, *Crimes without Victims*, pp. 172–73.

[87] Sebald, *Adolescence*, p. 207.

[88] Rubington and Weinberg, *Deviance*, p. 206.

[89] Ibid., p. 235.

[90] Ibid.

[91] Ibid., pp. 320–21.

A person may spend varying periods of time in a subculture. For example, the adolescent in a delinquent subculture can only be there for a specific period of his life. This is true because by definition that subculture requires a person to be within definite age limits to be a member. But there are also subcultures in which the person may spend his entire life. This is often the case in the black lower-class subculture. Persons who spend their entire lives in subcultures often have not been presented with the contrasting values of the dominant society. The background of many deviants shows that they were never originally socialized into the broader conventional society. In those cases early socialization occurred in the deviant subculture and was explicitly in terms of the deviant norms and values.[92]

Whatever the reasons for a person's being in the subculture, he must rationalize in some way meaningful to himself the differences between the values and norms of the broader society and those of his subculture. This is especially true when the subculture provides the means for sanctioning behavior that is not acceptable in the broader society. "The acquisition of status within the new group is accompanied by a loss of status outside the group. To the extent that the esteem of outsiders is a value to the members of the group a new problem is engendered. To this problem the typical solution is to devalue the good will and respect of those whose good will and respect are forfeit anyway."[93] But what is of overriding importance is the relative value of what has been left behind as compared with what has been acquired by moving into the subculture. As Cohen points out, over time the main ideas "of any particular individual are derived from the subculture to which he is most exposed and with which he most strongly identifies."[94]

Whenever a deviant examines what he feels he may gain from his participation in a subculture he must also look at the possible costs for him with regard to the broader society. That is, very often the patterns of behavior expected in the broader society will involve a clash of values for the deviant. For example, homosexuals may have problems in the social activities of a society in which heterosexual feelings and inclinations for marriage are taken for granted. In many businesses there are stages in a man's career during which it is almost required that he marry if he wants to move ahead. The homosexual who wants to succeed in his occupation may be faced with a real personal dilemma.

Ultimately the measure of successful indoctrination is the same in a subculture as in the broader society—the individual has been effectively socialized.

Individuals commit deviant acts because they have learned the sup-

---

[92] John DeLamater, "On the Nature of Deviance," *Social Forces*, June 1968, p. 447.

[93] Albert K. Cohen, *Delinquent Boys* (Glencoe, Ill.: Free Press, 1955), p. 68.

[94] Cohen, *Deviance and Control*, p. 85.

porting beliefs and values, from subcultures in which they have participated, in the same way people learn conventional beliefs and values from
their subcultures, and they are sustained in this behavior by the agreement
and approval of their reference groups. Social organization determines
the distinction of deviant behavior and conformity by structuring the
networks of social interaction in which reference groups are acquired and
cultural learning occurs.[95]

Always implied is that the broader society has the power to define the
subculture as deviant and to subject it to some forms of criticism or
punishment. Also, as previously indicated, it is often the factor of power
that creates a deviant subculture; that is, it is the power to punish, to
withhold, that is important to the subculture. While this is usually the
case it is not always true. The subculture must "recognize" the power of
the broader society. For example, the subculture could be indifferent, as
is often the case when "respectability" is withheld and the subculture
doesn't really care. In other words, knowing the power of the broader
culture relative to that of the subculture is not enough. One must also
know how each defines the power and what significance the power has
for each.

Another problem related to power distribution is that generally the
broader society sees deviant subcultures as behaving the way they do
because they are negatively willful or are victims of circumstances. This
implies the belief by the broader society that if the hostility can be
removed of if circumstances can be altered to give the subcultures a
chance they will choose the values of the dominant culture. However, a
subculture may reject the values of the broader culture because it does not
believe that they are worth pursuing *under any conditions.* When the
broader culture becomes aware of this assessment, the need to make the
subculture conform often becomes even greater. The broader culture
then finds it necessary to reaffirm the worth of its values to itself, and to
do this it must change the thinking of the subculture or in some way
discredit its "subversive" beliefs.

A problem which any social organization has to resolve is how much
deviance it can accept before it feels seriously threatened. This holds true
for the society in general, as well as for subcultures. For the broader
society, because of its size and complexity, the problem of accepted
deviance is generally a group one. That is, any threats will normally come
from deviant groups rather than from essentially unrelated deviant individuals. In the subculture internal threats may be from a group, or in
some cases from a few deviant individuals. But because the values of the
subculture deviate from the broader society in some significant ways it
must often insist on a high level of conformity to those values which
make it different from the larger society. If it doesn't, the basic reasons

---

[95] Ibid.

for its existence become blurred and less significant. So within the sub-culture conformity to value differentiation becomes increasingly important for all individuals. Also important for both the broader society and the subculture are the significance of the values from which deviation is occurring. "Even a subculture can tolerate values outside its value system so long as they do not disturb allegiance to its own existence, or the existence of its leaders and opinion-makers is not menaced."[96]

An important part of value sharing in the subculture is related to the need for a rationale for the members, and this is especially true when the subculture is in conflict with the broader society. The historical dimension of the subculture is important in providing a rationale for the members. This often gives the members a sense of belonging to something with permanence and stability. Certain events and incidents become the special histories of distinct subcultures. For example, "the subculture of delinquency possesses a rich folklore in which tales of injustice hold a prominent place. Thus, the subcultural adherent is not fully dependent on personal experience."[97]

One other important characteristic of the subculture is the development of specialized languages. Some specialized language is a characteristic of most groups, deviant and otherwise, in American society. In some groups specialized argots may develop because of the need for more precise communication among members. This is often the case for the specialized jargons of occupational groups. Other groups may develop specialized language forms because they don't want outsiders to understand them or because this gives a special quality to the things they consider important. Maurer suggests that "argots are more than specialized forms of language; they reflect the way of life in each of the numerous criminal cultures and subcultures; they are keys to attitudes, to evaluations of men and society, to modes of thinking, to social organization and to technology."[98]

The argots of a group may be very extensive or quite limited. For example, one writer talks about the relatively limited argot of the stock market subculture.[99] An illustration of a much more elaborate and complex argot would be that of the black lower-class subculture. This is the specialized language of an ongoing group which has found a special argot to be necessary in most areas of life. Hammond suggests that the use of a specialized jargon exists to a very substantial extent throughout the black lower-class subcultures of the United States. He further suggests that "while it may be true that each ghetto has its own local vocabulary, it is still tied in with the larger based subcultural system."[100]

---

[96] Wolfgang and Ferracuti, *Subculture of Violence*, p. 101.

[97] Matza, *Becoming Deviant*, p. 102.

[98] David W. Maurer, "The Argot of the Dice Gambler," *The Annals*, May 1950, p. 119.

[99] Paul Lerman, "Individual Values, Peer Values, and Subcultural Delinquency," *American Sociological Review*, April 1968, p. 210.

[100] Boone Hammond, "Jargon: The Language of the Ghetto," Occasional Paper #42,

The function of language often appears to be more than simply communication in the subculture. Language also helps to set the subculture apart from the broader society.

> Subculture segmentation is well reflected in the special languages, peculiar jargon, and secret symbolic accouterments that go with membership in one or more of these groups. They are "badges of belonging" that make for solidarity, social cohesive and *exprit de corps.* Communication among members is greatly facilitated, but the more cohesive their group becomes, the more difficult it is to maintain easy communication with outsiders.[101]

It also appears that in some areas of deviance a specialized argot serves the important purpose of allowing strangers to exchange cues as to their similar deviant inclinations. One way in which this is done is through casual kidding. Kidding provides an out which enables one to say he was only fooling if things get touchy. Simmons points out that such verbal exchanges provide freedom to explore others and to make suggestions without fear of great consequences. "In such encounters deviants often employ language innocuous to conventional people but with signal meanings for fellow deviants or the recruitable. You're saying several different things in the same breath and watching to see who picks up what."[102] In some cases the communication may be more subtle than language—it may be an inflection or intonation or even a gesture.

As suggested earlier, one important characteristic of deviance in recent years has been the increasing tendency of deviant groups to fight back. This may be through strikes and riots, as in prisons, or through the development of formal organizations. The recent development of deviant organizations is of particular interest. The common model for these organizations appears to have been the civil rights movement. For example, out of that movement came the tactics of passive resistance and confrontation now used by many protesting deviant organizations.

As deviants interact with one another they develop rationales toward their behavior. In some cases they may develop extensive historical, legal, and psychological justifications. One good illustration of this has been the development of formal organizations in the homosexual subculture. The organizations publish "magazines and books by homosexuals and for homosexuals that include historical articles about famous homosexuals in history. They contain articles on the biology and physiology of sex, designed to show that homosexuality is a 'normal' sexual response."[103] Recently there has emerged among some homosexuals an aggressive movement toward achieving greater civil liberties.

Washington University, May 1967, p. 10.

[101] Joseph Bensman and Bernard Rosenberg, *Mass, Class, and Bureaucracy* (Englewood Cliffs, N.J.: Prentice-Hall, 1963), pp. 36–37.

[102] Simmons, *Deviants*, p. 81.

[103] Becker, *Outsiders*, p. 38.

Today there are organizations representing such deviant subcultures as male and female homosexuality, extramarital "swapping," and the practice of birth control and abortion, as well as organizations representing groups who have abandoned deviant activities, for example, former alcoholics, criminals, mental patients, and drug users. How many deviants the various organizations represent and how much influence they have are not known. Many of the organizations put forward exaggerated claims as to their followings—a characteristic of almost all political, social, and special interest groups in the United States. Sagarin suggests that organized deviants generally speak for only a small percentage and that "the organizations' rates of success, as judged by the numbers of people who have, through them, either overcome a stigmatizing problem or adapted to it, are to be considered self-serving declarations never subject to verification."[104]

There is a risk for the deviant who becomes a part of an organized group. Public exposure can result in either greater understanding or greater ridicule, or it may result in both. Sagarin concludes from his study of deviant group organizations that the organizations have often sought publicity for its own sake rather than for its effectiveness in achieving goals. But "whatever good or harm publicity brings to the deviants themselves, it almost invariably strengthens their organizations."[105] Furthermore, one danger of organizations is that they can widen the breach between dominant and deviant groups. There is some evidence that this has been a result of the militancy of homosexual groups. But some deviants may feel that this is a price they are ready to pay.

CONCLUSIONS

In this introductory chapter out primary concern has been to present a broad conceptual approach to the study of social problems, social deviance, and subcultures. As has been suggested, these three concepts overlap, and in the chapters ahead they will be used in various ways as seems appropriate. Six major themes drawn from the discussion in this chapter will be applied to the areas of deviance discussed in each of the following chapters. Not all of them will always be appropriate, and themes other than the six will also be discussed. But our assumption is that in general these themes permit a systematic application of the theoretical considerations discussed in this chapter. The themes also serve as a guide for the organization of each chapter.

1.   *Historical background.* How long has this been an area of deviance

---

[104] Sagarin, *Odd Man In*, p. 235.
[105] Ibid., p. 238.

and why? Are there variations in different cultures? Have the views of the deviance varied in a given culture over time?

2. *Legal aspects.* What is the legal nature of the deviance and how important are the legal definitions for society? What are the relationships between the legal systems and the social values and norms?

3. *Causes and cures.* What are the various theories, and what does the evidence suggest about their utility and effectiveness? These matters are considered only when they are a major part of the discussion that centers on the substantive area, that is, when they are an intrinsic part of the deviance itself.

4. *Self-images.* How do the deviants see themselves in relationship to one another and to the broader society? Are they concerned with their deviance and with those who define them as deviant?

5. *Social organization.* To what extent have the deviants established values, norms, and roles that function for them in their relationships to one another and to the rest of society? Do they constitute a subculture, and if so to what extent?

6. *Specialized language.* Has one been developed? How is it different from the language of the broader society, and what functions does it perform?

Along with the above themes there are also three social patterns that are common to many of the areas of deviance discussed. The first is a rebellion against the institutional defining of personal behavior. That is, there is an increasing belief that one's behavior should be defined by oneself and not by the traditional social agencies of morality. This rebellion is evident in all areas of sexual behavior, abortion, and drug use. The second, seen in many areas of deviance, is that the major sources of conflict are generational and class based. It is not only the old against the young, but even more strongly the educated young against the less educated, lower middle-class, older generation. This conflict is also reflected in all areas of sexual expression, abortion, and drug use as well as among militant women and students. The third pattern is the increasing push for equality of women in the United States, based on the belief that they should have the same rights as men have. This push for equality is also seen in sexual expression, abortion, and drug use, and is discussed specifically in Chapter 15.

BIBLIOGRAPHY

Akers, Ronald L., *Deviant Behavior: A Social Learning Approach.* Belmont, Calif.: Wadsworth, 1973.

Bancroft, John, *Deviant Sexual Behavior: Modification and Assessment.* Great Britain: Clarendon Press, 1974.

36 Social deviance

Becker, Howard S., *Outsiders: Studies in the Sociology of Deviance.* New York: Macmillan, 1963.

Becker, Howard S., *The Other Side: Perspectives on Deviance.* New York: Free Press, 1964

Clinard, Marshall B., *Sociology of Deviant Behavior,* 4th ed. New York: Holt, Rinehart and Winston, 1974.

Cohen, Albert K., *Deviance and Control.* Englewood Cliffs, N.J.: Prentice-Hall, 1966.

Erikson, Kai T., *Wayward Puritans: A Study in the Sociology of Deviance.* New York: Wiley, 1966.

Gusfield, Joseph R., "Moral Passage: The Symbolic Process in Public Designations of Deviance," *Social Problems,* Fall 1967, pp. 175–88.

Lemert, Edwin M., *Human Deviance, Social Problems, and Social Control.* Englewood Cliffs, N.J.: Prentice–Hall, 1967.

Lofland, John, *Deviance and Identity.* Englewood Cliffs, N.J.: Prentice-Hall, 1969.

Matza, David, *Becoming Deviant.* New York: Prentice-Hall, 1969.

Sagarin, Edward, *Odd Man In: Societies of Deviants in America.* Chicago: Quadrangle, 1969.

Schur, Edwin M., *Crimes without Victims: Deviant Behavior and Public Policy.* Englewood Cliffs, N.J.: Prentice-Hall, 1965.

Simmons, J. L., *Deviants.* Berkeley, Calif.: Glendessary Press, 1969.

Wilkins, Leslie T., *Social Deviance.* Englewood Cliffs, N.J.: Prentice-Hall, 1964.

chapter two

Premarital sex

Traditionally in the United States premarital sex has been defined as an undesirable social problem from which the society must protect itself and its members. Like so many other social problems it has been defined within a strong moral context and has therefore been seen as something inherently bad and destructive. Premarital sex has been treated within the broader context of sexual values held to be important in American society. Human beings have developed a variety of means for satisfying their sexual needs, and all of those means are found among both the unmarried and the married population. The actual sexual behavior of the unmarried and the married do not differ nearly so widely as do the social and psychological definitions and interpretations. For the married population some forms of sexual outlet are approved, but for the unmarried *no* outlets are given explicit social approval. Yet the sexual needs of the unmarried do not lie dormant until the wedding day and then for the first time suddenly burst forth. Rather, the sexual needs of the unmarried exist with some change over time and with wide variation during the unmarried years. Often it is assumed that the sexual needs of the unmarried can be ignored, conditioned, or transferred, but in reality they usually find some form of expression.

It must be kept in mind that sexual intimacy between males and females is approved within the socially defined role relationship of monogamous marriage but that in all other role relationships sexual intimacy goes against the commonly stated and approved social values. When premarital sex is discussed it is almost always with respect to the attitudes and behavior of adolescents and young adults. The word *premarriage* clearly implies a stage in life *prior* to marriage, even though about 5 percent of the American population never marry. However, the sexual behavior of those who never marry is generally subject to premarital

37

values, regardless of their age or of any reasons they may have for not marrying. This chapter will be limited to a discussion of the premarital sexual activity of the young as deviant behavior.

While it has been common to define premarital sexual behavior as a social problem such behavior has not been examined within the context of social deviance. That is, there have been no attempts to look at it within the context of the concepts of deviance presented in Chapter 1. If, on the most general level, deviant behavior is defined as behavior which is seen by a large number of people in society as bad and as going beyond the limits of tolerance, then premarital coitus qualifies as deviance. Reiss points out that in the eyes of most adults (77 percent in a national sample of adults 21 years and older) premarital coitus is viewed as a violation of a norm, "and many people hold this view with sufficient intensity to place such behavior outside their tolerance limits."[1] Reiss goes on to suggest that the study of premarital coitus as deviance might contribute to a better understanding of related deviant behavior, such as prostitution, illegitimacy, and abortion. "The relation of these other substantive areas of sex deviancy is clear since one must often engage in premarital coitus before the possibility of illegitimacy, prostitution, or premarital abortion is present."[2]

The study of premarital sex as deviance is important in a broad sociological sense. That is, the present American society is characterized by rapid social change, and problems frequently develop around standards which are believed to be right and proper by the older generation but which are not adhered to by many in the younger generation. Two major social variables related to the understanding of the deviance discussed in this chapter and in many of the subject areas covered in forthcoming chapters are generational conflict and differential societal expectations for males and females. Therefore, the discussion of those two variables as crucial to the study of premarital sex is important in itself, but is also important in many other areas of deviance.

HISTORICAL BACKGROUND

To better understand the nature of deviance with regard to premarital sex it is necessary to look at how this behavior has been perceived and defined in the past. Views about premarital sex have been closely linked to values about sex in general, love, and the family. If one looks back at early Greek society it can be seen that love and sex were often closely linked. While love among the Greeks stressed physical beauty, the Greek

---

[1] Ira L. Reiss, "Premarital Sex as Deviant Behavior: An Application of Current Approaches to Deviance," *American Sociological Review*, February 1970, p. 78.

[2] Ibid., p. 85.

male often felt that beauty could not be found in the female, and certainly not in the wife. In fact the prestige of the female was so low that she was often considered unworthy of idealistic love and incapable of returning the male's love. The ideal Greek love was often homosexual, between a younger boy and an older man. That love was based on the belief that the essence of beauty, and therefore the realization of love, could be found by the male in the male. It is an ironic historical fact—one that many people find disconcerting—that love and sexual expression as it is viewed today, with the exchange of deep emotional commitment between members of the opposite sex, had some roots in male homosexuality.[3]

Restrictions against various forms of sexual expression have long been linked with religious beliefs and controls. However, nowhere in the Old Testament is there any prohibition of noncommercial unpremeditated fornication—apart from rape. "Once a girl had reached the age of twelve-and-a-half years, she was free to engage in sexual activity unless her father specifically forbade it. Prostitution, though frowned upon, was common, and in Jerusalem the whores were so numerous that they had their own market place."[4] The religious taboos against sex in general did not become strong until the development of Christianity. For the early Christians the highest form of achievement that a person could reach was as complete a rejection of the body as possible while still retaining life. Among early Christians sex was seen as carnal, sinful, and inferior to all things of the spirit.

In early Christianity the root of all evil was woman. Woman was believed to be inherently evil and therefore to be distrusted, watched, and controlled. "Woman was believed to inherit from Eve the natural propensity to lure man to his undoing. The sin in the Garden of Eden, St. Augustine maintained, had caused the sex organs to become the seat of lust. Thus, even with the sanction of marriage the sex act became a deed of shame."[5] The highest possible state for a woman was the glory of everlasting virginity. Early Christianity was characterized by severe ascetic attacks against the inherent sinfulness and implied witchery of woman. This view of woman was a basic part of early Christian beliefs, and celibacy (the taboo against woman) was believed to be the way that man could be saved from corruption.

The inferior status of the woman continued for many centuries. Isabel Drummond suggests that "the period of hatred and contempt of woman pervaded the Crusades, the age of Chivalry, and lasted well into the

---

[3] Morton M. Hunt, *The Natural History of Love* (New York: Knopf, 1959), p. 8.

[4] G. Rattray Taylor, *Sex in History* (New York: Vanguard Press, 1954), p. 241.

[5] Isabel Drummond, *The Sex Paradox* (New York: Putnam, 1953), p. 8.

Renaissance."[6] She writes that one of the most degrading examples of the
low value placed on women was the use of the "chastity belt" and that "it
was during this dark age of women that the doctrine of the Immaculate
Conception arose."[7] Morton Hunt suggests that by the end of the 15th
century the concept of the woman had become completely dualistic: "She
was not woman—she was either Lady or Witch, Blessed Virgin or sinful
Eve, object of adoration or vessel of abominable lust."[8] During the
Middle Ages and the Renaissance the influence of romantic love and
sexual expression varied. Hunt argues that three general influences e-
merged over time: (1) a greater emotional relationship between men and
women, which led to the eventual uplifting of woman's status; (2) sexual
fidelity to a single partner; and (3) the belief that love must be mutual,
which ultimately contributed greatly to the improvement of woman's
status.[9]

Many values basic to present-day American society originated with the
early Puritans who settled New England. Unlike many other patriarchal
systems, that of the Puritans believed in the premarital chastity of *both*
the male and the female. In Puritan theology premarital sexual behavior
was interpreted as succumbing to the temptations of the flesh—behavior
not found among the "chosen." The strength of the premarital chastity
norms was derived from, and supported by, economic as well as religious
values. But even with the strongly supported norms against premarital
sexual experience a number of Puritans deviated from those norms. The
records of Groton Church show that of 200 persons owning the baptismal
covenant there from 1760 to 1775, 66 confessed to fornication before
marriage.[10] Unlike many patriarchal societies, that of the Puritans did not
protect the sexual purity of women by providing a special group of
prostitutes to meet the sexual needs of men. And finally it should be
stressed that not only were the restrictions against premarital sexual
experience strong but that there were also strong restrictions against any
pleasure derived from sex. The sexual asceticism of the Puritans was
different only in degree from monasticism.

It may also be noted that in some peasant societies of Europe couples
do not marry until the girl gets pregnant. This may have resulted from
the high importance attached to fertility and maintaining the family
lines. The Groton Church records may reflect the same consideration.
Even a highly moral society may resort to "immorality" in order to insure
the perpetuation of its basic values.

---

[6] Ibid.
[7] Ibid.
[8] Hunt, *Natural History*, p. 175.
[9] Ibid., p. 171.
[10] Ibid., p. 133.

During roughly the first two thirds of the 19th century almost all aspects of sex were taboo for "good" women. During that period it was commonly believed that good women found the sexual relations of marriage an unspeakable and unpleasant duty neccessary for reproduction and sometimes for the satisifaction of the "animal" sexual needs of their husbands. Women were not expected to experience sexual pleasure, and their doing so often led to suspicion on the part of the husbands and guilt on the part of the wives. The view that good women had no sexual interest was strongly supported by the males in the patriarchal society of that period. The patriarchal male could conveniently seek out sexual partners before marriage and outside of marriage. Prostitution emerged as an important social institution for meeting the sexual needs of males. It was believed that among women only the prostitute felt sexual desire and enjoyed sexual relations. The patriarchal male could turn to "bad" women not only to satisfy his animal needs, but also to protect his good women from his uncontrollable sexuality. The dichotomy between good and bad women seems to have been accepted by most women. So the period between the Revolutuion and the Civil War was the period in American history most restrictive on the freedom of women.

World War I probably triggered the developing social forces that resulted in the new social patterns of the 1920s. In the area of sexual behavior a decrease in the "sinful" view of sex, along with new arguments for sexual expression provided by science, brought about important changes. Also during that period, the increasing use of contraceptive methods led to an increasing acceptance of the view that sexual intercourse could be an end in itself rather than merely a means to a procreative end.

The 1920s saw an increasingly important social force emerge in the United States—the intellectual community. During the decade the intellectual community was engaged in psychological and moral revolt against Puritan values, Main Street mores, and the complacency of a cold business culture. The intellectual movement with the greatest importance for values of sexual behavior centered on the Freudian view of human behavior. While during the early stages of science Social Darwinism was used to support the traditional views of male dominance and morality, in the 1920s many of the interpretations of Freudianism seemed "to provide scientific sanction of conventional standards and morals."[11] In the 1920s among many intellectuals, as Baltzell puts it, "the Social Gospel was replaced by the gospel according to Freud."[12]

Those who represented and supported the traditional morality were shocked by the revolt of the younger generation during the 1920s. In part

---

[11] Merle Curti, *The Growth of American Thought* (New York: Harper and Row, 1951), p. 706.

[12] E. Digby Baltzell, *The Protestant Establishment* (New York: Random, 1964), p. 218.

the shocked reaction can be viewed within a social class context. With rebellion often strong among those of middle-class background the traditionalists saw the rebels not just as accepting different values but also as rejecting the old values. It is easier for the dogmatic moralist to "understand" those who are different because their whole life pattern has been different than to understand those who have had all the "advantages" and then rejected them. (These points concerning generational confusion and hostility are just as applicable to the present as they are to the 1920s.)

The decade of the 1920s also saw a basic change in the traditional role of American women. The superiority of the male was no longer an accepted belief for many women as well as men. The "sexual rights" of the woman were held to be very important, and there was an increasing belief that her sexual drives both existed and needed to be satisfied.

Before ending this discussion of the historical background to premarital sex it is important to say something about the institutional influences of religion and the law. Religion has been the major social agency for the defining of American morality. The influence of religious institutions has been especially significant with reference to sexual behavior. In the United States every type of sexual activity *in and of itself* is a crime or a sin. "Marriage removes the stigma of criminality from vaginal heterosexual congress, but many Christians believe that it does not mitigate its sinful quality, unless engaged in for the sole purpose of procreation."[13] The most general values in the American society are that premarital sex is sinful, and in many cases it is also illegal.

In general the religious taboos against sex continue to be strong in American society. The religious values about premarital sex are a part of the broader values that see lawful monogamous marriage as the only acceptable means for sexual pleasure and procreation. Therefore, all other forms of sexual behavior are defined as wrong. The male-female sexual relationship is approved or disapproved according to the social role relationships of the two individuals when it occurs. If the couple are married then it is approved at least as a means to procreation; however, if the couple are not married, the act is condemned. American moral values probably condemn more strongly sexual relationships between individuals, one or both of whom are married, but not to each other, than between two unmarried individuals. There is rarely any stated belief by religious groups that premarital sex is less sinful than is extramarital sex. Yet, as Reiss points out, "premarital coitus is not adultery and thus is not part of the Ten Commandments."[14]

It is very possible that the strong positions taken by many religions against sexual behavior outside of marriage are given lip service but have

---

[13] Drummond, *Sex Paradox*, p. 3.

[14] Ira L. Reiss, *Premarital Sexual Standards in America* (New York: Free Press), 1960, pp. 162–63.

decreasing influence as significant determinants of behavior. This is not to argue that traditional religious values are unimportant, for many individuals have incorporated them into their personality structures, and often do have feelings of shame or guilt when their behavior is contrary to those values. The important difference is that in the past the strong sense of guilt was a result of a strong feeling of sin, and faith in God was almost the only relief, whereas today there are accepted alternative explanations, especially psychological ones, by means of which the individual can deal with his guilt feelings. The use of such explanations for guilt feelings is so common today that even the minister often acts in accordance with psychological explanations rather than traditional theological principles.[15]

The influence of religious beliefs on sexual laws has been very strong in the United States. This influence has been a part of the development of the state. Drummond points out that in common law "all the sexual transgressions other than adultery were at first merely torts, or civil wrongs, whatever the punishment inflicted." They were classified as "sins" and "wrongs," the former being offenses against God, the latter against one's neighbor. She further suggests that it was "only when the state became an entity that sins took on the aspect of crimes against the state and became indictable offenses."[16] One consequence has been that sexual laws have been altered little over time. "Today, in twentieth-century America, formal sex restrictions are—in their general outlines—much the same as they were in the times of Tertullian, St. Augustine, Martin Luther, or John Wesley."[17]

Premarital sexual relations are at present forbidden by more than two thirds of the states. However, the laws are rarely applied. That premarital virginity for the female is not of great legal importance is reflected in the fact that in only one state, Maryland, is female unchastity before marriage a ground for divorce. In summary it may be said that attempts to legislate controls over sexual morality in the United States have not been successful. Morris Plascowe points out that legislators have failed to recognize two factors that are necessary for effective legal sanctions: "(1) the support of public opinion; and (2) the ability of law enforcement agencies to get at the behavior involved. Neither element is present for much of the sexual behavior prohibited by the criminal law."[18]

---

[15] James M. Gustufson, "The Clergy in the United States," *Daedalus*, Fall 1963, p. 733.

[16] Drummond, *Sex Paradox*, p. 9.

[17] William N. Stephens, *The Family in Cross-Cultural Perspective* (New York: Holt, Rinehart and Winston, 1963), p. 259.

[18] Morris Plascowe, "Sex and the Law," in Edwin M. Schur, *The Family and the Sexual Revolution* (Bloomington: Indiana University Press, 1964), p. 195.

Some cross-cultural comparisons

While the basis of the sexual drive is physiological, in no known society is the frequency or form of sexual behavior determined completely by physiological factors. In all cultures some degree of social control is exerted over sexual expression. However, in many cultures premarital sexual activity is less restricted than other sexual outlets. For example, most cultures place far more severe restrictions on extramarital and homosexual activities. Murdock found that premarital license prevailed in 70 percent of the 148 cultures he analyzed and that in the rest the taboo fell mainly on the females and appeared to be a precaution against childbearing out of wedlock rather than a moral requirement.[19]

When a society does approve certain forms of adolescent sexual activity it does not leave matters of behavior to chance. There are usually special social institutions that provide facilities where young people can meet and spend time together. However, it is rare in human history to find a society like the American, in which premarital sexual activity is prohibited and, at the same time, wide opportunity is allowed for private interaction to occur. Ford and Beach point out that in most restrictive societies there is a public conspiracy against the acquisition of any sexual knowledge by children. In restrictive societies the methods used during adolescence "include segregation of the sexes, strict chaperonage of girls, and threats of severe disgrace or physical punishment."[20] But, as Ford and Beach further point out, "there are probably no societies in which methods of control are completely effective in preventing coitus among young unmarried couples."[21]

In the following sections premarital sexual attitudes and behavior will be discussed for two historical periods. First, the period of highly stabilized sexual behavior extending from about the 1920s until the mid-1960s will be examined. Second, evidence will be presented for the argument that premarital sexual behavior has been changing, at least among a number of college women, since the mid-1960s.

PREMARITAL SEXUAL BEHAVIOR: 1920s TO MID-1960s

Before the actual rates of premarital sexual behavior during this period are presented there will be an examination of some attitudes about premarital sex. The major contribution to the scientific study of premarital sexual standards in the United States has been made by Ira L. Reiss.[22]

---

[19] George P. Murdock, *Social Structure* (New York: Macmillan, 1949), p. 265.

[20] Clellan S. Ford and Frank A. Beach, *Patterns of Sexual Behavior* (New York: Harper and Row, 1952), pp. 180–82.

[21] Ibid., p. 182.

[22] Reiss, *Premarital Sexual Standards*, p. 80.

Reiss has suggested that in the United States two basic types of premarital sexual behavior, with their related attitudes, may be seen as extremes on a continuum: (1) *body-centered,* with the emphasis on the physical nature of sex, and (2) *person-centered,* with the emphasis on the emotional relationship to a given individual. Premarital attitudes may usually be classified into one of four categories falling along a continuum:

1. *Abstinence*—premarital intercourse is wrong for both the man and the woman, regardless of circumstances.
2. *Permissiveness-with-affection*—premarital intercourse is right for both men and women under certain conditions when a stable relationship with engagement, love, or strong affection is present.
3. *Permissiveness-without-affection*—premarital intercourse is right for both men and women regardless of the amount of affection or stability present, provided that there is physical attraction.
4. *Double standard*—premarital intercourse is acceptable for men, but is wrong and unacceptable for women.[23]

The traditional belief in the double standard continues to be accepted by many Americans of both sexes. And the attitude of abstinence is often found along with the double standard. In the past in the United States the double standard was often applied to the male and the abstinence standard to the female. Permissiveness-without-affection places value primarily on the sheer physical satisfaction derived from sex, although it is assumed that individuals will be sophisticated enough to control their pleasure in a careful way.[24] This standard tends to define sex as an end in itself, and while it has been accepted by only a minority there is some evidence that in recent years it has been winning increasing acceptance. Permissiveness-with-affection appeals to many. They believe that the feeling of love or affection justifies sexual intercourse. "Permissiveness-with-affection is an equalitarian standard, allowing premarital coitus for both men and women."[25]

In an earlier book the writer examined in detail many values that influence premarital sexual attitudes and behavior, but here only a few of the major variables will be examined.[26] Historically the family has been the most powerful agency for socializing the offspring. The family can transmit values to the child during the most impressionable years. Whatever values the family draws upon—religious, ethical, legal, or practical—the children, and especially the daughters, are almost always taught restrictions against premarital sexual intercourse. But it is clear that other

---

[23] Ibid., pp. 83–84.

[24] Ibid., pp. 118–23.

[25] Ibid., p. 144.

[26] Robert R. Bell, *Premarital Sex in a Changing Society* (Englewood Cliffs, N.J.: Prentice-Hall, 1966).

forces of great strength are also in operation because during their adolescence and early adult years many young people reject those restrictive values about premarital sexual expression. If the conservative force is the family the liberal force can be described as the peer group.

The adolescent, being neither child nor adult, and having no clearly defined role made available by the overall culture, often turns to peers for self-definitions. Frequently the adolescent desires some decisiveness and precision in role definitions and tries to create his/her own, and then often demands a high degree of conformity by other adolescents as 'proof' of the rightness of these definitions. One consequence is that while the adolescent peer group deviates in some ways from the adult world the requirements for conformity within the group are very strong. It seems clear that most peer groups take a more liberal view about premarital sex than do adults, and because this is true their members are important to one another in giving psychological support in this area. The values about premarital sexual expression may be the most functionally significant values the peer groups of the young are actually involved with.

Many of the activities engaged in by young people in their peer group activities contribute to increased premarital sexual possibilities. Some of the values are "high exposure to temptation via privacy, dancing, and drinking; youth culture approval of adventure and hedonism; and approval of youth culture for the importance of affection as a basis for sexual relationships."[27] How persons perform according to the values of the group determines how the group defines them. That is, the peer group can give status and take it away. And sometimes how an individual is labeled within the group will have a strong influence on future behavior. For example, labeling may affect premarital sexual permissiveness. "It is possible that a girl who is labeled by the boys or others in her school as an easy mark may react to this label and decide to continue or increase her sexual activities because of such a group label."[28]

It is clear that even within peer groups there may be differences in defining appropriate behavior. It would be a mistake to assume that within the peer group setting there is no conflict over sexual behavior. The most important source of conflict is between males and females. Studies have shown that even among college students strong male sexual aggression is quite common. One study found that over half of the coed respondents had been offended at least once during the prior academic year at some level of sexual intimacy. Of those coeds, 21 percent were offended by forceful attempts at intercourse, and 6 percent by aggressively forceful attempts at sexual intercourse in which menacing threats or coercive inflictions of physical pain were employed.[29]

---

[27] Reiss, *Premarital Sex*, p. 80.

[28] Ibid., p. 81.

[29] Clifford Kirkpatrick and Eugene Kanin, "Male Sex Aggression on a University Campus," *American Sociological Review*, February 1957, p. 53.

The values up until recent years were against premarital sex. For example, in 1939 80 percent of a national sample of men stated that it was either "unfortunate" or "wicked" when "young girls have sexual relations before marriage." And 83 percent of the women sampled gave the same answer with respect to young men having sexual relations before marriage.[30] In general the various studies from 1920 to the mid-1960s indicated that there were no significant changes in the rates of premarital coitus among women. During that period the most reliable and best-known statistics came from the Kinsey findings. These showed that about one half of the women studied who had ever married reported having premarital coitus. The data showed that for 44 percent of the women who had had premarital coital experience, the experience had been confined to one year or less. For almost one third it had extended over a period of two or three years, and for 26 percent it had extended over a period of four or more years. But only a very few women had had premarital sexual intercourse with any continuity over such periods of time.[31]

The Kinsey findings showed significant relationships between education and the probabilities of premarital coitus. There was a strong inverse relationship between education and male and female frequency of premarital coitus. By education level, the percentages for the females were: grade school, 30: high school, 47; and college, 60.[32] The percentages for the males were: grade school, 98; high school, 85; and college, 68.[33] Frequency of premarital coitus for the female went up with increased education because of the later age at marriage, more petting, and a less rigid view of the importance of virginity. The rates by the education of the male went down because of less coital opportunity and the use of other sexual outlets.

The Kinsey findings indicated that while there continued to be important differences between males and females with reference to premarital sexual relations, the double standard had undergone change. The important difference between the unmarried female and the unmarried male, at least in some groups, was no longer the virgin-nonvirgin double standard, but rather a double standard in which nonvirginity was found for both sexes, with the male often sexually promiscuous and the female generally restricting herself to a limited number of sexual partners. While the double standard has become less prevalent, it can still be found, even among those under age 25. Hunt found that where strong affection existed nine out of ten men under 25 considered premarital coitus to be all

[30] William J. Goode, *The Contemporary American Family* (Chicago: Quadrangle, 1971), p. 36.

[31] Alfred C. Kinsey et al., *Sexual Behavior in the Human Female* (Philadelphia: Saunders 1953), p. 291.

[32] Ibid., p. 293.

[33] Ibid., p. 330.

right for men and that eight out of ten considered it to be all right for women. "Six out of ten men and nearly four out of ten women sanction coitus for single males where strong affection is lacking; and four out of ten men and two out of ten women do so for single females."[34]

Several general points may be summarized from the various premarital sex studies made during the period up to the mid-1960s. First, while the major studies dealt with quite different samples the findings were in high agreement. In general the studies showed that of those women born after 1900 about half were not virgins when they married. And when women born after 1900 were compared by decades of birth there was no evidence to suggest any significant differences in their rates of premarital coitus. Second, the studies indicated that being nonvirgin at the time of marriage was not an indication of extensive premarital experience with a variety of partners. For the female, premarital coitus usually depended on strong emotional commitments and plans for marriage. Third, if the assumption of a temporary stabilization of premarital sexual coitus was correct, this meant that young people in the United States had been engaging in essentially the same types of behavior for three or four decades. It is the contention of the next section that these summary findings do not hold true for the period since the mid-1960s.

PREMARITAL SEX SINCE THE MID-1960s

It is suggested that there has been a change in the sexual experiences of unmarried college girls since the mid-1960s.[35] In recent years, more than ever, the group primarily responsible for rebellion among the young has been the college students. While there has always been rebellion by the younger generation against their elders, it has probably never been as great in the United States as it has been since the mid-1960s. In recent years youths have not only rebelled against their elders, but have also rejected many aspects of the major institutions in American society. The mid-1960s produced an action generation, and their modus vivendi was to experience, to confront, to participate, and sometimes to destroy. Since the mid-1960s a small but highly influential proportion of college students have been deeply involved in the civil rights movement and in the protest over the Vietnam War. What may be most important about that generation of college students is that many were not just alienated as others had been in the past, but that they were *actively* alienated.

Many college students believed that many adult norms were not only wrong but were also immoral. That view has been held by many college students toward the treatment of the black, toward the war in Vietnam,

[34] Morton Hunt, "Sexual Behavior in the 1970s," *Playboy*, October 1973, p. 74.

[35] Robert R. Bell and Jay B. Chaskes, "Premarital Sexual Experience among Coeds, 1958 and 1968," *Journal of Marriage and the Family*, February 1970, pp. 81–84.

toward American political procedures, and so forth. It seems logical that if large numbers of the younger generation view those adult norms as wrong and immoral, they are going to be suspicious and critical of other adult norms as well. Certainly adult norms one would expect the younger generation to view with skepticism would be those concerned with marriage and sexual behavior. Several other social factors also appear to be related to changes in the premarital sexual experiences of the young

One important factor of the 1960s was the development, distribution, and general acceptance of the birth control pill. On many large university campuses the pill is available to the coed, or it is not difficult for her to find out where to get it in the local community. While studies have shown that fear of pregnancy has not been a very important deterrent to premarital coitus for many years, it now seems to have been largely removed for most college girls. Another factor since the mid-1960s has been the legitimation of sexual candor. In part the new sexual candor has been legitimated by one of the most venerable of American institutions— the Supreme Court. (This point is discussed further in the chapter on pornography.) In recent years young persons have had access to a level of sexual expression far greater than was available just ten years ago. The new sexual candor, whatever its original cause, is often seen by the rebelling younger generation as "theirs" in that it also critically subverts the traditional institutions. As a result the sexual candor of the late 1960s was often both a manifesto and a guidebook for many in the younger generation.

Finally, it should be recognized that the rebellion of the younger generation has been given both implicit and explicit approval by many in the older generation. Many adults like to think of themselves as a part of the younger generation and its youth culture. For example, this is seen in the music and fashions of the youth culture, which have had a tremendous impact on adults. It would seem that if many adults take on the values of the youth culture, that would raise questions as to the validity of adult values for the youth world. In other words the very identification of many adults with youth culture contributes a lessening of the impact of adult values on college youths.

Reiss has suggested that in the past the groups that developed a tradition of sexual permissiveness were often groups that had the least to lose. "Men and Negroes would be examples, for men cannot get pregnant and Negroes have less social standing to lose."[36] But he goes on to say that the present movement toward permissiveness may be based differently than it used to be. It may be occurring within a context of general liberality. "It may be that liberalism emphasizes the types of social forces that maintain high permissiveness, for example, low religious orthodoxy,

---

[36] Ira L. Reiss, *The Social Context of Premarital Sexual Permissiveness* (New York: Holt, Rinehart and Winston, 1967), p. 54.

low value on tradition, high value on autonomy. The stronger the amount of general liberality in a group, the greater the likelihood that social forces will maintain high levels of sexual permissiveness."[37] Reiss's statement very clearly describes the type of college student considered here. It is being argued that the social forces developing since the mid-1960s have led to a rapid rise in the rejection of many traditional values and to the development of important patterns of behavior common to a general youth culture. And out of this has come an increased rate of premarital coitus among many college women, along with lessened feelings of guilt about their experiences.

The Kinsey data indicated that about one fourth of the women sampled had petted to orgasm by the time they reached age 25. But recent studies show much higher rates. The national study by Morton Hunt found that more than two thirds of the women in the sample had reached orgasm through petting in the year prior to the study.[38] This would suggest that petting is more intense, involved, and sexually fulfilling than was true in the past.

The writer conducted a study of premarital sexual behavior and attitudes among a sample of coeds in a large urban university in 1958.[39] In 1968 the same questionnaire was used with another sample of coeds in the same university. A careful effort was made to match the two samples by age and by class standings. The rates of coitus among those studied were determined for the different levels of the dating relationship. The coeds were asked about the highest level of intimacy ever reached while dating, going steady, and engaged. The number of girls having premarital coitus while in a dating relationship rose from 10 percent in 1958 to 23 percent in 1968, and the coitus rates while going steady rose from 15 percent in 1958 to 28 percent in 1968. The rates of premarital intercourse during engagement rose from 31 percent in 1958 to 39 percent in 1968.

> Further examination of the data suggests that in 1958, the relationship of engagement was very often the prerequisite to a girl having premarital sexual intercourse. Engagement often provided her with a high level of emotional and future commitment which she often felt justified having coitus. However, in 1968 it appeared that the need to be engaged and all it implied was much less a condition the coed thought necessary before sexual intercourse. Therefore, the data suggest that the decision to have intercourse in 1968 was much less dependent on the commitment of engagement and more a question of individual decision regardless of the level of the relationship. To put it another way, if, in 1958, the coed had premarital

---

[37] Ibid., p. 73.
[38] Hunt, *Sexual Behavior*, p. 74.
[39] Bell and Chaskes, "Premarital Sexual Experience," pp. 81–84.

coitus, it most often occurred while she was engaged. But in 1968, girls were more apt to have their first sexual experience while dating or going steady.[40]

Number of partners

As has been pointed out earlier, the Kinsey findings indicated that most women who had had premarital coitus had limited that activity to one person. It was mentioned that of all the women who had had premarital coitus 12 percent had had coitus with six or more partners. There is some evidence that younger women are having premarital coitus with a greater number of partners. In a nationwide study of 2,372 married women Bell and Balter found that 50 percent of the women had had premarital coitus with one partner, 36 percent with two to five partners, and 13 percent with six or more partners.[41] Generally the younger the woman the more premarital sexual partners she had had. There is also some evidence that those engaging in premarital coitus are doing so more often today than was the case in the past. Kinsey found that the rate of coitus for single women aged 16 to 20 was once every three weeks, but for the same age group Hunt found a rate of more than once a week.[42] The Bell and Balter study also found evidence of greater frequency for younger women. "Of the women 25 years of age and younger 72 percent had premarital coitus 9 or more times with each partner, but this was true of only 14 percent of the women respondents past the age of 50."[43]

There is also evidence that, as measured by their orgasm rates, younger women are getting greater satisfaction from premarital coitus. Kinsey found that about half of the young women engaging in premarital coitus were having orgasms. The Hunt study found that three quarters of the single women engaging in coitus were having orgasms. "The median frequency of more than one coital orgasm every two weeks is three times as high as in Kinsey's sample."[44] The Bell and Balter study found that 74 percent of the women 25 and younger had had orgasms in their premarital coitus. This compared with only 39 percent of the women past 50 years of age.[45]

---

[40] Ibid., pp. 82–83.

[41] Robert R. Bell and Shelli Balter, "The Premarital Sexual Experiences of Married Women," *Medical Aspects of Human Sexuality*, November 1973, p. 111.

[42] Kinsey, *Human Female*, p. 292; Hunt, "Sexual Behavior," p. 74.

[43] Bell and Balter, "Premarital Sexual Experiences," p. 111.

[44] Hunt, "Sexual Behavior," p. 75.

[45] Bell and Balter, "Premarital Sexual Experiences," p. 112.

Age at first coitus

The Kinsey data showed that in the past, age was an important factor in understanding the higher probability of premarital coitus among college-educated women. Many of these women did not have their first sexual experiences until they had reached an age at which the lower-educated woman was already married. The Kinsey data showed that of those women who had had premarital coitus, 18 percent of the grade school group were having premarital coitus by age 15, as compared with 1 percent of the college-educated girls, while between the ages of 16 and 20, the figures are about the same for all educational levels.[46] That 81 percent of the college-educated females who had had premarital coitus had had it past the age of 20 suggests that premarital coitus was not usually an event of their adolescence, but rather of their young adult years.

One nationwide study found that the average age at first coitus of white women was 18.6 years. A nearly identical figure—18.5 years—was found by the Bell and Balter study. The latter study indicates that the average age at first coitus has been somewhat lowered over the years. The average age of first coitus for women past age 50 who had had premarital coitus was 19.2 years as compared to an average of 17.3 years for women 25 years of age and younger.[47]

Nowhere in the research literature on premarital sexual behavior in the past has there been any information as to participation in certain types of sexual expression. That is, studies have asked about necking, various types of petting, and coitus, but not about oral-genital contact. Yet, the Kinsey study showed that oral-genital sexual experience was common among married couples, and that area of sexual expression has gained increasing acceptance in recent years (although it is almost completely ignored in the research literature about the means for sexual fulfillment, even among the married). Hunt found that more than 80 percent of the single men and women between the ages of 25 and 34 "had practiced cunnilingus or fellatio, or both, in the past year."[48] A study in a large Southern university in 1970 found a high frequency of oral-genital sex; 66 percent of the males and 54 percent of the females had engaged in this activity.[49] It is suggested that oral-genital sexual experiences have contributed to the wider repertoire of sexual behavior of college students and that not only do more of these students participate in coitus but also in oral-genital ac-

[46] Kinsey, *Human Female*, p. 292.

[47] Bell and Balter, "Premarital Sexual Experiences," p. 112.

[48] Hunt, "Sexual Behavior," p. 88.

[49] Ira E. Robinson, Karl King, and Jack O. Balswick, "The Premarital Sexual Revolution among College Females," *Family Coordinator*, April 1972, p. 191.

tivities. If this is true it would make such college students even more sexually experienced than the findings on coital experience would indicate.

The recent studies contribute to the general observation that engagement is less important as the stage for justifying premarital coitus than it was in the past. As previously mentioned, past studies have consistently shown that the coed who had premarital coitus usually limited it to one partner and then only during engagement. However, in the Bell and Chaskes study, when all girls in the 1968 sample who were ever engaged and who had ever had premarital coitus were analyzed, it was found that only 19 percent had limited their coital experience to the period of engagement. "Expressing it another way, of all girls who were ever engaged and ever had premarital coital experience, 75 percent had their first experience while dating, 6 percent while going steady, and 19 percent during engagement. For all coeds with premarital coital sexual experience, 60 percent had coitus while dating, going steady, and engagement."[50]

Closely related to the past condition of engagement before a coed had premarital coitus was the condition of love. It seems clear that this condition has changed, and while coeds do not usually have coitus with males they know in only a casual way they no longer demand that there be a strong emotional commitment on the part of both. It may also be that the younger generation defines love in a less complex and overwhelming way than it was defined in the past. While many of its members may say love is important, what they mean by love may be quite different from what was meant in the past.

There is some evidence that when a couple are in love the love is more likely to remain unchanged or to be heightened than to decrease after the first premarital coitus. The intensification of love after first coitus occurs most often for those who see themselves as very much in love. Those who state high love have the strongest desire for coitus with their love partners. "Clearly, from the subjective point of view, it appears that not only is love compatible with sex but that it also tends to be more compatible for those most in love, *both* for males and females."[51]

Religious influences

As suggested, historically in the United States religion has been the principal force defining appropriate sexual behavior. However, the influence of religious beliefs on premarital sexual activity has been decreasing steadily. In the Bell and Chaskes study it was found that in both 1958 and

---

[50] Bell and Chaskes, "Premarital Sexual Experience," p. 84.

[51] Eugene J. Kanin and Karen R. Davidson, "Some Evidence on the Aim-Inhibition Hypothesis of Love," *Sociological Quarterly*, Spring 1972, p. 214.

1968 the rates of coitus among coeds was lowest for Catholics, higher for Jews, and highest for Protestants. But what is of particular interest is that the proportionate rise in rates was the same for all three religious groups over the ten-year period.[52]

Whatever measure of religious intensity are used they appear to show higher rates of virginity among the more devout, regardless of the denomination. For example, just taking the type of educational institution coeds attend, Packard found that of the coeds in public institutions 49 percent were not virgins, and that this was true of 42 percent in private institutions, but of only 12 percent in church-related colleges.[53] A strong selection process takes place, with the most conservative girls going to the most conservative colleges. Another measure of religious intensity is religious attendance. In the 1970 study by the writer it was found that 67 percent of the nonvirgins and 51 percent of the virgins had not attended any religious ceremony during the past month.

The various studies indicate another social variable related to premarital sexual experience for coeds, and that is geographic region—especially if the coed is from the South. The South has the highest rural population, and it is also the most conservative in general moral values and religiously, all of which contributes to conservative sexual behavior. Also, as would be expected, the South has the highest proportion of double-standard adherents to premarital sexual behavior. For example, Packard found that in the eastern colleges studied 57 percent of the females and 64 percent of the males had had coital experience. By contrast, in the South the rates were 32 percent for the females and 69 percent for the males.[54]

When one examines the social variables related to present rates of premarital coitus it becomes clear that some of the old and reliable variables are no longer the absolute indicators they once were. For example, it used to be found that, whatever group one studied, the rate of premarital coitus for the male would be higher than the rate for the female. Yet when different types of college populations today are compared, this distinction doesn't always hold up. Packard writes that at 6 of 19 schools attended by males "*fewer* than 50 percent of the males reported that they had ever experienced coitus. And at 6 of 19 schools attended by females, *more* than 50 percent of the females responded that they had at some time experienced coitus."[55] Packard goes on to point out that for the females the lowest rates of coitus were reported at a Catholic university where less than one fifth reported coital experience. "The highest reported incidence for females was at the eastern woman's college

---

[52] Bell and Chaskes, "Premarital Sexual Experience," p. 83.

[53] Vance Packard, *The Sexual Wilderness* (New York: McKay, 1968), p. 507.

[54] Ibid., p. 188.

[55] Ibid., p. 186.

with liberal rules, where more than three-quarters of them reported coital experience."[56]

Guilt feelings

Given the argument that today many coeds engage in premarital sex in less emotionally demanding situations than existed in the past, what are the consequences of that behavior? If the norms of society are incorporated into the personality structure of the individual and the individual considers them to be important, any deviation from those norms will usually lead to guilt feelings. Certainly those who hold to the norms expect that to be true and assume that even when young people go "wrong" they will feel bad about it. "And what particularly bothers an older and more conservative generation is not only that the younger generation goes against the norms, but that it does not feel guilty about having done so. For the young person to have premarital intercourse *and* to be little influenced by the norms of the older generation is really the crux of the generational conflict pertaining to premarital sexual matters.

What evidence is there of feelings of guilt? In the Bell and Chaskes study the respondents were asked for each stage of the dating relationship, whether they had ever felt they had gone "too far" in their level of intimacy. Of coeds who had had coitus, the rates by the stage of the dating relationship for those saying they "went too far" were: "while dating, in 1958, 65 percent and in 1968, 36 percent; while going steady, in 1958, 61 percent and in 1968, 30 percent; and while engaged, in 1958, 41 percent and in 1968, 20 percent. In general, when the data of 1958 are compared with 1968 the coeds were more apt to have had intercourse at all levels of the dating relationship and at the same time felt less guilty than did their counterparts in 1958."[57]

Regardless of the limitations, the available evidence seems to indicate a change in the premarital sexual activity of an important minority of college students since the mid-1960s. From the point of view of the older members of society there has been no easing up of the traditional restrictive values about premarital coitus. Therefore, the differences by generation contribute to greater potential conflict. This chapter concludes by looking at the nature of generational conflict as it is reflected in the beliefs about premarital sexual behavior held by parents and their young adult offspring.

GENERATIONAL CONFLICT

Given their different stages in the life cycle, parents and children are

---

[56] Ibid., p. 187.

[57] Bell and Chaskes, "Premarital Sexual Experience," p. 83.

almost always going to show variations in how they define appropriate behavior for a given role. Values as to "proper" premarital sex-role behavior from the perspective of the parents are greatly influenced by the strong emotional involvement of the parents with their children. But by contrast the children are going through a life-cycle stage in which the actual behavior occurs, and must try to relate their parents' values to what they are doing or may do. There is a basic difference between defining appropriate role conduct for others and defining appropriate role conduct for oneself. What is important is that there is often more than one significant group of role definers that young persons may turn to as guides for their sex-role behavior. From the perspective of the young, what their parents think about how they should behave may be much less important than what their peers see as the correct mode of behavior. Some studies show the contrast in the attitudes toward premarital sex of the younger generation as compared with the values of parents and other adults.

In a study of college students and their parents Robert Walsh found that most parents felt that it was their duty to teach their children about sex and attempted to do so. He found that 93 percent of the mothers had discussed sex with their daughters and that 67 percent of the fathers had discussed it with their sons. What was most striking was the difference between the parents' perception and the children's perception of the parents' role as sex informant. "Seventy-three percent of the fathers and 63 percent of the mothers thought that they were indeed the major source of their child's sex information. Only 7 percent of the boys and 29 percent of the girls reported that their parents were the major source of sex information."[58]

Probably the most common technique used by the daughter for minimizing conflict is to avoid discussing her sexual attitudes or behavior with her mother. The entire area of sexual attitudes is highly influenced by emotion, especially for the mother as it concerns her daughter. The emotional reactions of some mothers may also be influenced by recollections of their own premarital sexual experiences. The Kinsey study, which provides data on the mothers' generation in its younger years, indicates that the mothers were actually no more conservative in their premarital sexual behavior than are many of their daughters.

There is a question as to whether the liberal sexual attitudes of coeds will be maintained as they get older. In the study discussed above it was found that differences in the educational background of the mothers did not produce differences in attitudes toward premarital virginity. It is quite possible that later in her life the college-educated daughter may be

---

[58] Robert H. Walsh, "The Generation Gap in Sexual Beliefs," *Sexual Behavior*, January 1972, p. 9.

as conservative as her mother, when her attitudinal rationales are not related to herself or her age peers, but rather to a daughter of her own. It is possible that the "sexual emancipation" of many college girls exists for only a short time in their life span—the time when they are personally involved in premarital sexual behavior.

In the mid-1960s Ira Reiss did research with several large samples of adults and high school and college students. In that study the respondents were asked to express their beliefs about different combinations of intimacy and degree of interpersonal commitment for both unmarried males and females. They were asked whether they believed that petting during engagement was acceptable for the engaged male and female. In the adult sample, 61 percent expressed the belief that petting during engagement was acceptable for the engaged male and 56 percent that it was acceptable for the engaged female. Of the student respondents, 85 percent approved for the engaged male and 82 percent for the engaged female.[59] Thus, not only were the adults' attitudes about petting during engagement more conservative than those of the student population, but for both the adult and student groups there is a single standard—that is, the acceptance rates are roughly the same for both males and females.

Reiss also asked his respondents whether they believed that premarital petting was acceptable when the individual felt no particular affection toward the partner. "Yes" was the response of 29 percent of the adult group with reference to the male, and of 20 percent with reference to the female. In the student sample, "yes" was the response for 34 percent of the males and 18 percent of the females.[60] These responses offer some evidence for a number of persons fitting into Reiss's category of "permissiveness-without-affection." The adult responses suggest a single standard of rejecting this kind of behavior, however, while the student sample gives some indication of a double standard—a higher proportion suggesting approval for this behavior pattern for males than for females.

Reiss asked his respondents whether they believed full sexual relations to be acceptable if the male or female was engaged. Approval was the response given by 20 percent of the adult group for males and by 17 percent for females. In the student group, acceptance was given by 52 percent for males and by 44 percent for females.[61] Finally, Reiss's respondents were asked whether they believed it acceptable for both males and females to have premarital coitus even if they felt no particular affection toward the partner. In the adult sample, 12 percent stated approval in the case of the male and 7 percent in the case of the female. In the student group, 21 percent approved for the male, 11 percent for

---

[59] Ira L. Reiss, "The Sealing of Premarital Sexual Permissiveness," *Journal of Marriage and the Family*, May 1964, pp. 190–91.

[60] Ibid., p. 190.

[61] Ibid., p. 190.

the female.[62] It should be remembered that these samples were taken in the mid-1960s, and it seems very likely that the rates of acceptance among college students would be higher today.

There is some recent evidence that an increasing number of college students are entering into living relationships that involve sexual participation. In a study conducted at Cornell University with a sample of 86 junior and senior women, Eleanore D. Macklin found that 34 percent had had an experience of cohabiting with a man. Those students generally did not see themselves as testing for a potential marriage. In most instances living together seemed a natural component of a strong, affectionate dating relationship—"which may grow in time to something more, but which in the meantime is to be enjoyed and experienced because it is pleasurable in and of itself."[63] A study conducted at Arizona State University found that 29 percent of the males and 18 percent of the females had cohabited at some time. That study also found that 57 percent of the males and 35 percent of the females who had not cohabited responded "yes" to the question "Would you want to cohabit?" The authors suggest that cohabitation patterns in the 1970s are what dating patterns were in the 1920s. "That is, expanding dimensions of the courtship process. Cohabitation among living-away-from-home college students will no doubt continue, and in fact increase, as more students are exposed to the idea and as administrators continue to relinquish their *in loco parentis* role."[64]

The values of parents and the adult community in general may in time become more liberal, and thus the conflict between the generations may be reduced. (There seems little possibility that the younger generation will become more conservative and reduce generational conflict in that way.) It appears most likely that parents and their children will continue to live with somewhat different value systems with regard to premarital sexual attitudes and related behavior. Many parents will probably continue to hold to traditional values and to assume that their children conform to those values unless the actions of their children force them to admit otherwise. The younger generation will probably continue to develop their own modified value systems and to keep those values pretty much to themselves, implicitly allowing their parents to believe they are behaving according to the traditional values.

In summary, it has been argued that premarital sexual involvement has increased in recent years and that it represents an important area of

---

[62] Ibid., p. 191.

[63] Eleanore D. Macklin, "Heterosexual Cohabitation among Unmarried College Students," *Family Coordinator*, October 1972, p. 470.

[64] Lura F. Henze and John W. Hudson, "Personal and Family Characteristics of Cohabiting and Noncohabiting College Students," *Journal of Marriage and the Family*, November 1974, p. 726.

social deviance as defined by older, more conservative elements of society. As suggested in Chapter 1, deviance often exists primarily in the eyes of the beholder, and therefore there are strong generational differences in defining whether or not premarital sex is deviance, and, if so, to what extent it actually exists. Related values held by different generations are important in understanding many other defined areas of deviance and social problems, and this will be seen in a number of the substantive areas to be discussed in the chapters ahead.

BIBLIOGRAPHY

Bell, Robert R., *Premarital Sex in a Changing Society.* Englewood Cliffs, N.J.: Prentice-Hall, 1966.

Bell, Robert R., and Shelli Balter, "The Premarital Sexual Experiences of Married Women," *Medical Aspects of Human Sexuality,* November 1973, pp. 111-18.

Bell, Robert R., and Jay B. Chaskes, "Premarital Sexual Experience among Coeds, 1958 and 1968," *Journal of Marriage and the Family,* February 1970, pp. 81-84.

Henze, Lura F., and John W. Hudson, "Personal and Family Characteristics of Cohabiting and Noncohabiting College Students," *Journal of Marriage and the Family,* November 1974, pp. 722-26.

Hunt, Morton, "Sexual Behavior in the 1970s," *Playboy,* October 1973, pp. 85, 88, 194, 197, 206; November 1973, pp. 74-75.

Macklin, Eleanore D., "Heterosexual Cohabitation among Unmarried College Students," *Family Coordinator,* October 1972, pp. 464-73.

Reiss, Ira L., *The Social Context of Premarital Sexual Permissiveness.* New York: Holt, Rinehart and Winston, 1967.

Robinson, Ira E., Karl King, and Jack O. Balswick, "The Premarital Sexual Revolution among College Females," *Family Coordinator,* April 1972, pp. 189-94.

Walsh, Robert H., "The Generation Gap in Sexual Beliefs," *Sexual Behavior,* January 1972, pp. 4-10.

chapter three

Extramarital sexual behavior

In the United States, while all sexual relations outside of marriage are morally condemned, the negative views toward extramarital coitus are generally stronger than those directed at premarital sexual intercourse. This is the result of two beliefs: first, that with marriage there is an approved sexual partner and that the individual therefore has the opportunity of having his sexual needs met within the marital relationship; second, that any extramarital sexual involvement threatens the highly valued relationship of marriage. In the past the American male could often discreetly indulge in sexual relations outside of marriage, but under no circumstances was the wife allowed any such sexual outlet. For many Americans the traditional double-standard values have been altered to the extent that both partners are expected to restrict their sexual activities to marriage; and if the husband has any extramarital "rights," then it is believed that the same "rights" should also exist for the woman. In this chapter the interest is first in examining extramarital sexual activity as it has traditionally been viewed, and second, in looking at "swinging," a fairly new type of sexual behavior outside of marriage that involves the husband and wife together with other married couples.

Under American law the specific legal restrictions placed on extramarital coitus fall under the heading of adultery.

ADULTERY

In the United States adultery is legally punishable, but actual prosecution is rare and in most states the penalties are mild. Adultery has its greatest importance as a legal ground for divorce, since it is the only legal ground for divorce recognized by all legal jurisdictions of the United States. It is useful to look first at views of extramarital coitus from a cross-cultural perspective.

All known societies have placed some restrictions on extramarital coitus and developed some means for enforcing the restrictions. However, the nature of the restrictions and the means to effectively enforce them vary widely among societies, and often within a given society over time. In most preliterate groups, ancient societies, and even recent civilizations adultery has not been restricted because of opposition to adultery per se or even because of morality. Adultery has most often been restricted because it was considered a threat to the economic stability of society.

As has been suggested, when one actually examines the many cultures, past and present, it is seen that the taboos against extramarital involvement are widespread—although sometimes honored more in the breach than in actual practice. Murdock found that taboos against adultery in 120 (81 percent) of his sample of 148 societies. "In 4 of the remaining 28, adultery is socially disapproved though it is not strictly forbidden; it is conditionally permitted in 19 and freely allowed in 5. It should be pointed out, however, that these figures apply only to sexual relations with unrelated or distantly related persons. A substantial majority of all societies permit extramarital relations with certain affinal relatives."[1]

Many societies reflect a double standard with regard to extramarital rights. In their study of various societies Ford and Beach found that 60 percent forbid a married woman to engage in extramarital relationships. They point out that in some societies the married man is also restricted, although most societies are much more concerned with the behavior of the wife. Yet, in those societies very often any man who seduces a married woman will be punished.[2] They go on to point out that "although in theory many societies accept a double standard of restrictions on extra-mateship liaisons, it is only in a few cases that the mated man can take advantage of his theoretical liberties."[3]

When it is seen that in most societies women have fewer opportunities for extramarital sex, and that even where the opportunities exist women have lower incidences and frequencies, it must be recognized that this is due to cultural rather than biological differences. That is, the evidence clearly indicates that if women are given the opportunity to engage in extramarital sex without strong social and psychological restrictions, many find it attractive and enjoyable. In those countries where strong progress has been made toward special equality of the sexes the evidence indicates increased incidence of extramarital sex behavior among married women. This appears to be a pattern for an increasing number of American women—especially among the higher educated.

Some cultures have allowed extramarital sexual involvement to take

[1] George P. Murdock, *Social Structure* (New York: Macmillan 1949), p. 265.

[2] Clellan S. Ford and Frank A. Beach, *Patterns of Sexual Behavior* (New York: Harper, 1952), p. 115.

[3] Ibid.

place under special circumstances. Often a society will be very restrictive about many areas of activity, but at special times of the year it will lift those restrictions. For example, there are societies which have special days or occasions for general license during which the members are allowed to violate the usual rules. This is seen during the Mardi Gras in New Orleans and similar pre-Lent activities in the Caribbean and South America. Ford and Beach write, "Sexual liaisons may be generally prohibited, but on certain special occasions the prohibitions are lifted for a short time and everyone is expected to have sexual intercourse with someone other than the spouse. The occasions for sexual license usually appear to have religious significance and may range from harvest festivals to mortuary feasts."[4]

It is also found that in some societies specific forms of extramarital sexual relationships take place. This is because with few exceptions every society that approves of extramarital liaisons limits them in some way. For example, some societies forbid extramarital relationships except between siblings-in-law.[5] And in some societies extramarital sex takes the form of "wife lending" or "wife exchange." "Generally, the situation is one in which a man is granted sexual access to the mate of another only on special occasions. If the pattern is reciprocal an exchange of wives occurs. Both wife lending and wife exchange may be involved in patterns of hospitality."[6]

Despite the exceptions to the absolute controls over extramarital sexual relationships, the strengths of these controls have been very powerful, especially in the Western world. According to Churchill all the sexual prohibitions in Judaism and Christianity originate in a profoundly *erotophobic* psychology, "a psychology in which sex is regarded not merely as somewhat inherently evil, but also as somehow inherently dangerous."[7] And this in turn relates to why extramarital sexual behavior has been so strongly controlled. Probably the most important reason has been the great influence of religion on the norms of sexual morality. The only sexual restriction in the Ten Commandments is against adultery. But biblically adultery referred to an offense against property and meant infringing on the rights of another man. It did not necessarily mean that a man must restrict his sexual attentions to his wife. In fact if his wife did not bear children she often gave one of her handmaidens to her husband. "Moreover, as the Bible often reminds us, men were free to maintain mistresses ('concubines') in addition to their wives; and on the number of wives a man might have there was no restriction."[8]

[4] Ibid., p. 115.

[5] Ibid., p. 114.

[6] Ibid.

[7] Wainwright Churchill, *Homosexual Behavior among Males* (New York: Hawthorn Books, 1967), p. 19.

[8] G. Rattray Taylor, *Sex in History* (New York: Vanguard Press, 1954), p. 241.

However, over time and especially with the emergence of Protestantism, the church gained increasing influence over sexual behavior.

In the United States religious restrictions against extramarital sex have had a great influence on the laws. The relationship between these two institutions in strongly controlling American behavior from the beginning is seen in the attempt to repress all sexual matters among the Puritans. The Puritans instituted the death penalty for adultery, although for ordinary fornication the penalty was the relatively mild one of three months' imprisonment. The death sentence was actually imposed, as there is on record the execution of a man of 89 for adultery in 1653.[9]

Down through the years the institutions of religion and law have worked together. In theory most laws about adultery are based on the assumption that it is a cardinal sin. But there has often been a wide disparity between the legal punishments in principle and in practice. This has been especially true for men, because exceptions have constantly been made. For example, in England less than a century ago a man could legally support his mistress on the earnings of his wife. "This is not an example of what was theoretically possible under the law of the day; it is an example of what did happen, alike in high and low society."[10] The study of all relevant data fails to reveal a society that has consistently suppressed and severely punished the extramarital sex relations of its males. This was true even among the early Puritans where even though the punishment was very severe and conformity was high there is still evidence of some sexual deviance. An anthropologist writes on this point that however much moralists push the obligation of chastity in marriage "this obligation has never been even approximately regarded: and in all nations, ages, and religions a vast mass of irregular indulgence has appeared, which has probably contributed more than any other single cause to the misery and degradation of man."[11]

There are many complex reasons for the breakdown of the traditional means of control over sexual morality. Certainly the decreasing influence of religion in defining behavior for many people is a major change. But on the broadest level the decrease in control has occurred because the American society is modern, industrialized, and urbanized. As a specialized society it has developed to the point where the traditional institutions of marriage and the family are of much less significance for survival and physical well-being. Adultery has ceased to be a serious threat to its economy. With this in mind it is possible to examine the contemporary scene in the United States with regard to extramarital sexual attitudes and behavior.

As is the case for all areas of deviance it is impossible to know with any

---

[9] Ibid., p. 173.

[10] E. S. Turner, *Roads to Ruin* (Middlesex, Eng.: Penguin Books, 1966), p. 135.

[11] William N. Stephens, *The Family in Cross-Cultural Perspective* (New York: Holt, Rinehart and Winston, 1963), p. 241.

accuracy how common extramarital sexual experience is in the United States. The Kinsey studies (done in the late 1940s and early 1950s) found that by age 40, 26 percent of the married women and 50 percent of the married men had had an extramarital coital experience.[12] In Bell and Peltz's 1972 study of 2,372 married women across the United States it was also found that 26 percent had had extramarital coitus. However, the average age of the women in that sample was 34.5 years, somewhat younger than the women in the Kinsey study. So if a projection of a few years is made to equalize the age variable it seems likely that the rate will be higher than Kinsey's. The key age group in the Bell and Peltz study may be the 26 to 30 group (17 percent had had extramarital coitus). It is predicted that by the time that group reaches age 40 its rate will be around 40 percent.[13]

Kinsey discovered important age differences for men and women; for men, the highest percentage was in the very young married group, and then the percentage gradually decreased with increasing age. For women, the highest percentage was in the age group 36 to 40, but the percentage was low for very young and older women.[14] The peak rates for extramarital coitus correspond to the different stages of greatest sexual interest and drive in the male and the female. The increase for women as they grow older may be a consequence of a decline in the husband's sexual activity as he gets older. Not only do many older women have a high sexual interest, but the sexual desire of some may increase because reaching the menopause has eliminated their fear of pregnancy.

The Kinsey studies also provided information as to the number of partners of those with extramarital coital experience. For women Kinsey found that at the time of the study 41 percent had limited their extramarital coitus to one partner; another 40 percent had had sexual relations with from two to five partners. The remaining 19 percent had had more than five partners in their extramarital activities. The rates for the married women in the Bell and Peltz sample were almost the same. One striking finding of the Bell and Peltz study was that extramarital sex as a single event was not a common pattern. The average number of times a woman had had sexual relations with each extramarital partner was almost six. Only 16 percent of the women had limited themselves to one sexual experience. By contrast one third had had extramarital coitus more than ten times with each partner. "Therefore, extramarital coitus is usually not an isolated event but clearly implies a willingness to maintain a series of experiences with the sexual partner."[15]

---

[12] Alfred C. Kinsey, Wardell B. Pomeroy, Clyde E. Marain, and Paul H. Gebhard, *Sexual Behavior in the Human Female* (Philadelphia: Saunders 1953), p. 437.

[13] Robert R. Bell and Dorthyann Peltz, "Extramarital Sex Among Women," *Medical Aspects of Human Sexuality.*

[14] Kinsey, *Human Female*, p. 416.

[15] Bell and Peltz, "Extramarital sex," p. 20.

Kinsey also provides information on other variables related to the frequency of extramarital coitus. For the female, the Kinsey data show no relationship between the frequency of extramarital coitus and educational level; however, for the male, the rates were significantly higher among the less educated.[16] By religion for women, the active incidence of extramarital experience was higher among the less devout, and this finding was true of Protestants, Jews, and Catholics alike. The same general relationship of extramarital experience to devoutness was also found for the male.[17] The influence of religious involvement was also found in the Bell and Peltz study. Among the women who attended religious services, 12 percent had had extramarital coitus, while this was true of 33 percent who did not attend religious services.[18]

The available data clearly indicate that a large number of both husbands and wives find some sexual experience outside of marriage. The data also suggest that this behavior cannot be attributed in all cases to chance circumstances or "momentary weakness." While there have been no socially approved changes in the values about extramarital coitus, it is clear that the traditional values and norms no longer exert effective control over the behavior of many husbands and wives. Of greatest significance may be the indicated behavioral changes in the sexual activity of many wives. The philandering husband has often had latent social acceptance in the United States, but the philandering wife has not, either in the past or the present. As suggested, the involvement in extramarital sexual activity is a result of many factors. The following are some suggestions as to possible reasons for becoming involved in extramarital coitus. It should be kept in mind that, for any given individual, the suggested influences may operate in varying degrees of intensity.[19]

1. *Variation of sexual partners.* The monogamous sexual relationship of man and woman is a result of cultural conditioning, which may not be as strong for some individuals as for others. In some cases the sexual relationship of marriage becomes routinized and boring, and the idea of another sexual partner seems different, new, and exciting. In other cases the person may feel that his spouse is no longer able to meet his sexual needs and, consequently, he seeks out someone who he believes will be a better sexual partner than the spouse. Within this setting the basic motivation appears to be the desire for the new experience of a different sexual partner.

2. *Retaliation.* If one partner in a marriage finds out that the other has had an extramarital affair, the reaction may be "If he can, so can I." Reiss suggests that this reaction is most commonly found among double-

---

[16] Kinsey, *Human Female*, p. 437.

[17] Ibid., pp. 424, 437.

[18] Bell and Peltz, "Extramarital Sex," p. 21.

[19] See Kinsey, *Human Female*, pp. 432–35. The following are partially drawn from this source.

standard men and women.[20] In the case of an affair on the part of a husband whose wife believes in sexual equality, the wife may respond by thinking that she should have an affair to show her sexual equality. Retaliation indicates that getting even may be a more important consideration than sexual interest in another partner.

3. *Rebellion.* Some people feel that the monogamous state of marriage places an unnecessary restriction on them, and that through extramarital coitus they can show their independence. The rebellion may sometimes be aimed at the spouse, who they feel restricts their sexual "rights." In other cases, the person may feel that the social norms of monogamy are unreasonable, and he shows his objection to and contempt for the norms by entering into a sexual liaison. The motivating force often appears to be not so much a desire for the extramarital sex partner, but rather to "show" the spouse or society in general.

4. *Emotional involvements.* Some individuals do not feel that their personal needs are being met in the marriage relationship, and as a result they may seek satisfaction (not always sexual) from a partner outside the marriage. But if a woman feels that the extramarital partner is satisfying some of her emotional needs, sexual activity may enter the relationship. Here the motive appears to be the need for an emotional relationship outside of marriage, which may then lead to sexual intimacy.

5. *Emerging from friendship.* In American society cross-sexual friendships among adults are often difficult because of the possibility of a shift to a romantic or sexual interest. In some cases men and women who are friends may find themselves developing an emotional and sexual interest in each other. In this setting, although there may be no conscious intention of establishing sexual relationships, a sexual interest may develop along with increased mutual interest and feeling.

6. *Spouse encouragement.* Kinsey found that in some cases husbands had encouraged their wives to have extramarital affairs. The motive of a number of husbands was the desire to find an excuse for their own extramarital activity.[21] Yet one of Kinsey's striking findings was that "most of the husbands who attempted or encouraged their wives' extramarital activity had done so in an honest attempt to give them the opportunity for additional sexual satisfaction."[22]

7. *The influence of aging.* It was pointed out that the highest frequency of extramarital coitus for women occurred among the age group from 36 to 40. Several influences may operate on women in this age classification. First, the woman's sexual desires and interests are often high as a result of a strong sex drive and the loss of many sexual inhi-

---

[20] Ira L. Reiss, *Premarital Sexual Standards in America* (New York: Free Press 1960), p. 170.

[21] Kinsey, *Human Female*, p. 435.

[22] Ibid.

bitions that influenced her when she was younger. During the same age period many husbands experience a decrease in sexual drive and interest. Second, in entering middle age a woman may see herself as leaving her youth behind and may find this aspect of aging very upsetting. She may want to prove to herself (and sometimes others) that she is still a desirable female, and an extramarital affair may be seen as one way of doing so.

8. *Hedonism.* This final category centers on the fact that while sex is usually highly enjoyable, most people will often forgo the pleasure because of various types of social conditioning. If the moral restrictions are not meaningful for an individual, he may take a hedonistic view toward sex. So some people may have extramarital sexual relationships simply because new sexual relationships are pleasurable, and they may do so with no negative consequences. Of course, in this day and age of belief in deep-seated and hidden motives (many of which are never empirically proven), a simple hedonistic approach to extramarital sex is denied. Yet, we would suggest that some people may enter "illicit" sexual activity not to prove anything—but simply because sex is pleasurable and because they are not subject to many of the usual social restrictions.

It is now possible to examine some of the effects of extramarital experience on the spouse who is left at home. Undoubtedly the most common reaction of the innocent spouse is jealousy. Stephens points out that while the urge to philander is strong, nevertheless in many cultures it collides with feelings of possessiveness and sexual jealousy. "When one spouse 'cheats,' the other spouse—if he or she knows about it—often suffers."[23] Stephens goes on to point out that even in societies which allow adultery the problem of jealousy still exists. "Some people are still hurt when their spouses engage in perfectly proper and virtuous adultery."[24]

Given the strong social restrictions against extramarital coitus, the sexual satisfactions and reactions of those who deviate are of interest. Kinsey found that about 85 percent of the females engaging in extramarital activity were responding, at least on occasion, to orgasm. But Kinsey also points out that selective factors were probably involved and that the most responsive females may have been the ones who had most often engaged in extramarital coitus.[25] However, the Bell and Peltz study found just the opposite, that among the married women who had never had orgasms 40 percent had extramarital coitus but that this was true of 24 percent of the women with at least some experience of orgasm. This suggests that some women who never have orgasm in marriage may be searching for that experience with partners outside of marriage.[26]

Kinsey also provides some information on the significance of extra-

---

[23] Stephens, *Family*, p. 254.

[24] Ibid., pp. 251–52

[25] Kinsey, *Human Female*, p. 418.

[26] Bell and Peltz, "Extramarital Sex," p. 22.

marital coitus for divorce. In general females rated extramarital coitus as a less important factor in divorce than did men, and both sexes assessed the extramarital coitus of the spouse as more significant than their own extramarital activity. Fourteen percent of the females and 18 percent of the males saw their own extramarital experience as a major factor in their divorce; however, when the extramarital activity was that of the spouse, 27 percent of the females and 51 percent of the males rated it as a major factor in their divorce.[27] Finally, pregnancy attributed to extramarital coitus appears to be quite rare. "Of our 2,221 ever-married women, 26 reported a total of 32 pregnancies known or believed to have been the result of extramarital coitus."[28]

Of great significance are the psychological reactions of women to their experiences in extramarital coitus. If the norms and values of society were fully accepted and integrated into the personality structures of individuals, then one would expect strong feelings of remorse and guilt by women who have had extramarital experiences. Kinsey found that "among the married women in the sample who had not had extramarital experience, some 83 percent indicated that they did not intend to have it, but in a sample of those who had had extramarital experiences, only 44 percent indicated they did not intend to renew their experiences."[29] These findings suggest that a number of women did not have severe enough negative feelings about their past experiences to deter them from anticipating the same experiences in the future. The Bell and Peltz study found that only 9 percent of the women who had had extramarital experience categorically said it would never happen in the future. In contrast, 62 percent of the women who had not had extramarital coitus said it would never happen in the future.[30]

With the traditional importance attached to the husband's exclusive sexual rights to his wife, it would seem that if a husband found his wife guilty of adultery he would either divorce her or drastically alter the nature of the marriage; yet Kinsey found that about 49 percent of the females who had had extramarital coitus believed that the husband knew or suspected. In those marriages where the husband suspected or learned of the wife's extramarital activities, 42 percent of the women reported no difficulty with the husband.[31] While it is possible that some of the women were interpreting their husbands reactions inaccurately, it is also possible that many were not. If so, this indicates a great change for some husbands from the traditional view of their wives' sexual exclusiveness for them.

   [27] Kinsey, *Human Female*, p. 438.
   [28] Paul H. Gebhard, Wardell B. Pomeroy, Clyde E. Martin, and Cornelia V. Christenson, *Pregnancy, Birth, and Abortion* (New York: Harper and Row, 1958), p. 85.
   [29] Kinsey, *Human Female*, p. 431.
   [30] Bell and Peltz, "Extramarital Sex," p. 22.
   [31] Kinsey, *Human Female*, p. 434.

Implied in the discussion thus far is the view that extramarital sex may follow many different patterns. One writer has suggested that today the two extremes are the new open and accepted affair and the old secret and guiltridden one.[32] The variation as well as the changing nature of extramarital sex is reflected in what extramarital relationships are called. Not too many years ago the term was *cheating*, but now it's an *affair*. In fact it is increasingly getting to be that only the lower middle and lower classes refer to cheating. And the term *adultery* is getting to sound old-fashioned and almost quaint.[33]

One type of extramarital sexual involvement that has always existed but has changed a great deal in recent years is the relationship of the mistress to the married man. This is an intimate relationship that involves far more than sex. It usually lasts for an extended period of time, and there are generally no real expectations that marriage will ever occur. By contrast an "affair" is much more sexually oriented and involves much less interpersonal commitment. Cuber has described the mistress relationship in some detail. He found that the mistress was as apt to be married as unmarried. When two married people enter into a mistress relationship it is usually because they feel that their respective marriages are lacking in interpersonal or sexual fulfillment. "However, for one reason or another they do not wish to terminate their marriages legally and so find their fulfillment in what is really a *de facto* marriage, without any legal or moral sanction by the community."[34]

Cuber found no simple configuration of attitudes and life-style which distinguished the wife from the mistress. Like a wife, a mistress may fit a wide variety of attitudes, life-styles, fulfillments, and frustrations.[35] Also, the importance of sex to the mistress relationship can be overdone. "Some mistresses are primarily intellectual companions, women who share some intellectual pursuit with their men, some important hobby, some political or ethical commitment in a way which neither has had or is able to have with anyone else."[36] Cuber goes on to point out that the stereotype of the young mistress and the aging man does not fit the facts. In fact he found that even in late middle age a number of men had mistresses of about the same age. Cuber suggests that perhaps the most startling finding of his study was that a considerable number of mistress relationships endured for long periods of time.[37]

---

[32] Nancy Love, "The '70's Woman and the Now Marriage," *Philadelphia Magazine*, February 1970, p. 56.

[33] Ibid.

[34] John F. Cuber, "The Mistress in American Society," *Medical Aspects of Human Sexuality*, September 1969, p. 86.

[35] Ibid., p. 85.

[36] Ibid., p. 86.

[37] Ibid., p. 87.

As suggested in Cuber's discussion of the mistress relationship, sex may not always be important and in some cases it may not occur. There may be nonsexual affairs that are based upon fairly strong emotional attachments. In fact a nonsexual emotional attachment may be a far greater threat to a marriage than a brief sexual nonemotional relationship. This distinction is very important to the "swingers" who will be examined later in the chapter.

The stress has been on the patterns of extramarital sexual experiences, but it should always be remembered that many Americans never have such experiences. For most of these people the traditional controls over sexual morality will continue to be strong. But for more and more people, especially among the young, the views about sexual morality are changing. In fact today many people who engage in extramarital sexual relationships suffer little or no social criticism if their behavior is discreet. Generally, extramarital sex is seen by many as a personal concern unless it becomes general knowledge. "Even then no legal action is likely unless the adultery, left unpunished, is thought to set a bad moral example for youth or otherwise to encourage wrongdoing."[38]

As is the case in so many areas of deviance, many persons who are involved in extramarital activity have moved from the defensive to the offensive. Put another way, they have often shifted from rationalizing their behavior to proselytizing it. For example, the Sexual Freedom League believes "that sexual expression, in whatever form agreed between consenting persons of either sex, should be considered an inalienable right. . . . Sex without guilt and restriction is good, pleasurable, relaxing, and promotes a spirit of human closeness, compassion and good will. We believe that sexual activity. . .has a wealth of potential for making life more livable and enjoyable."[39]

In the past the belief existed that extramarital sexual involvement would destroy a marriage, which it often did because the belief was so strong, even though there may have been no other logical reason for ending the marriage. However, there is no reason to believe that human beings, if they choose, cannot invent ways to reduce or remove the social conditions that make extramarital coitus hazardous for happily married people.

Whatever changes do occur will be a part of the new sexual morality that argues for equal rights of sexual expression for both men and women. This means that women will increasingly demand the same sexual rights for themselves as do men, whether in or out of marriage. As Love points out, "No matter what the outcome of the academic and ethical debates,

[38] Harper, "Extramarital Sex Relations," p. 387.

[39] Jack Lind, "The Sexual Freedom League," in Walt Anderson, *The Age of Protest* (Pacific Palisades, Calif.: Goodyear 1969), p. 184.

women are going to continue to demand equal time and equal rights to erotic pleasure, to self-realization, to self-respect—and if they can't find these qualities within marriage, they will quietly go on seeking them elsewhere."[40]

It is also of interest that the new sexual morality attaches great importance to women's sexual satisfaction. It is believed by many that women should have greater freedom to enjoy sex in the same way that men have always enjoyed it. But the irony of this liberation is that a woman may have greater apprehension if she doesn't fully enjoy the sexual experience. She knows she has a right to orgasm, and if she is not having it with the frequency or intensity she believes she should she may begin to wonder what is wrong. At the same time the man who also accepts the new morality may wonder what is wrong with himself if his mate doesn't reach full sexual fulfillment. These kinds of concerns are important both in and out of marriage. But in one sense they may be most important outside of marriage, where the affair is essentially sexual and any sexual failure undermines the limited tie of the relationship. In the next section we will consider an essentially avant-garde type of sex outside of marriage —"swinging"—the sexual exchange of marriage partners.

SWINGING

For years stories have been told about "wife-swapping" and "key clubs." When the tellers of these stories were pushed for evidence, it was almost always found that the stories were third or fourth hand, their origins lost in the foggy past of rumor. One story which it was possible to track down was based on one married woman having sexual intercourse with a number of neighborhood men. But this was not "wife-swapping" or "swinging." However, in recent years many stories about swinging have been tracked down and found to be based on fact. There has probably always been some swinging, but not to the extent that it has developed in recent years. Furthermore, swinging now seems to be prevalent throughout the United States, although it is probably less common in the South.

Swinging, as the term is used here, refers to the sexual exchange of partners between married couples. And the sexual activities of these couples with one another are viewed as primarily recreational and as an end in themselves. Swinging is a single standard of sex which insists that what is sexually right for the husband is also right for the wife. In this it contrasts with affairs, which usually involve guilt and dishonesty and often do not include any notion of fun and recreation. There are also

---

[40] Love, "'70's Woman," p. 93.

unmarried swingers who interact with one another. And sometimes single persons swing with married couples either as singles or as unmarried couples. However, our primary interest here is to examine swinging among married couples. The following sections draw on a study done by the author and a colleague.

The study is based on extensive interviews with about 25 swingers, sometimes as couples, but most often separately. Each interview lasted between two and five hours. While a number of different topics were consistently explored with all respondents the interviews were for the most part unstructured and carried out as free and open discussions. Observations were also made at "socials" and "open parties." The purpose here will be to describe and analyze some of the general social character-istics of swinging. The analysis must be general, and it is recognized that swinging may vary greatly in some situations from what is described here.

Two married couples may on occasion exchange sex partners, but never do this with any other couple. Many couples have probably had this experience, but they would not usually be thought of as swingers either by themselves or by others. In the broadest sense swinging can describe a wide range of events. A brief description of two extreme types will illustrate the range. One way of describing the variation is to see swinging as ranging from some interpersonal interaction and com-mitment to an almost totally impersonal relationship. This range is repre- sented by "closet swinging" at one extreme to "open swinging" or "orgies" at the other. A brief discussion of each follows.

Closet swinging

This occurs when two or more couples get together, usually at someone's home. Often the couples do not know each other, and the initial arrangements for getting together are made by telephone. Sometimes they will agree that the evening is to be "social," which means that there may or may not be sex, depending on how they feel about one another. The first part of the evening often involves a few drinks, talking, and sometimes dancing. The smoothness of the evening is often de-termined by the experience of the couples with swinging. If the couples decide to swing that evening a pair will usually leave and go to a bedroom. If a couple go into a bedroom and close the door they are truly "closet swingers" because the closed door means that no one else is to come into that room. However, if the door is left open that means that others may join them and watch, participate alongside of, or participate with. If there are more than two couples they will often go off with different sexual partners before the evening is over. Often between sexual experiences people will return to the living room either nude or partly dressed and talk and drink as at any party.

Open parties or orgies

In this setting the interaction may be almost completely physical, with little or no verbal communication. For example, after a "social," six or seven couples may go to a hotel suite, and most of them may not know one another. After a few minutes one couple may simply say, "Let's get started," strip, and within five minutes almost all are involved in various sexual activities. This can go on for several hours with almost no verbal exchange until people get tired, dress, and go home. There are many occasions when two people will have long, complex sexual exchanges and never say a word to each other. This extreme almost represents the ultimate sexual experience.

Between the two extreme types described there are many combinations and permutations. For example, a party may start out as closet swinging and turn into an orgy. Or at one party there may be one couple in one room swinging privately while in another room a number of couples are swinging together. Many swingers will not engage in all types of behavior, and that is often the factor that determines what direction the sexual activities will take at a given party.

RECRUITMENT

In some types of deviance many persons are recruited against their wills. For example, many homosexuals don't really make a choice as to the direction of their sexual expression. In other types of deviance some persons are recruited even though they are not sure they want to enter, as, for example, in some delinquent gangs. But recruitment into swinging always appears to imply that at least one partner wants to enter and that the other is willing at least to the extent that he knows that that is what his partner wants. Most often it is initially the husband who wants to try swinging and then persuades his wife. Many times the couple will enter swinging, but the wife resists and the couple drop out somewhere along the way. When couples stay for a relatively long period of time, that may be the result of two different responses by the wife. After wives enter swinging they may continue for a while because their husbands want them to stay. The wives may keep thinking their husbands will want to drop out. But after a while when they realize that the husband has no intention of stopping they may begin to convince themselves that they are in it because they (the wives) want to be. On the other hand it appears that when a couple stays with swinging for a period of time the wife does develop an enthusiasm for it that may become even greater than that of her husband. This pattern is similar to one sometimes found with regard to husband and wife views about sex in marriage. Often the husband enters marriage with great enthusiasm about having a sexual partner always available. The wife sometimes enters marriage with some inhibitions and anxieties as to her sexual participation. But as the newness of the sexual availability wears off, the husband's interests often decrease. But at the same time the wife's inhibitions are often removed and her sexual interests become greater.

One study found two factors that appeared to be important in making women favorably disposed to swinging. One was their perception of their marriage after entering swinging. If a woman felt that swinging had improved her marriage relationship she was encouraged toward swinging. The other was their subjective experience with swinging. If the experience was positive, then they were pleased with it. "Most women appear to attach more importance to the first factor, especially in the early stages of becoming a swinger. Later on, when assured that the relationship is not threatened, her subjective experiences take on greater priority."[41] It may also be that some general social factors are related to the entry of women into swinging. For example, in the Bell and Peltz study of married women it was found that those who had engaged in mate-swapping had had a higher rate of premarital coitus, with more different men, and more often with each man than had women without mate-swapping experience. There was also evidence of a high level of sexual interest as reflected in average monthly frequency of marital coitus. For mate-swappers it was 13.3 times as compared to 7.9 times for other women.[42]

There is no way of knowing how many swingers there are in the United States. This activity, like all areas of "hidden" deviance, is impossible to measure. The Bell and Peltz study provides a crude estimate, although the biases of its sample probably make the rates somewhat bigger than would be true for the general population. The study found that 5 percent of the married women said that they had had at least one mate-swapping experience. There was some indication that mate-swapping was more common among younger women. Seven percent of those under 30 and 3 percent of those over 30 had engaged in mate-swapping.[43] But probably the most that can be said is that there are more swingers than nonswingers believe, but not as many as swingers think. There are three general ways in which recruitment into swinging takes place. The three paths may be followed separately or in combination by different persons entering swinging.

---

[41] Charles A. Varni, "Contexts of Conversion: The Case of Swinging," in Roger W. Libby and Robert N. Whitehurst, *Renovating Marriage* (San Ramon, Calif.: Consensus 1973), p. 171.

[42] Bell and Peltz, "Extramarital Sex," p. 23.

[43] Ibid., p. 24.

Magazines

Several profit-making organizations directed at swingers have emerged, and one of the things they do is publish magazines. The main function of the magazines is to run personal ads. The ads have code numbers, and anyone who wants to respond must do so through the publisher. This offers some protection to the persons who place the ads and contributes to the profit of the organization. It may cost ten dollars to join a club and about five dollars to place an ad. (Single women can usually place an ad free because they are in great demand.) The clubs may charge a dollar to forward a letter. Often the ads are accompanied by a picture which bears only a remote resemblance to the real person. The ads are usually quite short and the following are actual illustrations:

S-115
Married couple, attractive, both late twenties. Wife 36-25-35, husband 5' 10", 170 lbs. New York City. Desire to meet other marrieds and single women. Both enjoy French culture, photography and erotic movies.

S-225
Married couple, middle thirties. Wife 37-25-36, husband muscular. Los Angeles area. Willing to try anything. Interested in French, Greek, and Arab culture. No single men.

While some of what is said in the ads would be understandable to most people, some of the phrases used are not commonly understood. For example, French culture means that the couple like oral sex, Greek that they like anal intercourse, while Arab refers to an interest in some sadomasochistic practices. Many of the ads are not genuine. For example, single men often place ads as if they were a part of a married couple, and this can create problems for couples who respond to those ads. But most swingers do not make their contacts through ads.

Socials

The same clubs that publish the magazines also sponsor parties, or "socials." These socials are held in hotel or motel ballrooms where a buffet dinner and a dance band can be presented. They are publicized through the magazines and are very well attended even though the price for the evening may run to $25 per couple. The socials are presented as opportunities for couples to get together, meet each other, and exchange phone numbers if they choose. And that is what happens—although there is often much more.

Many people go to socials out of curiosity and will never participate in swinging. However, for many who see socials as a major source for making sexual contacts, socials are in effect a "flesh market." This is an accurate description because the giving and receiving of phone numbers and party invitations is based primarily on physical appearance. This means that the youngest or most attractive couples are the most in demand. It is also reflected in the unadvertised function of the social, which is to provide contacts for swinging that night after it ends. Some couples go to a social and rent rooms, or if they live nearby plan on having a party at the end of the evening. The most attractive couples get the most invitations. As the evening draws to a close, some of the people who have not been invited to a party may become panicky. In some cases, almost out of desperation, rejects may seek each other out and have their own party.

Networks

Once people get into the swinging scene the most common way of making new contacts is through a network system. Initially these people make their contacts through advertisements, socials, or some couple they have met. Through their first contact they are often told of other couples to call, or that third couple may be asked to call them. This process continues, and contacts increase and are in turn passed on to others. There are networks that at times may involve 25 or 30 couples who each know some of the others and that get together as two or a number of couples. Some people are always coming in to the networks, and others are dropping out. But once a couple has successfully engaged in swinging with one or two couples it is not difficult to meet others.

Value system of swinging

Some swingers are very ideological and believe that they have found the answer to a good and happy life. As with any ideological commitment, there are some who believe with a religious fervor and want to proselytize their faith. Many who are not so ideological nevertheless believe that swinging leads to the best possible sex life. And, as suggested, swinging does mean a single standard of sex for both husband and wife. This single standard of participating sex implies important value changes for the wife and husband who accept it. For the wife it means separating sex from love, which she has been socialized to believe must go together. Her ability to make this distinction may be the best indicator of her ability to swing without serious personal problems. Varni found that for the wife the main effect of the first swinging experience was to reduce their level of anxiety. This provided a climate in which the experience could be evaluated more "objectively." "The typical response was that it was not such a big deal after all."[44] For the husband it means undoing the socialization process that has conditioned him to believe that a wife is the husband's exclusive sexual property. Not only are many swinging husbands able to do this, but some even find that seeing their wives in sexual contact with others is a highly erotic experience. Varni found that two types of men rejected the double standard and accepted swinging. One was the "user," who used his wife to gain entrance into swinging but did not appear very concerned about her feelings or desires. The other was the "encourager," who rejected the double standard on more idealistic grounds, mainly egalitarianism.[45] The ways in which husbands and wives are able to effectively undo their socialization to monogamous sex is an area worthy of future research.

Most swingers define sex as recreational and as an end in itself. Not only do they believe that swinging has nothing to do with love, but they develop strong sanctions to keep the two separate. What may be the most important value among swingers is that sex outside of marriage must be kept as physical and as impersonal as possible. Most swingers realize that if any interpersonal commitment develops this may constitute a real threat to the marriage. Swingers feel that sex doesn't threaten their respective marriages but that a developing emotional commitment could.

This taboo against interpersonal involvement is seen in the fact that if two couples swing together five or six times one of two things usually happens. Either they stop seeing each other altogether, or they develop a friendship and continue to see each other but drop the sex. And if they don't end or change their relationship their other swinging friends may take them to task for "going steady." The interpersonal restriction is also seen if any pair spend a good deal of time together and alone at a party and are *not* involved in sex—they are viewed with suspicion. Even in sexual activity there may be interpersonal limitations. That is, when a couple gets together foreplay is viewed as leading directly to possible orgastic experience. Couples are not expected to spend a lot of time in necking, petting, and romantic conversation.

While the above types of detached relationships are the common pattern, there are some exceptions among swingers. For example, some couples are able to maintain close friendships over time and still have sexual activities. These people will often say that they love and care about one another. What appears to happen is that the friendships are close but that there is not a strong emotional involvement. They are like any good friends who feel close but are not emotional interdependent. Such relationships do have the potential of developing into deep emotional ones

---

[44] Varni, "Contexts of Conversion," p. 171.
[45] Ibid., p. 170.

because they already have the strong ties of sex and friendship. It is our observation that a few couples have been able to maintain this type of relationship for several years.

If a man and woman want to see each other outside of swinging this is to be done only with the full knowledge of their respective spouses. "Single dating" is not very common, but if a man visits a woman both their respective spouses should know about it, and the couple would be together only for sexual purposes and not for interpersonal ones. This would be acceptable behavior to all so long as the sex is open and single standard. Not to tell one's spouse would be double standard, or, from the sincere swingers' point of view, dishonest and hypocritical.

ORGANIZATION

Because we have no idea of how many swingers there are we can't say with any accuracy who they are. About all that can be discussed are the visible swingers, the ones whom researchers have encountered. A few studies have found them to be quite conventional in their political views and essentially middle class, with swinging their only significant deviation from middle-class norms. This also appears to be true of what we have found in the Philadelphia area. The swingers we have met have generally been in their twenties and thirties with at least some college education and in business or the professions. They drink moderately and rarely use any kinds of drugs. (We know that lower middle-class as well as middle-aged swinging groups exist, but we have not encountered them.)

Swingers do have some fears. Some are concerned that their children will find out, and those couples will never swing at home. Because the woman places a high reliability on birth control methods pregnancy generally is not a great fear. Some are quite nervous about public exposure or even blackmail, although there is no evidence that these fears are well grounded. Probably most swingers do not consider themselves to be either immoral or lawbreakers. Swingers usually feel that the laws are wrong because there should not be legislation against personal morality. In fact many swingers feel superior because they believe that they have rid themselves of many of the sexual "hangups" that plague most American adults.

Oftentimes swingers will say that no rules govern their behavior, but in many ways and some cases already suggested this is not true. The most important rules are the sanctions against the development of interpersonal involvement. There are also rules governing who may participate in swinging. As suggested, physical attractiveness is important, and this means that one must be up to at least minimal standards. For example, people who are too heavy are usually excluded. Also, swinging couples tend to be alike in age. The fact that many parties involve nudity means that weight and age may be stigmata hard to hide.

Probably the more important rules center on the actual sexual selection and interaction among swingers. It is almost always true that no one is forced into any kind of sexual behavior if he lets it be known that he doesn't want to participate. The man usually initiates by asking the woman, and if she doesn't want to participate he is expected not to be overly insistent. And if he is turned down by most or all of the women present he will probably not be invited back. Sometimes a woman feels sorry for a rejected male and takes him on as a "charity" case. However, if a woman keeps refusing men then she and her husband will not be invited back. But the basic rule is that the wife does have the right to refuse any person, and if this happens when there are only two couples the evening ends, at least sexually. And many evenings do end this way. It appears to be a general rule that if the women take a dislike to each other there will be no swinging.

There is often greater pressure on the woman to participate sexually when there are only two couples than at an open party or orgy. This is because she knows that if she does not participate with the other husband the evening is over sexually. However, at an orgy, where there are a number of other women, she can say no and not be pressured. This is because there are enough women to take care of all the men sexually. It is common at orgies to find women who enjoy having sex with two or three men at the same time. Of course, any attempt to force a woman goes contrary to the basic belief of sincere swingers that sex must be voluntary and pleasurable for both partners.

SEXUAL BEHAVIOR

Basic to participation in the swinging movement is what persons believe they will get from the experience. It is clear that both men and women have many motives for entering swinging. For men there is often great excitement because they see the experience as giving reality to the sexual fantasies they have enjoyed for years. Swinging is also a chance for the man to fulfill the highly important male role of sexual activist. And, of course, it is seen as a highly exciting and pleasurable experience. When women are asked what they get out of swinging there are a variety of answers. For many of them the factor of pleasure is highly important, but swinging generally has nothing to do with fulfilling sexual fantasies or with meeting basic feminine needs for sexual expression. For some women the most satisfying aspect of swinging is the opportunity it gives them to be desirable and attractive to men. In some cases they say this makes them feel young again. Others have suggested that it is satisfying to be wanted by someone other than the husband and to be able to respond to that want. They feel not only that are they wanted but that they can control the situation in terms of their giving to the man who wants them.

Rarely does a swinger raise moral objections to any kind of sexual behavior. Swingers may say that something is not "their thing" but will make no moral judgments against any persons who engage in that behavior. Among swingers coitus is always acceptable, unless there is some reason on a given occasion for not indulging. Also oral-genital sex contact between men and women is practiced most of the time. Anal intercourse is accepted, although probably not practiced by most swingers. Many have tried it but choose not to indulge because they find it too painful.

As suggested, oral sex is very popular among both male and female swingers. Oral sex may be used both as foreplay or as a sexual end in itself. Often oral sex is used by the man when he is temporarily unable to get an erection for coitus. This is common when the men and women have had more than one orgastic experience over the course of the evening. Visual sex is also a very common practice among swingers. There is frequently a highly erotic influence on both men and women in seeing others have sexual relations. Often both husbands and wives find it very sexually exciting to see each other having sex with other partners.

One important area of sexual behavior among swingers is homosexuality. In the Bell and Peltz study 38 percent of the women with some swinging experience had also had homosexual experience. The study also found that 60 percent of the mate-swappers said that they would enjoy homosexual experiences in the future.[46] Male homosexuality is rare among swingers, but female homosexuality is quite common. This difference is due to several important reasons. First, most men would find a homosexual experience to be very threatening to their sense of masculinity. Such sexual activity carries with it a potentially severe threat to the basic male sex-role image. But this same sex-role concern is not true for women. Generally women have no strong fears about homosexuality and do not see it as threatening to their sense of femininity. Second, most men find the idea of two women having sexual contact highly erotic, but most women do not find the notion of two men having sexual relations at all sexually exciting. Therefore, men often encourage women to have sexual experiences with each other in the swinging situation. They often find that while they rest from a previous orgastic experience it is exciting and sexually stimulating to watch the women having sex with each other.

Among many swingers there is competition among the men to be the top sexual performers. The man is generally expected to have at least one erection to orgasm in an evening. But frequently a man feels that he has to have sex with as many women as possible. If half a dozen women are present he may feel a strong need to have some kind of sexual experience with each of them. For some men it is like being a boy with a box of candy who feels he must sample every piece—even if it gives him a stomachache.

The women are also interested in satisfactory sexual experiences during

---

[46] Bell and Peltz, "Extramarital Sex," p. 25.

the evening, but this doesn't always mean that they feel orgasm is necessary. It appears that for the more experienced swinging women orgasm is often not a measure of sexual satisfaction. That the woman always reach orgasm with each partner is often far more important to the man than to the woman. The man often sees her orgasm as a measure of his ability as a sexual "artist." It is common to hear a woman tell how she has mentioned to a man not to worry about her orgasm because it is hard for her to make it. And the man interprets this as a challenge and may try for hours to bring the woman to a climax. This effort doesn't necessarily mean that the man is interested in his partner's sexual welfare; it may mean that he sees her orgasm as a measure of his sexual ability.

To most Americans swinging seems so morally deviant and abhorrent that they immediately feel that people who engage in it are mentally sick and must have terrible marriages. By contrast many swingers believe that nonswingers are hung up on a hypocritical sexual monogamy and that they rarely have good marriages. As is often the case the truth probably falls somewhere between the two extreme points of view. The ideological swingers, those who are philosophically committed to swinging as a way of life, believe that swinging is no solution for a marriage in trouble. They believe that swinging would probably intensify the problem and should be avoided. But there are also many swinger who use swinging for their own psychological needs and hangups.

Swinging appears to work for a couple when the couple are able to separate sex with other partners from their relationships to each other. This means that sex with other partners is seen by both partners as serving a recreational end, and therefore the constant concern that swinging not develop into any interpersonal involvement. So those who believe that they are successful swingers argue that sex with others is recreational and *different* from the emotional sex they have with their spouse. Sex in swinging is physical, while in marriage sex is physical *and* emotional. Because they see sex as different in the two settings some argue that swinging sex helps marital sex because it makes each partner more sexually sophisticated and aware of the other as a desirable sex object.

Bartell found that one advantage of swinging couples was that they spent more time together. They often became involved in looking for new contacts. They planned weekend trips and vacations to other parts of the country to meet swingers.[47] Bartell also suggests that divorce rates are no higher among swingers than among nonswingers. He observes that in the cases he followed of couples who dropped out of swinging and were then divorced the evidence indicated deep incompatibility on many points prior to swinging.[48] Another study found that neither personal happiness nor marital happiness is different among swingers than among non-

---

[47] Gilbert D. Bartell, *Group Sex* (New York: Wyden, 1971), pp. 281–82.
[48] Ibid., pp. 26–27.

swingers.[49] Gilmartin and Kusisto came to the conclusion that mate-swapping by itself can neither help nor harm a marital relationship. They say that what is of vital importance is how the couples view their behavior. "If both partners can be both mentally and emotionally satisfied in a swinging situation, then this type of sexual expression will not do any harm to their relationship. If both partners see swinging as an essential part of their relationship, then swinging is 'right' for them."[50]

Sociologically the emergence of swinging in the United States is a logical extension of increased sexual freedom. This is a part of a value pattern, how large nobody knows, that believes that sex can be an end in itself and that participation in sex is to be determined by the individuals themselves and not by moral norms or legislated controls. The same pattern has been shown in recent years in studies of premarital sex where the woman is less concerned with sex's being a part of any interpersonal commitment than has been true in the past. That is, sex is becoming viewed by more and more females as a recreational end in itself on at least some occasions outside of marriage. Given this change, one may speculate that in the future the recreational nature of sex will continue to increase.

Many in the younger generation are growing up with a philosophy that sex can be recreational and privately decided upon. It is logical to predict that, as they marry, more and more people will have swinging experiences. In fact it is striking that many swingers today are in their early twenties and that many have been married only a few years. It may also be that many people have not tried swinging because they have not been aware of it as a possible activity.

Most Americans will continue to be monogamous in their married sexual experiences and will find the idea of swinging immoral, indecent, and generally reprehensible. Yet, no real moral forces control the behavior of many people. For many people the traditional arguments of religion with a stress on sin or the psychological arguments with a stress on "guilt" are ignored or seen as irrelevant. So the swinging phenomenon appears inevitable in a society where norms are rapidly losing their strength and where values centered on individual moral decisions are becoming increasingly powerful, especially among the younger generation.

POSTMARITAL SEX

Before concluding this chapter we will discuss briefly the sexual behavior of persons who were once married. This is appropriate because premarital and extramarital values extend to postmarital sexual behavior

---

[49] Brian G. Gilmartin and Dave V. Kusisto, "Some Personal and Social Characteristics of Mate Sharing Swingers," in Libby and Whitehurst, *Renovating Marriage*, pp. 152–53.

[50] Ibid., p. 163.

in defining appropriate behavior. This is true whatever the reasons for ending the marital interaction, that is, death, divorce, separation or desertion. While it is generally assumed that the postmarital are sexually experienced because of their previous marriage, once their marriage ends they are expected to conform again to the sexual values that operated for them when they were young and unmarried.

Regardless of the reason their marriages ended, the postmarital constitute a group of sexually experienced individuals. The American society, in effect, says that even though an active, socially approved involvement was a part of their lives for many years, and even though their sexual needs and interests may continue to be very strong, once they are no longer legally married they must give up all personal interest and involvement in sex. In reality, the postmarried, especially the women, are treated in somewhat different fashion according to how their marriages ended. The widow is assumed to have had a satisfactory sexual relationship with her deceased husband, and if she shows an interest in sex she may be viewed as being disloyal to the memory of her husband. Frequently implied for the widow, if she does not remarry, is that she can and should live with her memories.

Toward the divorced woman there is often a different view—she is frequently viewed by men as sexually exploitable. After divorce, the assumption is that the marriage was a failure and that the sexual aspect had also been unsatisfactory. The divorced woman is often seen as sexually experienced, but without "good" sexual memories of her past marriage, so many men define the divorcée as in "need" of a good sexual partner—a role that these men see themselves as eminently capable of filling. Jessie Bernard points out that in theory the mores of chastity apply to the divorced woman as to all unmarried women, but that in reality the divorced woman is considered fair game.[51]

Kinsey found that for males whose marriages had ended through death, separation, or divorce, the frequency of sexual outlet was considerably higher than for single males of the same age, and nearly as high as for married males of the same age. In his postmarital years the male tends to follow sexual patterns similar to those of the married man. This appears to be true even though he no longer has marriage to provide the physically convenient and legally approved sexual partner. Kinsey found that among postmarried males between the ages of 16 and 30 total sexual outlet was 85 to 95 percent that of married men, and 40 to 50 percent higher than that of single men. However, after age 30 the rates of total sexual outlet for the postmarital males were about three fourths the married male rates, and "this actually places them below the rates of even the single groups after age 30."[52] The above statement refers to total

---

[51] Jessie Bernard, *Remarriage* (New York: Dryden Press, 1956), p. 155.

[52] Kinsey et al. *Sexual Behavior in the Human Male* (Philadelphia: Saunders 1948), p. 262.

sexual outlets; if only coitus between the postmarried and single males is compared, then the previously married group has the higher frequency.

In the Kinsey study the rates of sexual involvement for postmarital women were lower compared to married women than was the case for postmarital males in comparison with married males. For previously married women between the ages of 26 and 50, Kinsey found that from 80 to 86 percent had some sexual outlet.[53] Of the women between the ages of 36 and 40, 95 percent of the married, 96 percent of the previously married, and 71 percent of the single had some sexual activity. As to weekly frequency for this age group, the rates were 1.2 for the married, 0.7 for the postmarried, and 0.5 for the single.[54] These data suggest that the incidence rate for the postmarried women places them closer to the married than to the single, but that with regard to weekly frequency of sexual activity they are closer to the single.

It is also useful to look at some comparisons of various sexual outlets of the never-married, postmarried, and married. "The most notable aspect of the histories of these previously married females was the fact that their frequencies of activity had not dropped to the levels which they had known as single females, before they had married."[55] In types of sexual outlets the general sexual patterns for the single, postmarital, and marital females was the same as those found for the males. For women between the ages of 36 and 40 heterosexual coitus accounted for 88 percent of the sexual outlets of the married women, 70 percent of the postmarried, and 43 percent of the single. By contrast, masturbation accounted for 13 percent of the sexual outlets of the married, 28 percent of the postmarried and 39 percent of the single. Homosexual outlets accounted for 0 percent of the married, 2 percent of the postmarried, and 19 percent of the single.[56]

Kinsey's data clearly show that sexual involvement of some type is a common experience for many postmarried men and women. For most of them the decision is an individual one, and they must cope with any guilt feelings by themselves. However, for some postmarried, particularly the divorced, there emerges a subculture that helps them in their adjustment to their deviant status. Morton Hunt has provided a picture of the subcultural world of the divorced and how it helps provide a setting for many decisions and activities with regard to sexual behavior. Hunt suggests that divorced people, while they are a part of the overall American culture and interact with it, "elsewhere have a private and special set of norms that guide them in their interactions with each other, and from

[53] Kinsey et al., *Human Female*, p. 394.
[54] Ibid., p. 533.
[55] Ibid.
[56] Ibid., p. 562.

which they derive their own customs, moral values, rules of fair play, and devices for coping with the problems special to their condition." Hunt goes on to suggest that many of their life patterns are quite different from those of the inhabitants of the wider culture.[57]

The subculture of the divorced is not highly restrictive; in fact in most respects it is quite permissive. The individual can arrange the details of his new dating life to suit his personal needs. "No one need consent to any suggestion he or she dislikes, but it is not impossible for the other to have made it."[58] This value of permissiveness without force is very similar to that found among swingers.

The divorced people that Hunt studied were predominantly urban and highly educated. Therefore, their behavior was no doubt much different from that of many other divorced persons in the United States. This limitation should be kept in mind. In his sample Hunt found that almost none of the men and only about 20 percent of the women had had no sexual experiences since their marriages ended. Hunt found that about 80 percent of the "formerly married" started having sexual intercouse during the first year after their divorces, most of them with more than one partner. Nearly all of the men and a fairly large number of the women found their sex life more intense, less inhibited, and more satisfying than it had been during their marriages.[59] Hunt suggests that divorced persons who did not have sexual relations typically had problems. He writes that a common type of divorced woman without sexual experience had been characterized by a limited amount of sexual excitement in the past in what was an unhappy marriage. "Her innate negative feelings about sex gradually gained the upper hand and anesthetized her sexual feeling or even caused her to find the act somewhat repellent." Hunt goes on to point out that the common male abstainer was generally of normal sexuality, "who lost potency or desire in the course of a deteriorating marriage and avoids sex afterward out of fear of failure."[60]

Many of the divorced entered into their first sexual encounters with a great deal of fear and anxiety. They were faced not only with the general moral restrictions but with the fact that their previous sexual experience had been in a relationship that had failed. Therefore the anxiety was often both sexual and interpersonal. As would be expected, the anxiety about entering into a sexual affair was greater for the woman than for the man and greater for those married a long while than for those married only briefly. But except for those with real neurotic problems about sex,

---

[57] Morton M. Hunt, *The World of the Formerly Married* (New York: McGraw-Hill, 1966), pp. 4–5.

[58] Ibid., pp. 112–13.

[59] Ibid., p. 144.

[60] Ibid., p. 146-47.

the great majority did have successful sexual experiences, most only after some initial failures, the fortunate few at once.[61]

The subcultural world of the divorced is like other areas of deviance in that many members often feel it necessary to hide some of their subcultural activities from the broader society. Even when the divorced woman is able to adjust successfully to her extramarital activities she often feels it necessary to hide them from her friends, her parents, and especially her children. If she has older children she usually says in effect that there is one set of values to govern her nonmarital sexual behavior and a different one for her unmarried children. Hunt says that divorced women are caught between two cultures; "while they permit themselves their present conduct and justify it, they also have a nagging residual feeling that it is not really proper, and do not want their children to emulate them."[62]

The contrast between the generally stated values controlling all aspects of sex outside of marriage and the actual behavior of many postmarried persons points up the conflict in the United States. Because the general values do not change, individuals must adapt to them. They can accept them, they can deviate as individuals with no support from others, or they can deviate and seek support from others who share their position. That more and more people follow the third choice is not surprising because that choice provides some adaptation to a situation in which they find the dominant values intolerable for their life patterns.

BIBLIOGRAPHY

Bartell, Gilbert D., *Group Sex.* New York: Wyden, Inc., 1971.

Bell, Robert R., *Premarital Sex in a Changing Society.* Englewood Cliffs, N.J.: Prentice-Hall, 1966.

Bell, Robert R., and Dorthyann Peltz, "Extramarital Sex among Women," *Medical Aspects of Human Sexuality,* March 1974, pp. 10, 18–26.

Cuber, John F. "The Mistress in American Society," *Medical Aspects of Human Sexuality,* September 1969, pp. 81–91.

Gilmartin, Brian G., and Dave V. Kusisto, "Some Personal and Social Characteristics of Mate-Sharing Swingers," in Roger W. Libby and Robert N. Whitehurst, *Renovating Marriage.* San Ramon, Calif.: Consensus, 1973, pp. 146–65.

Hunt, Morton M., *The World of the Formerly Married.* New York: McGraw-Hill, 1966.

Johnson, Ralph E., "Some Correlates of Extramarital Coitus," *Journal of Marriage and the Family,* August 1970, pp. 449–56.

---

[61] Ibid., pp. 154–55.
[62] Ibid., p. 163.

Neubeck, Gerhard, *Extramarital Relations.* Englewood Cliffs, N.J.: Prentice-Hall, 1969.

Varni, Charles A., "Contexts of Conversion: The Case of Swinging," in Roger W. Libby and Robert N. Whitehurst, *Renovating Marriage.* San Ramon, Calif.: Consensus, 1973, pp. 166–81.

chapter four

Factors related to birth control

This chapter concerns two separate but related problem areas. At its broadest, one of these problem areas—that of population size and composition—is on the national and even the international level. The basic problem for many countries is their economic development and their ability to meet the needs of their populations. The second problem area concerns the various birth control measures used by individuals. At this level the problem is usually the inability of some individuals to control the number of children they have in accordance with their desires. This level is clearly related to the first but involves problems in a number of different ways. Our discussion of these problem areas starts with a brief look at the historical development of birth control methods. This is followed by an examination of the "population explosion," of some social variables related to birth control success, and finally the various methods of birth control, their usage, and their reliability.

The conceptual approach used in this chapter to examine the data is more from a social problem than a social deviance view. Population limits are a social problem because large numbers in society define them as such. Also, many who contribute to the overall problem by having large numbers of children see themselves as having a difficulty. In this country we know that poor people often do not have access to adequate birth control information and techniques and therefore have more children than they can afford.[1] So from the perspective of the individual deviant there is often a strong desire to correct the problem—having a large number of children. There was a time when using birth control methods was defined as eccentric or deviant behavior. For most of mankind's history the general value has been that having large families is desirable

[1] Lee Rainwater, "Family Planning in Cross-National Perspective," *Journal of Social Issues*, October 1967, pp. 2–3.

and usually inevitable. And anyone who tried to change this "natural" process has been seen as deviant. While this viewpoint is still held by some groups of people it is no longer a major belief in most societies, including that of the United States.

HISTORY OF BIRTH CONTROL

While most societies, preliterate and literate, past and present, have accepted large birthrates as natural and inevitable it is also probably true that in many of those societies at various times some people have attempted to control conception. To the problems of birth control there have always been two general approaches. The first has been a mystical formula, and practices stimulating emotional responses.[2] The second general approach has been based on rationality. This approach has centered on whatever were believed in a given society to be the processes whereby procreation occurred on the one hand, and the powers of the substances used to stimulate or defeat them on the other.[3] Both approaches were used not only among primitive tribes but also among the civilized nations of antiquity. The Egyptians, the Jews, the Greeks, and the Romans all possessed beliefs about the reproductive process and some knowledge of contraceptive devices.

In most societies of the past there was no knowledge of how conception occurred and therefore no awareness of a process that could be halted by some contraceptive measure. The rational development of birth control methods assumes the knowledge that conception occurs as a result of sexual intercourse. When this knowledge did not exist, societies had to wait to try to do something about birth control until pregnancy could be seen or the infant was born. Therefore, in primitive societies the chief method of birth control was abortion, and in many societies infanticide was also used. These methods were much commoner than contraception. A study of anthropological monographs shows that other practices were also used by some preliterate groups, for example, "delayed marriage and celibacy, both almost negligible among primitive peoples; sex taboos limiting the time and frequency of connection, pre-puberty coition, sex perversions (more or less neglected by most writers), prolonged lactation, and conception control, both magical and rational."[4]

Because preliterate societies often developed magical systems to cope with many aspects of their lives it is logical that they would attempt to control births in that way. Among primitive groups there has often

---

[2] Elizabeth Draper, *Birth Control in the Modern World* (Baltimore: Penguin Books, 1965), p. 53.

[3] Ibid.

[4] Norman E. Himes, *Medical History of Contraception* (New York: Gamut Press, 1963), p. 4.

existed the belief in a panacea or elixir—something that could be taken to resolve a given area of difficulty. This might be a potion that would give all men great strength, make all women beautiful, make all men great hunters, and so forth. Also common among preliterates was the belief that some magical potion existed that would prevent conception. That belief took many directions. For example, a symbolic kind of contraceptive potion was the drinking of water used for the washing of a dead person. A more medical kind of potion has been the infusions of the bark of different trees, (especially the willow), the yolk of the egg, and so forth.

The anthropological data show that thousands of materials have been used in primitive societies in attempts to control conception. Because so many methods were tried, on the basis of chance some had to be successful. For example, women in Guiana and Martinique used a douche solution containing lemon juice mixed with a decoction of the husks of the mahogany nut which worked fairly well. This is because lemon juice is an effective spermicide. Another related and more ingenious approach is reported to have been used in the 18th century. "This consisted of cutting a lemon in half, extracting most of the juice, the disk being used as a cervical cap."[5] Among the Djukas the women inserted into the vagina an okralike seed pod about five inches long from which one end was cut off. "The intact end probably lies against the cervix, or in the posterior fornix, the open end receiving the penis. This is, therefore, a kind of vegetable condom held in place by the vagina."[6]

The above illustrations of successful contraceptive developments in preliterate societies should not be overstressed. The successes were due to chance and not based on knowledge. It should be remembered that not until the late 1600s was it first known that contact between the sperm and the egg had to occur for fertilization to take place. And not until 1850 was it understood that the spermatozoa had to penetrate the egg for fertilization to take place. Himes, after his extensive research into birth control methods, writes: "It cannot be too strongly emphasized, therefore, that whatever primitive peoples may have known about contraception, they hit upon by trial and error, by trial-success-and survival processes, not as a consequence of a thorough understanding of the physiology of conception."[7]

The failure of contraceptive attempts in the past was not entirely due to ineffective methods. Because the modern techniques are effective they control conception, but even the less effective techniques of the past could have been more effective if used consistently and with care. Had such attempts been made the population of Europe would not have risen so

---

[5] Ibid., p. 18.

[6] Ibid., pp. 18–19.

[7] Ibid., p. 53.

greatly during the 18th and 19th centuries. "We must instead say that the modern *demand* for better control has led to the *development* of more adequate techniques; i.e., has created a large market for the new, improved devices."[8]

The societies of the Western world have used a variety of means to influence their overall birthrates on at least some occasions. However, this was not true for the majority of persons in most countries in the past. With the high death rate in societies of the past, a high birthrate was needed to meet the economic and military demands of most societies. The concern for developing the means of birth control existed among the wealthier and upper-class levels of society. There was generally little concern about the "inevitably" high birthrates of the lower classes. This social class distinction has continued over the centuries and still holds true in many parts of the world.

Probably the first significant breakthrough in the development of a reliable means of mechanical birth control was the invention of the condom. A treatise published in 1564 by Gabriele Fallopio contained the first written account of the condom or sheath which Fallopio claimed to have invented. This was not initially seen as a contraceptive device, and over the years it gained popularity as a measure against venereal infection. During the 18th century, the condom was used mainly in brothels, both in England and on the Continent, but it was also sold in London and other cities. "At the end of the century, contraceptives were still associated exclusively with immorality and vice, but by the close of the nineteenth century, this position had been deeply undermined and the way prepared for the general acceptance of contraceptives which has been so marked a feature of our time."[9] During the 18th century, associating the condom with the protection of the male from possible diseases from prostitutes meant that a husband did not consider using the same method to protect his wife from pregnancy. In a patriarchal society where pleasurable sex was associated with prostitutes and the danger of disease the condom seemed appropriate, while in marriage where sex was often chaste and merely a means to the procreative end the condom did not seem appropriate.

It was not until the 19th century in the Western world, especially in England, Germany, and France, that contraceptive practices started to spread rapidly. France was the only country to use contraception as early as the end of the 18th century. This was 50 to 100 years before any other country. No other countries in the Western world experienced so early

---

[8] William J. Goode, *World Revolution and Family Patterns* (New York: Free Press, 1963), p. 53.

[9] Norman St. John-Stevas, "History and Legal Status of Birth Control," in Edwin M. Schur, *The Family and the Sexual Revolution* (Bloomington: Indiana University Press, 1964), pp. 333–34.

and so rapid a decline in population.[10] In brief, in the Western world the major reasons for the rapid spread of contraceptive practices were growing industrialization, urbanization, lessened church authority, and greater freedom for women. Himes points out that concern with the social and economic desirability of birth control was a characteristic of the 19th century and did not exist to any extent before that time. "Medical discussion is old; the economic and social justification, the body doctrine known as Neo-Malthusianism, is new."[11] In the 1820s in England there developed a fairly extensive amount of birth control propaganda. This was led by Francis Place (1771-1854), who appears to have been the first individual to venture alone upon an organized attempt to educate the masses on techniques of contraception. "Place holds, therefore, the same position in social education on contraception that Malthus holds in the history of general population theory."[12] A pamphlet written by Place presented in clear language to poor women some ways in which they might avoid having more children than they wanted. The reliability of the pamphlet was limited by the knowledge of effective means of birth control that existed at that time. But what is most important is that the publication launched the birth control movement.

During the early years of the birth control movement it had little support. And in the first century of its history the birth control movement was more opposed than supported by the medical profession. The leading activists were not physicians. For example, Francis Place started his career as a maker of leather breeches, Marie Stokes was a botanist, and Margaret Sanger was a nurse. Organized religion was also indifferent or opposed to the birth control movement for much of its history. No major religion advocated the use of contraception prior to its popular adoption. "The common people took it over in the face of almost universal ecclesiastical opposition."[13]

But the greatest resistance to the birth control movement probably came from the belief that having children was inevitable and natural. This belief assumed that nothing could be done or should be done about it—having children was the natural order of things. Most of humanity has seen attempts to tamper with births as being like attempts to influence death—trying to alter what is believed to be beyond the power of human beings. This belief in the inevitability of birth was further supported by the fact that most of humanity has lived in patriarchal societies.

---

[10] Pierre Goubert, "Historical Demography and the Reinterpretation of Early Modern French History: A Research Review," in Theodore K. Rabb and Robert I. Rotberg, *The Family in History: Interdisciplinary Essays* (New York: Harper and Row, 1971), p. 23.

[11] Himes, *Contraception*, p. 211.

[12] Ibid., p. 212

[13] Kingsley Davis, "Values, Population, and the Supernatural: A Critique," in William Petersen and David Matza, *Social Controversy* (Belmont, Calif.: Wadsworth, 1963), p. 30.

Therefore, in male-controlled societies having babies was the woman's problem. The fact that women often had problems associated with giving birth was taken as a reflection of their "inferior" status. Men in most societies have seen the question of controlling the birthrate as one for the woman to worry about. The patriarchal male has traditionally seen sexual intercourse with his wife as his right and her getting pregnant as a measure of his masculinity. Therefore, to ask him to influence his sexual activity in some way that might affect the frequency of his wife's pregnancies was to try to influence his basic beliefs about his masculine rights as a husband. So birth control problems have traditionally been seen as problems for women to deal with if anything was to be done about them.

The values that existed with regard to birth control among the early settlers in the United States were the same as the values found in Europe and especially in England. There is some evidence that during the colonial period American fertility was among the world's highest, with the average woman having about eight children. "In those days, high infant and general mortality rates claimed perhaps half of these children before they reached marriageable ages. Nevertheless, despite this higher mortality, the size of families was much greater than now."[14] But during the 19th and 20th centuries there was an almost consistently decreasing birthrate that reached its all-time low in the 1930s.

During the 1800s in the United States the birth control movement slowly developed in strength and influence. However, the movement was drastically restricted in 1873 with the passage of the Comstock Law. This was a statute enacted by Congress which excluded contraceptives and contraceptive information from the mails by defining them as obscene. Many states also passed statutes banning the sale and distribution of contraceptives. At that time no major social institutions supported the birth control movement. Not until 1888 was the first medical symposium on the prevention of conception presented in an American medical journal. That symposium came about as a result of an editorial in the *Medical and Surgical Reporter* that declared that while the subject demanded "discretion" for its discussion, "even so delicate a subject may be regarded with too much timidity." The editorial added that "no medical man of any experience can fail to know that the propriety and feasibility of preventing conception engages, at some time or other, the attention of a large proportion of married people in civilized lands." It went on to say that "the woman who lives in dread of her husband's sexual appetite cannot satisfy him as a wife, and, with this poison in her

---

[14] Charles F. Westoff, "The Fertility of the American Population," in Ronald Freedman, *Population: The Vital Revolution* (New York: Anchor Books, 1964), pp. 110-11.

life, must find it hard to be a kind and wholesome mother to her children."[15]

The most influential person in the American birth control movement was Margaret Sanger. Through her educational or propaganda campaigns she did more than any other American to make birth control known to the public. Margaret Sanger was a woman of great vision, personal courage, and organizing ability, and she gave unity to the American birth control movement. She published a monthly magazine, *The Woman Rebel*, and was arrested and indicted under the Comstock Law. In 1916 she opened the first birth control clinic in the United States. The clinic was raided by the police, and Margaret Sanger and her sister were both sentenced to thirty days in jail. Over the years she continued her work and propaganda, basing her appeal on the suffering caused women by unlimited childbearing rather than on any theoretical Malthusian arguments.[16]

It was not until the 1930s that the birth control movement in the United States began to take on influence through some of the institutional forces of society—principally religious, legal and medical institutions. For example, in 1931 the Federal Council of the Churches of Christ was the first religious group to publish a report favoring birth control. During the same year support also came from the American Neurological Association, the Eugenics Society, and the Central Conference of Rabbis. In the middle 1930s there were also some important legal breakthroughs. The Court of Appeals upheld a ruling of the District Court in 1936 that contraceptives imported for a lawful purpose did not come within the restrictions of federal law. And in 1937 the American Medical Association unanimously agreed to accept birth control "as an integral part of medical practice and education."[17]

There have also been legal and governmental influences on birth control in a variety of more subtle and indirect ways than through direct intervention. Draper has argued that "the influence of government upon population size is immense and is by no means confined to legislation directly concerned with birth control."[18] For example, birth control is affected by government influence in many countries through the provision of family allowances and maternity benefits. Or, as in the United States, income tax allowances for children give financial encouragement or ease the burden on the family budget. Also, such factors as free education, vocational training, and in many countries free medical

---

[15] Himes, *Contraception*, p. 289.
[16] St. John-Stevas, "Birth Control", pp. 337–38.
[17] Ibid., p. 338.
[18] Draper, *Birth Control*, p. 179.

services provide for the cultural and occupational rewards and general "physical and mental well being which makes it good to live and worth having children to share."[19] Other indirect legal influences are laws providing minimum ages for marriage. In the United States these are four to six years after the female is capable of reproducing. Because most women do not have their children until after marriage the early years of childbearing are usually eliminated. Probably no society encourages reproduction up to the limits of the biological capacity of the female. Some limits, if not in the laws then in the values of the society, are imposed on the reproductive potential of women.

Even when governments have been concerned with birth control problems they have generally restricted themselves to policy statements and have not advocated contraceptive rights for the individual. However, in some countries explicit population policies attempting to influence birthrates became important before World War I, when many European countries appointed population commissions to investigate their declining birthrates and to develop policies they thought would reverse that trend. It has been in recent decades that first mortality and then fertility became subjects of government policy, "not only to further the health and welfare of the individual citizens, but also to influence the rate of growth, size, and age structure of populations."[20]

All in all, by the 1930s in the United States birth control was accepted by many in the general population. For example, a poll in 1936 asked, "Do you believe in the teaching and practice of birth control?" and 63 percent of the respondents answered "yes." In 1943 another poll asked a group of women aged 21 to 35: "Do you believe that knowledge about birth control should be available to all married women?" and 85 percent of them answered "yes." By 1965 when a national sample of women was asked: "Do you think birth control knowledge should be available to anyone who wants it?" about 80 percent of *both* Protestant and Catholic women answered "yes."[21]

The view that family size can and should be controlled is accepted today in many parts of the world besides the United States. In fact, Ryder suggests that there is now a remarkable demographic consensus throughout the modern world to the effect that marriage should occur at a rather young age and that the couple should have a small number of children at regulated intervals. He further states that celibacy and voluntary infertility are highly improbable and that at the other extreme the large family is becoming an anachronism. "The range of fertility dif-

---

[19] Ibid.

[20] Freedman, *Population*, p. 8.

[21] *Trans-Action*, April 1967, p. 3.

ferences among modern nations depends essentially on the question of whether the proportion of couples who have three children is greater or less than the proportion who have two children."[22] Many persons feel that the most threatening problem facing the world today is the "population explosion."

THE POPULATION EXPLOSION

The concern with population growth became very great during the 1960s, and many saw the problem of population growth as potentially more dangerous to the world than even atomic warfare. Before examining the problem of recent population growth it is of interest to look at the way in which the world's population expanded in the past. It has been estimated that the population of the world at the end of the neolithic period (8000–7000 B.C.) was between 5 million and 10 million. By the beginning of the Christian era the world's population probably numbered between 200 million and 300 million. At the start of the modern era (1650) world population had reached about 500 million. The present world population is about 3½ billion. "In the course of man's inhabitation of this globe, then, his rate of population growth has increased from about 2 percent per millennium to 2 percent per year, a thousandfold increase in growth rate."[23] Put another way, of all persons who have ever lived it is estimated that about 4 percent are alive today.

The population explosion was a result of a high birthrate and a somewhat lower death rate. The population of the world can only increase for a given period of time when the number of births is greater than the number of deaths. During the initial population explosion the death rate was high but the birthrate was even higher. For example, the expectation of life at the time of birth was about 30 years at the beginning of the Christian era and remained at that level until well through the 19th century. By 1900 death rates had decreased to the point where life expectancy in western Europe and the United States was 45 to 50 years. And by 1960 another 20 years of life had been gained, with life expectancy having reached about 70 years.[24]

If the present rate of population growth continues there will be well over 6 billion people in the world by the year 2000. This potential growth is seen by many experts as leading to severe problems. It is argued that with a world population today of about 3½ billion, more than two thirds of the people in the world are undernourished or starving. As a result

---

[22] Norman B. Ryder, "The Character of Modern Fertility," in Jeffrey K. Hadden and Marie L. Borgatta, *Marriage and the Family* (Itasca, Ill.: F. E. Peacock, 1969), p. 344.

[23] Freedman, *Population*, p. 16.

[24] Ibid., p. 20.

birth control is seen by many as a major weapon of civilization and as an essential part of any satisfactory solution to population problems, from the personal to the international.[25]

In recent years there has also been some argument that rapid population increase leads to various ecological problems. For example, more people make greater demands on natural resources, many of which are becoming increasingly scarce. It has also been argued that more people means more pollution, but there is disagreement on how significant this need be. Some argue that values are what is important, not the number of people. According to this view if people really want to deal with the problems of natural resource use and pollution they can do so regardless of number. If this position is correct all it does is lift the acceptable number for population expansion. But obviously at some time population limits would have to be imposed because we live in a finite world.

The population explosion may be examined in several ways. On the practical level the modus operandi for the reduction of fertility must take one of three forms: first, the reduction of the probability of intercourse; second, the reduction of the probability of conception if intercourse occurs; and third, the reduction of the probability of birth if conception occurs. "The first of these is control through nuptiality, the latter two constitute control of marital fertility."[26] The control of marriage has existed for centuries, so the stress when it does occur is on marital fertility. In most societies abortion has been used as a supplement or an alternative to contraception. Historically abortion has probably been the most important influence in holding population expansion below what it could have been. But the extent to which abortion has influenced population growth in time and space is not yet known and probably never will be. "Nevertheless, the more we learn of the ineffectuality of most efforts at contraception, the more we are inclined to suspect a major covert role for abortion as a second line of defense against the unwanted birth."[27]

Davis suggests that abortion does not compete with contraception but rather serves as a backup when the latter fails or when contraceptive devices or information are not available. "As contraception becomes customary, the incidence of abortion recedes even without its being banned."[28]

In recent decades abortion has been used in many countries as a major means for controlling the birthrate. First Japan, then Russia, and subsequently all the countries of eastern Europe, with the exceptions of East

---

[25] Draper, *Birth Control* p. 15.

[26] Ryder, "Modern Fertility," p. 340.

[27] Ibid., p. 341.

[28] Kingsley Davis, "Population Policy: Will Current Programs Succeed?" in Daniel Callahan, *The American Population Debate* (New York: Doubleday, 1971), p. 234.

Germany and Albania, have permitted abortion on socioeconomic grounds. As a result of legal abortion the birthrates of those countries dropped rapidly, and the lowest fertility rates in the world today are found in them. "Controls associated with legalization have reduced the health risks appreciably. Nevertheless, and entirely apart from moral considerations, abortion is an expensive alternative to contraception. Consequently, we may expect a persistent effort to induce a shift from abortion to contraception."[29]

Abortion probably continues to be the most common method of birth control throughout Latin America. But this method is rejected by almost all national and international population control programs. In fact American foreign aid is used to help stop abortion. "The United Nations excludes abortion from family planning, and in fact justifies the latter by presenting it as a means of combating abortion. Studies of abortion are being made in Latin America under the presumed auspices of population control groups, not with the intention of legalizing it and thus making it safe, cheap and available, and hence more effective for population control, but with the avowed purpose of reducing it."[30] But it is becoming increasingly clear throughout the world that no society can remain indifferent to reproduction, and therefore every society maintains some fertility norms. "The society indoctrinates its members into conformity with these norms, by explicit and implicit rewards and punishments."[31]

The problems of population vary with different societies and even in the same society over time. Many of the poorer countries appear to be condemning themselves to continued poverty if they don't control their population growth. The technologically advanced societies often find that they too have population problems. They may be able to control population, but they still find that the distribution of population at a given time creates problems for them. For example, in a technological society fewer persons are needed in the labor force, and therefore one problem is what to do with the young and the old who are not occupationally needed. It would seem safe to suggest that while a society may cut down on many of its population problems it never succeeds in eliminating all of them.

It has been contended in recent years that the population increase in the world is slowing down and becoming somewhat less of a problem, although this is still an area of great disagreement. One reputable spokesman for this interpretation is the demographer Donald Bogue. He argues that the trend of the movement around the world toward fertility

---

[29] Ryder, "Modern Fertility," p. 341.
[30] Davis, "Population Policy," p. 234.
[31] Ryder, "Modern Fertility," p. 342.

control has reached the point where declines in death rates are being surpassed by declines in birthrates. Because possible new developments of controls over death are slackening and the means for controlling births are rapidly increasing, the world has entered a stage in which population growth has begun to slow down. Bogue has suggested that this switch occurred in about 1965 and that from then on the rate of world population growth has declined each year. "The rate of growth will slacken at such a pace that it will be zero or near zero at about the year 2000, so that population growth will not be regarded as a major social problem except in isolated and small 'retarded' areas."[32]

Bogue points out that all over the world wherever studies of attitudes of the public on family size have been made the majority of couples with three living children do not want any more. Of the populations studied, a large proportion approve of family planning and would like to have more information about it, and they also approve nationwide health service that includes family planning. In other words, among the great masses of people objection to birth control on cultural, moral, or religious grounds is becoming increasingly minor. "This is true in Asia and Latin America, and seems to be developing in Africa. Thus, at the 'grass roots' level, the attitudinal and cultural conditions are highly favorable."[33] Bogue also finds that the leaders of nations with population problems openly accept family planning as a moral and rational solutuion. "Heads of state in India, Pakistan, Korea, China, Egypt, Chile, Turkey, and Colombia, for example, have made fertility control an integral part of the national plan for economic development. The national ministers of health and welfare not only are permitted but are expected to provide family planning services."[34]

Bogue's arguments for a leveling off of the "population explosion" may be summarized as follows. Wherever one looks in the underdeveloped segments of the world there is evidence of established and functioning family planning activities. It is clear that a large share of their populations are using modern contraceptives, and this has had an inhibiting effect on their birthrates. "Even conservative evaluation of the prospects suggests that *instead of a 'population explosion' the world is on the threshold of a 'contraception adoption explosion.'* Because of lack of adequate vital statistics, the effects of this 'new explosion' will not be readily measurable for a few years."[35]

However, many experts are not nearly so optimistic about the future.

---

[32] Donald J. Bogue, "The End of the Population Explosion," in C. H. Anderson, *Sociological Essays and Research* (Homewood, Ill.: Dorsey, 1970), p. 333.

[33] Ibid., p. 327.

[34] Ibid., p. 328.

[35] Ibid., p. 332.

For example, while Bogue's arguments make sense if one assumes that he is right about the use of birth control methods, the world's population nevertheless could be drastically increased in another way—through the extension of life. While life expectancy in industrial countries like the United States has changed very little in recent decades there is great potential for change in the near future. If (and it is a big if) there are significant breakthroughs in heart research, cancer control, and other major killers in the United States, and if safety devices in automobiles, factories, and the home are developed, then it can be expected that people will live longer. It is very possible that by the end of the 20th century defective human organs will be replaceable by artificial organs. All in all, there is a strong possibility that by the end of the century life expectancy could be increased by 10 or even 20 years. If this happens the population explosion will be great even though birth control methods are highly effective.

At the present time it is highly important that as births become increasingly under control greater social value is attached to the small family. In fact, contrary to a popular belief, the increase in the average number of children per couple has not been the main reason for the high fertility levels of the past two decades. More important has been an increase in the proportion marrying, as well as a trend toward marrying at younger ages.[36] In the United States increasing social pressure is developing among some groups against having large families. It used to be that middle- or upper-class couples who had large numbers of children were applauded. (The lower classes were seen as "irresponsible.") Invariably the "mother of the year," one of our many commercialized honors, was a woman with six or seven children. Yet, in 1970 one United States senator suggested that it might be more sensible to give the "mother of the year" award to a woman who had had her tubes tied and adopted two children. This symbolizes dramatically the changed attitude to family size among some social groups.

An increasing body of evidence has been emerging in the 1970s that the size of families is being reduced. One influence has been the recent trend of postponing marriage which leads to an overall older age at marriage. Because the female is more fecund in the first than in the second half of her reproductive span the postponement of marriage tends to reduce births. Sociologically this gives women more time to educate themselves, to acquire interests not related to the family, and to develop a cautious attitude toward pregnancy. "Individuals who have not married by the time they are in the late twenties often do not marry at all."[37] And even after a woman has married the longer a "wanted" birth is delayed the less

---

[36] Westoff, "Fertility," p. 113.
[37] Davis, 'Population Policy," p. 250.

likely she is to have that birth or a subsequent birth. "This is because the delay provides the woman time to assume roles which are not compatible with early childcare responsibility, and also increases the likelihood that she or her husband will become subfecund."[38]

A shift in values may have a powerful impact on the birthrate. Various social actions could have a further impact. One action could be to remove some of the financial punishments that are directed at people with no or few children. They, in effect, are forced to subsidize those who have large families. Even stronger changes could be made through government policy. The government could pay people to agree to sterilization and could pay all costs for abortion. Or a substantial fee could be charged for a marriage licence, or a child-tax could be levied on those who want children.[39]

For many years there was a belief that children were better off being reared in large families. But that may have been an exaggeration. As Guttmacher points out, children raised in large families tend to have small families when they grow up and marry—in fact, smaller than average.[40] It would seem that the large family in the United States is on its way out; and studies indicate that the vast majority of couples believe that the control of fertility is desirable and that the ideal number of children is two or three.

The decreased birthrate discussed above has reference to the rate per woman in her childbearing years. This decrease doesn't mean that the overall number of births in the United States has been going down. The continued rise in the number of births has been due to the changing number of women aged 20 to 34, who account for about three quarters of all births. The size of that group remained fairly constant between 1955 and 1965, but from 1965 to 1970 it increased from 18 million to 21 million. In the period from 1970 to 1985 it will increase by about 10 million. This wave of younger women is the result of the baby boom that followed World War II.[41] Even if each of these women has fewer children there are so many more childbearing women that the net effect is an increase in the total number of babies born.

USING BIRTH CONTROL METHODS

In this section our discussion moves more directly to questions of who uses what birth control methods and under what social conditions. More

---

[38] Larry Bumpass and Charles F. Westoff, "Unwanted Births and U.S. Population Growth," in Callahan, *Population Debate*, p. 271.

[39] Davis, "Population Policy," pp. 250–51.

[40] Alan F. Guttmacher, *The Complete Book of Birth Control* (New York: Ballantine Books, 1963), p. 22.

[41] Lawrence A. Mayer, "U.S. Population Growth: Would Fewer Do Better?" in Callahan, *Population Debate*, p. 3.

specifically, our interest is in some of the social variables that are related to the use of birth control methods. In any society where birth control methods are available there will be many variations between groups of people who use them as against those who do not.

Religion

In the United States certain religious values have been the greatest overall force against the use of birth control. This religious interest in birth control has not been common to most religions of the world. The major religions of the Eastern world do not have explicit ideologies with regard to birth control. Some aspects of some Eastern religions do encourage large families, but these religions do not object to family planning. So religious beliefs in the Eastern world have not been a major factor in resistance to population control. However, in many parts of the Western world, and specifically in the United States, religious values *have* had a major impact on population control.

Protestant groups are now almost unanimous in giving strong endorsement to birth control. This was strongly demonstrated in a statement adopted in 1961 by the General Board of the National Council of Churches of Christ in the United States. This is a federation of 25 major Protestant denominations with about 40 million members in the United States. The Protestants' point of view is based on their notion of the basic purposes of marriage. Those purposes include not only parenthood, but also the development of the mutual love and companionship of the husband and wife, and their service to society.[42] The Protestant position is illustrated by that of the Methodist church, the largest single Protestant denomination. In 1960 it adopted the unequivocal position that "planned parenthood, practiced in Christian conscience, fulfills rather than violates the will of God."[43] It should be stressed that among almost all Protestant groups birth control methods are not just accepted, but are encouraged.

The support for birth control methods among Jews has paralleled the developments among the Protestants. The initial endorsements among Jews first appeared in 1931. Now all Jewish groups, except for the most extreme Orthodox group, endorse birth control. And even the extreme group sanctions female contraceptive methods under special health circumstances.[44] Not only do Jews accept the use of contraceptives, but all the available evidence indicates that they use contraception most effectively. For example, Westoff found that Jews had the highest rates of

---

[42] Ibid., p. 108.
[43] Ibid., p. 109.
[44] Ibid., p. 111.

any religious groups in using contraceptive methods and chose to use the most effective methods that were available.[45] It has been estimated that the fertility of American Jewish women is more than 20 percent below that of the urban population, more than 25 percent below that of the entire white population, and nearly 30 percent below the national level.[46] It is clear that whatever problems exist in birth control methods among Protestants and Jews, they are not due to ideological rejection of birth control but rather to the limitations of birth control methods and inefficiency in using them. However, by contrast, the primary problem for Roman Catholics is the ideological position of the church, and secondarily for many, the choice and effective use of the various methods. It is therefore important to devote some attention to the Catholic position with regard to birth control.

Catholics

The basic theological difference between Catholic doctrine and that of Protestants and Jews relates to the basic purpose of marriage. The Catholic church believes that procreation is the primary reason for marriage, with companionship and vocation being secondary. Therefore, according to the Catholic church, birth control by any chemical or mechanical means would frustrate the primary purpose of marriage and as a result violate natural law. The position of the Catholic church can be seen more clearly by looking briefly at its position with regard to several different means of birth control.

For whatever purpose it might be used, *sterilization* is outside the moral pale as far as Catholics are concerned. "The Catholic Church conceives of direct sterilization as an unwarranted attack upon the dignity of the human person."[47] Because it goes against the natural manner of sexual intercourse, coitus interruptus is also ruled out if it is used in any way to influence birth control.

The Catholic church opposes *artificial birth control,* which it defines as the use of any mechanical, chemical, or other procedures for the purpose of keeping the sperm from entering the uterus and/or reaching the Fallopian tubes. "The precise type of contraception is not the important issue; neither is the fact that there are different rates of effectiveness. Rendering the sperm nonviable, or impeding its normal motility, is

---

[45] Charles F. Westoff, et al., *Family Growth in Metropolitan America* (Princeton, N.J.: Princeton University Press, 1961), p. 79.

[46] Leslie Aldridge Westoff and Charles F. Westoff, *From Now to Zero* (Boston: Little, Brown, 1968), p. 20.

[47] William J. Gibbons, "The Catholic Value System and Human Fertility," in Petersen and Matza, *Social Controversy,* p. 21.

included under the general heading."[48] The fact that conception will not be the result of a particular coital act does not make that act unnatural or illicit in the eyes of the Catholic church. "The governing principle enunciated by moralists is that the act of intercourse must be performed in a natural manner and without the interposition of any positive obstacle to conception."[49]

There is confusion by many on the Catholic church's position with regard to the rhythm system. Approval of the rhythm method was given by Pope Pius XI in his 1930 encyclical *Casti Connubii [On Christian Marriage]*. However, Gibbons, a Catholic spokesman, states that the advocacy of periodic continence must never be such as to obscure or ignore the purpose for which marriage exists according to Catholic doctrine. "Such would be the case were the impression left that rhythm is the Catholic answer to the query of the selfish: how to achieve the gratification of marriage, while avoiding its major responsibility."[50] Gibbons goes on to say that the precarious health of a mother or the well-based fear that another child cannot be cared for properly are valid reasons for having recourse to continence. Nor, he continues, should the motivation of those who look ahead and try to foresee how they will care for future offspring be condemned. "Such an approach to fertility is rational and legitimate, provided of course the parents avoid the opposite error of thinking the fewer the children the better."[51]

The contention of Catholic spokesmen is that Catholicism does not tell married people that they must have a high birthrate, but that it does warn them about the abuse of marriage and the dangers of undersized families. "It opposes selfishness and excessive individualism, whether it be in the use of sex or in the utilization of material wealth."[52] It may be argued that while Catholicism does not tell its members that they must have large families it usually makes that result occur if the members follow the church's restrictions with regard to birth control. It seems safe to say that if all Catholics followed the restrictions of their church with regard to birth control most of them would have very large families. In fact their families would be far larger than they actually are. This raises the question, Is the restrictive view of the Catholic church on birth control being accepted and used by its members? In other words, How successful are the restrictions against birth control methods on the actual lives of Catholics?

---

[48] Ibid., p. 23.
[49] Ibid.
[50] Ibid., p. 24.
[51] Ibid.
[52] Ibid., p. 28.

On the broadest level it would seem that many Catholics are not too different from non-Catholics in controlling their family size. For example, the annual birthrate is 18.1 per 1,000 for all the Catholic countries of Europe. The corresponding figure for the non-Catholic countries of Europe is 18.0 per 1,000. In the United States about a third of all Catholics restrict themselves to abstinence or the rhythm method as a means of birth control. One study found that 46 percent of lower middle-class Catholics practiced the use of withdrawal, condom, diaphragm and jelly, or a combination of these methods. As Westoff points out, "One assumes that these couples must be highly anxious about their child-spacing in order to use methods disapproved by their church. To practice efficient methods of contraception, Protestants do not have to overcome the same religious inhibitions."[53] It seems possible that guilt would make Catholics less effective in the use of birth control. It is also possible that many Catholics do not feel any guilt about using birth control. Some of them may feel that birth control is really not the church's business. That is, simply because the Catholic church defines areas of behavior it has jurisdiction over does not always mean that its members accept those jurisdictional imperatives.

There are variations among American Catholics in their acceptance and use of birth control methods. Religious education is related to whether or not Catholic women follow the dictates of the church. The factor of education in religious schools has been one of the strongest single predictors of differentials in Catholic fertility. "Catholics who did not go to Catholic schools behave more like Protestants with respect to fertility— than like the more indoctrinated members of their own faith."[54] Studies have shown that Catholic women who are highly devout and highly educated are most effective in using the rhythm method. This is because they have the knowledge and sophistication to use the method most efficiently as well as a strong religious motivation to do so. Another study indicates that fertility is closely related to the frequency with which the person receives the sacraments. "The average most likely expected total number of births rises from 3.2 for Catholic wives who never received the sacraments to 4.4 for those who received them once a week or more."[55]

All of the evidence indicates that there is a wide gulf between the position of the Catholic church on birth control and what a majority of Catholics actually do. One of the basic measures of the strength of any social institution is the extent to which the behavior patterns of its stated

---

[53] Westoff, *Family Growth*, p. 94.

[54] Ibid., p. 201.

[55] Paseal K. Whelpton, et al., *Fertility and Family Planning in the United States* Princeton, N.J.: Princeton University Press, 1966), p. 83.

value system are followed by its members. For example, the military institution states as a basic value assumption that there must be un-questioning obedience by those in subservient positions to those in superi-or positions. On occasions the military elite finds that this is not occur-ring. It immediately institutes various means for punishing deviants and forcing behavior back in line with the values of obedience. This is roughly analogous to the situation the Catholic church is confronted with. Basi-cally the leadership of the church has two possibilities. First, it can attempt through various methods to bring the behavior of the member-ship into line with the values of the leadership. Hypothetically the Catholic church could impose strong sanctions on its members to abide by the values of birth control and, if necessary, excommunicate those who will not conform. If all members who did not go along with the values of the church on birth control were excommunicated there would then be congruence between the stated values and the actual behavior of the members. Second, the church could modify its values with regard to birth control methods to fit more closely the actual behavior of its members. For example, many have argued that if the church allowed the use of some chemical means of birth control, then its members would have something reliable to turn to. At the present time there seems to be little chance that this will occur. Yet, it is also clear that there are great pressures from within the Catholic church to bring about changes with regard to birth control. This is one of the major issues around which the liberal and conservative forces of the Catholic church are struggling.

In the United States there is great opposition by many non-Catholics to the Catholic church's position on birth control and abortion. This is because the Catholic church's concern with individual obligations for procreation and parental responsibility presents the only major theologi-cal obstacle to population control. The Catholic church contributes to the conflict when it opposes legislative change to more liberal laws on birth control methods or abortion wanted by many Protestants. In other words the Catholic power groups find themselves arguing on their religious grounds for restrictions that affect an overwhelmingly non-Catholic population. One danger of the Catholic position on birth control and abortion in the United States is that of stimulating an increase in anti-Catholicism.

Next we will examine briefly some other social variables related to the use of birth control methods. Education is one important variable. It is highly correlated with the most effective use of birth control methods, although not necessarily with families having the smallest number of children. That is, highly educated women often have large families, but when they do it is most often from planning rather than chance. By contrast studies show that women who have a low level of education not only expect to have larger families but do, in actual fact. In general the higher educated woman knows more about available means of birth control and knows how to use most effectively whatever methods she does choose. Closely related to the difference by education is the variation by social class. The lower the social class of the women the greater the average number of children she has. One exception to this is the upper upper class in the United States, who often have large families. One major reason is that they can afford to have all the help they need in taking care of their children and their homes.

There is a common belief that one reason many women in the lower social classes have more children is that they have a higher level of sexual coitus. In other words, they have larger families because their greater frequency of sexual coitus leads to a greater chance of pregnancy. There are several misconceptions in this assumption. First, there is no evidence that a high rate of sexual coitus increases fertility. In fact there is a counterargument that it reduces fertility because it lessens the sperm count in a given act of coitus. Second, there is no reason to believe that the lower classes actually have a higher rate of coitus than the higher social classes. And in fact it may be that because of hard physical labor and malnutrition the coital rates of the lower classes are lower. However, studies show that the lower classes are less informed and least effective in their use of birth control methods. This could be the major reason for the large families.

The birthrate among blacks has been higher than that among whites. But the higher birthrate among blacks is not due to greater fertility. The differences in birthrates between blacks and whites can be explained primarily by their differences in education, income, and occupation. In general educated women, and wives of educated husbands, have fewer children. Because only a small number of blacks are highly educated and because most blacks are unskilled workers with low incomes, high fertility among blacks is to be expected. Well-educated blacks in white-collar occupations with high incomes are somewhat less fertile than whites of the same general status. It is quite possible that the relationship between race and high fertility is a spurious one, and that other variables are the important causal ones.

Most American couples attempt to control fertility. It has been estimated that about one fifth of all births are unwanted. The percentage of unwanted births increases sharply by birth order: 5 percent of first births; 30 percent of fourth births; and 50 percent of sixth or higher-order births. There is also a social class relationship to unwanted births. "Fifteen percent of births to nonpoor families were declared unwanted, compared to 23 percent among the near poor and 37 percent among the poor."[56] It also appears that the timing of births is often not what the parents would

---

[56] Bumpass and Westoff, "Unwanted Births," p. 269.

have preferred. It has been estimated that two thirds of wanted births would have occurred at another time if the women had been successful in controlling the timing of births.[57]

Working women

One of the most important consequences of the birth control development over recent decades has been the large number of married women in the work force. The development of birth control methods has been the single most important factor in the emancipation of the American woman. For almost the entire history of humanity most women have been locked in the home because of having large numbers of children. Birth control methods have allowed women to have fewer children and to have them when they want them. At the same time women have developed the willingness to turn their children over to schools and other agencies for care while they work. In general, when a woman decides to work she has fewer children. Whelpton found that those wives who worked after their marriage not only had fewer births than those who had not worked but also anticipated a significantly smaller total number of children. Furthermore, the longer the wife worked the fewer the births she had or expected to have.[58] However, the causal relationship between women working and their fertility is a complex one. "Many wives are probably motivated to limit the size of their families because of their desire to work, and many wives who cannot have as many children as they want as a result of fecundity impairments probably work primarily because they have comparatively few responsibilities at home."[59] Whelpton also found that wives who said that they worked primarily because their families needed the income had and expected to have significantly more children than did wives who worked because they liked to. This suggests that some wives work because of the economic needs that arise from the fact that they have or expect to have a fairly large number of children.[60]

Birth control use is also related to certain views that are held about the sexual nature of marriage. Historically, in the vast majority of cultures, sex in marriage has been important in two ways: first, as the means of reproduction, and second, as a means of satisfying the sexual needs of the husband. In the past, with few effective means for controlling con-

---

[57] Jeanne Clare Ripley, "The Effects of Population Change on the Roles and Status of Women: Perspective and Speculation," in Constantina Safilios-Rothschild, *Toward a Sociology of Women* (Lexington, Mass.: Xerox College Publishing, 1972), p. 380.

[58] Whelpton, *Fertility*, p. 108.

[59] Ibid.

[60] Ibid.

ception, pregnancy frequently resulted from marital coitus. This resulted in large numbers of children, high rates of maternal and infant mortality, and a short life span for the reproductive wife. Also in the past, while women could and did receive personal satisfaction from the sexual aspect of marriage this was not usually an expected right. In the patriarchal system sexual need was generally assumed to be a need of the man. The woman who also received sexual satisfaction was sometimes viewed by her husband (and herself) as somewhat "unnatural." "Good women," at least in terms of accepted sexual values, did not usually derive pleasure from the sexual act. Their role as sexual partner was one of duty to the husband. However, all of this has changed for many American women in that they now see their own sexual satisfaction as their right and as a goal to be achieved separately from any decision with regard to reproduction.

It might also be added that overwhelmingly the sex act of marriage is performed with no anticipation of pregnancy. An estimate based on a 6.7 average frequency of intercourse per month came to the conclusion that about 2 billion acts of sexual intercourse occurred in the United States in one year. Given the fact that 3.5 million births occur each year to married women living with their husbands, this indicates a ratio of about one live birth for about every 600 acts of sexual intercourse.[61]

Views about birth control methods also enter into the thinking about many aspects of premarital sexual intercourse. When the birth control movement was first emerging one of the common arguments against it was that contraceptive methods would lead to greater sexual promiscuity among the unmarried. The argument went that if the fear of pregnancy were removed through the use of contraception the unmarried would become highly active sexually. There is some indication that new contraceptive devices did contribute to greater premarital sexual activity, although they probably have not been a major force. The difficulty with this argument is that even if there are possibilities of greater premarital intercourse among the unmarried, is that sufficient reason for restricting the overall use of contraceptive devices? In reality the only way in which one could be sure that no unmarried persons used contraceptives would be to make them unavailable to all persons. This would, of course, infringe on the rights of the married to use these methods for important and accepted reasons.

At the present time there is general acceptance in the United States that the young and unmarried should learn about birth control methods. For them to learn may mean, of course, that some will use the knowledge before they are married. In a Gallup poll conducted in 1969, 71 percent of a national sample said that they approved of schools giving courses in

---

[61] Westoff and Westoff, *From Now to Zero*, p. 24.

sex education. And of those who approved, over half said that they approved of courses that included the discussion of birth control methods. However, most people do not approve of providing birth control pills to unmarried girls. For example, a national sample was asked whether they approved of giving birth control pills to unmarried girls in college. Seventy percent of the men and 77 percent of the women answered "no."[62]

It is generally overlooked that the sale of birth control devices is a fairly large business. Most contraceptives, whatever the type, are manufactured, distributed, and sold by private concerns. The sales in the United States run into the hundreds of millions of dollars every year. The attitudes associated with the sale of contraceptives are of interest because contraceptives are usually defined as either a medical concern or a public health issue. Governments usually classify contraceptives as pharmaceuticals. However, many consumers see contraceptives as personal rather than medical products. "In England barber shops are popular sources of supply; in Jamaica rum shops and groceries serve the same purposes, as do peddlers in India, and vending machines and fraternity brothers in this country."[63] There tends to be an implicit standard in the United States against encouraging the private sales of contraceptives for profit, except through drug stores. "Surprisingly, this standard seems to be shared by a composite of some clubwomen, contraceptive manufacturers, physicians, churchmen, public health officials, foundation executives, and social scientists. While many favor population control in general and many of these, contraception in particular, they either ignore or abhor broad distribution of contraceptives."[64] This is largely a result of a lack of respectability associated with contraceptive devices that exists in the minds of many. This is illustrated in the sale of some types of contraceptives, especially of condoms. About half of all condom sales in the United States take place in semiprivate settings, such as men's rooms (and ladies' rooms), often through vending machines. They are sold "for the prevention of disease," and many are bought for nonmarital sexual intercourse.[65] Condoms also tend to be associated with the lower class and are probably most often used in that group, especially in nonmarital coitus. Among the higher educated it is common for the female to provide the contraception through the use of a diaphragm or the pill. This indicates that in the middle class the woman commonly takes the responsibility for not getting pregnant.

---

[62] *Trans-Action*, April 1967, p. 3.

[63] John U. Farley and Harold J. Leavitt, "Population Control and the Private Sector," *Journal of Social Issues*, October 1967, pp. 136–37.

[64] Ibid., p. 143.

[65] Ibid., p. 136.

Conception problems

The great interest in birth control methods often clouds over an opposite problem that exists for many couples. That is the problem of having children. It is estimated that about 10 percent of all married couples will be childless, but that only 1 to 3 percent are personally satisfied with their childlessness. So about one out of every 12 couples is childless even though the couple desires children. Draper points out that the reverse of the birth control penny is the side concerned with greater help for couples unable to have children. As science finds ways of reducing the percentage of couples unable to have children it will contribute to the overall birth expansion number. And medically the problems of fertility and infertility are closely linked and often represent medical problems and processes that apply to each other in reverse.[66]

METHODS OF BIRTH CONTROL

Birth control methods, in the broadest sense, refer to the various ways used to stop either pregnancy or live births. Sometimes the concept of birth control applies to "positive" aspects of controlling family size through the spacing of children over time. Ultimately this means not having children except when desired. There are a variety of birth control methods that may be applied in a number of ways. First, there is *destruction* after conception. This ranges from destroying the fetus by induced abortion to ending the life of the child after giving birth. Second, there is birth control through *sterilization,* a process by which a person is made biologically incapable of producing or transmitting the ovum or the sperm. Third, there are the *processual* ways of controlling pregnancy. These include the withdrawal of the penis prior to ejaculation of sperm, or the use of a system in which the sperm is present but no ovum is available for fertilization. Last, there are the various contraceptive methods. The term *contraception* is generally applied to "mechanical or chemical barriers that prevent the access of spermatozoa to the uterus and Fallopian tubes at times when fertilizable ova are present."[67]

The arguments for the means and ends in using birth control methods fall into two groupings; one is generally medical and the other social. When birth control methods are prescribed by physicians in the United States today it is mainly to achieve the goals of better maternal health, improved child care, financial stability, and family happiness.[68] Several

---

[66] Draper, *Birth Control,* p. 22.

[67] Edgar S. Gordon, "Taking Physical Factors into Account," in Howard Becker and Reuben Hill, *Family, Marriage, and Parenthood* (Boston: Health, 1955), p. 337.

[68] Guttmacher, *Birth Control,* p. 17.

related reasons have been suggested by McCary. They are: (1) to aid in early sexual adjustment in marriage, (2) to space pregnancies, (3) to limit the number of children, (4) to avoid aggravation of any existing illnesses or diseases, and (5) to prevent the perpetuation of inherited diseases.[69] We now examine some of the different types of birth control methods and give some attention to their reliability.

Abstinence

Abstinence is obviously the most reliable method of birth control, but it is also the most extreme. It represents the total linking of coitus with reproduction because coitus would never be engaged in unless the intention were pregnancy. This method has been used by many individuals or groups of individuals in various cultures. Of course, if a social group used it completely that group would never replace itself unless it did so by bringing in new members from the outside.

The rhythm method

The rhythm method is based on refraining from sexual intercourse during the period when the female ovum is at the stage in the menstrual cycle when conception is possible. The most difficult problem with making this method work is that extreme care must be used in the calculation of dates so that sexual abstinence will occur during the mid-stage of the menstrual cycle when conception can occur. In general the more irregular the menstrual cycle the less dependable is the rhythm system. About 15 percent of all women have such irregular menstrual periods that they cannot safely use this method. And after childbirth the first few menstrual cycles are often so irregular that the rhythm method is unreliable at that time.[70] So this is not a highly dependable method, although the unplanned pregnancies among women who use it are often the result of insufficient care in following the basic requirements of the method.

Withdrawal (coitus interruptus)

Like the rhythm method, withdrawal is a "processual" means of controlling conception in that it does not involve artificial impediments. Sexual intercourse is interrupted immediately before the male orgasm by withdrawal of the penis and ejaculation outside the vagina. Withdrawal is one of the least used methods in the United States today. A number of

---

[69] James L. McCary, *Human Sexuality* (New York: Van Nostrand, 1976), pp. 131–32.
[70] Ibid., p.143.

problems are associated with this method. One problem is that it calls for strong willpower on the part of the male. He must be willing to give up the final and often most satisfying stage of sexual intercourse. Another problem involves the ability of the male to anticipate accurately when he is ready to ejaculate. Yet another difficulty is that even if the male withdraws ahead of ejaculation, there is still some possibility of pregnancy. The danger rests with the "sperm cells in the few drops of seminal fluid which often escape from the penis before the orgasm is reached."[71] The reliability of this method, like that of the rhythm system, depends to a great extent on the user. This is the major disadvantage of the method.

Douche

The douche is the cleansing of the vagina with a mildly acidic sperm-killing solution after sexual intercourse. The douche is often used as a supplement to other methods; for example, it may be used with the diaphragm. The assumption of this approach is that douching will flush the semen from the vagina before it has a chance to enter the mouth of the womb. "Actually, however, sperm move so quickly that the douche often fails to reach them."[72] The douche is probably the least reliable of all birth control methods and really serves better as a means to cleanse the vagina than to prevent pregnancy.

Sterilization

Sterilization prevents parenthood without destroying the sexual abilities of the individual. The usual methods are the cutting of the vas deferens (vasectomy) of the male and the Fallopian tubes (salpingectomy) of the female. Vasectomy removes no organs (nor does salpingectomy). It is relatively simple surgery which interrupts the seminal duct so that the male fluid that reaches the female no longer contains sperm cells. The operation is safe and only takes about twenty minutes. This operation is totally reliable and is the most effective means for making sure that pregnancy does not occur. The female operation costs far more and requires about ten days in the hospital.

Some fears associated with the male vasectomy have proved to be unfounded. First, some women have been fearful that vasectomy would lead to unfaithfulness by their husbands. The available evidence indicates that this is not common. Second, it does not in any way influence the sexual ability or drive of the male. Follow-up studies show that very

---

[71] Gordon, "Physical Factors," p. 354.
[72] McCary, *Human Sexuality*, p. 140.

rarely do men have regrets about the operation. For example, one study found that 98 percent of the men would have the operation again. Of those men 73 percent had experienced an increase in sexual pleasure, and 2 percent a decrease. "The health and sexual enjoyment of the wives improved even more than that of the husbands."[73]

However, vasectomy does have one major disadvantage for some who use it, and that is that its effects are often permanent. If at a later date a man wants to undergo an operation that reverses the effects of vasectomy there is only about a 50 percent chance of success. It is estimated that in the United States about 2 million couples have had surgical birth control. For most of them there is probably no great concern about changing the operation at some later date because they do not want children or because they already have all the children they want.

Sterilization has often been involved in governmental policy decisions involving the control of pregnancy potentials. Sterilization for eugenic reasons has been sanctioned in some states, particularly in state-supported institutions. There the physician can perform the operation on mentally deficient patients without fear of legal consequences. There appears to be approval of sterilization in the United States, at least under certain conditions. In the mid-1960s 67 percent of the respondents in a national sample approved of sterilization for persons with mental or physical afflictions who asked to be sterilized. In the same sample 78 percent approved of sterilization when the health of the mother would be endangered by having more children.[74] In 1970 in Great Britain male sterilization operations were made free under the National Health Service Law if both the husband and wife agreed.

Condom

As has been indicated, the condom may be the oldest of the artificial methods of contraception. It is the most widely used method of contraception in the United States because it is commonly used more in nonmarital than in marital coitus. When the condom is used correctly it is a highly reliable method of contraception. While there is some danger of breakage this has been reduced greatly because the manufacture of condoms is now under government supervision, and there are now far fewer failures due to tearing and to defects than was the case in the past. Some men object to the condom because it dulls pleasurable sensations. "Also, its use may interfere with the natural progress of mounting sexual tensions because sexual play must be interrupted in order to put it on."[75]

---

[73] Helen Edey, "Psychological Aspects of Vasectomy," *Medical Counterpoint*, January 1972, p. 23.

[74] *Trans-Action*, April 1967, p. 3.

[75] McCary, *Human Sexuality*, p. 1.

Historically the condom has been linked with venereal diseases, giving it a "bad image," and some people do not like to use it for that reason. The condom is unique in another way—of all the present mechanical and chemical means for controlling pregnancy it is the only one that the man uses.

Diaphragm

The disphragm is a flexible rubber disk that is coated with a spermicidal jelly and covers the cervix, thereby preventing the sperm from reaching the ovum. It must be left in place for 8 to 12 hours after coitus. The diaphragm can be obtained only by prescription from a physician and must be fitted by him the first time. Prior to the pill the diaphragm was the birth control method used by the most highly educated women in the United States, and it was used with a high level of reliability.

Intrauterine contraceptive devices (IUCDs)

IUCDs are small plastic or metal devices of various sizes and shapes that are designed to fit into the womb and may act as an irritant to prevent implantation of the fertilized ovum in the uterine wall. The placement of IUCDs is a simple and usually painless process. It can be done without danger by a physician or a medical technician. Once in place the device can be allowed to remain for years or be removed if the woman wants a baby.

At first IUCDs seemed ideal—they were almost as effective as the pill; they did not affect the body's natural hormonal balance; and once in place they could be forgotten. But recently it has been argued that they pose serious hazards. This is important because in 1973 about 3 million American women were using them. There is evidence that IUCDs cause perforation of the uterus, pelvic infection, spontaneous expulsion, and excessive menstrual bleeding. But there is also evidence that the negative claims are exaggerated.[76] One clear fact is that the risk of death from pregnancy far exceeds the risk associated with IUCDs. Another problem is that IUCDs are not as reliable as was originally thought. The average pregnancy rate of women using IUCDs is 3 percent as compared with 0.1 percent for those using the pill.

Oral contraceptives (the pill)

The pill works through: (1) suppressing ovulation or spermatogenesis, (2) preventing fertilization, or (3) preventing the implantation of the

---

[76] *Newsweek*, "The Risks of IUD," June 25, 1973, p. 54.

fertilized ovum in the uterus.[77] The so-called steroids, pills that contain synthetic hormones, have been the most effective of the oral contraceptives. When they are taken daily from the 5th to the 25th day of the menstrual cycle, they halt conception by halting ovulation. The pill's advantages over older methods are that it offers a high degree of reliability—not only biologically but also psychologically, in that the human errors often associated with the use of the condom or the diaphragm are minimized. The pill also contributes to greater spontaneity in the sexual act because it can be taken prior to sexual intercourse. Because of the pill's great simplicity of use, it can be taken by many not willing or able to use the condom or diaphragm. Taken as prescribed, the pill is virtually 100 percent effective, and its success is unequaled by any other means of contraception.

It has been recognized that there are side effects from the pill for some women. "The most common symptoms reported are mild gastrointestinal disturbance, nausea and bloated feeling, increase in weight, and spotting and irregular bleeding. Other occasional negative side effects are persistent menstrual-like cramping and painful swelling of the breasts."[78]

The federal Food and Drug Administration in 1959 approved for public sale the first pill to be used for purposes of birth control. By 1969 the pill was being used by an estimated 7 million women in the United States. This meant that approximately one seventh of all women in the childbearing years were using it. The wholesale value of annual domestic sales was estimated at $100,000,000, and export sales were about equal to that. All indications were that the pill would be used by an ever greater proportion of women, but in 1969 came the "pill scare."

The pill scare came about as a result of congressional hearings on oral contraception. In 1969 a congressional committee heard testimony that the pill was dangerous and had not been adequately tested as to side effects and possible dangers for the user. The hearings received a great deal of publicity, and panic set in among many users. By the winter of 1970 it was clear that many women had stopped using the pill. A Harris poll found that 50 percent of a national sample of women said they had stopped using the pill because they thought it to be injurious to their health. The same poll asked: "From what you have heard or read, do you feel the birth control pill is dangerous to use or not?" Of the respondents to this question, 60 percent felt that the pill was dangerous. However, most of the respondents did not feel that the pill should be outlawed.

There are other indications of the panic related to the pill. A number

[77] Hans Lehfeldt, "Contraception," in Albert Ellis and Albert Abarbanel, *The Encyclopedia of Sexual Behavior* (New York: Hawthorn Books, 1961), p. 297.

[78] McCary, *Human Sexuality*, p. 136.

of New York City obstetricians said that they had been approached to perform abortions on women who had stopped using the pill. Also, birth control clinics in New York funded by the Office of Economic Opportunity reported that before the congressional hearings on the pill about eight out of every ten women asked for the pill, but that after the hearings only about 60 percent chose oral contraception.[79]

Some countersupport for the pill has developed, but it has received much less publicity. At the congressional hearings most of the testimony emphasized the hazards of the pill and little attention was paid to the pill as the most effective means of family birth control. Guttmacher has argued that blood-clotting problems, some of which can be fatal, are the only proven risks associated with oral contraceptives. Death from clot complications occurs in about three out of every 100,000 women on the pill, but for women who become pregnant the risk is 15 times as great.[80] Guttmacher further points out that if all the women who quit the pill turn to the next most effective method, intrauterine devices, almost 50,000 will become pregnant because of the higher failure rate of that method.[81] A recent five-year study based on a sample of 18,000 women found that pill users had higher blood pressure, faster heart rates, higher blood sugar levels, and a greater tendency to form blood clots than nonusers. On the plus side, the pill users seemed to have better hearing than nonusers, and pill users over 40 had lower blood cholesterol levels than did nonusers of the same age.[82] There is need for a careful and objective study of the pill with a clear statement on the dangers and the advantages of that method.

The discussion of birth control methods may be summarized in terms of their relative effectiveness. The most effective methods are oral contraception, IUCDs, the diaphragm and jelly, the condom, and withdrawal; the least effective are the rhythm system and the douche. Many times the failure of contraception is mistakenly attributed to the method rather than to the person using it. The fact is that the most reliable methods used by careful individuals can and do effectively control pregnancy.

There is a constant attempt by experts in the area of birth control methods to discover new or better procedures. Some physiologists argue that the present methods are crude and that superior, cheaper methods are being developed. Actually huge sums of money are being poured into research in this area both through the public and the private sector. "The giants of the drug industry know that huge markets can be gained by

---

[79] *Newsweek*, March 9, 1970, p. 46.

[80] Ibid.

[81] Ibid.

[82] *New York Times*, Sept. 23, 1973, p. 8.

improving upon present contraceptive technology—and that huge markets will be lost if a competitor discovers and markets a superior product."[83] The ideal contraceptive they all seek would be harmless, reliable, free of unpleasant side effects, cheap, and simple to use. It would also have to be easy to reverse so that a woman could become pregnant if she desired. "And, finally, one should be able to apply it at a time completely removed from the sexual act, so that the couple does not have to bother about birth control whenever they have intercourse."[84]

A number of new birth control methods are being worked on. These include: (1) lower dosage minipills whose lower hormonal concentration would cause fewer side effects; (2) an implanted capsule of slowly released birth control hormones which could be changed yearly, lessening the chances of failure from forgetfulness; (3) a pill that a woman could take before intercourse which would change the chemical makeup of the mucus in the cervix, so that the sperm would not fertilize an egg; (4) vaginal pessaries containing prostaglandins, inserted once a month so that menstruation would occur whether or not the woman was pregnant (if pregnant, she would have an early abortion without being aware of it); (5) a male pill which would combine progesterone with the male sex hormone, androgen, rendering the man infertile.[85]

Yet, with all the attempts to develop new and better methods of contraception it should not be assumed that any method will ever be developed that will reduce the frequency of unwanted pregnancies to zero. This is true because unwanted pregnancies occur most often among the underaged, the overaged, and the psychologically disturbed. "The underaged become pregnant because they cross the sexual threshold before they think they are going to, and do so unprepared. The overaged, entering the menopause, neglect contraceptive precautions because they *think* they are sterile. The psychologically disturbed, typically a neurotic woman involved in a marriage that is going on the rocks, behave impulsively and sometimes with destructive intent."[86]

Of all the areas of social problems and deviance discussed in this book there is the greatest irony with regard to birth control. Since the beginnings of humanity, having children has been seen as inevitable, natural, and in most cases highly desirable. For a man to marry and not have children was in most societies a loss of face as well as an economic deprivation. When this occurred the blame was usually placed on the

---

[83] Bogue, "Population Explosion," p. 330.

[84] Guttmacher, *Birth Control*, p. 55.

[85] *New York Times*, Sept. 23, 1973, p. 8.

[86] Garrett Hardin, "The History and Future of Birth Control," *Perspectives in Biology and Medicine*, Autumn 1966, p. 10.

woman, and in many societies barrenness in marriage was grounds for the man to divorce his wife. However, in recent years the problem has come to be associated with just the opposite—with those who will not control the number of children they have. Today there are often dominant values that say a small family is desirable and possible in the very same societies in which many individuals continue to believe that having large numbers of children is highly desirable. So in many societies technological knowledge and broad social and governmental encouragement of birth control often exist while the value of the large family of the past is still basic to many persons in those societies.

BIBLIOGRAPHY

Callahan, Daniel, *The American Population Debate*. New York: Doubleday, 1971.

Draper, Elizabeth, *Birth Control in the Modern World*. Baltimore: Penguin Books, 1965.

Edey, Helen, "Psychological Aspects of Vasectomy," *Medical Counterpoint*, January 1972, pp. 19–24.

Farley, John U., and Harold J. Leavitt, "Population Control and the Private Sector," *Journal of Social Issues*, October 1967, pp. 135–43.

Freedman, Ronald, *Population: The Vital Revolution*. New York: Anchor Books, 1964.

Guttmacher, Alan F., *The Complete Book of Birth Control*. New York: Ballantine Books, 1963.

Hardin, Garrett, "The History and Future of Birth Control," *Perspectives in Biology and Medicine*, Autumn 1966, pp. 1-18.

Himes, Norman E., *Medical History of Contraception*. New York: Gamut Press, 1963.

McCary, James L., *Human Sexuality*. New York: Van Nostrand, 1967.

Ridley, Jeanne Clare, "The Effects of Population Change on the Roles and Status of Women: Perspective and Speculation," in Constantina Safilios-Rothschild, *Toward a Sociology of Women*. Lexington, Mass.: Xerox College Publishing, 1972, pp. 372–86.

Westoff, Leslie Aldridge, and Charles F. Westoff, *From Now to Zero*. Boston: Little, Brown, 1968.

chapter five

Pornography

Of all the areas of deviance discussed in this book there is probably none where there is a greater gap between the low significance of the problem and the high social indignation toward it than is found with pornography. The word *pornography* seems to denote to most Americans something that is obscene, sinful, and childish. As a result almost all Americans are against pornography, and while some are indifferent very few are openly for it. Probably most people who use pornography with any frequency do so surreptitiously and rarely volunteer any indication of their interest. So one major purpose of this chapter is to try to analyze why the social problem of pornography leads to so much public indignation despite its slight behavioral consequences.

The word *pornography* is basically a negative one, as is the word *obscenity*. A more positive term referring to the same thing is *erotica*. Later in the chapter there will be an examination of the uses of the term *pornography*. However, at this time pornography may be defined as some appeal to the human senses to bring about the arousal of sexual desire. This implies that the creator of pornography has the purpose of sexual arousal in mind and in fact that that is the main reason for the pornographic product. However, one cannot always know the intent of the producer, and oftentimes what is used pornographically may not have been intended to be pornographic. In the past, for example, excerpts were sometimes taken from literary works not considered to be pornographic and were reprinted and sold as pornography. The interest in this chapter is with those things that are deliberately created to be erotically stimulating, that is, wih consciously created pornography.

In all societies there have probably been some types of erotic productions or pornography. Even the earliest drawings of preliterate humanity included pictures that were sexual in nature and that probably

120

represented something more than simply a graphic record of sexual behavior. This fits the fact that man's sexual involvement is something more than just physical drive and release. The records of the development of humanity indicate that at an early stage people used their senses of touch, sight, and smell in their sexual activities. Therefore, it is logical to assume that pornography existed fairly early in human development.

With the emergence of written language people had a new means for pornographic expression, and as more people were able to read, the potential of this form of expression became greater. Written pornography had its origins in the Western world in the 17th century, but it probably did not come into full flower until near the end of the 18th century. In England the growth of written pornography was closely related to the development of the novel. Marcus suggests that those social forces which acted to contribute to the rise of the novel "and to the growth of its audience—acted analogously in contributing to the development of pornography."[1]

In 18th century England there was little concern over pornography or obscenity, "though it had been ruled in 1729 that an obscene *libel* constituted a common-law misdemeanor."[2] In the latter part of the 18th century a pornography of unprecedented richness developed. There are striking differences between that pornography and the pornography of Victorian England. Taylor points out that Cleland's *Memoirs of a Woman of Pleasure* is frankly sexual in character but that it also has a human warmth and that its characters are convincing by their naturalness and the activities in which they are engaged. He goes on to point out that this is very different from Victorian pornography, "which is shot through and through with sado-masochism, and which is quite unredeemed by an air of the protagonists even getting any enjoyment from their desperate attempts to stimulate lust. All spontaneity is gone."[3] But it should be recognized that what is depicted in pornography must have some appeal to readers, or they won't respond to it. For example, sado-masochistic pornography has never been very popular in the United States. But the sadomasochistic stress in Victorian pornography appealed to the sexual interests and the patterns of sexual expression common to many during that period.

Early in the 20th century a new form of pornographic expression developed—the movie film. Pornographic films initially appeared and gained notoriety in houses of prostitution. Prostitution has had a long history of using visual methods to heighten sexual stimulation. For example, many houses of prostitution had erotic murals, tapestries, and pictures. The early visual erotica were presented in some cases like the

---

[1] Steven Marcus, *The Other Victorians* (New York: Basic Books, 1964), p. 282.

[2] G. Rattray Taylor, *Sex in History* (New York: Vanguard Press, 1954), p. 216.

[3] Ibid., p. 217.

films to serve as ends in themselves. That is, the observer received his sexual pleasure from viewing them. But far more often the visual approaches were used as means for encouraging sexual arousal and the use of the prostitutes. This kind of exposure of stag films led to their increased popularity. "By the end of *la belle Époque,* no self-respecting brothel in any of the large cities on the continent considered its facilities complete without a stock of these films for showing either as an artistic *whore d'oeuvre* or as an entertainment in their own right."[4]

Given the Victorian heritage in Great Britain and the United States, it is not surprising that any public knowledge of pornography was often followed by great moral indignation, sometimes leading to attempts to legally restrict or eliminate pornography. The Victorian view that sex was evil was accompanied by a belief in the need to control that evil in the same way that other varieties of evil were controlled. The Victorian mode of thinking has never concerned itself with whether or not there are social and personal dangers from pornography—that has always been assumed to be the case. Therefore, the problem has always been viewed as one of how to eliminate what has been believed to be very dangerous. In recent decades this belief in the United States has led to a wide and complex variety of legal decisions with regard to pornography.

LEGAL ASPECTS

In most modern societies there have been some restrictions on the public sale of at least some types of pornography. Generally societies are more restrictive about visual than about written pornography. In the past pornographic stag films have been shown in most countries only clandestinely. One well-known exception was the Shanghai Theater in pre-Castro Cuba, which offered a continuous show of stag films to the general public. Knight and Alpert, in their extensive study of the history of stag films, write that there was evidence that a sizable market for such films "did exist as early as 1904, with Buenos Aires then a principal center of production. Movies of fully detailed sexual activity were shot and shipped to private buyers, mostly in England and France, but also in such distant lands as Russia and the Balkan countries."[5]

There has been a recent trend for many countries to become more liberal about what can legally be sold. This has been the case in the United States, and later in the chapter the limits that continue to prevail on what may be legally sold will be examined. At the present time Denmark provides the best illustration of permissiveness toward all forms of pornography. In Denmark there are shops that sell all kinds of written

---

[4] Arthur Knight and Hollis Alpert, "The History of Sex in Cinema: The Stag Film," *Playboy,* November 1967, p. 158.

[5] Ibid., p. 156.

and pictorial pornography, and one may buy their pornographic films or pay for a showing in the shop. In 1969 a great deal of attention was directed at Denmark when the first international pornography fair was held there. In a large convention hall various manufacturers of different types of pornography displayed their products to prospective buyers in the same way that other types of products are shown at international trade fairs. However, Denmark represents an extreme degree of social acceptance of pornography which is far more permissive than that found in the United States.

Traditionally the legal concern with pornography has been linked to its "impact" on women and children. Kanowitz points out that singling out women and children as persons to be spared the ordeal of hearing obscene, vulgar, or abusive words is "reminiscent of the common laws' time honored practice of treating women like infants or, at times, idiots."[6] Kanowitz goes on to state that any constitutional doubts attending various obscenity statutes are intensified if these statutes apply only to women. He argues that most statutes against obscenity can be invalidated because they violate the free speech guarantees of the 1st Amendment. "When courts have an occasion to invalidate them for these reasons, the respect that men and women bear toward one another as fellow human beings will be enhanced rather than diminished."[7]

Increasingly the major concern with pornography in the United States has centered on legal questions. This has been because of legal restrictions that have developed around the question of obscenity. As a result many things other than pornography have been lumped together under the general category of obscenity. As pointed out in Chapter 4, the Comstock Law of 1873 excluded the sending of contraceptives and contraceptive information through the mails by defining them as obscene. In recent years the question of control over pornography has become complexly linked with questions of censorship. It is therefore useful to look at several recent decisions made by the United States Supreme Court. A major decision was handed down in 1957 in the case of *Roth* v. *United States*. The majority opinion declared that "obscenity is not within the area of constitutionally protected speech or press" but that "sex and obscenity are not synonymous. Obscene material is material which deals with sex in a manner appealing to prurient (lustful) interests."[8] This decision said that some things about sex were all right and some were not, and therefore a part of the *Roth* decision was its definition of obscenity. It was believed that the legal tests must set up standards of judgment that would protect

---

[6] Leo Kanowitz, *Women and the Law* (Albuquerque: University of New Mexico Press, 1969), p. 176.

[7] Ibid., p. 178.

[8] Harry M. Clor, *Obscenity and Public Morality* (Chicago: University of Chicago Press, 1969), p. 14.

socially important literature. The Court said that literature dealing with
sex in a manner not appealing to prurient interest was socially important
literature and that the authoritative test would be "whether to the
average person, applying contemporary community standards, the
dominant theme of the material taken as a whole appeals to prurient
interest."⁹

The test was not whether the material would arouse sexual desire in
people making up a particular segment of the community but whether it
would arouse sexual desire in the average person. "You judge the circu-
lars, pictures, and publications which have been put in evidence by the
present day standards of the community. You may ask yourselves does it
offend the common conscience of the community by present day
standards."¹⁰ As Clor points out, it is very difficult to determine how the
"community standards" test is supposed to function. "Is an obscene
publication one which violates the community's current standards of
right? Or which offends the average person in the community? Or which
arouses the sexual desires of the average person?"¹¹ But the even more
difficult question is how one determines who the average person in the
community is.

A second important recent Supreme Court decision on obscenity was
handed down in the *Ginzburg* case in 1966. In that case the Court did not
explicitly hold the defendant's conduct to be "the central issue, but it did
pave the way for an increasing interest and stress on the behavior of the
purveyor and a decreasing concern with the nature of the materials."¹²
The concern with *Ginzburg* centered in part on his stressing of sexually
provocative aspects of his publications, and that fact may be decisive in
determining whether something is obscene. To the Court, one proof of
Ginzburg's motives was his request for second-class mailing privileges
through the post offices at Intercourse and Blue Ball, Pennsylvania.
Ginzburg finally obtained mailing privileges at Middlesex, New Jersey.

Gagnon and Simon have suggested that the Supreme Court's concern
with pornography has had two dimensions in recent years. The first
dimension has dealt with sexual representations that are held to be
offensive to public morality or taste. This was the primary concern in the
Ginzburg case. The second dimension has centered on the effects of
pornography on specific individuals or groups. This has been the focal
point of most public discussions of and prior court decisions on pornography. "This dimension was mentioned only twice in the array of
decisions of 1966, but much of the confusion in discussions of por-

⁹ Ibid., p. 31.
¹⁰ Ibid., p. 37.
¹¹ Ibid., pp. 37–38.
¹² Ibid., p. 82.

nography reflects a difficulty in distinguishing between these dimensions or a tendency to slip from one to the other without noting the change."[13]

There has been a strong demand on the part of many Americans to put controls on pornography, especially on what are perceived to be obscene materials being sent through the mail. A 1969 Gallup survey asked respondents whether they would like to see stricter state and local laws dealing with obscene literature sent through the mails, and 81 percent of the men and 88 percent of the women answered "yes." The survey also indicated that those who most wanted the stricter laws were the older respondents and the ones with the least amount of education.

A third important Supreme Court decision was handed down in June 1973. Essentially the Court said that obscenity could best be defined at the "community" level. According to the Court, lewd conduct "must be specifically defined by the applicable state law, as written or authoritatively construed." However, many states had lost their obscenity laws to the earlier and more permissive Supreme Court decrees. The 1973 decision turned over to state and local legislative bodies the problem of drawing up new laws or guidelines. Many experts felt that the Court decision was a bad one because of the vast variations in what different communities might define as obscene. And in fact one consequence of the decision was to close down movies that were seen as pornographic in very few places. Because of the confusion that has resulted from the decision the Supreme Court has agreed to reexamine it. It might also be added that few states have come up with "community" standard laws. One recent attempt (March 1974) was an antipornography bill passed by the Pennsylvania legislature but vetoed by Governor Milton J. Shapp. The bill was vetoed because it was seen as unconstitutional and as excessively harsh. Of interest was the strong opposition to the proposed law. In fact all three Philadelphia newspapers urged the governor to veto it, mainly on the grounds that it was a legal mess and would result in real problems of censorship. One of the newspapers also opposed the law on the grounds that pornography was not harmful and that if adults wanted it that was their business so long as children were protected. This position would probably have been unthinkable for a newspaper a few years ago.

The federal government's interest in the question of pornography has also been expressed on another level. In October 1967 Congress established the Commission on Obscenity and Pornography, and in January 1968 the president appointed its members. The commission was assigned four specific tasks. First, with the help of leading constitutional law authorities it was to analyze the laws pertaining to the control of obscenity and pornography and to evaluate and pass on recommendations

---

[13] John H. Gagnon and William Simon, "Pornography—Raging Menace or Paper Tiger?" *Trans-Action*, July 1967, p. 42.

for defining obscenity and pornography. Second, it was to determine the means used in distributing obscene and pornographic materials and to study the nature and volume of traffic of such materials. Third, it was to study the effects of obscenity and pornography upon the public, especially upon minors, and the relationship of obscenity and pornography to crime and other antisocial behavior. Fourth, it was "to recommend such legislative, administrative, or other advisable and appropriate action as the Commission deems necessary to regulate effectively the flow of such traffic without in any way interfering with constitutional rights."[14] The commission reported its findings to the president and Congress in the early fall of 1970.[15] When the report appeared it was met with great indignation and hostility. Basically the findings of the commission were that no link had been established between exposure to pornography and criminal or antisocial behavior. The report also indicated that pornography should be available to adults if they choose to use it. The report appeared several months before the congressional elections of November 1970. Therefore, most politicians violently attacked it and few defended it. The president of the United States refused to accept the report. Rarely were the attacks on the report made for methodological or theoretical reasons. Rather, the critics simply *knew* that they were right and that the report was wrong. In the discussion that follows some references will be made to the findings of the report.

INTERPRETATIONS OF PORNOGRAPHY

Before examining the various forms of pornography it is important to say something about attempts to understand this kind of deviance. At the present time there are two different approaches to the study of pornography. One is the approach of social science, and the other is that of literary criticism. Rosen and Turner suggest that there have been two major approaches in the social science attempt to define and understand pornography. The first is a cultural relativist position that sees pornography as anything which a society defines as such. "In other words pornography is that which violates the societal norms of sexual expression."[16] The second tries to discover objective, universal characteristics which make an item pornographic. Rosen and Turner suggest that the best illustration of this is the assertion by the Kronhausens in 1964 that

---

[14] Commission on Obscenity and Pornography, "Progress Report" (Washington, D.C.: July 1969), pp. 1–2.

[15] *The Report of the Commission on Obscenity and Pornography* (New York: Bantam Books, 1970).

[16] Lawrence Rosen and Stanley H. Turner, "Exposure to Pornography: An Exploratory Study," *Journal of Sex Research*, November 1969, p. 235.

"hard core pornography is erotic material which is unrealistic, voyeuristic, and contains infantile sexual fantasies."[17]

Ned Polsky has speculated on the relationship of pornography to society. He suggests that pornography and prostitution are, at least in modern societies, functional alternatives. By this he means that they are different roads to the same social end because both provide for the discharge of what society defines as antisocial sex, that is, "impersonal, nonmarital sex: prostitution provides this via real intercourse with a real sex object, and pornography provides it via masturbation, imagined intercourse with a fantasy object."[18] Gagnon and Simon also suggest that pornography and prostitution are the forms of collective sexual deviance most intermixed with and linked to the conventional social order."[19] Both prostitution and pornography are found in all societies large enough to have a fairly complex division of labor. Polsky writes that although pornography develops in only a rudimentary way in preliterate societies, "whenever a society has a fair degree of literacy and mass-communication technology then pornography becomes a major functional alternative to prostitution."[20]

The sexual needs and desires of individuals cover a wide range. As discussed in Chapter 9, one of the functions of prostitution is to provide the customer with the opportunity to express his sexual deviance because a woman may not be willing to participate unless she is paid. Pornography is also produced to meet all forms of sexual deviance. Whatever the reasons, it is clear that although a great deal of pornography presents sexual relations that are not highly deviant a large amount of pornography offers fantasy involvement in sex acts that society proscribes as "unnatural."[21] Pornography may be the only outlet for many who can't or won't find a prostitute to meet their deviant sexual needs.

Although societies use both prostitution and pornography, the extent to which one is used in preference to the other varies widely among societies. Polsky points out there are also variations within a given society. He suggests that there may be variations in what is considered appropriate in different social situations. "For example, a group of adolescent boys might collectively visit a prostitute but masturbate to pornography only singly and in private, with group contemplation of pornography serving merely to convey sex information or as the occasion for

---

[17] Ibid.

[18] Ned Polsky, "Pornography," in Edward Sagarin and Donald E. MacNamara, *Problems of Sex Behavior* (New York: Crowell, 1968), p. 271.

[19] John H. Gagnon and William Simon, "Sexual Deviance in Contemporary America," *The Annals*, March 1968, p. 117.

[20] Polsky, "Pornography," pp. 270–71.

[21] Ibid., pp. 276–77.

ribald humor."[22] Another type of variation may be related to broad social variables. For example, the Kinsey data indicated that masturbation to pornographic materials was most common among the higher educated. "At the lower levels of our society, this is generally put down (as is long-term masturbation *per se*), and, conversely, prostitutes are visited much more often."[23]

Recent research indicates that erotica do not serve as a major source of sexual arousal leading to masturbation. One study found that erotica were but one set of sexual stimuli to which male teenagers reacted. In fact real people were far more potent sexual stimuli for these teenagers than any kind of pornography.[24] The study also found that if a boy had developed feelings of confusion and guilt concerning his sexuality during preadolescence his reactions to erotic materials as an adolescent would reflect this internal conflict. "Sexual arousal will elicit guilt and disgust, emotions that will serve to reinforce his sense of distaste regarding his own sexual desires."[25]

One functional value of pornography that has generally been over-looked is its use in social situations in which heterosexual outlets are highly limited or unavailable. For example, pornography is commonly found in boys' schools, the military (particularly aboard naval vessels), and so on. But the best illustration of its use is in prisons. Polsky suggests that sociologists have been so concerned with the extent to which prisoners use homosexuality that they have neglected their use of pornography.[26] There is a great deal of written but unpublished pornography within prisons. Polsky points out a major difference between prostitution and por-nography. "Hardly any man can, as it were, be his own prostitute (although many try, by attempting autofellation), but every man can be his own pornographer."[27] Some of the published pornography was origi-nally written to aid the writer in masturbation. "For example, Jean Genet indicates this was why he wrote *Our Lady of the Flowers*. And it is apparently to this motivation that we owe the pornography produced by the most noted pornographer of them all, the Marquis de Sade."[28]

The social science approach to the study of pornography is not con-cerned with it morally, but rather functionally. Because pornography has prevailed for so long and is of interest to so many people it is of social relevance. By contrast the approach of literary criticism is primarily concerned with making moral and aesthetic judgments about por-

---

[22] Ibid., p. 271.

[23] Ibid.

[24] Michael J. Goldstein and Harold S. Kant, *Pornography and Sexual Deviance* (Berkeley: University of California Press, 1973), p. 151.

[25] Ibid., p. 149.

[26] Polsky, "Pornography," p. 273.

[27] Ibid.

[28] Ibid., pp. 273-74.

nography. Some literary critics believe that it is legitimate for literature to attempt to sexually arouse its readers. Marcus writes that "if it is permissible for works of literature to move us to tears, to arouse our passions against injustice, to make us cringe with horror, and to purge us through pity and terror, then it is equally permissible—it lies within the orbit of literature's function—for works of literature to excite us sexually."[29] But then Marcus follows this up by saying that pornography is not literature. The argument then is that nothing written as pornography can ever be literature. Yet, there is nothing inherent in pornography, however it is defined, that makes it incapable of being literature. If written pornography is material designed to sexually arouse the reader, it often achieves that goal. But if a man writes something which he believes to be pornographic and it is read with laughter and no sexual excitement, then he has not produced pornography. But, as Gebhard points out, "There is no reason why in skilled hands pornography could not be an aesthetically legitimate art form."[30] Many literary critics disagree. They believe that something inherent in pornography makes it incapable of being true artistic expression.

Literary critics are often highly subjective observers, and this means that some of them can see social worth and significance where others cannot. For example, some critics now see the works of Genet as literature while only a few years ago those writings were dismissed as pornographic. The same may also be said of the works of the Marquis de Sade. For many readers, having something defined as literature allows them to read and be titillated with less guilt than they would feel if it were defined as pornography. It is doubtful that the erotic response of the reader changes because a work is called literature instead of pornography. In other words, what is erotic exists however it is labeled—but the label often removes guilt for the reader and may even give him the feeling of being avant-garde and aesthetically sophisticated.

It also appears that the acceptance of erotic scenes in a book may be determined by the context in which they are presented. That is, does the plot of the book suggest that the sexual scenes are a part of guilt, shame, fear, or frustration? When this happens, it is a soul-searching book and the sex becomes acceptable. As David Loth points out, however, if the book treats sex in a spirit of bravado with everyone capable of intense sexual activity at all times and to a rousing climax on every page, it is doomed to be called pornographic.[31]

It is commonly observed that American novels since World War II have presented sex with all its variations in highly descriptive detail. Yet, amidst all the frank and open descriptions of sexual behavior in novels there also continues to be a strong Puritan influence. With few exceptions

---

[29] Marcus, *Other Victorians*, pp. 277–78.

[30] Paul H. Gebhard et al., *Sex Offenders* (New York: Harper and Row, 1965), p. 669.

[31] David Loth, *The Erotic in Literature* (New York: Messner, 1961), p. 19.

the sexual life of characters in novels either leads to or results from severe individual problems. Rarely does one find a character in the modern novel who engages in sexual behavior (even in marriage) without problems. The common theme appears to be that, while a character may indulge in all types of sexual experiences, he rarely enters into such experiences simply for pleasure or leaves them satisfied and free of personal and social problems. The modern novel seems to suggest that sexual involvement is bad, not in the sense of "sin," but in terms of psychological and social problems. Punishment is the overwhelming consequence of sexual behavior—either because that behavior is a manifestation of some deep-seated problem or because it leads to new problems. In his analysis of the erotic aspect of the modern novel Loth writes that "most of us disapprove (for consumption by others) of fictional characters who enjoy sex or its perversions frankly and heartily without shame or pain. We want them to suffer in mind or body (or both) before the last page."[32]

The sexual motivations of characters in modern novels are very often presented as resulting from a need to "prove" something. Characters may attempt to "prove" that they are sexually adequate, that they can cut the umbilical cord, that they are not latent homosexuals, and so forth. However, it is striking that in few cases do the characters in modern novels ever successfully "prove" anything by their sexual involvement— except that sex was not the answer. That sex might be entered into for its own sake, and simply be a relationship of pleasure without complex causes and effects, is rarely suggested.

In the 1960s in the United States a genre of the modern novel developed that was presented to the public as pornographic. This kind of novel was strongly rejected by critics as not being literature. Such novels should also be rejected as not being pornographic because they are not erotically stimulating. The best illustrations of this genre have been the novels written by Jacqueline Susann. The characters of her novels are miserable, sad human beings. As one critic points out, "The love in *Love Machine* is joyless, violent, and cruel. This is the kind of sex which probably discourages going out and trying it."[33] It is hard to imagine how anyone could become sexually aroused by reading a Susann novel. While literary critics see her books as insulting to the novel it may also be suggested that to call them pornographic is insulting to pornography.

When a person buys something which he hopes will arouse him sexually he generally doesn't care whether it is literature or not. The user of pornography may get what he wants from "hard core" pornographic literature or from erotic "art" literature. "So far as he is concerned, the only significance is that in the latter he usually gets less for his money."[34]

---

[32] Ibid., p. 30.

[33] Sara Davidson, "Jacqueline Susann: The Writing Machine," *Harper's*, October 1969, p. 66.

[34] Polsky, "Pornography," p. 279.

But it is clear that the literary critic is looking for different things than is the user of erotic literature. When critics define a work as pornographic this may mean that they are hostile to and contemptuous of that work. Many critics are doing more than just making literary judgments about various works—they are also trying to define appropriate sexual behavior. For example, one literary critic states that sex is an obsession in the United States today, that this has brought about a new wave of pornographic literature which "approaches the quality of mechanical repetition and unreality," and that this new pornography makes sex dull.[35] (It is obviously not dull for many who read it.) The critic goes on to say that there is no use for pornography in society today. Consequently the purpose of pornography is not fulfilled, making it a useless part of literature. This critic also states that the purpose of sex is serious and that the purpose of sex in literature is to help convey the feeling of meaning of life as it is.[36] What is striking about this type of view is its narrowness with regard to both sex and literature. It is also important that such social observers make categorical statements but are never troubled with presenting evidence.

Another rather tortured argument of the literary critic is that sex is private and that pornography invades that privacy. Elliott writes that "the trouble with pornography in our culture is that it offends the sense of separateness, individuality, and privacy and it intrudes on the rights of others." He goes on to say that one should wish to remove oneself from the presence of men and women enjoying sexual intercourse. "Not to withdraw is to peep, to pervert looking, so that it becomes a sexual end in itself."[37] This seems a rather silly argument because those who feel that pornography invades their privacy wouldn't use it. And the argument that fantasies about fictional characters invade the privacy of real persons doesn't make sense.

But probably the most common literary argument directed against pornography and its use is that it is adolescent and therefore demeaning to adults. Marcus writes that pornography is, after all, "nothing more than a representation of the fantasies of infantile sexual life, as these fantasies are edited and recognized in the masturbatory daydreams of adolescence. Every man who grows up must pass through such a phase in his existence."[38] The critics' only evidence that using pornography is an adolescent behavior is that the strong interest in pornography and masturbation first develop in adolescence. By the same logic one could refer to a man's sexual interest in women as adolescent because it is during the same adolescent period that he becomes highly oriented to females and masturbates to all kinds of fantasies about them.

---

[35] "The New Pornography," *Time*, April 16, 1965, p. 29.

[36] Ibid.

[37] George P. Elliott, "Against Pornography," *Harper's*, March, 1965, p. 53.

[38] Marcus, *Other Victorians*, p. 286.

It has been necessary to say something about the literary critics' view of pornography because literary critics are often the intellectually respectable "authorities" who write about the subject. Their expertise in this area is assumed because they are authorities on literature. But, as suggested, the critics very often go beyond literature and become authorities on the causes and consequences of pornography. And these are areas where there is very little empirical evidence, and where pronouncements from any source should not be taken as factually verified statements.

The discussion thus far has implied that the primary purpose of all types of pornography is to evoke erotic responses from the persons subjected to it. We may take this a step further and see what the actual purposes of pornography are. The Kronhausens state that "pornographic writings are 'meant' to function as psychological aphrodisiacs and are successful only to the extent that they accomplish this particular purpose."[39] Wayland Young goes further and says that all-out pornography is "a determination that the customer shall have his money's worth, and that the purpose of the whole operation is to provide male consumers with something to masturbate over."[40]

Polsky has pointed out that pornography is not simply limited to its role as an adjunct to masturbation. He suggests that for some persons pornography serves as a sex instruction manual, that it may be used as a form of foreplay to stimulate coitus, as in, "say, the case of whorehouse murals from Pompeii to the present."[41] But probably most people who read pornography with any regularity generally do so for erotic titillation that does not lead to any physical sexual release.

As indicated earlier, the public reaction in the United States to all forms of pornography often conveys the notion that pornography is highly significant and dangerous to society. But as Gagnon and Simon point out, what is most important about pornography is not that it is particularly relevant to sexuality, but that it brings forth special treatment when it confronts the law.[42] They go on to suggest that the danger from pornography itself is minor, that the real danger may be in the methods being used in dealing with pornography because those methods may become "prevalent in controlling the advocacy of other ideas as well."[43] To many the attempts to control the buying and use of pornography by adults is censorship.

The importance of pornography is also linked to what is defined as

---

[39] Eberhard and Phyllis Kronhausen, "The Psychology of Pornography," in Albert Ellis and Albert Abarbanel, *The Encyclopedia of Sexual Behavior* (New York: Hawthorn Books, 1961), p. 849.

[40] Wayland Young, *Eros Denied* (New York: Grove Press, 1964), p. 88.

[41] Polsky, "Pornography," p. 272.

[42] Gagnon and Simon, "Pornography", p. 48.

[43] Ibid.

such. The 1957 Supreme Court decision makes clear that pornography or obscenity is what the community says it is, and the community's definitions vary over time. As a result the definitions of the past are no longer adequate today. Not very many years ago people smuggled copies of such books as *Fanny Hill* and Frank Harris's *My Life and Loves* into the United States but these can now be bought legally in bookstores and drugstores in most parts of the country.

Labeling a work as pornographic produces significant consequences. If persons of authority define something as pornographic or obscene, then it becomes such in the minds of many people. For example, family planning pamphlets and pictures of human birth have in the past been defined as pornographic and in some cases have been treated under the obscenity laws. There is an opposite consequence of labeling something as pornographic, and that is to make it sell better. For many years "banned in Boston" was great publicity for a novel and helped make it financially successful. A recent illustration of the sales boost given to a movie by the attacks of moralists was *Last Tango in Paris*. In the summer of 1970 a road troupe of *Hair* came to Detroit, and according to the manager ticket sales were not good until two city councilmen got a lot of mass media coverage for protesting that their fair city was being besmirched by that production. So having something labeled as obscene may be harmful in some cases, but in others it may be highly profitable.

TYPES OF PORNOGRAPHY

In this section we will look at various types of pornography. As suggested at the start of the chapter, pornography is defined as something created to bring about sexual arousal in its users. The three types of pornography to be discussed here share in common the deliberate attempt to bring about sexual arousal in at least some people. The three types are exposure of the body, movies or films, and written narratives.

Exposure of the body

Under the broadest interpretation of the definition of pornography one could argue that any women who deliberately dress to be sexually provocative (and are successful) are pornographic. However, this instance can be eliminated by adding one other criterion to the definition of pornography—that the primary motive behind pornography is to make money for the sale of the product. Within the profit context are certain occupational groups of women who expose their bodies in what may be defined as a pornographic fashion. The exposure of the nude body for profit is not enough in itself to define that behavior as pornographic—there must also be the conscious intent to bring about sexual arousal.

Women in nudist colonies are not pornographic because they are neither exposing their bodies for profit nor deliberately trying to bring about sexual arousal. By contrast most erotic dancers are doing both. If the customers have no erotic response to a stripteaser she will be a failure in her occupation. (Some strippers see themselves as artists and get indignant when it is suggested that their function is to sexually stimulate the customers. But few customers will go to see a stripper because they are art connoisseurs.) Because stripping is the most common type of pornographic body exposure it is useful to look briefly at that occupation.

There has been a long tradition of burlesque theater in the United States, and over the years it has come to center more and more on the strippers. Even with the general sexual liberalization of today stripping is still considered deviant or at best a marginal occupation. In a recent study of strippers it was found that almost every one of them believed that most people's conception of their occupation was that it was dirty and immoral. "This belief affects their behavior in public; for example, many of the girls avoid identifying themselves in public as strippers, preferring to call themselves dancers, entertainers, and the like."[44]

To achieve success the stripper must have a body that is erotically attractive to many of the male customers. As a group the physiques of strippers, particularly their bust size, are larger than average for women of their age. That the primary function of strippers is their visual erotic appeal is also reflected in the fact that most strippers begin with little or no training. It was found that the career sequence for most strippers involved three contingencies: "(1) a tendency toward exhibitionistic behavior for gain, (2) an opportunity structure making stripping an accessible occupational alternative, and (3) a sudden awareness of the easy economic rewards in stripping."[45]

Legal definitions of what is obscene for strippers vary greatly. This is because the enforcement of obscenity laws in the states where strippers work is left up to the local officials. Thus strippers find considerable variation in interpretation of what is obscene. In some cities performers are allowed to "bare their breasts completely and are permitted to 'flash.' Flashing consists of lowering the G-string so that the pubic area is displayed. Although the G-string may be lowered to the knees or ankles its complete removal is apparently considered obscene."[46] Overall it is estimated that about 7,000 women in the United States earn their living by removing their clothes in a titillating fashion.

The successful stripper erotically excites the viewer. She does this by revealing her body within a context, often with "mood" music, of sexual

---

[44] James K. Skipper, Jr., and Charles H. McCaghy, "Stripteasers: The Anatomy and Career Contingencies of a Deviant Occupation," *Social Problems*, Winter 1970, p. 392.

[45] Ibid., p. 402.

[46] Ibid., p. 394.

seduction. For example, the traditional bumps and grinds of the stripper are the movements of sexual intercourse. And as with all pornography, the stripper sometimes erotically arouses the viewer to the point where he masturbates.

There are other ways in which the body may be used pornographically, but they are not common in the United States. One way is to present sexual shows for customers. People are hired to perform all types of sexual acts in all kinds of erotic combinations. These performances are roughly to the stag film what the legitimate stage play is to the movie. The viewer sees persons act out pornographic scenes in person rather than on film. However, the legal risks are so great that sexual shows are quite rare in the United States, although this is not true in some other countries of the world.

Pornographic movies, or stag films

In addition to pornographic movies, or stag films, visual pornography includes cartoons, drawings, and photographs. These are used along with written pornography or by themselves. In the past the cartoon book was a common form of pornography. It was usually a takeoff on some well-known comic strip characters with exaggerated sex organs engaged in sexual activities, and the quality of the drawing was usually very poor. In general, pornographic photographs range from crude to highly sophisticated products and can be highly erotic. In recent years the photograph has become a part of a legally acceptable kind of pornography which is presented within a pseudomedical context. Brochures are sent through the mail telling one how he can learn to be more successful sexually. One approach is to talk about sexual positions and to include illustrative photographs. This kind of literature, often sent indiscriminately through the mails, has raised a great deal of indignation among many Americans. Legally it appears to be acceptable because the brochures have "redeeming social qualities." But limits continue to be set on what can be shown legally in these types of photographs. Both the male and female sex organ can be shown, but the erect penis cannot be. And photographs of the penis in the vagina are not permitted. These restrictions appear to be informally imposed by the postal authorities and could ease up or become tighter in the future.

Pornographic movies, or stag films, have been a part of the American scene for many years. Stag films have in the past been subject to uniquely ambivalent social attitudes. Publicly stag films have been almost universally condemned, but in private they have been endorsed by a large and responsive element of the community. The support of the community is evidenced by the sub rosa stag screenings frequently sponsored by "our nations leading—and most patriotic—civil, social, fraternal and veteran's organizations."[47] Gagnon and Simon point out that stag films are commonly seen by two kinds of male groups. "First are those living in group housing in colleges and universities and second are those belonging to upper lower-class and lower middle-class voluntary social groups."[48]

One basic ingredient in stag films is a simple and contrived situation to provide initial motivation. The plot is often "sexual excitation of the female by visual means, comparatively rare in real life but a persistent theme in these films: a direct and rapid seduction—so direct and rapid that in many films it cannot properly be called a seduction at all; and, finally, sexual activity, which of course is the focal point of the film."[49] The world of movie pornography is often a fantasy world. This means that all females are in a state of constant sexual arousal and waiting to be sexually serviced by the first male to come along. As Knight and Alpert point out, the beginning of countless stag films concerns a female who becomes sexually aroused "by reading an erotic book, masturbating, dreaming, watching a nude male, watching horses have sex, sunning herself, doing housework, listening to the radio—or even being hit by a car."[50] All of this buttresses the view that stag films present male audiences with highly sexed women who fit their male fantasy of the sexual nature of at least some women.

Stag films cover the range of both heterosexual and homosexual activities. Included are fellatio, cunnilingus, sodomy, bestiality, and mutual masturbation. But the sexual activities that are usually included reflect the American males' preferences and prejudices. For example, Knight and Alpert found in their analysis of over 1,000 stag films that male homosexuality was relatively rare while female homosexuality was quite common. Heterosexual oral-genital contact has been quite common, especially in recent stag films. "But, once again, the men come out ahead, with 89 percent of the films including fellatio and only 46 percent including cunnilingus."[51] In recent years a number of male homosexual films have been produced for the male homosexual audience. However, female homosexual films have been produced for male audiences and not for a lesbian market.

The stag films have traditionally reflected certain social values. While the main function of stag films is sexual stimulation they sometimes also serve as an outlet for pressures created by social and sexual taboos. "In strongly Catholic countries, for example, there is a significantly anticlerical strain in the local pornography. As a less rigidly religious country, the United States has no marked anticlerical feelings of any kind, so that

---

[47] Knight and Alpert, "Sex in Cinema," p. 155.
[48] Gagnon and Simon, "Pornography," p. 43.
[49] Knight and Alpert, "Sex in Cinema," p. 158.
[50] Ibid.
[51] Ibid., p. 170.

the irreverent themes so common in the stag films of Mexico, Cuba, and France are almost unknown here."[52] American prejudices control what may be seen in American-produced stag films. For example, while a black female may be involved in these films it is rare to find a black male.

In their extensive study of stag films Knight and Alpert found that a number of changes had occurred over the years. The main difference between the early films produced in the 20s as contrasted with those of the 30s was the increased concentration on sexual activity and the lessened concern with the narrative development of the story. "Particularly pronounced in the thirties was a pervasive antiwoman theme, with the female treated as a sex object rather than as a sexual partner."[53] In the 40s and early 50s, U.S. stag films generally declined in quality, with less attention given not only to humor but to plots, sets, and editing."[54] By the 60s youthful and attractive actors had become common rather than the exception. Most of the females in present stag films are in their late teens or early twenties. This is about ten years younger than their counterparts of a generation ago. Although most of the females are recruited from the ranks of professional prostitutes, "many films are now being made with semipro and nonprofessional females, who may agree to perform more for erotic and egotistical reasons than for the traditional economic considerations."[55] Whatever their motives the actors in today's films are much less inhibited than their predecessors and have a far greater erotic effect on the viewer.

Over the years changes have also occurred in the nature of the sexual activity shown in stag films. Only about one third of the films produced in the 20s included fellatio, but in the 1960s this was found in over three fourths of the stag films. Also the "increasing sexual emancipation of women in the intervening years is reflected clearly in an equally striking increase in the incidence of oral-genital activity performed on the female by her male partner. This was found in only about 10 percent of the films of the 20s but in two thirds of those produced in the sixties."[56] Also in contrast with the past there is more variety in sexual position and more group activity. The changes over the years in stag films correspond with changing views about the greater sexuality of the woman.

In the early 1970s the stag film became available in commercial theaters. These films were shown in many cities, both in small storefront theaters and in former first-run movie houses. Some theaters continued to show "medium core" X-rated movies, in which there continued to be restrictions on what was shown. X-rated films do not show the erect penis

---

[52] Ibid.
[53] Ibid., p. 176.
[54] Ibid., p. 178.
[55] Ibid.
[56] Ibid., p. 180.

or the sex organs in coital position. The best way of knowing whether you are going into a medium-core or a hard-core theater is the price. In general the price for hard-core films is three to five dollars while that for medium-core films is often under two dollars. Among the hard-core theaters are a few that specialize in homosexual films. However, the vast majority show films that include heterosexual behavior and female homosexuality, with no hint of male homosexuality. The sex in hard-core films is explicit and detailed. The performers, with few exceptions, are young, white, and reasonably attractive. These films tend to run about an hour and have a general plot line that is usually secondary to the purpose of showing a maximum of sexual action. Some performers and films have achieved great notoriety, as, for example, Linda Lovelace in *Deep Throat*.

There appear to be two general types of audiences at hard-core theaters. The first, and by far the most common, is the all-male audience. These men represent all ages and social class levels. They almost always attend by themselves, and their overwhelmingly common seating arrangement is as isolated individuals. These men rarely react to anything shown on the screen. They rarely laugh (even though some scenes deserve laughter), and rarely look at or speak to each other. One gets the feeling that many of the men are somewhat guilty or nervous about being there. The second type of audience includes a lot of couples as well as unmixed groups of men and women. This audience is most commonly seen often on the weekend, in the better theaters showing the more publicized pornographic movies. It is often vocal, making remarks about what is going on on the screen.

The future of hard-core films will be determined by how the 1973 Supreme Court decision is applied. If the restrictions become stronger the hard-core film will be driven out of the legal movie house and there will be a return to the medium-core film in legitimate theaters and to the stag film for illegal showings.

Novels

The deliberately pornographic novel is usually short. In the past, when hard-core pornography was illegal, pornographic novels were often no more than 20 or 30 pages in length and cheaply printed with many printing errors. However, this type of pornographic novel is now primarily a collector's item because in many parts of the United States there is no longer a distinction between what can be written legally and illegally. Nothing that can be said in print about sexual activity cannot be sent through the mails or sold in various paperback shops in many cities. The new pornography is written with a skill equal to that usually found in the cheaper types of paperbacks, and the quality of pornographic book production is about the same. One difference is the higher price. Pornographic novels run to about 175 to 200 pages of large print and sell for between two and four dollars. The prices vary from one location to another, and the same book may sell for a dollar more in one city than in another. Pornographic novels are generally not sold in drugstores or neighborhood paperback stores. They are most often found in the center of cities, in the nonresidential hotel and business areas. And they are usually sold in stores that sell other kinds of paperbacks, although they generally have a section of the store or even a room to themselves. So that they can be found more easily the books may have a sign over them that says a person must be 21 or older to read them. It is rare to see women looking at the pornographic books in these types of stores. The commission report states that a vast majority of "adults only" books are written for heterosexual males, "although about 10 percent are aimed at the male homosexual market and a small percentage (less than 5 percent) at fetishists. Virtually none of these books is intended for a female audience."[57]

A recent study describes the behavior of patrons in an "adult" book store that sells pornographic materials. Often such stores sell not only books, magazines, and pictures but also such sexual objects as dildos, vibrators, vaginal creams, and so forth. In most cities the store operators are very careful to keep minors out. The patrons are almost always men. When women do enter they are rarely alone. McKinstry found that they were either with other women, their boyfriends, or their husbands. "When making a purchase they almost always choose one of the funny greeting cards, novelty towels, or otherwise purposefully humorous items."[58] Like that of the all-male audiences in the hard-core movie theaters, the password in the bookstores is silence. Although a number of men in a store may be standing quite close together there is clear physical separation. "Individuals are especially careful not to come into close contact with one another—not showing any facial espression, particularly expressions of pleasure."[59] Many men seem to feel guilty about being there. McKinstry found that while able at first to maintain both their silence and their adult presentation of self, at the counter many of these men reverted to a little-boy approach. "One has the distinct feeling when watching them that they feel guilty about what they are doing, are putting themselves at the mercy of the clerk, and want to get the whole thing over with as soon as possible."[60]

---

[57] *Report of the Commission*, p. 18.

[58] William C. McKinstry, "The Pulp Voyeur: A Peek at Pornography in Public Places," in Jerry Jacobs, *Deviance: Field Studies and Self-Disclosures* (Palo Alto, Calif.: National Press Books, 1974), p. 36.

[59] Ibid., p. 37.

[60] Ibid., pp. 38–39.

The pornographic novel assumes that some plot is necessary if its description of sexual behavior is to take on erotic character for the reader. In the past illegal hard-core pornography had a minimal plot because its authors knew that the readers bought the books for the sexual scenes. But the more recent, legal pornography appears to be trying to attract readers who want both a story and sexual description. The sexual description is the main part of the book, though the new books appear to be aiming at a higher educated readership, one that wants some setting of realism to the sexual scenes. This approach seems logical because the evidence indicates that it is the higher educated male who is most responsive to written pornography.

As indicated earlier, almost all pornography is aimed at the male consumer, and as a result women are described by its authors in ways that they think men want to perceive at least some women to be sexually. For example, one common scene in pornographic novels describes the woman as looking at her body, caressing herself, and masturbating in the privacy of her room. What is of interest is that the women are presented as seeing their bodies in the same way as would men, and as sexually responding to the thoughts they have about their own bodies. "Thus, the main sex object is frequently for both the men and women the female body and the same descriptions are seen as appropriate for the reactions of both sexes to that stimulus."[61]

The main female character in pornographic novels is almost always one who is highly inhibited sexually at the start of the story. She is described as being puritanical and as repelled by sexual relationships even with her husband. She is seduced by another man, often while under the influence of alcohol or aphrodisiacs, or while seeing another couple having sexual relations (often her husband being willingly seduced by her seducer's wife). She resists mentally, but physically she can't control herself, and there always comes a moment when she gives in and tells her seducer to "do it to her." By the end of the novel she has had all kinds of sexual experiences with a variety of persons, and she and her husband decide that it is a good life and that they enjoy each other even more sexually. So with their newfound sexuality they together and with others sexually live happily ever after.

In written pornography all disturbing elements of life are avoided. One never reads about unwanted pregnancy, abortion, venereal disease, or other unpleasant side effects of sexual activity.[62] The novels might be described as presenting a "happy world of pornography," a world in which the characters seek and accept sexual pleasure with no problems. Not only are there no difficulties in that world, but it becomes thera-

---

[61] Michael Gordon and Robert R. Bell, "Medium and Hard Core Pornography: A Comparative Analysis," *Journal of Sex Research*, November 1969, p. 266.

[62] Kronhausen, "Pornography," p. 849.

peutic for many problems—for example, the problem of frigidity is always solved. Even putting aside the obvious errors and exaggerations of the pornographic novel the notion they convey of simple and uninhibited sex is difficult for many Americans to accept. We usually insist that sexual behavior be intricately interwoven into the complex web of human behavior. For example, if a novel deals with sexual behavior within the context of psychological struggles it is treated seriously and is defined in most communities as acceptable literature. Yet, it is doubtful that the "happy world of pornography" is any more an exaggeration of reality than the presentations in many of the "serious" literary works or psychoanalytic treatises on sexual behavior that are viewed as telling it "like it is."[63]

As suggested, pornographic books are written almost entirely for male audiences. However, the more specific aim of the books may vary. For example, many pornographic books are written for male homosexuals. The male with homosexual interests is seen as a potential buyer of pornography in the same way as is the heterosexual male—basically all that is varied is the gender of the sex object. By contrast it appears that there is no market for female readers with either heterosexual or homosexual interests. There do not appear to be any significant number of books written for female homosexuals. However, there are a large number of books about lesbians written for male readers, and sexual experiences between women are common to a majority of pornographic books. This is because many men, especially among the higher educated, find the description of sex between women very erotic.

There is no evidence that contact with either heterosexual or homosexual pornography influences an individual's sexual direction. One study found that most homosexuals had already started experimenting with same-sex activities prior to any significant exposure to homosexual erotica. The study found that erotica were first encountered in late adolescence or early childhood when the sexual patterns of the respondents were already pretty well established. "Homosexuals, then, rarely if ever develop their sexual preferences as a result of exposure to homosexual erotica."[64]

Given the various forms of pornography available to many people in the United States, it is important to look at how people view this availability. One would assume that of the types of pornography discussed the display of the female body would be the least offensive. However, the evidence indicates that nudity in any form is offensive to most Americans. One study found that a large percentage of people rate nudity, even without genital exposure, as obscene, and that this was especially true

[63] Gordon and Bell, "Pornography," p. 267.
[64] Goldstein and Kant, *Pornography*, pp. 149–50.

among the lower socioeconomic groups.[65] It should be remembered that
the display of *any* part of the body was considered obscene during the
Victorian period, and residues of that thinking continue.

In recent years strong public reaction has developed and polarized
against all types of sexual materials, whether visual or written. It seems
clear that a large number of Americans are upset and often indignant
because they believe that their country is suffering from "moral decay."
This reaction tends to be most common among the older and the lower
educated, and it contributes to the great hostility that many of them feel
toward the young and higher educated—the college student. Many older
people see things they find sexually objectionable in areas that are far
from pornographic. For example, the most conservative of the mass
media is television, but 38 percent of the respondents to the Gallup survey
of 1969 said that they had seen something involving sex on television that
was objectionable. The hostility is reflected in the Gallup finding that 50
percent of the respondents said that they would be willing to join a
neighborhood group to protest the sale of objectionable literature on
newsstands.

It is clear that in the United States the legal rights given for sexual
expression through all possible outlets are far greater than what most of
the adult population believe to be right. For many Americans, to be
against pornography is like being against sin. That is, they see no rational
reason for not being against it, and in fact find being for pornography
almost incomprehensible. It is important to recognize that there are few
things that such a large number of Americans so unquestioningly believe
to be wrong. This is even reflected in the fact that many people who buy
pornography often do so with some guilt. It may be that many customers
feel that they are a little "sick," or at least immature. This is also why
even persons who purchase pornography do not publicly resist those
groups trying to halt the sales. To support pornography in the local
community would be equivalent in the minds of many to admitting being
a moral degenerate.

THE USERS OF PORNOGRAPHY

It has been stressed throughout this chapter that pornography is for the
most part produced and used by men. In the past the use of pornography
was best typified by the stag party, which tended to be a group of
respectable men in the community. For those men the stag evenings were
a kind of ritual that allowed them to express crude emotions in a masculine context.[66] And in the past when the medium was written pornogra-

---

[65] Marshall Katzman, "Obscenity and Pornography," *Medical Aspects of Human
Sexuality,* July 1969, p. 82.

[66] Knight and Alpert, "Sex in Cinema," p. 172.

phy it was produced, bought, traded, and exchanged by men. Yet, there may have been some change in recent years, with some women becoming more interested in pornography, and it is therefore useful to look at how women respond to pornography. In a recent study of college student exposure to pornography it was found that males and females had had about equal access.[67] This means that encountering pornography is now much less sex segregated than was the case in the past, a reflection of the greater display of legitimate pornography.

The commission report found that experience with explicit sexual materials varied according to a number of characteristics in the potential viewer. As has been pointed out, the report found that men were more likely to be exposed to erotic materials than were women. "Younger adults are more likely to be exposed than are older adults. People who have more education are most likely to have experience with erotic materials. People who read general books, magazines, and newspapers more, and see general movies more, also see more erotic materials. People who are more socially and politically active are more exposed to erotic materials. People who attend religious services more often are less likely to be exposed to erotica."[68]

The study by Goldstein and Kant was concerned in part with users of pornography. They found that among their sample of adult males, users of pornography had the most liberal sexual attitudes. When they compared users of pornography to a control group of male nonusers of pornography they found that both groups had about the same rates of intercourse. But the users of pornography employed a wider variety of means to reach orgasm and reported greater overall sexual pleasure than did the control group.[69] This would suggest that many men who use pornography use it as a part of a broad repertoire of activities related to their general sexual interest. For such men pornography tends to be used, not as a substitute for other sexual activities, but rather as a means to a greater degree of sexual expression and activity.

The Kinsey studies provide some evidence on the difference between male and female responses to various sexual stimuli. In his sample Kinsey found that 88 percent of the females and 46 percent of the males said that they had never been erotically aroused by observing portrayals of nude figures.[70] In observing portrayals of sexual action 68 percent of the females and 23 percent of the males said that they were never erotically aroused.[71] And as to being stimulated by the reading of erotic stories, 86

---

[67] Rosen and Turner, "Pornography," p. 236.

[68] *Report of the Commission*, pp. 23–24.

[69] Goldstein and Kant, *Pornography*, p. 145.

[70] Alfred C. Kinsey, et al., *Sexual Behavior in the Human Female* (Philadelphia: Saunders, 1953), p. 652.

[71] Ibid., p. 662.

percent of the women and 53 percent of the men said that they were never aroused.[72]

Masters and Johnson found in their extensive research into physiological sexual responses that none of their subjects could fantasize to orgasm. But they did examine the excitement phase levels of sexual response by providing suggestive literature for their subjects. "A clinically obvious tumescent reaction of the clitoral glans could be demonstrated in only a few of the women who normally developed this reaction during somatogenic stimulation."[73] They further found that a minimum of a half hour of exposure to stimulative literature was necessary to produce any observable glans tumescence in a woman. In the same study the response to suggestive literature showed "fewer than one-third of the responding women produced a demonstratable increase in clitoral shaft diameter and no shaft-elongation reaction was observed."[74]

Women are not only much less stimulated by pornography than are men, but they are much less likely to be involved in writing it. The Kronhausens state that very rarely do women produce clearly erotic art and writing, despite the fact that pornographic books are often presented as having been written by women. Most such books were written by men using female pseudonyms. The Kronhausens point out that this pretense is one of the tricks used in the trade "in order to give the illusion that the supposedly female author was as sexually active and lascivious as the male author wished us—or himself—to believe."[75]

While the evidence clearly indicates that men are more responsive to and interested in all types of pornography this may be changing, at least to some extent. The women who do show interest are most apt to be among the younger and the higher educated. These are the women who are most apt to be sexually emancipated and to feel that they have the same rights to sexual expression as men. The commission's report found some link between age and sex in responses to erotic stimuli. Men and women in their early 20s reported a higher frequency of erotic dreams and sexual fantasy after exposure than older people. Thirty-five percent of men in their 20s and 30 percent of women in their 20s reported having erotic dreams frequently or occasionally, as against smaller proportions for older men and women.[76] Knight and Alpert wrote that not too many years ago it was understood that no "nice girl" could have anything but a negative reaction to the crudities of a stag film. But they found that viewing stag films has become more and more a heterosexual activity in

---

[72] Ibid., p. 671

[73] William H. Masters and Virginia E. Johnson, *Human Sexual Response* (Boston: Little, Brown, 1966, p. 55).

[74] Ibid., p. 55.

[75] Kronhausen, "Pornography," p. 856.

[76] *Report of the Commission*, p. 228.

recent years. They believe this to be true because of "the increasing availability of home movie equipment and because of the increasing acceptance of erotica in our more sexually permissive society."[77] Further evidence of this change was found by the writer in his study of sexual behavior among 2,372 married American women. Of that group 38 percent said that they had seen a pornographic (stag) movie. This was much more common among the younger women. Among the women who had seen such films the responses were: 45 percent, became sexually aroused or excited; 19 percent, no reaction; 16 percent, shock, disgust, or surprise; 8 percent, amusement or laughter; 5 percent, interest or curiosity; 4 percent, boredom; and 3 percent, other reactions.[78]

The Goldstein and Kant study examined the influence of erotica on their male respondents. They found that erotica affect adults significantly only by increasing their interest in sex and arousing their sexual impulses. The behavior that erotica stimulate is usually their ordinary sexual activity and not some new and novel behavior. "In most heterosexual males, an exciting erotic stimulus will provide a momentary boost to the sexual drive, increasing the likelihood of sexual activity if a regular partner is available."[79]

Another study examined the effects of pornography on a sample of middle-aged, middle-class Americans. In general it found that both men and women responded more to film depictions of heterosexual coitus than to heterosexual and homosexual practices generally considered deviant. Men reported generally higher levels of arousal to all themes than did women. The author suggests that the great arousal reported by men may have been due to the orientation of the movies he used—commercial "porno" films aimed at male audiences.[80]

In the above study the couples almost unanimously rated the sadomasochistic film "disgusting." The point is made because most anti-pornography groups claim that depictions of deviant sex acts arouse one's interest in such acts. However, the evidence doesn't support that view. "It appears instead that portrayals of deviancy are arousing only to those who have already developed a corresponding interest or orientation."[81]

Also of interest was the impact of the erotic movies on the sex lives of the middle-aged couples who viewed them. There was sexual arousal among a number of such viewers, as evidenced by greater marital sexual activity on film-viewing nights, but there was no increase in extramarital activity. The movies did not have much effect beyond a

---

[77] Knight and Alpert, "Sex in Cinema," p. 174.

[78] Robert R. Bell, unpublished data.

[79] Goldstein and Kant, *Pornography*, p. 151.

[80] Jay Mann, "The Effects of Erotica," in Leonard Gross, *Sexual Behavior: Current Issues* (Flushing, N.Y.: Spectrum, 1974), p. 52.

[81] Ibid., p. 53.

24-hour period. "Couples reported little change in sustained patterns of frequency of intercourse, choices of partners, or variety of sexual techniques. Unconventional activities, such as homosexuality, sadomasochism, anal intercourse, spouse swapping, and group sex, which few couples had reported before the study, did not increase."[82]

The products of pornography are produced primarily because they are economically profitable. The pornographer is in business to make money, and if he were not successful he would have to change to another occupation. Gagnon and Simon have suggested that there are two different images of the pornographer in the United States. One image is that he is "self-consciously evil, a representative of the antichrist, the Communist conspiracy, or at the very least, the Mafia. We also tend to see him in terms of the obscenity of ill-gotten wealth as he deals in commodities that are assumed to generate high prices."[83] The other image sees the pornographer more as a public nuisance. "Here we find not a sinister villain but a grubby businessman producing a minor commodity for which there is a limited market and a marginal profit and which requires that he live in a marginal world."[84]

It appears that part of the public indignation against pornography is based on the fact that a lot of money is being made from it. This was especially true with the movie *Deep Throat*. After it had been out a few months it was reported to have grossed 3.2 million dollars in theaters across the country. All of this for a movie that only cost $25,000 to make! Many people become very upset when they learn that pornography can be both pleasurable and profitable. This seems to make it a two-pronged attack on our puritanical values. It is also assumed that if there is money to be made then organized crime must be involved. As a result pornography becomes linked with prostitution, drugs, crime, and so on. However, there is no evidence that this assumed linkage exists.

Consequences of pornography

After one states that he is morally and ethically opposed to all pornography his next argument against it is that it "harms" people. One of the difficulties in determining whether pornography does harm people is that what is defined as pornography varies so greatly. For example, one study found that there was a "strong, statistically significant relationship between the personality rigidity of the observer as measured by a standard personality test, and the number of works of accepted great art

---

[82] Ibid., p. 57.
[83] Gagnon and Simon, "Pornography," p. 43.
[84] Ibid.

considered to be obscene."[85] So there are variations in who defines what as pornography and in what the consequences of exposure to pornography are believed to be.

One must make a distinction between how people respond to pornography for others and how they respond to pornography for themselves. That is, a person may feel that pornography is very bad for others and yet be erotically stimulated by it himself. But probably most people who are exposed to pornography for any length of time become satiated and bored. Many people who are quite sexually aroused by the first pornographic novel they read find that after reading many of them their level of arousal decreases sharply. Gebhard and his associates found that the possession of pornography did not differentiate sex offenders from non-sex offenders. "Even the combination of ownership plus strong sexual arousal from the material does not segregate the sex offender from other men of a comparable social level. We have often found that men with large collections of long standing lose much of their sexual response to the materials, and while their interest in collecting may continue unabated, their motivation is no longer primarily sexual."[86]

The most commonly expressed concern as regards pornography is that it corrupts and harms young people. Many people believe that pornography will erotically arouse adolescent boys and contribute to their masturbation. And this belief is undoubtedly correct because the major users of at least pictorial pornography are adolescent males. For many of those boys such materials are used as an aid in masturbation. Yet, there is no evidence that the availability of pornography increases the rates of masturbation among adolescents. (And there is no evidence that increased rates would cause problems of any kind.) Adolescence is the period of life when male rates of masturbation are highest, particularly among middle-class boys. Given this high sexual interest, when pornography is not available the boys may create their own stimulation from mail-order catalogues, magazine ads, and so on.[87] It should also be kept in mind that the use of erotic literature as an aid to fantasies in masturbation is not limited to adolescents but is often found among adult males. The point is that adolescents will masturbate with or without pornography and that there is no evidence that pornography is harmful to them.

In his extensive study of sex offenses, Gebhard examined the possible influences of pornography on all types of sex offenses. He came to the conclusion that all that can be said about a strong response to pornography

---

[85] I. R. Stuart and W. G. Eliasberg, "Personality Structures which Reject the Human Form in Art: An Exploratory Study of Cross-Cultural Perceptions of the Nude—Cuban *vs.* The United States," *Journal of Social Psychology*, 57 (1962), p. 384.

[86] Gebhard, *Sex Offenders*, p. 678.

[87] Gagnon and Simon, "Pornography," p. 46.

is that it is associated with imaginativeness, ability to project, and sensitivity, "all of which generally increase as education increases, and with
youthfulness, and that these qualities account for the differences we have
found between sex offenders, in general, and non-sex offenders. Since the
majority of sex offenders are not well educated nor particularly youthful,
their responsiveness to pornography is correspondingly less and cannot be
a consequential fact in sex offenses."[88]

The overwhelming reaction of clinicians and researchers who have
studied pornography is that it has little or no relation to sex offenses. The
Kronhausens observe that "it is extremely doubtful whether even continued exposure to specific pornographic stimuli will result in behavior
changes, unless they are accompanied by actual contacts with individuals
who are so predisposed."[89] A survey of psychiatrists and psychologists in
New Jersey found that 94 percent of the respondents had not had normal
patients who were incited to antisocial acts by exposure to sexually
stimulating materials. "Further, two-thirds believed that erotic materials
might provoke a substitute outlet for some individuals who might
otherwise engage in antisocial acts."[90] Of a sample of 3,400 clinicians in
mental health professions 84 percent said that they believed that persons
exposed to pornography were no more likely to engage in antisocial sexual
acts than persons not exposed. Furthermore, 86 percent of the clinicians
said that they believed that people who vigorously sought to suppress
pornography were motivated by unresolved sexual problems of their
own.[91]

The research by Goldstein and Kant takes up the possible consequences
of pornography on the user. They found that child molesters had seen less
pornography than had those men they defined as their "normal" group.[92]
They also found that the data suggested that the rapists they studied came
from repressive backgrounds with regard to sexuality. The rapists said
that "fear of sex" was the reason that pornography did not stimulate them
to engage in or even desire sexual activity. In general Goldstein and Kant
found that erotica do not appear to be important stimuli for antisocial
sexual behavior in the potential sex offender. "In fact, there is some
evidence that for rapists, exposure to erotica portraying 'normal' heterosexual relations can serve to ward off antisocial sexual impulses."[93]

However, as is the case for so many other areas of deviance, there may
be a wide range in who gets defined as an expert and in how he defines
pornography. For example, when the question was asked, "Do you think

---

[88] Gebhard, *Sex Offenders*, p. 673.

[89] Kronhausen, "Pornography," p. 858.

[90] Katzman, "Obscenity," p. 83.

[91] *Detroit Free Press*, August 23, 1969.

[92] Goldstein and Kant, *Pornography*, p. 61.

[93] Ibid., p. 152.

that reading obscene books plays a significant role in causing juvenile delinquency?" only 12 percent of a sample of professional workers in the delinquent area answered "yes" in contrast with 58 percent of a sample of police chiefs.[94] The general finding from the commission's report that upset so many read as follows: "In sum, empirical research designed to clarify the question has found no evidence to date that exposure to explicit sexual materials plays a significant role in the causation of delinquent or criminal behavior among youth or adults. The commission cannot conclude that exposure to erotic materials is a factor in the causation of sex crime or sex delinquency."[95]

A recent study, drawing on data from the President's Commission on Pornography, discusses the kinds of persons most upset by pornography. It found that the typical opponent of pornography was "female, over 40, with a grade school education, a frequent church-goer of conservative attitudes, restrictive of civil liberties, and claiming little or no exposure to erotic materials." Those persons who believe that pornography has harmful effects seem to hold this belief as a matter of faith and not with reference to its effects on themselves or on anyone they know.[96]

There is a recent study of groups of people in two towns who became actively involved in antipornography campaigns. One part of that study was interested in whom these people saw as opposing their efforts to end pornography. When the antipornography crusaders were asked who opposed their efforts a majority (58 percent) cited, not smut peddlers or users, but "radicals," "young people," "college students," "hippies," and "university professors." "Producers and users of pornography were assessed variously to be atheists, deviates or criminals, and immature, irresponsible, mentally ill, perverted, lower-class, immoral, or amoral individuals."[97] Among the antipornography crusaders there was a common feeling that most people were weak and that they as stronger people had to help them even if the help was not requested.

The study pointed out that people who are very upset about pornography are not necessarily personally familiar with it. Twenty-six percent of those actively opposed to pornographic films said that they had never seen one, and 67 percent of those opposed to pornographic books said that they had never read one.[98]

---

[94] *Report of the Commission*, p. 194.

[95] Ibid., p. 32.

[96] C. Gary Merritt, Joel E. Gerstl, and Leonard A. LoScuiuto, "Age and Perceived Effects of Erotica—Pornography: A National Sample," Institute for Survey Research, Temple University, 1973, pp. 1–2.

[97] Louis A. Zurcher, R. George Kirkpatrick, Robert G. Cushing, and Charles K. Bowman, "The Anti-Pornography Campaign: A Symbolic Crusade," *Social Problems*, Fall 1971, p. 226.

[98] Ibid., p. 224.

The researchers found that what was ultimately achieved by the antipornography campaigns was more symbolic than utilitarian. That is, to show a belief in a particular set of values, "to have a large number of others join in the demonstration, and to have the demonstration recognized by significant others seemed often to be even more important to the crusaders than implementing restrictions which more effectively could eliminate the problem of pornography as they defined it."[99]

One major reason for concern about the efforts being made to control the sale of pornography is the fear of censorship. Many people who have no personal interest in pornography are afraid that restrictions on the sale of that kind of material could lead to restrictions in other areas. In the above study of clinicians two thirds of them felt that censorship was socially harmful "because it contributed to a climate of oppression and inhibition within which creative individuals cannot express themselves adequately."

It appears that the sale of legal pornography in the United States is fairly well controlled. The young person is not exposed to pornographic materials unless he seeks out the stores that sell them, and often he will not be sold the materials. Even if he is not sold pornography he can get it if he wants in the same way that he gets cigarettes or alcohol. When written pornography was prohibited it was still available, and it may be that with written pornography now legal, and for the most part in a few restricted stores, its sale will be controlled. What may happen is what appears to be occurring in Denmark—access to pornography often means that the user quickly reaches his satiation level. Continued experiences with alcohol or drugs may become increasingly exciting, but such is not the case with continued use of pornography.

It would appear from the discussion in this chapter that the use of pornography constitutes a special type of deviance. That is, people believe the use of pornography to be wrong although it has no significant negative consequences either personally or socially. This is a deviance of values rather than of behavior. It may be that in a changing society where so many beliefs are undergoing questioning and rejection, many people resist the idea that pornography may not be harmful. It is almost as if they were saying, "If one can't believe that pornography is undesirable and harmful, what is there left that one can believe is evil?" People not only need things to believe in but also things to believe against.

BIBLIOGRAPHY

Clor, Harry M., *Obscenity and Public Morality.* Chicago: University of Chicago Press, 1969.

Gagnon, John H., and William Simon, "Pornography—Raging Menace or Paper Tiger?" *Trans-Action*, July 1967, pp. 41–48.

---

[99] Ibid., p. 236.

Goldstein, Michael J., and Harold S. Kant, *Pornography and Sexual Deviance*. Berkeley: University of California Press, 1973.

Gordon, Michael, and Robert R. Bell, "Medium and Hard Core Pornography: A Comparative Analysis," *Journal of Sex Research*, November 1969, pp. 260-68.

Katzman, Marshall, "Obscenity and Pornography," *Medical Aspects of Human Sexuality*, July 1969, pp. 77, 81-83.

Knight, Arthur and Hollis Alpert, "The History of Sex in Cinema: The Stag Film," *Playboy*, November 1967.

Kronhausen, Eberhard and Phyllis, "The Psychology of Pornography," in Albert Ellis and Albert Abarbanel, *The Encyclopedia of Sexual Behavior*. New York: Hawthorn Books, 1961, pp. 848-59.

Loth, David, *The Erotic in Literature*. New York: Messner, 1961.

McKinstry, William C., "The Pulp Voyeur: A Peek at Pornography in Public Places," in Jerry Jacobs, *Deviance: Field Studies and Self-Disclosures*. Palo Alto, Calif.: National Press Books, 1974, pp. 30-40.

Mann, Jay, "The Effects of Erotica," in Leonard Gross, *Sexual Behavior: Current Issues*. Flushing, N.Y.: Spectrum, 1974, pp. 45-58.

Polsky, Ned, "Pornography," in Edward Sagarin and Donel E. MacNamara, *Problems of Sex Behavior*. New York: Crowell, 1968, pp. 268-84.

The Report of the Commission on Obscenity and Pornography. New York: Bantam Books, 1970.

Rosen, Lawrence, and Stanley H. Turner, "Exposure to Pornography: An Exploratory Study," *Journal of Sex Research*, November 1969, pp. 235-46.

Zurcher, Louis A., R. George Kirkpatrick, Robert G. Cushing, and Charles Bowman, "The Anti-Pornography Campaign: A Symbolic Crusade," *Social Problems*, Fall 1971, pp. 217-38.

chapter six

Alcohol

The origins of alcohol go back into the unknown past of prehistory. It has been established that breweries flourished in Egypt almost 6,000 years ago, and there is even some evidence that prehistoric Stone Age humans made alcoholic beverages long before that. The use of alcohol has appeared in varying degrees in most societies throughout recorded history and "has traditionally played an important symbolic as well as pharmacological role in many social, religious and medical practices and customs."[1] For hundreds of years there has been controversy over the value and use of alcoholic beverages. Probably in most societies the issue has not been whether or not alcohol should be used, but rather who should use it and where, when, and under what conditions it should be used. So in various cultures alcohol has been used as a means of social facilitation, to celebrate or commiserate, as a part of religious ritual, to try to psychologically "escape," and for many other purposes.

Alcohol has been used in the United States from the very beginning. In colonial America there was general acceptance of some alcoholic beverages, such as rum, beer, wine, and cider. Contrary to what is generally believed the Puritans were not against the use of alcohol—but they did punish drunkenness. Yet, as Blum points out, there were condemnations of alcohol during the early colonial period, when Increase and Cotton Mather both preached against the "demon rum."[2] But in general during that period drinking was common to most adult men and was not seen as either a personal or a social problem.

Historically in the United States it was not until the westward movement that a widespread concern with heavy drinking began to

---

[1] *Non-Medical Uses of Drugs: Interim Report of the Canadian Government's Commission of Inquiry* (Middlesex, Eng.: Penguin Books, 1971), p. 60.

[2] Richard H. Blum, *Society and Drugs* (San Francisco: Jossey-Bass, 1969), pp. 36–37.

develop and that it came to be defined as a social problem. The new social problem of heavy drinking was the result of a combination of factors. First, there was the general social disorganization and lawlessness that were a part of the western frontier. Second, there was the developing industrialization, urbanization, and heavy migration that were expanding and transforming the cities. Third, there was an increasing availability of rum in the East. Finally, there was an increase in the frontiersmen who wanted a strong, cheap, and potable liquor.[3]

The campaign that developed against drinking was based on moral disapproval and sought total prohibition of alcohol. In the early 1800s a new definition of the drinker emerged which pictured him as an object of social shame. Some observers argue that after the 1850s American drinking became very extreme, most people being either heavy drinkers or totally abstinent. By the 1870s rural and small-town America had developed middle-class morals that included the dry attitude of abstinence and sobriety. Gusfield suggests that "moral persuasion, rather than legislation, has been one persistent theme in the designation of the drinker as deviant and the alcoholic as even further debased."[4] Well into the 20th century the alcoholic was viewed as a sinner. This definition affected how the family of the alcoholic was viewed. Fifty years ago the members of an alcoholic's family were usually seen as innocent victims of the willful self-indulgence of an irresponsible, weak, and sinful person. The drunkard was seen as someone for the family to hide, the police to control, and the clergy to reform. The family was to be pitied and shown charity.[5]

The antidrinking view reached its peak of power and influence in January 1920, when national prohibition was enacted. It may have been that drinking was so much a part of society that it could not be legislated out. During prohibition even many nondrinkers saw drinking or nondrinking as a matter of individual choice. As a result ignoring and circumventing prohibition became increasingly acceptable to large numbers of Americans. Many powerful proalcohol forces with a vested interest in the sale of alcohol were also anxious to have prohibition repealed. In general since the repeal of prohibition there has developed on the broadest social level in the United States a basic indifference to alcohol. People do become concerned about problems resulting from drinking—alcoholism, drunken driving, adolescent drinking, and so forth. But there does not appear to be any general strong opposition to the

---

[3] Ibid., p. 38.

[4] Joseph R. Gusfield, "On Legislating Morals: The Symbolic Process of Designating Deviance," *California Law Review*, January 1968, p. 63.

[5] Joan K. Jackson, "The Adjustment of the Family to the Crisis of Alcoholism," in Earl Rubington and Martin S. Weinberg, *Deviance: The Interactionist Perspective* (New York: Macmillian, 1968), p. 50.

use of alcohol because it is immoral or bad, especially when it is used in moderation.

Before taking up the views of other societies we will discuss the meaning of alcohol and its effects on the user. Many people believe that alcohol is a stimulant. But in fact alcohol is a protoplasmic poison with a depressant effect on the nervous system. If alcohol is taken in large enough quantities it can render a person unconscious, and in the past alcohol was sometimes used as an anesthetic. So as alcohol is absorbed into the system it functions as a continuous depressant of the central nervous system. What appear to be stimulation effects are the result of the depression of inhibitory control mechanisms. "Alcohol is thought to exert first its depressing action on the more primitive parts of the brain responsible for integrating the activity of other parts of the central nervous system, thereby releasing the higher centers from control."[6] In general the drunker a person gets the less control over himself he has physically, psychologically, and socially.

The views of various societies toward alcohol cover a wide range. It has been argued that there may be a universal tendency for valuations of alcoholic beverages to become polarized in any given society. "At one extreme liquor, wine, and beer are glorified in song, poetry, and drama as keys to ecstasy and sublimity; at the other extreme, they are viewed as perverters of human morality and the chief causes of the ills of society as well as of the sorrows of individuals."[7] It has also been suggested that there are three general ways in which a society can influence its rates of alcoholism. One is the extent to which a society creates tensions in its members that would lead them to alcohol as a possible source of reducing their tensions. Second are the kinds of attitudes that a society develops in its members toward drinking. Third is the degree to which a society provides means of tension reduction other than alcohol.[8]

The ways in which different cultures use alcohol may be closely related to various social institutions. Alcohol may be used at a variety of social functions, including religious functions. When alcohol is used in religious setting is centers on ceremonial functions. For example, among Roman Catholics wine is used in Holy Communion. Or alcohol may be used at a Bar Mitzvah or a wedding. Often alcohol is used hedonistically—to show solidarity between friends and relatives. And in some societies alcohol is used in a utilitarian way—to gain some advantage over another person or for medicinal purposes.[9]

---

[6] Helen H. Nowlis, *Drugs on the College Campus* (New York: Anchor Books, 1969), pp. 85–86.

[7] Edwin M. Lemert, *Human Deviance: Social Problems and Social Control* (Englewood Cliffs, N.J.: Prentice-Hall, 1967), p. 73.

[8] Robert F. Bales, "Cultural Differences in Rates of Alcoholism," in William A. Rushing, *Deviant Behavior and Social Process* (Chicago: Rand McNally 1969), p. 283.

[9] David J. Pittman, *Alcoholism* (New York: Harper and Row, 1967), p. 14.

At the present time in the United States alcohol is recognized as an official drug although the various alcoholic beverages as such are no longer listed for medical use. "Alcohol has been cited over the past few thousand years as a cure for nearly every ailment or disease. Most of the medical benefits were probably more imagined than real."[10]

One may describe social patterns of drinking for societies, but it should be recognized that the more complex societies rarely ever follow any single, clear-cut pattern. In fact many societies are unclear and ambivalent about their drinking patterns. It has been suggested that the American culture may be the prototype of ambivalent cultures. The reason is that the cultural attitudes toward drinking are not uniform, and, moreover, this "social ambivalence" is reinforced by the conflict between the drinking and abstinent values that coexist in many communities. On the one hand there are those who support alcohol for religious reasons and for being a traditional expression of hospitality and sociability. And there is the powerful and influential liquor industry, which supports alcohol for economic reasons. On the other hand, "the abstinent groups are characteristically composed of ascetic Protestant groups who believe the use of alcohol is sinful and who therefore see little difference between the occasional social drinker and the chronic inebriate, since the former is the beginning stage for the latter."[11]

Another group may be emerging in opposition to alcohol among the more sophisticated young, who are usually college students. There has developed in recent years an increasing awareness and concern about things harmful to life. This is true with regard both to ecological dangers and to mental and physical dangers, and many young people who have become aware of the dangers of alcohol to the body reject it for that reason. Many see drinking as the irrational crutch of the older generation who put them down for using marijuana, which they feel is less harmful than alcohol. Generally the more that people use marijuana the less they use alcohol. So marijuana may be replacing alcohol for many in the younger generation.

The amount of drinking and the rates of alcoholism in various countries cannot be determined. However, it does appear that the proportion of alcoholics varies from country to country "but does not seem to exceed in any country 5 percent or 6 percent of all users of alcoholic beverages."[12] There seems to be little question that in those cultures with strong social and religious pressures for proscribing the sale and distribution of alcohol the arrests for drunkenness are quite high. By contrast the rates of arrests for drunkenness are much lower in countries that have permissive laws with regard to alcohol. "It seems clear that

---

[10] *Non-Medical Uses of Drugs*, p. 64.

[11] Pittman, *Alcoholism*, p. 8.

[12] E. M. Jellinek, "Phases of Alcohol Addiction," in Simon Dinitz et al., *Deviance* (New York: Oxford University Press, 1969), p. 254.

arrests for drunkenness as a reflection of deviant behavior are higher where a background of proscription is greater."[13]

As mentioned earlier, drinking patterns vary among the various religious groups. Mizruchi argues that among ascetic Protestant and Mormon groups the norms against drinking are proscriptive. Therefore, any deviation from the abstinence pattern, even in what is usually defined as socially approved drinking in the broader society, is seen as an almost complete absence of directives. "So if in the ascetic religious groups drinking behavior is adopted variation must be the rule because for those groups there are no norms for drinking but only against. As a result extremes often occur in drinking because the behavior itself represents rejection of social rules."[14] The contrast to this pattern is seen among Jews, whose drinking is governed by elaborate norms. There are directives as to what, when, where, with whom, how much, and why a person is expected to consume alcoholic beverages. "The norm is predominantly *prescriptive* in nature, and deviation from the drinking norms is associated with gradual and predictable patterns of deviant behavior."[15]

Another way of looking at the norms and sanctions governing drinking is to examine the extent to which those norms and sanctions stress abstinence or prescriptions. That is, one does not drink *or* one does drink but only under certain limits and conditions. Prescriptions allow drinking but set up limits that will make it acceptable. There are other variations in the norms that influence responses to drinking. For example, there are ambivalent learning environments with vague definitions that do not effectively prohibit drinking or adequately prescribe guidelines for proper drinking. There are also permissive groups that positively sanction drinking, including frequent and heavy drinking. So the range of controls over drinking varies among different groups and are often in conflict with one another.

LEGAL ASPECTS OF ALCOHOL USE

Probably in all societies some controls over drinking have developed, and in most societies the controls are at least in part built into the legal systems. In many societies, including our own, there are elaborate legal controls over who may sell alcoholic beverages, where they may sell, to whom, and under what circumstances. But our main interest is in the controls over people who are using alcohol. And the legal view of the

---

[13] Ephraim H. Mizruchi and Robert Perrucci, "Prescription, Proscription, and Permissiveness: Aspects of Norms and Deviant Drinking Behavior," in Mark Lefton et al., *Approaches to Deviance* (New York: Appleton-Century-Crofts, 1968), p. 163.

[14] Ibid., p. 157.

[15] Ibid., p. 158.

drinker is closely related to the social view of his use of alcohol and the effects it is believed to have on him. As suggested, whether or not drinking alcoholic beverages is deviant behavior is culturally defined. In the United States the use of alcohol is generally defined as deviant behavior when the user is defined as an alcoholic or as an excessive and problem drinker, or when he commits offenses related to the influence of alcohol. This last would include such things as driving an automobile while under the influence of alcohol or being drunk and disorderly.

Large numbers of persons are arrested for public drunkenness. There are about 2 million arrests each year on this charge, and this accounts for about one out of every three arrests made in the United States. These arrests place a very heavy burden on the criminal justice system. The laws provide maximum jail sentences ranging from 5 days to 6 months; the most common maximum sentence is 30 days. "There is strong evidence, however, that a large number of those who are arrested have a lengthy history of prior drunkenness arrests, and that a disproportionate number involve poor persons who live in slums."[16]

Drunkenness arrest practices vary greatly from one place to another. Some police departments strongly enforce the laws against drunkenness, while others are far more permissive. "In fact, the number of arrests in a city may be related less to the amount of public drunkenness than to police policy."[17] After a drunk is arrested he is usually placed in a barren cell called a "tank" where he is held for at least a few hours. The tanks in various cities may hold anywhere from 1 to 200 people. In the tank one major problem is that medical care is rarely provided and that it is difficult to detect or to diagnose serious illness which resembles intoxication.[18] Most drunkenness offenders are picked up at night and therefore stay in the tank until the next morning before they are brought before the judge. He usually sees them in groups of 15 or 20, and rarely are the normal procedural or due process safeguards applied to these cases.

One area of great social concern has been drinking and driving. A recent study points out some of the social variables that are related to driving and the use of alcohol. This study found that persons with higher education and in more prestigious occupations were more likely to drive and drink.[19] There was also evidence to suggest that certain social and cultural factors affect behavior after drinking. The middle-class person learns to behave "properly" even after consuming a good deal of alcohol. This can extend to his driving, where he may give the appearance of

---

[16] *The Task Force Report*, "Drunkenness Offenses," in Dinitz et al., *Deviance*, p. 244.

[17] Ibid., p. 245.

[18] Ibid.

[19] Harvey Marshall and Ross Purdy, "Hidden Deviance and the Labelling Approach: The Case of Drinking and Driving," *Social Problems*, Spring 1972, p. 542.

being well in control and not attract attention from the police. By contrast lower-class persons may not have such proscriptions, and as a result their driving may be more expressive. "Moreover, both groups may respond differently when stopped by police officers; specifically, middle class persons may not only appear to be in greater control, their demeanor may be more acceptable to the officer."[20]

It seems clear that the criminal justice system is ineffective in deterring drunkenness or in meeting the problems of the chronic alcoholic offender. What the legal system does in effect is remove the drunk from where he can be publicly seen, "detoxify him, and provide him with food, shelter, emergency medical service, and a brief period of forced sobriety."[21] Built into the arrest system is inherent discrimination against the homeless and the poor. "Due process safeguards are often considered unnecessary or futile. The defendant may not be warned of his rights or permitted to make a telephone call. And although coordination, breath, or blood tests to determine intoxication are common practices in driving while intoxicated cases, they are virtually nonexistent in common drunk cases."[22]

THE CAUSES

We next look at some beliefs about the causes of heavy drinking and alcoholism. It should be stressed that the vast majority of those who use alcoholic beverages stay within the limits of the culturally accepted drinking patterns and drink predominantly as an expression of their socialization. But some drinkers suffer from alcoholism, and this may be defined as a complex chronic illness although it is not very well understood. According to the American Medical Association alcoholism is a form of drug dependence characterized by preoccupation with alcohol and loss of control over its consumption, usually leading to intoxication once drinking has started. The alcoholic has a high tendency to relapse and usually suffers physically, emotionally, occupationally, and socially because of his addiction. And too, the very size of the problem—the large number who are alcoholics—makes the question of causes and cures extremely difficult to determine.

Whatever the causes of alcoholism, becoming an alcoholic takes time. This is true because repeated ingestion of alcohol results in tolerance so that a higher level of alcohol is needed in the bloodstream to produce a given level of intoxication. Thus, both physical and psychological dependence may result from prolonged use. It has been found that psychological dependence occurs in about 10 percent of all users and that the development of physical dependence requires the consumption of

---

[20] Ibid., p. 543.
[21] *Task Force Report*, p. 246.
[22] Ibid., p. 247.

large amounts of alcohol over a period of about 3 to 15 years or more. "In the dependent individual, even a few hours of abstinence precipitates the beginning of the alcohol withdrawal syndrome, a syndrome similar to that following withdrawal of the barbiturates or other depressant drugs."[23]

As suggested, many social factors are related to the development of drinking patterns. One study states that among persons who drink those who have received few, if any, restrictive guidelines defining appropriate drinking behavior are more likely to become heavy drinkers than those who are given specific directives about their drinking. "In other words, heavy drinking is associated with a *relative* lack of norms regarding the consumption of alcoholic beverages in an environment which does not prohibit drinking."[24]

What makes the problem of drinking difficult to define in the United States is that it is less a question of whether one should drink than of *how much* one should drink. Of course, the amount of drinking varies greatly among individuals and groups, and what may be defined as appropriate for some may be seen as inappropriate for others. So at certain times and in certain situations drinking meets with at least some degree of social approval. "The positive orientation to drinking is based on its usefulness in decreasing feelings of tension and anxiety and in fostering pleasant and sociable moods in most individuals."[25] This is in contrast to the attitude taken toward the person defined as a heavy drinker or an alcoholic, who is often seen as self-destructive and a social detriment.

Yet, society is also mixed in its views concerning drinking that is generally seen as acceptable; drinking that may be seen as reducing tension and contributing to sociability is also seen as lowering sensitivity, efficiency, and caution. It has been argued that in a complex society these influences can be socially dangerous because a complex society puts strong emphasis on self-control and on inhibitions and repressions of aggression and irresponsibility. Alcohol releases those inhibitions and can wreck regularity of behavior.[26] "The need for imagination and perception, for control over responses, for timing and balance, is greatly increased by the complex culture; just to get things done is a more delicate task, and the penalty for not getting things done has far greater social implications than in the simpler society."[27]

We have indicated the relatively high rate of drinking in the United States, and now we will look more specifically at some rates of drinking

---

[23] Nowlis, *Drugs on Campus*, p. 87.

[24] Donald E. Larsen and Baha Abu-Laban, "Norm Qualities and Deviant Drinking Behavior," *Social Problems*, Spring 1968, p. 449.

[25] Nowlis, *Drugs on Campus*, p. 87.

[26] Seldon D. Bacon, "Alcohol and Complex Society," in Dinitz et al., *Deviance*, p. 225.

[27] Ibid.

and alcoholism. In 1965 about 60 percent of women and 77 percent of men would on occasion take a drink. This was a significant increase over the figures for 1940, which were 38 percent and 64 percent, respectively.[28] Millions of persons may be variously classified as light drinkers, moderate drinkers, heavy drinkers, problem drinkers, and alcoholics. The most recent estimate is that there may be as many as 9 million adult American alcoholics and that millions more are on the verge of having serious drinking problems. The World Health Organization defines alcoholism as "a chronic behavior disorder manifested by repeated drinking of alcoholic beverages in excess of dietary and social uses of the community and to the extent that interferes with the drinker's health or his social and economic functions."[29] There is evidence of a turnover in the population having major alcohol-related problems. "Thus, problem drinkers do not represent a permanently fixed population when large samples are considered."[30]

The most important cost of alcohol is death. It has been estimated that alcohol-related problems are the cause of more than 85,000 deaths in the United States each year. This would include about half (30,000) of the annual highway fatalities. There are many other costs. One half of the 5 million yearly arrests in the United States are related to misuses of alcohol; this includes 1.5 million offenses for public drunkenness. "And one half of all homicides and one fourth of all suicides are alcohol related, accounting for a total of 11,700 deaths annually."[31] The total annual economic loss to the country from alcohol-related problems is an estimated $15 billion. "Of this, $10 billion is attributed to lost work time in business, industry, civilian government, and the military; $2 billion is spent for health and welfare services provided to alcoholic persons and their families. Property damages, medical expenses, and other overhead costs account for $3 billion or more."[32]

As a medical problem alcoholism is outranked only by mental illness, heart diseases, and cancer. Furthermore, it is estimated that 20 percent of the people in state mental hospitals are there because of alcoholic brain disease and that 50 percent of the people in prisons have committed their crimes in association with alcoholic consumption. Alcohol also generates enormous marital breakdown and welfare costs. In total, alcoholism is very costly to American society.

---

[28] Richard S. Shore, "The Alcoholic," in Patricia Keith-Spiegel and Don Spiegel, *Outsiders USA* (San Francisco: Rinehart Press, 1973), p. 229.

[29] Ibid., p. 231.

[30] Ibid., p. 229.

[31] *Marihuana: A Signal of Misunderstanding, The Official Report of the National Commission on Marihuana and Drug Abuse* (New York: New American Library, 1972), p. 17.

[32] Shore, "Alcoholic," p. 229.

The effects of the alcoholic on his family have always been of great concern. Joan Jackson has done extensive research on the relationships between the alcoholic and his family. The impact of the alcoholic on his family is usually a gradual one, and how the various members of the family respond to the alcoholic is influenced by their respective personality structures and family roles. The actions directed toward the alcoholic are influenced by the past effectiveness of those actions. The family members' views of the alcoholic are affected by the broader cultural definitions of alcoholism as evidence of weakness, inadequacy, or sinfulness; "by the cultural prescriptions for the roles of family members; and by the cultural values of family solidarity, sanctity and self-sufficiency. Alcoholism in the family poses a situation defined by the culture as shameful but for the handling of which there are no prescriptions which are effective or which permit direct action not in conflict with other cultural prescriptions."[33] This is in contrast to such family crises as illness or death where there are cultural definitions that family members may draw on.

In most states where drunkenness may be used as a ground for divorce no distinction is made between aggrieved husbands and aggrieved wives. However, in some states such distinctions are made. For example, in Kentucky a wife may be granted a divorce from her husband on the ground of drunkenness only if his condition has been "accompanied by a wasting of the husband's estate and without any suitable provision for the maintenance of the wife or children. A husband, however, can be granted a divorce from his wife on the ground of her mere drunkenness alone, without the necessity of showing any additional factors."[34]

Jackson suggests that a family goes through a number of different stages in its response to the alcoholic father. In the first stage excessive drinking begins, and although at this stage the drinking is sporadic it does place a strain on the husband-wife relationship. In the second stage the family's social isolation begins as incidents of excessive drinking multiply. Increasingly behavior and thought become drink-centered, and the marital relationship breaks down as tension between the husband and wife increases. During the third stage the family give up their attempts to control the drinking and start to develop their behavior to relieve tension rather than to achieve long-range ends. At this stage there is no longer any attempt to support the alcoholic in his roles as husband and father. At the fourth stage the wife takes over control of the family and the husband comes to be defined as a recalcitrant child. The family becomes more stable and is organized in a way that minimizes the disruptive behavior of the husband. The wife begins to rebuild her self-confidence. During the

---

[33] Jackson, "Adjustment to Alcoholism," pp. 52–53.

[34] Leo Kanowitz, *Women and the Law* (Albuquerque: University of New Mexico Press, 1969), p. 97.

fifth stage the wife separates from her husband if she is able to resolve the problems and conflicts surrounding that action. At stage six the wife and children reorganize the family without the husband-father. Finally there may be a seventh stage if the husband achieves sobriety and the family attempts to reorganize itself to include a sober husband-father. There are often problems in reinstating him to his former roles within the family.[35]

Data on the impact of an alcoholic on the family have been limited to the husband-father. No empirical studies have been made of the alcoholic wife's effect on her family. There is some indication that the alcoholic wife is able to hide her drinking from her husband longer than can a male alcoholic hide his drinking from his wife. One reason may be that the alcoholic woman is more concerned about hiding her drinking. Also, the man is often in a variety of social situations because of his occupation, and it is therefore more difficult for him to hide his alcoholism. The alcoholic housewife follows a workday that permits more frequent drinking, "and most of her tasks can be accomplished despite a state of mild intoxication."[36]

The sexual area of marriage is affected by the husband's heavy drinking. Often the wife begins to avoid sexual contact with her husband when he is drinking. She may define sex under those circumstances as sex for its own sake rather than as an indication of his affection toward her. "The lack of sexual responsiveness reflects her emotional withdrawal from him in other areas of family life. Her husband, on his part, feels frustrated and rejected; he accuses her of frigidity and this adds to her concern about her adequacy as a woman."[37] The relationship between alcohol usage and sexual impotence in the male is a strong one. Masters and Johnson found that impotence that developed in the male in his late 40s and early 50s was more closely associated with excessive alcohol consumption than with any other single factor. The sexual tensions and desires of the truly alcoholic male simply disappear as he deteriorates physically and mentally.[38]

Over the years there have been many beliefs concerning the effects of alcohol on sexual behavior. Alcohol does not have a specific aphrodisiac effect. However, it may be reduce inhibitions and thus lead to an increase in sexual activity as well as in other usually restricted behavior. But an increase in sexual desire can often be negated for the male by an increased probability of impotence. Hunt asked his national sample about the effects of alcohol on their sex lives. Of his respondents 36 percent of the women and 30 percent of the men said that it made intercourse more

    [35] Jackson, "Adjustment to Alcoholism," pp. 53–54.
    [36] Ibid., p. 57.
    [37] Ibid., pp. 57–58.
    [38] William H. Masters and Virginia E. Johnson, *Human Sexual Response* (Boston: Little, Brown 1966), p. 268.

pleasurable; 12 percent of the women and 27 percent of the men said that it made intercourse less pleasurable.[39]

As would be expected, children are more affected by living with an alcoholic than are other family members. The personalities of the children are developed in an unstable social setting that is characterized by conflict and social disapproval. The children must model their behavior on roles that are being filled in a distorted fashion. "The alcoholic shows little adequate adult behavior. The nonalcoholic parent attempts to play the roles of both father and mother, often failing to do either well."[40] It is somewhat ironic that there is a common tendency among some children to feel more affection for the alcoholic parent than for the nonalcoholic parent. This is probably because the "alcoholic parent is rewarding when sober, while the nonalcoholic parent tends to be irritable and rejecting under the constant situation pressure."[41]

As suggested, the family with an alcoholic member suffers some shame, knowing that society generally defines alcoholics as weak and shameful persons. Even though the family may have no responsibility for the alcoholism it still must suffer some stigma because of the alcoholic member. The family is stigmatized in basically the same way that it gains prestige in the community because of some personal success of the father. But alcoholism is deviance, and in its efforts to handle the problem the family labors under the imputation of blame. It often feels "guilty, ashamed, inadequate, and, above all, isolated from social support."[42] Often friends contribute to the feeling of shame. Frequently when the wife consults friends about her alcoholic husband the friends discount her concern and tell her the situation is really not so bad. This may contribute to her tendency to deny that a problem exists and can also add to her guilt by making her remorseful over her "disloyal" thoughts about her husband.[43]

The problems for the family do not end even when the husband-father stops drinking. It is often the case that he has stopped before and then gone back to alcohol. The wife often finds it very difficult to believe that her husband is sober permanently, and she is therefore unwilling to relinquish her control over family affairs even though she knows that that is necessary for her husband's continued sobriety. The wife vividly remembers the time when his failures to handle responsibilities created severe problems for herself and her children.[44] There is a difficult

---

[39] Morton Hunt, "Sexual Behavior in the 1970's" *Playboy*, October 1973, p. 200.

[40] Joan K. Jackson, "Alcoholism and the Family," in Jeffery K. Hadden and Marie L. Borgatta, *Marriage and the Family* (Itasca, Ill.: F. E. Peacock, 1969), p. 277.

[41] Ibid., p. 577.

[42] Ibid., p. 582.

[43] Ibid.

[44] Ibid., p. 584.

dilemma for the wife. To turn over more and more responsibilities to him is to increase the risk of problems for herself if he doesn't stay sober. But not to turn some responsibilities over to him may contribute to his sense of failure and inadequacy and push him back toward the use of alcohol.

SOCIAL VARIABLES RELATED TO DRINKING

A number of social factors other than the family are related to drinking patterns. One area of high concern in most societies is drinking among young people. Generally the concern is not so much with whether they drink but rather with whether they drink to a degree defined as socially excessive. For the most part the drinking patterns of the young can be predicted from the drinking patterns of their parents. In most cases in the United States the first drinking experience among the young occurs in the home under parental supervision. Among the various social groups those with the lowest risk of developing alcoholism are those in which drinking is learned at an early age in a context of complex social and ceremonial activities supervised by persons who themselves drink safely.[45]

In the United States most adolescents at some time enter social situations in which there is a temptation to experiment with alcoholic beverages. This may be because they are curious, "because their parents include them in their drinking habits, because they wish to imitate adult behavior patterns, or because they find it a means of expressing their rebellion against being classified as less than adults."[46] Because the peer group is very powerful among adolescents and the pressures to conform and thereby achieve one's identity are so great the introduction of drinking as a positive force is very hard for the individual to resist. Also, because drinking is defined as adult behavior and the adolescent often wants to be seen as an adult he will turn to drinking because he thinks it will give him adult status. Studies of high school students have found that anywhere from one third to four fifths have had some experience with the use of alcohol. The average age at first experience appears to be about 14 or 15.[47]

A common pattern for many teenagers is to learn about alcohol from observing their parents and other adults drink. Teenagers often drink at home in the presence of and with the encouragement of their parents. They often describe such at-home use of alcohol as "tasting" or "sipping," whereas its use with their peers is described as "drinking"—meaning the consumption of entire glasses or bottles of wine, beer, or whiskey.[48] One

---

[45] Blum, *Society and Drugs*, p. 39.

[46] Hans Sebald, *Adolescence: A Sociological Analysis* (New York: Appleton-Century-Crofts, 1968), p. 470.

[47] Muriel Sterne et al., "Teen Agers, Drinking, and the Law: A Study of Arrest Trends for Alcohol-Related Offenses," in Pittman, *Alcoholism*, p. 57.

[48] Ronald L. Akers, *Deviant Behavior: A Social Learning Approach* (Belmont, Calif.: Wadsworth, 1973), pp. 125–26.

study of high schoolers states that about one third to one half of the boys and one fourth of the girls drink to an extent that would be recognizable as a pattern of moderate drinking in an adult. "Little of the drinking that teenagers do is high-frequency-high-quantity, and an average of only about 3 percent can be characterized as 'problem' drinkers."[49]

Only a small percentage of adolescents are alcoholics. This is reflected in the finding that the median age of alcoholics is in the mid-40s. A small minority of adolescents who drink will eventually become alcoholics. It has been suggested that involvement with alcohol by adolescents can be seen as a matter of degree and may range from: "(1) relatively harmless, occasional drinking, consisting of nothing more than mere imitation of a permissible adult custom; to (2) peer-associated drinking that has overtones of rebelliousness against and alienation from adult institutions; to (3) heavy "escapist" drinking symptomatic of serious personality problems."[50]

Over the past 20 years various Gallup polls have consistently found that the highest proportion of drinkers are in the 21 to 29 age category and the lowest proportion among those over 60 years of age. "The peak years for heavy and alcoholic drinking are middle to late 40s, but there are relatively few heavy drinkers among persons 60 and older."[51] It has been suggested that older people drink less because they grew up at a time when drinking was less common or that they drink less because the process of aging influences them to cut down on their drinking.[52] It may also be that the heaviest drinkers have died or have been institutionalized and that those with lower drinking rates represent the "survival of the fittest." Also, older people are more often under the care of a physician on at least some occasions and would therefore often have their drinking patterns subjected to medical control.

Male-female differences

Far fewer females than males drink, and when women do drink they consume less than do men. There are also four or five times as many male alcoholics as there are female ones. However, one may predict that the rates of drinking and alcoholism among women will come closer to those of men. This expectation is predicated on the fact that women are achieving greater equality in the United States. One consequence of equality is the right and opportunity of women to acquire the socially undesirable problems of men. For example, if many men drink because of occupational pressures, then as women become increasingly involved in

[49] Ibid., p. 126.
[50] Sebald, *Adolescence*, p. 477.
[51] Akers, *Deviant Behavior*, pp. 116–17.
[52] Genevieve Knupfer and Robin Room, "Age, Sex, and Social Class as Factors in Amount of Drinking in a Metropolitan Community," *Social Problems*, Fall 1964, p. 229.

these occupations they too will probably turn more and more to alcohol. One measure of the achievement of total sexual equality will be the equalization of alcoholism rates among men and women.

Race differences

Most studies suggest that male alcoholism rates, whether crude or standardized by age, are usually higher for blacks than for whites. Rates of alcoholism for black females are also uniformly higher than those for white females. Furthermore, the rates of arrest, conviction, and incarceration for public intoxication tend to be higher for blacks than for whites.[53] This would be at least in part a reflection of higher arrests for all causes in the black population. Studies have also indicated that the tavern is a major focal point for public drinking among blacks and is often an important institution in the black community. "Although church and tavern represent the extremes of respectable and nonrespectable behavior, they serve analogous functions: Each is an accepted area for seeking individual recognition and for relatively uncircumscribed behavior, provides a mode of relief from problems, attracts a regular clientele to customary, ritual-like attendance, and is run by and for Negroes."[54]

Social class

Drinking is much less visible in the middle class than in the lower class. This is because among the middle class there is a high rate of drinking at home and therefore less visibility on the street while under the influence of alcohol. In general the public defines the middle-class drinker in much less harsh terms than it does the lower-class drinker. "On the other hand, the same public considers lower-class alcoholics and excessive drinkers as derelicts, beggars, petty thieves, and worthless drunks unable to support themselves."[55] The middle-class drinker, unless he clearly shows otherwise, is believed to be a good provider and is generally believed to be able to handle his drinking. In effect the lower-class drinker is condemned as much for being lower class as he is for being a drinker.

In the middle class a system of norms and behavior patterns related to drinking has developed. Permissive drinking goes with a notion of cosmopolitanism, and abstinence is often seen as a negative symbol of a life-style. To drink socially is to be cosmopolitan and often carries with it

---

[53] Muriel W. Sterne, "Drinking Patterns and Alcoholism among American Negroes," in Pittman, *Alcoholism*, p. 74.

[54] Ibid., pp. 85–86.

[55] Pittman, *Alcoholism*, p. 114.

the implication that one is emancipated from traditional Puritan values.[56] The person who doesn't drink is often looked down upon as a "square"—as one who lacks sophistication. Hence, it is often the case that the use of alcohol is important, not in itself but as symbolizing a certain life-style. The style is sometimes reflected in what one chooses to drink. A martini (very, very dry) is a sign of sophistication while a rye and coke is "square" or lower middle class.

The evidence indicates that there is proportionately more drinking in urban and suburban areas than in small towns and more in small towns than in rural areas. The rate of drinking in the large cities is close to double that of the farming areas. "The urbanized regions of the Northeast and the Middle-Atlantic states have the highest rates of drinking and heavy drinking, the South the lowest rates, and the West and Midwest have the intermediate rates."[57]

One of the lowest social class levels is that of the "skid rows" to be found in most large cities. On skid row most of the inhabitants are heavy drinkers or alcoholics. They constitute a crude and relatively simple subculture. They appear to show little interpersonal concern, and they cooperate on occasion primarily because this is more effective than not cooperating. One purpose for cooperating is in order to get alcohol. When they don't individually have enough money to buy a bottle of wine a number of skid row inhabitants may pool their resources as a "bottle gang." Generally they meet, pool their money, get a cheap bottle of wine, drink it, and split up once the bottle is empty.

The drunkenness of the skid row alcoholic tends to be prolonged and steady. He is dependent not so much on a large intake of alcohol as on a constant intake. For many skid row men the term *sobering up* means more than just clearing the system of alcohol. It also refers to "coming down," a change in perspective from optimism to pessimism.[58] Jacqueline Wiseman observes that the life of the skid row man is neither as sexless nor as homosexual as has often been portrayed. There are also some women on skid row. "If the woman has enough money, or shelter for two, they would share resources and dispel their mutual loneliness. Such women usually have clerical jobs, are well past middle age, and have 'been around.' Most of these liaisons last anywhere from one night to six months.[59]

The tavern or bar

How and where one drinks is important in that there are different

---

[56] Ibid., p. 18.

[57] Aker, *Deviant Behavior*, p. 117.

[58] Jacqueline Wiseman, *Stations of the Lost* (Englewood Cliffs, N.J.: Prentice-Hall, 1970), p. 15.

[59] Ibid., p. 36.

social patterns for the different settings in which drinking occurs. For example, the alcoholic will often drink alone and in secrecy. But most people who drink prefer to do so with other people, and thus the drinking becomes social and contributes to what is often enjoyable interaction. This can be done in one's home or in a tavern. It is not known how many taverns there are in the United States, but the number is probably somewhere between 200,000 and 300,000. Many people go to taverns or bars on a regular basis. One study of persons going to taverns in Dane County, Wisconsin, showed that about half the men and 15 percent of the women were regular patrons. In neighborhood taverns and bars drinking is often a secondary function because while people go to drink they also go for other reasons. Often when one person says to another, "Let's have a drink," he actually means, "Let's talk."[60]

Taverns and bars are often viewed as potential trouble spots both legally and socially. "In general, and unlike houses of prostitution and opium dens, bars in America are not, by law, as much deviant settings as they are places of potential deviant activity."[61] But since the end of prohibition the public bar has been seen as a legitimate retail business. However, it is different from other retail businesses in that special restrictions are placed on where it can be located, when it can open for business, and who may trade there. All of the restrictions serve to define a setting in which, from the point of view of the conventional order, trouble is apt to occur.

As suggested, the tavern or bar is a public meeting place where individuals may actively interact with one another. The degree and nature of the interaction are determined by the type of tavern. In the neighborhood bar the clientele know one another and constitute a kind of subculture. The bar is seen as important by the regulars. For example, the bar can be very important in a rooming house area, because there it serves as a meeting place for persons who have no other way of meeting people. In this kind of bar the regular customer often finds a sense of belonging and a place in the community.

There are also bars that serve quite different functions. Among them are what Cavan calls marketplace bars, and she points out that next to liquor the commodity most frequently handled in public drinking places is sex, on either a commercial or a noncommercial basis.[62] There are also bars that market narcotics, gambling, stolen goods, and a variety of other illegal products and services. In general the marketplace bars do not sell to anyone walking in off the street. Generally the buyers and the sellers must be vouched for before they can enter into the activities of such

[60] Marshall B. Clinard, "The Public Drinking House and Society," in Dinitz, *Deviance*, p. 235.

[61] Sherri Cavan, *Liquor License: An Ethnology of Bar Behavior* (Chicago: Aldine, 1966), p. 37.

[62] Ibid., p. 171.

bars. Even in bars that are commonly known to provide information about prostitutes, "patrons walking into the bar cannot always receive such information, since it can be used by the police as evidence of pimping, even though the one giving the information may be getting no fee from any transaction that may take place."[63] There are many other types of bars, but the most common is probably the neighborhood bar and the second most common the bar that deals in sex either for a fee or free, and both heterosexually and homosexually.

In general the research evidence suggests that drinking behavior is a social phenomena in two important and related ways. First, what a person does with and thinks about alcohol is a function of his group membership and feeling of identification. Second, almost all drinking takes place in social group settings in which the drinker believes his behavior is socially approved by the people who matter to him.

Cures for alcoholism

For centuries there have been attempts to cure alcoholism. The attempts have been closely linked to what has been believed to be the cause. When it was believed that people became alcoholics because they were possessed of the devil or were committing a sin it was the church that tried to cure them. But the problems of drinking have for the most part been removed from religion and placed in the hands of medical clinics. So the tendency to handle drinkers through protective and welfare agencies, rather than through the police or the clergy, has become stronger.[64]

With the increased use of drugs in recent years there has been an interest in the relationships between alcohol use and drug use. Some research indicates that while a user may be able to distinguish subjectively between the effects of alcohol and the effects of barbiturates it is very difficult for the observer to tell the difference on the basis of the user's behavior. One serious problem has been that heavy alcohol users "are usually resistant to the effects of barbiturates, minor tranquillizers, volatile solvents and anaesthetics although the cross-toleration does not significantly affect the lethal dose. Consequently, many overdose deaths occur due to the mixing of these drugs in chronic users."[65]

There has developed the establishment of detoxification centers. Many experts argue that these should replace the police station as the first detention for drunkards. If this were done the drunkard would be brought to a public health facility by the police and kept there until sober. After that the decision to continue treatment would be left to the individual. There has also been some work with "inpatient programs"

---

[63] Ibid., pp. 172-73.

[64] Gusfield, "Legislating Morals," p. 67.

[65] *Non-Medical Uses*, p. 71.

where the patients are given high-protein meals with vitamin and mineral supplements and appropriate medication to help cut down on withdrawal symptoms. In these settings bath and laundry facilities are also available, as are basic clothing and limited recreation facilities. For any continued success "aftercare" programs are also needed. There is little reason to believe that the chronic drinker will change a long-term pattern of drinking after a few days of sobriety and care at a public health unit. It has been suggested that a network of aftercare facilities should be expanded to include halfway houses, community shelters, and other forms of public housing.[66]

Alcoholics Anonymous

The approach of Alcoholics Anonymous is by far the best-known attempt to help the alcoholic stop his drinking. This group is important not only in itself but also because it has served as a model for many other attempts to deal with problems. Programs to deal with the drug addict, the chronic gambler, and so forth have been modeled after Alcoholics Anonymous. This means that the public image of the organization is very high and that the organization is generally seen as the only really successful way to "cure" alcoholism. Therefore, it is important to look at how it operates and to examine its successes and failures.

Alcoholics Anonymous (AA) was founded by a medical man and a stockbroker as a result of a chance meeting they had in 1935. The stockbroker, through some kind of mystical experience, had stopped his own drinking and wanted to share his new sobriety with others. Initially there was a 12-step program to stop drinking. Some of the steps were: you admit you are licked; you get honest with yourself; you talk it out with someone else; you make restitution to the people you have harmed; you try to give of yourself without stint, with no demands for reward; and you pray to whatever God you think there is, even as an experiment, to help you do these things.[67]

The various Alcoholics Anonymous groups are very powerful and pervasive subcultures. Basically one enters AA because he has been a deviant through his alcoholism and wants to give up that deviant role. He does so by joining a powerful subculture made up of persons with similar motivations. He is rewarded for making the changes by persons in the same situation who confirm his new self-in-transition. "When these conditions are met, transforming a deviant identity is encouraged."[68]

---

[66] *Task Force Report*, p. 250.

[67] Milton A. Maxwell, "Alcoholics Anonymous: An Interpretation," in Pittman, *Alcoholism*, p. 216.

[68] Earl Rubington and Martin S. Weinberg, *Deviance: The Interactionist Perspective* (New York: Macmillan, 1968), p. 323.

One supporter of the AA approach says that the subculture provides a way of life "which is more realistic, which enables the member to get closer to people, which provides one with more emotional security, and which facilitates more productive living. Thus, the AA group becomes an important new reference group—a new point of orientation."[69] The high value and importance of conformity in the subculture is a major value in AA. It is argued that when the alcoholic seeks help it is the great strength of AA that he is interacting with persons who have been through the program and have stopped drinking. So the subculture says, "Come on in, do what we say, and you can be like us—people who no longer drink."

A basic belief of AA is that there are no ex-alcoholics. This is because, according to AA, alcoholism cannot be cured and the person who has stopped drinking must therefore give constant vigilance to his own urge to drink as well as to the like urges of other AA members. For AA members there are only alcoholics in control (for the time being) of their temptations and never ex-alcoholics. In the jargon of the group such persons are referred to as dry or sober alcoholics.

The subculture of the AA members develops in a number of other ways. For example, a ritualism of behavior develops. Initially all members were called by their first names as a means of protecting their identity, but this now continues as a ritual.[70] As is true of all subcultures, the members of AA develop an argot of their own which contributes to their sense of solidarity and exclusiveness. The argot often has meaning in reference to the special experiences that the members have in common or have actually shared. It includes, for example, such phrases as "nickel therapy" for "phoning another AA member to avert a 'slip'" and "the guy Upstairs" for "God as you conceive him."[71]

Alcoholics Anonymous sees alcoholism as a disease that is arrested when a person stops drinking and erupts again if he or she resumes drinking. AA refuses to consider alcoholism as a symptom rather than a disease. Sagarin says that if it did there would be more need for psychotherapy and much less need for AA. As a result the organization has become, almost by nature and in spite of itself, antitherapy. At its meetings and in its publications AA strongly denounces those who argue that alcoholics are psychopathological or that they have behavior disorders in any way similar to those of manic-depressives and persons with obsessions.[72]

An important part of the AA subculture is the pressure for honesty about oneself, which is reflected in a strong need to confess. Sagarin

---

[69] Maxwell, *Alcoholics Anonymous*, pp. 218-19.

[70] Edward Sagarin, *Odd Man In: Societies of Deviants in America* (Chicago: Quadrangle, 1969), p. 51.

[71] Ibid., p. 42.

[72] Ibid., p. 47.

suggests that the great need to confess brings about a catharsis "similar to that produced by religious confessions and psychoanalysis."[73] This contributes to the high sense of personal and spiritual commitment of the AA member. The subculture not only influences his behavior and interaction with others but, more important, becomes his reason for being. This appeal to the alcoholic often appears to transcend many social factors. AA is found in prisons, in hospitals, in small towns and large cities, and among the rich and the poor. In fact there are AA branches in several police departments, and other branches that cater especially to priests.[74]

There is disagreement about the success of Alcoholics Anonymous. It is quite likely that more contemporary alcoholics have reached sobriety through AA than through all other agencies combined. However, while the AA plan works for some it does not work for many, and there is no clear understanding of why it works when it does. A critical view is that of Sagarin, who states that many of AA's claims and assumptions about its success are unproven, obviously self-serving, and of doubtful validity. "They may be not only wrong but actually harmful. Some of these claims are: that alcoholism is a disease; that it is incurable but can be arrested; that AA has had a 50 percent success rate with its members; and that only an alcoholic can understand—or help—another alcoholic."[75] But another observer has suggested that the major contribution of AA has been not only in rehabilitating alcoholics, but also in dramatizing that alcoholics can be helped. "By virtue of their interest, they have made work with the alcoholic legitimate."[76]

It has been suggested that one possible consequence of arresting or halting deviance is that stopping the undesirable may have undesirable consequences. It is possible that the results of halting a deviance may be worse than the deviance itself. But more often there are negative consequences that tend to be ignored in light of the fact that the primary problem has been solved. For example, possible consequences for the individual who stops drinking are loneliness, frustration, and other difficulties.[77] This is especially true if the individual became an alcoholic because of personal problems. When he stops drinking these problems return, and he is therefore in the same situation as when he originally developed his alcoholism. And because AA does not accept the approach of psychotherapy the alcoholic usually has not been helped with his original problems.

---

[73] Ibid., p. 37.

[74] Ibid., p. 40.

[75] Ibid., p. 45.

[76] Morris E. Chefetz and Harold W. Demone, Jr., "Alcoholics Anonymous," in Dinitz et al., *Deviance*, p. 272.

[77] Sagarin, *Odd Man In*, p. 47.

The alcoholic who goes on the wagon may also create problems for his family. In many cases his wife has been managing the family, and with his continuing sobriety he usually wants to return to his former family roles. There is often resistance by both the wife and the children. "Their mother has been both parents for so long that it takes time to get used to the idea of consulting their father on problems and asking for his decision. Often the father tries too hard to manage this change overnight."[78]

Jackson found that if a man's sobriety comes about because of AA he very often commits himself so totally to AA activities that his wife sees little of him and feels neglected. And as she worries less about his drinking she may push him to cut down on some of his outside activities. But this can be dangerous because AA activity is correlated with success in Alcoholics Anonymous. The wife also learns that even though her husband is off alcohol she is by no means free of alcoholics. "In his Twelfth Step work, he may keep the house filled with men he is helping. In the past her husband has avoided self-searching; and now he may become excessively introspective, and it may be difficult for her to deal with this."[79]

In conclusion it can be said that alcohol in the American society is not the cause of deviance, but rather that deviance is related to the degree to which alcohol is used. In general social drinking that is personally controlled is not viewed as deviance and in fact is often given some positive social value. The problem of deviance is associated with the heavy drinker and the alcoholic. And even when there is agreement that this is a problem there is little agreement on what to do about it. Most medical persons define alcoholism as a psychological problem that should be treated through some form of physical and psychological therapy, whereas Alcoholics Anonymous defines it as a disease that can never be cured. So, although alcoholism refers to something that most people would agree is a problem there is limited knowledge and high disagreement on what should be done about it.

BIBLIOGRAPHY

Bacon, Seldon D., "Alcohol and Complex Society," in Simon Dinitz et al., *Deviance.* New York: Oxford University Press, 1969, pp. 217–27.

Cavan, Sherri, *Liquor License: An Ethnology of Bar Behavior.* Chicago: Aldine, 1966.

Jackson, Joan K., "The Adjustment of the Family to the Crisis of Alcoholism," *Quarterly Journal of Studies of Alcohol,* December 1954, pp. 564–86.

---

[78] Jackson, "Adjustment to Alcoholism," p. 60.
[79] Ibid., p. 64.

Knupfer, Genevieve, and **Robin Room,** "Age, Sex, and Social Class as Factors in Amount of Drinking in a Metropolitan Community," *Social Problems,* Fall 1964, pp. 224-40.

Larson, Donald E., and **Baha Abu-Laban,** "Norm Qualities and Deviant Drinking Behavior," *Social Problems,* Spring 1968, pp. 441-50.

Marshall, Harvey, and **Ross Purdy,** "Hidden Deviance and the Labelling Approach: The Case for Drinking and Driving," *Social Problems,* Spring 1972, pp. 541-53.

Mizruchi, Ephraim H., and **Robert Perrucci,** "Prescription, Proscription, and Permissiveness: Aspects of Norms and Deviant Drinking Behavior," in Mark Lefton et al., *Approaches to Deviance.* New York: Appleton-Century-Crofts, 1968, pp. 151-67.

Pittman, David J., *Alcoholism.* New York: Harper and Row, 1967.

Shore, Richard S., "The Alcoholic," in Patricia Keith-Spiegel and Don Spiegel, *Outsiders USA.* San Francisco: Rinehart Press, 1973, pp. 328-41.

Wiseman, Jacqueline P., *Stations of the Lost.* Englewood Cliffs, N.J.: Prentice-Hall, 1970.

chapter seven

Drugs

In recent years a great interest has developed in the "drug problem." Drug use is often presented as a major social problem that is undermining the morality of society and destroying many of the younger generation. The use of drugs is a form of deviance that operates within the context of passionate response frequently based on limited knowledge. This is true whether the view is that all drugs are evil and dangerous or that drugs are the way for the individual to find his true identity. In this chapter our interest is in the various types of drugs and their consequences as well as in the social settings in which drugs are used.

Drugs have been a part of most cultures in the world. The evidence indicates that only a few societies have been without mind-altering drugs. The American society places great stress on the use of drugs under many circumstances, but it also makes many strong distinctions between the kinds of drugs to be used and the circumstances under which drugs may be used. However, this has not always been true in the United States. For many years many remedies that had narcotic contents of 5 to 10 percent were sold over the counter without any controls. Through such wonder-working medications as Mrs. Winslow's Soothing Syrup, Dr. Cole's Catarrh Cure, and Perkins' Diarrhea Mixture large amounts of opium, codeine, and cocaine were fed to children as well as adults. Also, every well-equipped home had a rosewood chest, an earlier version of today's medicine cabinet, with its ball of opium and its bottle of paregoric. It is estimated that by 1863 addiction in the United States ran to as high as 4 percent of the population.[1] By 1900 there were institutions of different types for the treatment of drug addiction at various locations around the

---

[1] Marie Nyswander, "History of a Nightmare," in Dan Wakefield, *The Addict* (New York: Gold Medal Books, 1963), p. 21.

country. Before the attempt to suppress the drug trade started in 1915 the drug addicts were mostly scattered throughout respectable society and did not form a deviant subculture.

There had been some initial concern with the possible dangers of drug use as early as the 1830s. But for the most part during the 19th century the problem of drug dependence was handled through the continued availability and consumption of the drug. The discomforts of abstaining from drugs were seen as just another set of aches and pains that could be eliminated by the use of drugs that were seen as the panacea for all ills.[2] The first law that tried to control drug addiction was the Boylan Law, passed by the New York legislature in 1904. The Harrison Narcotic Law, enacted in 1914, was modeled on the Boylan Law, but it omitted the important measures that were concerned with the physician's role in treating addiction. The Harrison Act was designed to control the production, manufacture, and distribution of addictive drugs by making it necessary to register all transactions in such drugs and by specifying that only physicians could prescribe them.[3] Over the years the Harrison Act has been supplemented by a number of other antinarcotics statutes under which the unauthorized possession, sale, or transfer of drugs has been severely punished. "Rather than constituting a rationally planned program for dealing with the narcotics problem, this legislation has mainly represented an emotional response to periodic crises."[4] During this period the Federal Narcotics Control Board came up with what it saw to be the solution to drug use. That solution was compulsory treatment, and the board's successor since 1930, the Bureau of Narcotics in the Treasury Department, still considers compulsory treatment the only road to complete cure.[5]

What antinarcotics laws have meant for the drug addict is that it has stopped him from being a respectable member of the community and made him a common criminal. This is because the law requires the registration of all legitimate drug handlers and the payment of a special tax on drug transactions, resulting in a licensing system for the control of the legitimate domestic drug trade. Schur suggests that through a combination of restrictive regulations, attention only to favorable court decisions, and harassment, the Narcotics Division of the United States Treasury Department and its successor, the Federal Bureau of Narcotics, have effectively and severely limited the freedom of medical practitioners to treat addicts as patients. Physicians have not been allowed to provide

---

[2] John A. Clausen, "Drug Addiction," in Robert K. Merton and Robert A Nisbet, *Contemporary Social Problems* (New York: Harcourt, Brace and World, 1961), p. 185.

[3] Nyswander, "History," p. 22.

[4] Edwin M. Schur, *Crimes without Victims: Deviant Behavior and Public Policy* (Englewood Cliffs, N.J.: Prentice-Hall, 1965), p. 133.

[5] Nyswander, "History," p. 24.

addicts with drugs even when that has been believed medically advisable.[6]

It must be recognized that the highly restrictive laws with regard to drug addiction have been enacted in a society that is quite permissive about drugs in general. In fact the American public places a high positive value on the use of *"legitimate"* drugs. In the United States drugs are usually acceptable and approved when they are seen to relieve some kind of pain, illness, or disability or, more generally, to help bring a person from some negative state toward a condition seen as "normal."[7] More and more drugs are seen as legitimately used not only in reducing physical pain but also in alleviating mental anguish.

About 60 percent of the patients who appear in general practitioners' offices or clinics do so for largely nonspecific medical reasons. "Patients seek the help of a physician because they are lonely, depressed, anxious, dissatisfied or unhappy."[8] This means that a great many of them will be treated through drugs. In 1971 physicians wrote 230 million prescriptions for various drugs with psychoactive agents, less than 30 percent of which were written by psychiatrists. "During 1970, five billion doses of tranquilizers, three million doses of amphetamines and five million doses of barbiturates were produced in the United States. About one third of all Americans between the ages of 18 and 24 used a psychoactive drug of some type."[9] While the legitimate drugs help many there are dangers of overdependence, and even more serious, there is danger of death. There are, for example, approximately 3,000 deaths per year resulting from overdoses of barbiturates.

Often physicians who prescribe drugs have no special qualifications to deal with psychological problems. Frequently the treatment is given to alleviate symptoms and does not get at the roots of the problem. As Bernstein and Lennard have pointed out, when drugs are given to a middle-aged woman who is upset about her child's rebellion or to an elderly man who has been isolated from children or community the problems are being masked. "The drugs decrease the anxiety or unhappiness of the individual but, more important, they decrease the amount of trouble his anxiety, misery or unhappiness is causing others."[10]

Another danger from the legitimate use of drugs is that along with the widespread and intense belief in the power of medicine there is often a tendency to ignore the limitations and the side effects of drugs. There is also some indication that with the breakdown of the traditional patient-

---

[6] Schur, *Crimes without Victims*, p. 130.

[7] John H. Weakland, "Hippies: What the Scene Means," in Richard Blum, *Society and Drugs* (San Francisco: Jossey-Bass, 1969), p. 359.

[8] Arnold Bernstein and Henry L. Lennard, "The American Way of Drugging," *Society*, May 1973, p. 16.

[9] Ibid., p. 14.

[10] Ibid., p. 22.

doctor relationship and an increasing amount of medical specialization, people depend more on medication than on the physician. The patient often sees the physician simply as the one who prescribes the drugs that will take care of his problem. Once the patient has the medication, he sometimes uses it excessively or indiscriminately. One writer suggests that there is a kind of patient who "uses medication as a kind of magical protector and depends on medication rather than people to handle certain emotional drives and needs."[11]

Adult society, with its use of many kinds of drugs, and not always according to medical prescription, has socialized many of the younger generation to the use of drugs. The generation that is sometimes now looking for new values in LSD or marijuana received its orientation in a society that had been using various pills for adjustment to its psychic imbalances. Over the years, among the adults, barbiturates and "bennies" had been finding their way into the hands of many, and this had been increasingly reflected in accident and suicide statistics.[12] So in one sense the medicine cabinet in the middle-class home has been a socializing experience that in some ways predisposed children toward experimentation with drugs.

Illegal drugs are believed to provide a wide range of benefits. At one extreme, the believers in drug use see the psychedelic compounds, such as LSD and mescaline, as a way of counteracting the "depersonalization," "commercialization," and "inhumanity" of modern American society. For such people the use of drugs is a modern means to mystical experience and to the great "inward journey of self-exploration and self-discovery."[13] At the other extreme, those who oppose drug use see it as self-indulgent, degenerate, and both psychologically and physiologically damaging. "Drug use is viewed as a 'symptom'—either of profound psychological problems or of some fatal weakness in the moral fiber of American youth. It is a form of moral depravity, and it must be ruthlessly stamped out, its users thoroughly punished, and the young indoctrinated in the 'hazards' of drugs."[14] These two extremes help set the stage for the discussion ahead and indicate that the area of drug use is one that brings forth great passions and doctrinaire points of view in the United States.

Before looking at the various kinds of drugs and their use and consequences it is necessary to define some terms. The word *narcotic* is used to refer to opium and the various painkilling drugs that are made from opium, such as heroin, morphine, paregoric, and codeine. These, as well

---

[11] Helen H. Nowlis, *Drugs on the College Campus* (New York: Anchor Books, 1969), p. 25.

[12] Warren Young and Joseph Hixson, *LSD on Campus* (New York: Dell, 1966), p. 52.

[13] Nowlis, *Drugs on Campus*, p. x.

[14] Ibid., p. xi.

as other opiates, are taken from the juice of the poppy fruit. Several synthetic drugs, such as Demerol and Dolophine, are also classified as narcotics. The opiates are widely used in medicine to kill pain. Cocaine, made from cacao leaves, and marijuana are legally classified as narcotic drugs although they are not narcotic in chemical makeup. Pharmacologically the term *narcotic* is applied to a drug which, in most people under most circumstances and at the right level of dosage, will produce sleep and relieve pain. However, from the legal point of view the term *narcotic* has been applied to almost any drug assumed to be habit forming or addictive. The general public has gone even further in its definition of the term *narcotic*, using it to refer to any drug which is socially disapproved or associated "with delinquency, crime, and the underworld, as well as any drug which was controlled by the Federal Bureau of Narcotics."[15] The term *drug* refers to any chemical substance that alters mood, perception, or consciousness. The social and legal settings define the nature of drug use. The term *drug addiction* refers to a state of periodic or chronic intoxication brought about by the repeated use of a drug of either a natural or a synthetic nature. The characteristics of drug addiction are: "(1) an overpowering desire or need (compulsion) to continue taking the drug and to obtain it by any means; (2) a tendency to increase the dose; (3) a psychic (psychological) and generally a physical dependence on the effects of the drug; (4) an effect detrimental to the individual and to society."[16] It has been suggested that the term *drug addiction* has taken on so many different meanings that even the pharmachologist no longer has a specific definition for it. In 1965 the World Health Organization Expert Committee on Addiction-Producing Drugs came to a similar conclusion and suggested using the term *drug dependence* in place of *drug addiction*. The two terms will be used interchangeably in this chapter.

The major difference between the United States' handling of drug addiction and that of other countries is that this country sees drug addiction as a legal matter whereas other countries see it as a medical concern. This has not always been true. Before 1914 the American drug addict had little or no involvement in any kind of criminal behavior. He did his job and maintained his home and family life, and for the most part his drug dependence did not inflict injury on anyone other than himself. But under the controls of the Harrison Act the treatment of the addict was basically ignored, and amendments and various court decisions expanded that approach. As a result "the addict was gradually forced out of the role of the legitimately ill into the role of the willful

---

[15] Ibid., p. 34.

[16] Expert Committee on Addiction- Producing Drugs, *Seventh Report*, World Health Organization Technical Report Series No. 116, (1957), Reprinted in Schur, *Crimes without Victims*, p. 122.

criminal."[17] Like so many legal control systems in our society this development was not a result of rational and planned decisions. Rather, as legal agencies developed a vested interest in the handling of drug addicts they helped to bring about the laws that made them more significant and gave them greater control. In other words once the direction of handling drug addicts was toward the legal rather than the medical approach, the process snowballed.

One of the strongest critics of the present legal handling of drug addiction in the United States is the sociologist Alfred Lindesmith. He argues that the fatal weakness of our present system is that it fails to take into account the basic human situation with which it is supposed to be dealing. By not allowing the physician to relieve the addict's suffering during drug deprivation the idea of the sanctity of human life and the desirability of preventing needless suffering are rejected. Lindesmith says that "the narcotic laws are basically immoral and essentially unjust because of the manner in which they affect the addict, the way in which they distribute punishment, and because they require that the police engage either in immoral or criminal behavior, or both, in enforcement of the laws."[18]

The American system has also been severely attacked on the ground that the legal approach to drug addiction has failed. Obviously the laws have failed in that they have not eliminated drug addiction. Actually they have contributed to the narcotics problem. The addict, because he is cut off from any legal supply of drugs, must seek out illegal drug sources. The strong demand of addicts for the satisfaction of their drug needs means that huge profits can be made on the illegal market. Because there are great profits to be made, illegal activity is seen as worthwhile by the drug sellers. One indication of the vast profits is an estimate that the retail value of a thousand dollars worth of heroin may surpass 3 million dollars.[19] The traffic in illegal drugs has been estimated to gross hundreds of millions of dollars per year. So narcotics smuggling and distribution are big business for the criminal syndicates. Yet, as has been pointed out, at the beginning of the century little illegal profit was being made from drug sales. Therefore, it seems clear that the illegal view of drugs that has developed since 1914 has been the major factor in creating the highly profitable criminal business of selling illegal drugs.

As indicated, the legal restrictions on the medical distribution of drugs place the drug addict in an almost impossible position. As Lindesmith points out, the dilemma for the drug addict is that if he does not secure drugs he is punished by his disease; if he does secure them he is punished

---

[17] Nyswander, "History," p. 23.
[18] Alfred R. Lindesmith, "Torture by Law," in Wakefield, *Addict*, p. 41.
[19] Schur, *Crimes without Victims*, p. 134.

by the police. He goes on to point out that the drug user or anyone who knows him at first hand knows that drug withdrawal is usually a serious, frightening, and dangerous experience. "To deny him his medical care on the grounds that he should not have acquired the habit in the first place is the moral equivalent of denying medical treatment for gonorrhea on the same grounds."[20]

Having seen that the legal system with regard to drug treatment in the United States has been a failure both in *not* treating the addict as a medical problem and in *not* controlling the distribution of drugs, one might question why the system continues. One explanation is that using heavy criminal sanctions to control drug addiction rather than to treat the addict as a sick person may continue because the drug laws are primarily symbolic rather than instrumental in their effect. The severe treatment of addicts is evidence that policymakers may be more interested in expressing disapproval than in controlling the problem effectively. "The stereotype of the drug addict suggests that this hostility is related to the view of the drug addict as representing a world outside conventional society."[21] In fact the constant publicity given to various drugs by politicians and some of the police have sensationalized many drugs and stimulated curiosity about them. New drug laws have almost always been enacted on the basis of anecdotal, unscientific, and illegal testimony. Their enactment has often occurred in a climate of hysteria which may have been consciously developed and reinforced through the mass media. For example, recent laws against the use of LSD were passed with little medical, sociological, or scientific testimony.[22] Often politicians are against drugs in the same way that they are against sin. That is, drugs are something safe to be against and in fact being against them may win votes because most people are against drugs—at least when used by others.

A commonly heard argument is that there should be drug reforms, but the argument almost always takes it for granted that the current policies are still desirable. In other words the legal view of drugs, rather than the medical approach taken in other countries, is rarely questioned by politicians. But some experts, who receive little attention, state that what is needed is an absolute reversal of the present attitudes and laws. These experts argue that the addict will get his drugs no matter how hard the law enforcers try to stop him, and that "the only sensible course of action is to try to substitute medical supervision for police persecution."[23]

---

[20] Lindesmith, "Torture by Law," p. 33.

[21] Joseph R. Gusfield, "On Legislating Morals: The Symbolic Process of Designating Deviance," *California Law Review*, January 1968, p. 71.

[22] Joel Fort, "Social Problems of Drug Use and Drug Policies," *California Law Review*, January 1968, p. 20.

[23] Schur, *Crimes without Victims*, p. 160.

The drug laws also show the irrationality often found in society, since drug use is often not as harmful as the use of some legally accepted materials. Judged impartially, alcohol is probably more harmful to the user than even heroin, because the use of alcohol over a long term causes physical and nervous deterioration, which heroin does not. In fact, if alcohol were invented today it would probably be severely controlled through law.[24] But alcohol has been around for centuries, and in the United States it is a part of large, legitimate business enterprises. Therefore, all attempts to control alcohol have met with little success. It is quite possible that if around 1914 the drugs of addiction had developed as legitimate business enterprises, they too would be accepted today. Another illustration of this point is the reaction to cigarettes. Since the mid-1960s the evidence has been overwhelming that the use of cigarettes is dangerous. Yet, cigarettes are not being taken off the market and probably will not be in the foreseeable future.

Society also often reacts in another way toward things that are defined by many as bad. For example, with cigarettes, an economic argument is advanced for their continued manufacture and sale, namely, that if the sales of cigarettes were drastically reduced many people would be put out of work and the tobacco regions would become depressed areas. It is also common to hear a similar argument about war or the need for at least the continued threat of war, namely, that if defense industries were closed down people would be out of jobs. There is something strange about the argument that the killing of people is needed to maintain jobs for other people—but it is advanced, nevertheless.

TYPES OF DRUGS

In this section our interest is in examining various types of drugs. However, the hallucinogens are one group that cuts across several categories of drugs. In this group are included such drugs as LSD, mescaline, psilocybin, and marijuana. These drugs have a hallucinatory effect and influence the user's perception of the world both within and outside of himself. The drugs are not addictive, although under some personality conditions they may become habit forming. This group is also sometimes referred to as the *psychedelic* drugs. The black market for the sale of hallucinogens is loosely organized, with friends often supplying one another and covering their mutual costs, rather than an organized network of pushers. "The non-addictiveness of the drugs makes for a frustration in demand that hardly attracts the established operators, who prefer the stability of the opiate market."[25]

Variations in the effects of drugs on the individual may be related to

---

[24] Peter Laurie, *Drugs: Medical, Psychological, and Social Facts* (Baltimore: Penguin Books, 1967), p. 15.

[25] Ibid., p. 123.

how they are taken. The injection of the drug directly into the vein delivers the total dose immediately, and this produces a rapid maximum response of minimal duration. Smoking and inhalation cause rapid but less efficient delivery of the dose because a quantity of the drug is destroyed during burning or escapes into the air and does not reach the lungs. Oral ingestion produces different effects, according to the system in which the drug is dispensed. Generally oral ingestion diminishes but prolongs the effect of drugs.[26]

Barbiturates

The first barbiturate appeared in 1903 and was called barbital (Veronal). Barbiturates are classified among the general depressants. They are not specific in effect and are capable of depressing a wide range of functions. Their influence on the central nervous system ranges from a mild sedation to coma, depending on the level of dosage. At moderate dosage levels the barbiturates often produce disinhibition and euphoria, much as does alcohol (also a depressant). The drugs depress other functions, such as nerves, skeletal muscles, smooth muscles, and cardiac muscles. Addiction to barbiturates differs from addiction to opiates in several important ways. It appears to be more destructive to personality; "the barbiturate addict tends to dope himself until he is completely intoxicated—his object is oblivion."[27] Barbiturates are estimated to be the cause of about 3,000 deaths per year.

Barbiturates are under the regulation of the Bureau of Narcotics and Dangerous Drugs, Department of Justice. The federal laws provide for a strict accounting of drug supplies by the manufacturer, distributor, and seller, and they limit the refills of the prescription, at the discretion of the physician. This means that barbiturates can be obtained legally only through a physician. The illegal manufacture and dispensing of barbiturates can lead to fines as high as $10,000 and prison sentences of up to 5 years. Those convicted of selling the drugs to persons under 21 years of age can be fined $15,000 to $20,000 and can be sentenced to 10 to 15 years in prison. To be in possession of these drugs illegally can bring a fine of from $1,000 to $10,000 and/or imprisonment of 1 to 3 years. There are also state laws that control the illegal use of barbiturates.

Amphetamines

The amphetamines, which were first produced in the 1920s for medical use, stimulate the central nervous system and are best known as a means

---

[26] *Marihuana: A Signal of Misunderstanding, The Official Report of the National Commission on Marihuana and Drug Abuse* (New York: New American Library, 1972), pp. 61–62.

[27] Laurie, *Drugs*, p. 63.

to fight against fatigue and sleepiness. They are also sometimes used to limit appetites in medically controlled weight reduction programs. The
most commonly used are amphetamine (Benzedrine), dex-
troamphetamine (Dexedrine), and methamphetamine (Methedrine).
These drugs are also known under the slang terms of *pep pills* and
bennies.

The amphetamines produce effects resembling those resulting from the
stimulation of the sympathetic nervous system, that part of the nervous
system which has major control over bodily functions. There is a high
potential for psychological dependence in some individuals if they use
amphetamines regularly over a period of time. The psychological
dependence appears to be a function of the drugs' ability to bring forth
feelings of energy, initiative, self-confidence, and well-being. After a
period of usage many people find it very difficult to meet the demands of
life without this uplift. There is some evidence that women are more apt
to use amphetamines than are men. By contrast men use hallucinogens
more often.

There is little doubt that amphetamines can improve a person's
performance on a wide variety of tasks, especially those involving an
element of fatigue or boredom. They are in a way "superman" drugs
because they can increase the capacity for simple physical and mental
tasks, and becuase they increase intelligence, as measured by simple tests,
by an average of up to eight points. "However, highly coordinated tasks
like playing golf or flying an airplane are unaffected in quality, though
they can be prolonged beyond the normal duration."[28] One of the most
dangerous uses of amphetamines is "speeding." This is a series of in-
jections, each of which is followed by a general climax of intense feelings
and bodily sensations.

Production figures for the United States for 1962 showed that four and
a half billion tablets were produced, about twenty-five tablets per capita.
The Food and Drug Administration estimates indicate that half of these
were consumed without a medical prescription. Continued use can lead
to a habit which is reinforced by physiological as well as psychological
distress upon withdrawal.

Marijuana

Marijuana is a drug found in the flowering tops and the leaves of the
Indian hemp plant. The plant grows in mild climates in countries all over
the world. The marijuana plant is a relative of European hemp and looks
like a scrawny, six-foot nettle. The term *marijuana* has become
synonymous with *cannabis* and all of its products and derivatives, in-

---

[28] Ibid., pp. 70–71.

cluding the natural and synthetic tetrahydrocannabinols. The substance cannabis is derived from the resin exuded by the female hemp plants. This substance has been used by man throughout recorded history. It is the leaves, stems, and flowering tops that are dried and chopped to produce the marijuana common to the United States and Mexico. The chopped-up product is usually rolled and smoked in short cigarettes or in pipes, and may be taken in food. The cigarettes are commonly known as "reefers," "joints," and "sticks." The smoke from marijuana is harsh and smells like burnt dried grass, and the rather sweetish aroma is quite easy to identify.

At one time in the United States extracts of cannabis were used almost as commonly for medicinal purposes as is aspirin today. Cannabis could be purchased without a prescription, and it was often prescribed by physicians for the treatment of a broad range of medical conditions, from migraine headaches and excessive menstrual bleeding to ulcers, epilepsy, and even tooth decay. Many medical reports were written about the use of cannabis but hardly ever did they refer to any intoxicating properties of the drug. "Rarely, if ever, is there any indication that patients— hundreds of thousands must have received cannabis in Europe in the nineteenth century—were 'stoned' or changed their attitudes toward work, love, their fellow men, or their homeland."[29]

Well before the Marijuana Stamp Act of 1937 the use of cannabis in general medicine was already declining. This was because there had always been problems in prescribing the drug. It is insoluble in water and cannot be injected intravenously for rapid effect. "Moreover, the delay before it begins to take effect when given by mouth, one or two hours, is longer than with many other drugs."[30]

How common is the use of marijuana in the United States? One survey estimates that about 24 million Americans over the age of 11 have used it at least once.[31] Up until recently about twice as many males as females had used it, but this differential appears to be decreasing. Various surveys uniformly indicate that more than 40 percent of the college population has tried marijuana.[32] In part this is a reflection of their younger age. A national survey indicated that 39 percent of all young adults between the ages of 18 and 25 had tried marijuana. In fact of all the "ever users" about half fell into this age group. By contrast only about 6 percent of all adults past age 50 had ever tried marijuana.[33] Other variables have been related to the use of marijuana. Its use does not seem to vary significantly by race.

---

[29] Solomon H. Snyder, *Uses of Marijuana* (New York: Oxford University Press, 1971), p. 13.

[30] Ibid., p. 14.

[31] *Marihuana*, p. 38.

[32] Ibid., pp. 7–8.

[33] Ibid., p. 39.

With respect to religious affiliation, Jews and Catholics appear to be slightly overrepresented as compared to Protestants.[34] One study found that youths who came from broken homes or did not live with their parents had higher rates. That study suggests that "the likelihood of marijuana use increases when demands made by the family are perceived as unfair and excessive and are not accompanied by 'warmth.'"[35]

The effects of marijuana vary not only among different individuals but also with a given individual over time. The wide variety of responses to marijuana seems to be more closely related to personality differences and the cultural setting in which it is used than to any specific property of the drug itself.[36] The effects of the drug also vary as one learns to smoke in the most effective manner and then becomes sensitized. In most individuals these effects are pleasurable at low dosage levels and unpleasant at higher dosage levels.[37]

More specifically the effects of marijuana include a euphoric state accompanied by motor excitation and mental confusion. These reactions are frequently followed by a period of dreaminess, depression, and sleep. The only notable physical changes brought about by marijuana are slight increases in the heart rate and the dilatation of the blood vessels in the conjunctivas, which results in the common "red eyes" of the marijuana smoker. This is probably the most efficient way of detecting whether someone is stoned.[38] Marijuana has usually been found to inhibit the expression of aggressive impulses by pacifying the user, "interfering with muscular coordination, reducing psychomotor activities and generally producing states of drowsiness, lethargy, timidity and passivity. Only a very few marijuana users have been arrested and convicted for such violent crimes as murder, forcible rape, aggravated assault or armed robbery."[39]

Snyder says that an impression emerging from recent research is that marijuana is a mild intoxicant. He points out that moderate users, when high, have rich fantasies and enhanced perceptions but are still in general control of their thoughts and actions and are able to behave quite normally if the need arises. "Hallucinations and psychotic reactions can occur with preparations of cannabis more potent than marijuana, but only rarely with marijuana itself."[40]

---

[34] Ibid., pp. 38–39.

[35] Neehama Tec, "Family and Differential Involvement with Marijuana: A Study of Suburban Teenagers," *Journal of Marriage and the Family*, November 1970, p. 663.

[36] Donald D. Pet and John C. Ball, "Marijuana Smoking in the United States," *Federal Probation*, September 1968, p. 82.

[37] Ibid., p. 40.

[38] Snyder, *Marijuana*, p. 58.

[39] Nowlis, *Drugs on Campus*, p. 96.

[40] Snyder, *Marijuana*, p. 71.

Intellectually the use of marijuana tends to increase imagination but reduce concentration. For example, intelligence test scores are slightly lower or unchanged, "and if attention is held, say in a game of poker, an expert player can more than hold his own against other good players. Jazz musicians claim that they can play more excitingly under the influence than without; in simple—but musically sterile—laboratory tests of note identification and beat duration, their performance is worse on the drug."[41] What often happens is that the person "thinks" he is better at performing tasks than he is by any objective criterion. This is a result of the psychological lift and optimistic interpretation marijuana generally induces in the user. It should also be pointed out that there is no conclusive evidence that marijuana is responsible for academic failure. "Many studies reported that the majority of young people who have used marijuana received average or above-average grades in school."[42]

Snyder suggests that marijuana may facilitate the kinds of problem solving that are most dependent on intuition and that it hinders the performance of tasks that require cool, analytical thinking. "On the other hand, it is possible that marijuana impairs all kinds of thinking without exceptions and that the drug user is merely deluded in the grandiose conviction that he is doing better than ever, much as a drunk may feel he is driving in Grand Prix style."[43]

It appears that a person who is accustomed to the effects of marijuana can compensate for any impairment of mental and physical functioning. This view is supported by the testimony of smokers who say that a marijuana high is much more manageable than alcohol intoxication. In driving tests it has been found that in terms of total scores subjects performed no worse when they were stoned on marijuana than when they were sober. "They did show somewhat more speedometer errors when under the influence of marijuana. In contrast, after consuming the equivalent of about 6 ounces of 86-proof whiskey, there was a marked impairment in all measures of the driving simulator test."[44]

Many people will argue that sexual experiences while under the influence of marijuana are more erotic and exciting. It may be that the loss of inhibitions induced by marijuana makes them feel that such is the case. It is not known whether marijuana actually makes for a physiological heightening of sexual response or whether this impression may be explained on psychological grounds.

The writer, in his study of 2,372 married women, found that of those women who had had sexual experiences while under the influence of

[41] Laurie, *Drugs*, p. 85.
[42] *Marihuana*, p. 123.
[43] Snyder, *Marijuana*, p. 51.
[44] Ibid., p. 63.

marijuana 72 percent said that it contributed to good sexual experiences, 14 percent said that it sometimes did, 10 percent couldn't say, and 4 percent said that it made no contribution.[45] In a study by Goode it was found that both men and women who had used drugs were significantly more likely to have had intercourse more often and with a greater variety of partners than those who had not used drugs.[46] Sex and marijuana are linked in another way. They often go together as parts of a life-style. For example, both variables are linked to more radical life-styles. In the writer's study only 7 percent of these women who defined themselves as conservative had had any sexual experiences while under the influence of marijuana. But this was true of 26 percent of those who defined themselves as liberals and of 62 percent of those who said they were politically radical.[47]

There has often been confusion over the "expert's" views about marijuana. Generally, reliable authorities have publicly taken opposite views regarding it, not only on moral and social policy grounds, but also on the basis of the supposedly "hard" scientific facts. This confusion is reflected in the fact that of several thousand publications on marijuana being published only a few actually meet the standards of scientific investigation. "They are often ill-documented and ambiguous, emotion-laden and incredibly biased, and can, in general, be relied upon for very little valid information."[48]

In a recent study 302 selected professionals who were involved in research of some kind with psychedelic drugs were asked to assess the danger to the user's mental health from marijuana. Six percent said "very much," 22 percent "somewhat," 33 percent "only in rare cases," 21 percent "none," and 17 percent "insufficient evidence." Fifty-nine percent of the researchers felt that marijuana should be at least as available as alcohol. Fifty-seven percent regarded marijuana as less likely to cause genetic damage than such commonly used drugs as caffeine and tranquilizers.[49] In general these experts saw the risk level of marijuana as not very great.

There is no evidence that marijuana is a drug of addiction. There is also no evidence that marijuana has a direct causal relationship with criminal behavior in the sense that it leads the user to commit criminal acts. Most authorities have dismissed the lurid charges that have been a part of the traditional "marijuana menace." The current medical thinking is that "tolerance and physical dependence do not develop and

---

[45] Robert R. Bell, unpublished.

[46] Erich Goode, "Drug Use and Sexual Activity on a College Campus," *American Journal of Psychiatry*, April 1972, p. 95

[47] Bell, unpublished.

[48] *Non-Medical Use of Drugs, Interim Report of the Canadian Government's Commision of Inquiry* (Middlesex, England: Penguin Books, 1971) pp. 109–10.

[49] Walter H. Clark and G. Ray Funkhauser, "Physicians and Researchers Disagree on Psychedelic Drugs," *Psychology Today*, April 1970, p. 50.

withdrawal does not produce any abstinence syndrome."[50] Although the use of marijuana is not seen as a cause of crime it is often associated with illegal acts. "First, many persons who are otherwise delinquent or criminal may also smoke marijuana. Second, marijuana use is often pursued in a hedonistic peer-group setting in which laws are violated. Third, use of more dangerous drugs is frequently preceded by the use of marijuana."[51] The link between the use of marijuana and that of hard drugs can be overdone. It is obviously true that many drug addicts started out on marijuana, but many of them also started out on cigarettes and alcohol.

The failure to link in a causal way the use of marijuana with drugs of addiction is a fact that many young persons are fully aware of. The attempt by authorities to present a causal link where none exists makes them suspicious and skeptical of statements that are true. For example, when the Federal Bureau of Narcotics writes "that it cannot be too strongly emphasized that the smoking of marijuana is a dangerous first step on the road which usually leads to enslavement by heroin" many persons know that scientific knowledge does not support this kind of assertion and they often become distrustful.

There have been many statements attempting to link marijuana use to various kinds of anti-social behavior. But by itself marijuana does not lead to acts of violence, juvenile delinquency, or aggressive behavior. Nor is there any conclusive evidence that physical damage or disturbances of bodily processes are due to high uses of marijuana. "However, there is very little evidence as to the long term effects of heavy use of marijuana on the body. Although it appears that the long term consumption in moderate doses has no harmful effects."[52]

Up until very recently the sale of marijuana was a felony under federal law, and the penalty for possessing the drug was 2 to 10 years' imprisonment for the first offense. For the sale or transfer of the drug a first offense could bring a 5-to 20-year sentence and a fine of up to $20,000. However, a great amount of pressure emerged in the late 1960s to ease the severity of the punishments. Beginning in 1966 the proportion of defendants ultimately convicted declined gradually, as did the percentage of defendants who were incarcerated and the average length of their sentences. "This response reflected an attempt to mitigate the harshness of the law as applied to this new user population."[53]

The former laws were changed, and possession of marijuana was reduced to a misdemeanor. Special treatment was set up for first offenders, and their records could be wiped clean after satisfactory completion of a probationary period. After a series of hearings Congress

---

[50] Dan Wakefield, *The Addict* (New York: Gold Medal Books, 1963), p. 18.

[51] Pet and Ball, "Marijuana Smoking."

[52] *Non-Medical Use*, p. 115.

[53] *Marihuana*, p. 133.

passed the Comprehensive Drug Abuse Prevention and Control Act, and in October 1970 the president signed it into law.[54] Many of the states also eased their laws. It has been suggested that also important to the 1969–70 official response was a recognition of uncertainty. "No longer perceived as a major threat to public safety, marijuana use had now become primarily an issue of private and public health."[55]

In general the views of society have remained hostile toward the use of marijuana. One writer has observed that much of the hostility comes from people who have never examined the facts. He suspects that "what makes them dislike cannabis is not the belief that the effects of taking it are harmful but rather a horrifying suspicion that there is a source of pure pleasure which is available, for those who have not *earned* it, who do not deserve it."[56] This would help to account for some of the hostility of some older people who consider marijuana to be a part of a hedonistic society they deplore. Some people see the use of marijuana as a result of a manipulative society's control over the young. They believe that an evil, criminal influence is at work to get the young to use marijuana. This fits a theory of society which holds that there are the corrupted and the corrupters. These people see healthy youngsters being corrupted by a few psychologically disturbed and economically motivated individuals.[57]

Undoubtedly the greatest resistance to marijuana use comes from the older members of society. The attitude to marijuana is a value area in which the amount of generational conflict is very great. In part this is reflected in the fact that very few people past age 50 have ever used marijuana. One study reported that only 9 percent of the over-50 generation agreed with the statement that "most people who use marijuana lead a normal life." By contrast half the young adults (18 to 25) considered most marijuana users to be normal.[58] Another study asked parents what they would do if they found that their teenage children were smoking marijuana. Forty-seven percent said that they would try to stop them through persuasion and reason, 23 percent said that they favored a punitive approach. "Interestingly, 9 percent of the latter group felt so strongly about the matter that they were willing to report their own child to the police. A considerable number, 35 percent, indicated they were uncertain about what to do."[59]

Another study reported that about one fourth of the American public

[54] Ibid., p. 135.

[55] Ibid., p. 52.

[56] Alastair MacIntyre, "The Cannabis Taboo," *New Society*, December 1968, p. 848.

[57] Jock Young, "The Role of Police as Amplifiers of Deviancy, Negotiators of Reality and Translators of Fantasy," in Stanley Cohen, *Images of Deviance* (Middlesex, Eng.: Penguin Books, 1971), p. 43.

[58] *Marihuana*, pp. 116–17.

[59] Ibid., p. 147.

was convinced that criminal sanctions should be withdrawn entirely from marijuana use. Another fourth was fully convinced that existing social and legal policy was appropriate, and would ordinarily jail possessors, with the exception of young first offenders. About half of the public was confused about what marijuana meant and unsure about what society ought to do about its use. "This half of the population is unenthusiastic about classifying the marijuana user as a criminal, but is reluctant to relinquish formal control over him."[60]

A good summary statement on society's view of marijuana was provided by the National Commission on Marihuana and Drug Abuse. The commission believed that three interrelated factors had led to the definition of marijuana as a major national problem. First, the illegal behavior associated with its use was highly visible to all segments of society. Second, the use of the drug was seen as a threat not only to the health and morality of the individual but of the society itself. Third, "and most important, the drug has evolved in the late sixties and early seventies as a symbol of wider social conflicts and public issues."[61]

LSD (lysergic acid diethylamide)

LSD is an odorless, colorless, and tasteless drug that is taken in very small amounts. It is a powerful man-made chemical that was first developed in 1938 from one of the ergot alkaloids. Ergot is a fungus that grows as a rust on rye. LSD is so powerful that one ounce is enough to provide 300,000 average doses. It is legally classified as a hallucinogen. The story of LSD in the United States begins in 1949 with the first shipment to a Boston psychiatrist for the possible treatment of mental illness. At first there were no legal controls on LSD, but in 1963 the American Medical Association asked for an editorial on LSD from Harvard University campus physician Dana L. Farnsworth. He wrote, in effect, that he thought that legal restrictions should be imposed on LSD.[62]

There is a belief that LSD is cheap and easy to produce, but such is not the case. It takes the investment of a lot of time and several thousand dollars to produce even poor-grade LSD. Obtaining the lysergic acid is also a problem. As a result, while "LSD is not scarce, it requires considerable skill to make it, considerable financing to set up the lab, and fairly good contacts to get the raw ingredients."[63]

LSD is important because it is the most powerful mind-affecting substance known. However, the observable effects are slight, and it is

---

[60] Ibid., p. 129.

[61] Ibid., pp. 6–7.

[62] Young and Hixson, *LSD*, p. 17.

[63] James T. Carey, *The College Drug Scene* (Englewood Cliffs, N.J.: Prentice-Hall, 1968), p. 39.

often not easy to tell that a person is on LSD. The most noticeable effects are usually goose pimples and enlarged irises. Of all the effects, the perceptual changes are probably the most dramatic. Of the senses, vision seems to be the most affected. Objects and patterns appear to come alive and shift or become wavy; colors may seem very vivid, intense, and beautiful. White light may seem much brighter with numerous colors surrounding it. Also smell, taste, hearing, and touch may seem more acute. Even the experience of hearing music may seem more intense than ever before. Walls appear to move; unusual patterns unfold; and flat objects become three-dimensional. In some instances one sensory impression may pass over into another, and sounds appear as colors, or colors appear to have a taste. However, true hallucinations are relatively rare.[64]

The subjective effects of LSD are what make the use of the drug so attractive to most users. It is therefore useful to list some of the main subjective effects. First, as suggested, sense perceptions are stronger. Second, the mechanism that relates one sense impression to another is altered so that a person touching himself may find it difficult to be sure that it is *his* hand touching *his* leg. Third, the relationship between current and past sense impressions is eliminated so that one sees things as if for the first time. Fourth, muscular coordination and pain perception are often reduced. Fifth, learned patterns of behavior, logical thinking, and role playing that allow persons to function as social beings may dissolve. Sixth, emotional repressions are altered, and users often behave more fundamentally. For example, LSD users often become more sensitive to each other's personalities.[65] Yet, with all the descriptions of LSD "trips" it must be recognized that many never "see" what others do. An LSD "trip" may be described as "the greatest experience of my creative life" or as "a living hell I'll never forget," as "restoring my vision of the infinite" or as "a shattering nightmare."[66]

What are the dangers of LSD? Recently 302 professionals involved in some kind of research with LSD were asked whether they believed there was a danger to the mental health of those taking it. Forty percent answered "very much," 32 percent "somewhat," and 20 percent "only in rare cases." This indicates that most experts define LSD as at least potentially dangerous. However, 59 percent of the researchers said that the danger of LSD type drugs to chromosomes had been exaggerated.[67]

A great deal of publicity has centered on the possibility that LSD may effect hereditary transmission through alterations of the chromosomes. Some have argued that LSD will produce changes in the white blood cells that resemble leukemia and that it will adversely affect the development

---

[64] Nowlis, *Drugs on Campus*, p. 104.
[65] Laurie, *Drugs*, pp. 99–100.
[66] Young and Hixson, *LSD*, p. 31.
[67] Clark and Funkhauser, *Psychedelic Drugs*, p. 50.

of the human fetus. However, the various studies have been contradictory and provide no clear answers. "In the few controlled studies in which chromosomes were examined in humans before and after clinically supervised administration of known doses of pure LSD; little evidence of significant change was noted."[68]

There is no evidence that physical dependence on LSD develops even in cases where the drug has been used more than two hundred times in a single year. In some instances psychological dependence has been reported for individuals who became preoccupied with the drug experience and felt emotionally depressed and dissatisfied without it. "Normally, however, LSD use is intermittent and periods of weeks or months may separate 'trips' in even 'confirmed' users."[69]

There are five rough categories of danger when LSD is used without close medical supervision. First, there may be panic reactions as the user feels that he cannot stop the drug's action and that he is losing his mind. The panic reaction usually subsides after 8 to 12 hours. Second, there may be a feeling of paranoia where the user becomes increasingly suspicious and feels that someone is trying to harm him or control his thinking. This feeling often lasts for about three days after the drug has worn off. Third, for days, weeks, and even months after the person has stopped taking LSD there may be momentary recurrences of LSD-type perceptual phenomena. Fourth, there are accidental deaths. For example, the user may feel that he can fly, and may then jump off a high building to his death. Such occurrences are uncommon, and this incidence may range from 1 in 1,000 "trips" to 1 in 10,000 trips.[70] How many deaths there are from LSD use is unknown because there is no way to distinguish conscious suicides from deaths that occurred because the person really thought he could fly. A fifth danger of LSD is psychosis following its use. However, with all the dangers, LSD is not a drug of addiction.

At the present time there is no widely accepted medical use for LSD. However, it has been employed experimentally for therapeutic purposes. There have been a number of reports of LSD successes in the treatment of alcoholics, opiate narcotic dependents, criminals, and psychiatric patients. LSD has also been used to alleviate the anxiety and pain of patients dying from cancer, and to help them adjust to the prospect of death. However, most of these leads have not been followed up with any scientific investigations. Some recent controlled studies have not substantiated the claim that LSD adds to the effectiveness of conventional psychotherapy.[71]

The present legal controls over LSD in the United States are very strong. In 1965 a federal law gave federal narcotics agents increased

---

[68] *Non-Medical Use*, p. 104.

[69] Ibid., p. 106.

[70] Fort, "Drug Use," p. 24.

[71] *Non-Medical Use*, p. 93.

power to seek out and arrest pushers of LSD and other hallucinogenic drugs. There are also stronger penalties, including longer jail sentences and heavier fines, for those caught distributing hallucinogenic drugs. In 1968 even stricter federal laws were passed. By 1968 about half of the states had enacted legislation against the possession of LSD. The penalties for a conviction under federal law are a fine of $1,000 to $10,000 and/or imprisonment for up to 5 years. For persons over 18 years of age who sell or give drugs to anyone under 21, the law provides penalties of 10 to 15 years in jail and fine of up to $20,000. Merely the illegal possession of LSD can bring a fine of from $1,000 to $10,000 and/or 1 to 3 years in prison. And some of the state laws are even more severe.

Drugs of addiction

Drugs of addiction are also called opiates. These are drugs with pain-killing and euphoria-producing properties and include chemicals which are derived from or are the equivalent of opium. The best known are morphine and heroin. The term *narcotics* is also often used to describe the opiates. Addiction implies a physical dependence that is far more than just habit or some vague emotional craving. The morphine or heroin addict's organism depends on a regular supply of the opiate just as a normal organism depends on a regular supply of important vitamins. In this section our interest is limited to heroin and morphine. Heroin, the most common drug of addiction, is classified as a depressant. It can be purchased in the United States only in illegal markets. Therefore, people who become addicted to heroin are engaged from the first shot in what they know to be an illegal activity. The second most common drug of addiction is morphine, which is similar in its effects to heroin. But many people who become addicted to morphine develop their addiction unknowingly, often through its medical use as a pain killer. In fact a number of physicians become addicted to morphine, a drug they have access to. Often the morphine addict with no legitimate sources from which to get the drug may get pushed into the illegal drug market to meet his addiction.[72]

Morphine and heroin are depressants, and this is contrary to the misconception that addicts are dangerously "hopped up." Actually these drugs produce a general lowering of the level of nervous and other bodily activity.[73] Also, no known organic diseases are associated with chronic opiate addiction, though these are often found with alcohol addiction, cigarette smoking, and even chronic overeating. "Although opiate use does produce such effects as pupillary constriction, constipation, and sexual impotence, none of these conditions need be fully disabling, nor

[72] Wakefield, *Addict*, pp. 16–17
[73] Schur, *Crimes without Victims*, p. 120.

are they permanent.[74] The great danger with drugs of addiction does not lie in what they do to the organism but rather in their consequences for the person. The extreme physical and psychological need for such drugs means that the addict will usually do almost anything to meet his needs, and this is often what is most harmful.

There have been recent changes in the patterns of heroin use. Before 1970 it was rare for anyone to use heroin more than five or six times without becoming addicted. But in the 1970s heroin became more and more a drug in a pattern of multiple drug use, especially among young drug users. It is still rare for someone to use heroin occasionally without becoming addicted if he uses no other drugs, but the terms *heroin addict* and *heroin user* are no longer synonymous. "It may be that mixing other drugs, especially barbiturates, with heroin during the initial stages of heroin use makes the road to addiction slower, but no less sure."[75]

The "causes" of drug use

In this section our interest is in the "causes" of drug addiction. By this is meant not only why persons become drug addicts but also how addiction takes place. Our first interest is in the process of drug addiction. There is a great difference between using something that is addictive and using something that becomes habit forming. A habit is primarily mental and emotional—the smoker's desire for a cigarette, the drinker's desire for a cocktail. However, addiction is as physical, as urgent, and as implacable as a person's need for water. One study of young addicts suggested that three conditions were necessary for them to emerge as addicts: first, a psychological and predisposing inadequacy; second, a crisis that occurred in their lives; and third, a timely offer of drugs.[76] Of course, those same conditions might have led the young person to get drunk for the first time, but what appears to be crucial is a state of readiness and the availability of the drug. When one first takes drugs there may be some positive feelings in one's reactions to the drugs, but this seems to last only during the early stages of addiction. "In the later stages, a reversal of affects occurs, in which the drug is no longer taken primarily to obtain positive pleasure but rather to avoid the negative effects of withdrawal."[77]

As suggested, some persons who get started on morphine unknowingly, may wind up as addicts against their wills. But other persons do make conscious moves toward addiction. It takes deliberate acts to become addicted to heroin, and a first step may be taken because of a feeling of

---

[74] Ibid., p. 121.

[75] James V. Delong, "The Methadone Habit," *New York Times Magazine*, March 16, 1975, p. 92.

[76] Laurie, *Drugs*, pp. 38–39.

[77] Schur, *Crimes without Victims*, p. 122.

uselessness and despair. But the addict must see some positive hope through his involvement in drugs; "to him, if to no one else, they offer some improvement to his present condition."[78] It would seem that few nonaddicts could ever anticipate what it means to become an addict. For most who try narcotics there is undoubtedly an exaggerated expectation of what they will gain and an unrealistic anticipation of what the costs will be. It is often only when it is too late that an accurate understanding develops.

The most difficult question is why people consciously turn to the drugs of addiction, especially in light of all the negative publicity about those drugs. The availability of drugs does not seem to be an important factor in drug addiction. Almost all studies show that people who become drug addicts do so because of personality factors rather than the availability of the drugs. That is, drug addiction is a symptom of some need rather than a disease. Some persons see the use of drugs as a means of finding their sense of identity. A part of personality training may derive from socialization experiences to the use of drugs. One study pointed out that users of drugs of addiction, in contrast to nonusers, had been ill more often as children, had been taken more often to a physician, and had been given more medications.[79]

There is no single cause for addiction, as there is no single type of addict. For example, the physician who becomes an addict is very different from the lower-class black who is a part of a delinquent and addict subculture. "However, individuals in certain socioeconomic categories run a relatively greater risk of encountering and using narcotics than do those in other categories. Also, it seems likely that of those individuals in the high-risk categories it is the more troubled or the more disadvantaged, situationally, who are especially likely to take up drugs."[80] Addiction is not distributed around the United States in a random fashion. Broadly it exists where there are social and economic squalor and the opportunity to get drugs. There is a "southern pattern" which is a survival from the early part of the century. This is found in Alabama, Georgia, and Kentucky where the addicts are about 90 percent white, middle-aged, and using old morphine mixtures. By contrast the modern pattern is to use imported heroin, and this pattern is found in New York, Puerto Rico, the District of Columbia, and Chicago. There two thirds of the addicts are black or Puerto Rican, and the average age of addicts is about 27. There is also a narrower belt of heroin users along the Mexican border in Arizona, New Mexico, and Texas.[81] Almost all of these groups have to resort to illegal ways of getting money to support their drug habit.

---

[78] Laurie, *Drugs*, p. 46.
[79] Nowlis, *Drugs on Campus*, p. 24.
[80] Schur, *Crimes without Victims*, pp. 128–129.
[81] Laurie, *Drugs*, p. 30.

Sociologically the studies clearly show a relationship between poverty and drug addiction. Addiction comes in settings where many other social problems also exist. The slum areas in which addiction develops are also characterized by high rates of delinquency, dropping out of school, truancy, unemployment, family disintegration, poverty, and so forth. However, most drug addicts are adults, not adolescents.

Drug addiction "cures"

The great concern with drug addiction as a social and psychological problem has resulted in many attempts to find solutions. At the same time there is often indifference or even hostility to the drug addict. Most Americans probably believe that the drug addict could cure himself if he would only put his mind to it. They believe that for some reason—being lazy, or sinful, or irresponsible—he will not take the responsibility of curing himself. But persons who work with drug addicts know that addiction is very powerful and that severe methods are often needed if the addict is ever to be cured. When a person stops taking drugs his most difficult problem—the problem of staying off drugs—is usually just starting.

This problem has been well documented in Ray's study of the drug abstainer caught between continued abstinence and a relapse into drug use. Stopping addiction often means major life-style changes. So, often in the early phases of an episode of cure the drug abstainer may show considerable ambivalence about where he stands in the addict and non-addict social situation.[82] The tendency to relapse occurs if he develops an image of himself as socially different from nonaddicts, and actual relapse occurs when he redefines himself as an addict. "It is at this point, when the old values and old meanings he experienced as an addict are still immediate and the new ordering of his experience without narcotics not well established, that the ex-addict seems most vulnerable to relapse."[83]

One problem for the ex-addict is to adjust to his new role of how others view him. This is because the addict has established an image of himself in the eyes of others who knew him as an addict—members of his family, social workers, law enforcement officers, physicians, and so forth. Through their gestures the nonaddicts indicate their doubts about the addict's right to participate in their worlds. And the former addict is highly sensitive to the nonaddicts' cues. The nonaddicts have their expectations about the abstainer's future conduct. In general they exhibit skepticism concerning his "cure" and his future success. Often when the abstainer becomes an addict again he has redefined himself as an addict and consequently has taken the actions necessary for relapse. "But it

---

[82] Marsh Ray, "Abstinence Cycles and Heroin Addicts," in Earl Rubington and Martin S. Weinberg, *Deviance: The Interactionist Perspective* (New York: Macmillan, 1968), p. 402.

[83] Ibid., p. 403.

should be noted that the seeds of a new attempt at abstinence are sown, once addiction has been reestablished, in the self-recrimination engaged in upon rememberance of a successful period of abstinence."[84] Ray's study suggests that whatever the approach to a cure many addicts have the expectation of failure.

Synanon

Synanon's approach has received a great deal of publicity through the mass media although it has only been tried on a small number of drug addicts. But as will be seen the methods are dramatic and therefore prone to evoke interested response and some sensationalism. Synanon had its origins in Alcoholics Anonymous, in that its founder was a member of AA and was an ex-alcoholic (but not an ex-drug addict). Not long after its start the organization left Alcoholics Anonymous and became fully involved with drug addicts, and Synanon was founded in May 1958. One writer points out that it is ironic that the dominant person in Synanon was never a drug addict, which contradicts the Alcoholics Anonymous type of slogan, "Only an addict can help an addict."[85]

Admission into a Synanon house appears to have two principal functions. First, the newcomer is forced to admit, at least on the verbal level, that he is willing to try to conform to the norms of the group he is entering. He knows that the members will tolerate no liking for drugs or drug addicts. From the moment he enters the house he is tested as to his willingness to conform to *all* the demands made on him by the members of Synanon. For example, he has to have his hair cut off, give up all of his money, and sever all family ties. Second, the admission process seems to weed out those who simply want to rest for a few days, to get a free place to stay, or to keep out of the hands of the police. So the new person is expected to want to completely stop his drug addiction. "This means that he must *say* that he wants to quit using drugs once and for all, in order to realize his potentials as an adult; he must not indicate that he merely wants a convenient place in which to go through withdrawal distress so that he can be rid of his habit for a short time because he has lost his connection, or for some other reason."[86]

The most difficult requirement for the addict entering Synanon is that he must withdraw "cold turkey"—simply stop using drugs without any medical help. If he is able to stop he must live in the community for a minimum of two years. The main feature of the actual treatment is the

---

[84] Ibid., p. 407

[85] Edward Sagarin, *Odd Man In: Societies of Deviants in America* (Chicago: Quadrangle, 1969), p. 143.

[86] Rita Volkman and Donald R. Cressey, "Differential Association and the Rehabilitation of Drug Addicts," in Rubington and Weinberg, *Deviance*, p. 411.

seminars, where the members meet in small groups several times a week and subject each other to extreme criticism, abuse, and ridicule. The members of each seminar are rotated so that all members of the community come under fire from one another. What this means is that Synanon is like "a mental institution, a prison, or a nineteenth century American utopian community in that one's entire life is lived within its walls. Like monks and nuns, the members give themselves over to the place, but the keys to the doors are always in their hands."[87]

What is nearly unique to the Synanon approach is that the addict is treated almost as a nonhuman and is made to feel completely worthless. This technique is the opposite of the therapy approach in which the subject is told that the basis of his problem is his lack of feeling as to his own self-worth. In that kind of approach, the most common one, the subject is made to believe that he is a worthwhile person and that his problem comes primarily from the fact that he has failed to realize that. But at Synanon just the opposite occurs as the addict's self-contempt and self-hate are developed.[88] The lowness of his worth is drummed into him from the very beginning. The newcomer starts by cleaning out toilets and works his way up to doing the dishes. And at every point those above him are constantly demeaning him to insure his continued humility and abasement.

Synanon has a clearly stated program for distributing status symbols to members in return for their conformity to the values of the community. The Synanon experience is organized into a career of roles that represent stages of graded competence. And at the peak are those roles that might later be used in the broader society. Because the member does not have the status of "inmate" or "patient," as in a prison or hospital, he can achieve any position in the status hierarchy. But no member can go up the status ladder unless his "attitude" is correct, no matter what degrees of skill he might have.[89] So any success must be achieved within the context of total conformity to the values of the Synanon program, and individual initiative is of negative value.

The Synanon program usually evokes strong support or severe criticism. It has been argued that Synanon reaches only a small number of addicts and doesn't work for many of those. But the leaders of Synanon do not claim to "cure" drug addicts. The contribution that this program makes is that it helps some to stay away from drugs. The statistics on dropouts suggest that the group relations method does not begin to have effect until newcomers are fully integrated into the antidrug, anticrime value system that is Synanon. This means that great time and expense are needed to help those few who are able to stay on and be aided.

---

[87] Sagarin, *Odd Man In*, pp. 143–44.

[88] Ibid., p. 148.

[89] Volkman and Cressey, "Drug Addiction," p. 416.

It has also been argued that in reality the members have substituted a dependence on Synanon for their dependence on drugs. Therefore, it has been suggested that Synanon should be seen as a protective community rather than as a truly therapeutic community aimed at the eventual reintegration of the patient with the outside world.[90] A more critical view has been taken by Sagarin. He suggests that because Synanon is so hostile to the outside world the members develop no real will to get out. Therefore, it may be that Synanon has modified the Alcoholics Anonymous type statement "once an addict always an addict" to "once an addict to narcotics, always an addict to Synanon." It is a convenient modification, one similar to AA's statement that "alcoholism cannot be cured, and one which performs the same function; to keep the individuals tied to the organization, thus preserving its present state and insuring its further growth."[91]

Methadone

One attempt at curing drug addiction has been the methadone approach. This approach is based on the fact that one drug can sometimes be substituted for another without producing increased addiction. This approach was used a number of years ago with heroin before it was recognized as a drug of addiction. Heroin was then substituted for morphine. Methadone is a synthetic opiate which is less active than heroin. It is given to the drug user in decreasing doses. Most of the work with this approach has been done in New York City where applicants are voluntarily hospitalized for six weeks after being examined by physicians and psychiatrists. They are given methadone after their discharge and are then usually still dependent on methadone but no longer dependent on heroin. There is evidence that the methadone approach produces a much higher rehabilitation rate than any other treatment program.

By early 1973, 70,000 addicts were in methadone programs. The number then rose slowly, leveling off at about 80,000. This figure, according to government estimates, represents a little less than 20 percent of the addict population. "Another 45,000 are in treatment other than with methadone, 85,000 are in jail and 250,000 are on the street."[92]

Methadone is as potent a painkiller as morphine and heroin, and its other effects are also similar. For major purposes all three drugs are interchangeable, and all are highly addictive. Another common characteristic of heroin and methadone is that neither is known to cause organic damage—neither appears to cause cancer, rot the liver, deform

---

[90] Schur, *Crimes without Victims*, p. 149.

[91] Sagarin, *Odd Man In*, p. 158.

[92] Delong, "Methadone Habit," p. 16.

fetuses, or destroy brain cells.[93] One important difference between heroin and methadone is the timing of effect. Heroin peaks and fades away rapidly, and after four to six hours the user wants and needs more. Oral methadone peaks more slowly and lasts longer. "As a general proposition, a dose once every 24 hours is sufficient, and methadone variations are under development to make it effective for three days."[94]

Methadone treatment is seen by many as a means of allowing an addict to live a "normal" life. Because it is longer lasting the addict can take his methadone in the morning and work comfortably all day, unlike the heroin addict who may need several fixes in that time. There is also some evidence that methadone programs relieve many family strains and improve family relationships. "As an interim measure, methadone programs offer immediate social rewards for the married addict living with his family. The gain in this respect may offset any failure to accomplish a complete 'cure' of the addiction."[95] Yet, methadone has no attraction for at least half of the addicts on the streets. In fact there is evidence of a good deal of cheating by addicts on methadone programs. One study reported that 50 percent of the methadone users admitted to using some heroin for special crises or special kicks.[96]

The methadone approach is still highly controversial and has drawn especially strong opposition from law enforcement groups because in most cases it does not resolve the addiction problem but substitutes a legal drug for an illegal one. This is what bothers many law enforcement agencies—because their vested interest is in drug addicts and not in what makes them addicts. Another point of view is that methadone has helped to alleviate the addiction problem by allowing the addict to function without the results of increased addiction, thereby helping him to become a more productive member of society.

In a recent discussion of methadone use it was pointed out that one basic weakness in the methadone position was the limited support by professionals in the drug area. However, despite the many criticisms and restrictions, the Methadone Maintenance Training Program and other methadone programs that are run with care seem to be helpful. Patient retention seems to range from 55 percent to 75 percent; "arrest rates among patients who stay in drop significantly; there are increases in socially productive activity and precipitous declines in illicit drug use."[97]

---

[93] Ibid.

[94] Ibid.

[95] June S. Clark et al., "Marriage and Methadone: Spouse Behavior Patterns in Heroin Addicts Maintained on Methadone," *Journal of Marriage and the Family*, August 1972, p. 501.

[96] Walter R. Cuskey and William Krasner, "American Way of Drugging," *Society*, May 1973, p. 48.

[97] Delong, "Methadone Habit," p. 90.

DRUG SUBCULTURES

In this section our interest is in the various social settings in which persons use drugs. Some drug addicts have little or no contact with drug users or pushers. For example, one study of physician addicts found that they rarely associated with other physician addicts. "They did not have any occasion for doing so, either for the purpose of getting drugs or for passing time or for emotional support. They were solitary about their addiction."[98] However, we will look at several types of drug subcultures. These have some factors in common but are also different in many important ways. The three to be discussed are the addict subculture, marijuana users, and LSD in the college subculture. Members of all three subcultures typically participate in a group setting with persons they know well rather than with strangers. These relationships usually last for some time. There develops some consensus of values and social cohesion with greater and greater group involvement. The participants view their activity as an important basis for their own identity. "They define themselves, as well as others, partly on the basis of whether they have participated in the drug activity or not."[99] These are values common to many of the subcultures discussed in this book. Of course, the strength of the subculture for its members will vary widely, and one would expect it to be much stronger for the addict than for the marijuana user or the LSD group on college campuses. This difference is predicated on the fact that the addict has a much greater personal commitment and need in his use of drugs. Each of the various subcultures has contact with many people who are not a part of it. For example, in all high-drug-use neighborhoods nonusing "squares" live alongside of addicts. And even though drug distribution is closely related to the underworld, delinquent gangs as such are not a major factor in the promotion of addiction.[100]

The addict subculture

It has been pointed out that the subculture of the drug addict has its symbols of status, its mythology, and to some extent its own language. (For example, a "pusher" is one who sells drugs, a "fix" is a drug dose, "horse" is heroin, and so forth.) These help create social solidarity among addict outcasts from the broader society. "The addict acquires skills at the necessary transactions to secure drug supplies, often including the skills of some type of professional criminal activity to provide a source of funds for

---

[98] Charles Winick, "Physician Narcotic Addicts," in Howard S. Becker, *The Other Side* (New York: Free Press, 1964), p. 267.

[99] Erich Goode, "Multiple Drug Use among Marijuana Smokers," *Social Problems*, 1969, p. 54.

[100] Schur, *Crimes without Victims*, p. 144.

purchasing supplies."[101] Important to all subcultures is the development of rationales to explain who they are to themselves and to boost their morale and lessen their feeling of being isolated. Schur suggests that "drug addicts, like homosexuals, benefit psychologically from knowledge of and contact with others who share their plight."[102]

Regardless of the patterns of interaction that develop in the addict's subculture the reason for its existence is simple—getting drugs. The addict's relation to drug sources is the overriding force determining his subcultural membership. "This point is borne out by the experience in Britain, where the availability of drugs eliminates the need for addicts to involve themselves in underworld distribution processes and thus prevents the significant development of an addict subculture."[103] The subculture gives the addict some insurance that he will have contact with several potential sources of narcotics if his usual source of supply is blocked. He must be known by others to be an addict in case he needs to approach them for drugs, or for an introduction to a new source of drugs. It is possible that of all deviant subcultures that of the drug addict may be the most utilitarian.

As indicated, sellers or pushers of drugs are very important to the addict subculture. In one sense they have the ideal product to sell—one where there is always a seller's market with buyer demand based on extreme need and compulsion. The sellers can push their prices to an upper limit because they know the buyers must purchase what they sell. Schur suggests that in the American system of drug traffic there are at least four classes of sellers. There are *importers* who bring the drugs into the country, and these people are rarely themselves drug addicts. There are the professional *wholesalers* of the drugs, and they too are rarely addicts. Then there are the *peddlers*, who may be addicted, and the *pushers*, who sell drugs to get the money for their own drug supplies.[104]

The subculture of the addict is illegal because addicts use drugs that are illegal and also because they usually pursue illegal means of getting money to buy the drugs. However, there is no known drug that by itself can be shown to cause crime.[105] In fact the use of drugs may have a negative consequence with regard to most types of crime. For example, in a statement from a joint committee of the American Medical Association and the American Bar Association it is said that "crimes of violence are rarely, and sexual crimes are almost never, committed by addicts. In most instances the addict's sins are those of omission rather than commission;

---

[101] Clausen, "Drug Addiction," p. 221.

[102] Schur, *Crimes without Victims*, p. 140.

[103] Ibid., pp. 144–45.

[104] Ibid., p. 137.

[105] Blum, *Society and Drugs*, p. 290.

they are ineffective people, individuals whose great desire is to withdraw from the world and its troubles into a land of dreams."[106] As Schur points out, the specific effects of opiates tend to decrease the likelihood of any violent antisocial behavior. Opiates bring about a reduction in sexual desire, and long-term addiction usually results in impotence.[107]

With the exception of a few physician addicts and some others who have the money, addicts in the United States must enter into the subcultural world where the distribution of illegal drugs takes place. The addict is by necessity thrown into contact with drug peddlers and pushers. When crimes are committed by addicts they are usually undertaken to buy illegal drugs. In the United States the amount of money needed is great because the drug cost may run over a hundred dollars a day.

It is probable that most addicts seek out a subculture as soon as they are hooked. Just looking for illegal sources of drugs will usually mean moving into subcultural contacts. There is a belief that pushers look for nonaddicts to hook them and thereby build a market, but this is probably not common. Usually the addict is first introduced to drugs by friends, and after being hooked he needs to find a pusher. One writer points out that to hand out free or cheap drugs randomly and hope to hook customers would be uneconomical as well as dangerous because there would be nothing to stop the recipients from betraying their drug supplier.[108] Both the addict and his drug source have a vested interest in keeping away from the police.

As suggested, the subcultural world of the addict has some social system and some patterns of defined behavior. Of importance to all subcultures is the transmission of information. Addict subcultures pass on information about the police, about what kinds of drugs are available, and about where to get them. Information may be sifted out according to consensus concerning the general reliability of various individuals. "In particular, there is a belief that informers can be spotted so that they can be excluded from the grapevine. In some periods, information can be so valuable that it is paid for by the addicted."[109] The accuracy and reliability of the grapevine as a general source of information is basic to the survival of the members, and they all have a vested interest in its maintenance.

One study notes the highly developed jargon that is found in the addict subculture. Agar says that "two *junkies* who have not previously met and who are of different regions, races, or ages can converse over a wide range of topics in a manner not understandable to an outsider." He goes on to point out that while some terms are specific to addict subcultures

[106] Wakefield, *Addict*, p. 9.

[107] Schur, *Crimes without Victims*, p. 121.

[108] Laurie, *Drugs*, p. 33.

[109] Schur, *Crimes without Victims*, p. 143.

nationwide, others are used by nonaddict cultures, and still others may be special to a regional, racial, or other subgroup. "To give a quick example, junkie is a well-established term. *Jones* on the other hand, is not. In Boston, *jones* is a 'heroin addict'; in Detroit it refers to heroin itself."[110]

Because the addict is a deviant and feels rejected by the broader society he turns more and more to the subculture. At the same time the more deeply involved he becomes with drugs the less likely he is to associate with straight people. So the gradual immersion of drug addicts in their subcultures is interwoven with the general process by which they have been rejected by the broader "respectable" society. The social image of the addict as a criminal influences both his behavior and his self-image. Schur notes that although the physician-addict and the subcultural addict are addicted in exactly the same way, their self-images are generally very different.[111] He also points out that drug addicts get caught up in a self-fulfilling prophecy. The addict is aware that respectable people see him as a criminal, and he begins to see himself acting as one. As a result he must turn increasingly to the drug world for interpersonal support as well as for drug supplies. And as the need to support his habit occupies more and more of his time and energy, and his other worlds recede into the background or fade away completely, addiction becomes a way of life.[112] As the addict becomes more immersed in meeting his drug need he often becomes more careless about his personal appearance and cleanliness. Consequently nonaddicts may come to define him as a bum and, because he continues to use drugs, to conclude than he has no willpower or is even a degenerate. The addict is aware of these definitions, and while he may attempt to reject them that may be hard to do because he in part believes them. "They assume importance because they are the medium of exchange in social transactions with the addict and non-addict world in which the addict identifies himself as an object and judges himself in relation to addict and non-addict values."[113]

Marijuana users

Marijuana subcultures do not have the significance for marijuana users that the addict's subcultures have for addicts, becuase while marijuana is illegal it is not a drug of addiction. Therefore, marijuana users do not have a severe need for the drug. Marijuana is also cheaper and is easier to get legally. Marijuana subcultures develop around the group use of marijuana and group experimentation with it and other drugs.

The first experience with taking marijuana or being "turned on" is

---

[110] Michael Agar, *Ripping and Running: A Formal Ethnology of Urban Heroin Addicts* (New York: Seminar Press, 1973), p. 43.

[111] Schur, *Crimes without Victims*, p. 145.

[112] Ibid.

[113] Ray, "Heroin Addicts," p. 353.

almost always a group experience. Goode's study found that only 3 percent in his sample were alone the first time they tried marijuana. Only 5 percent said that they smoked at least half the time alone, and 45 percent said that they never smoked alone. Marijuana is not just smoked in groups: it is smoked in intimate groups. "The others with whom one is smoking are overwhelmingly *significant* others."[114] Therefore, marijuana may be described as probably the most social of all drugs. The group experience often offers the shy, lonely, socially awkward beginner a means of entrance into the group. Often repetition of the behavior serves to increase overall closeness and commitment to the group.[115]

It is not usual for one to just start smoking marijuana and get high pleasure from it immediately. Rather, an individual will be able to use marijuana for pleasure only when he learns to see it as something that can be used for pleasure. Becker argues that no one becomes a user without first learning to smoke the drug in a way that will produce real effects. One must also learn to recognize the effects and connect them with the drug being used. In other words one must learn to get "high." Furthermore, the person must learn to enjoy the sensations he perceives. In time he develops motivation to use marijuana which he did not have when he first started. And on completion of this process he is willing and able to use marijuana for pleasure.[116]

There is common belief that repeated exposure to marijuana causes an individual to need lesser amounts to achieve the same degree of intoxication. However, this has not been substantiated in an experimental setting.[117] Yet, most people who use marijuana do not become heavy users. Using it once in a while does not inevitably lead to its frequent use. In fact most users either discontinue use altogether or use it infrequently.[118] These people are not really a part of the marijuana subculture, whose members are generally heavy marijuana users. Goode describes the consequences of heavy marijuana use. He points out that it implicates the user in intense and involved social interaction with other heavy users. The user also becomes involved in activities related to marijuana use. But most important, his chances of taking other drugs besides marijuana are increased.[119] The most common other drug experimented with by the marijuana subculture is LSD. Of the 204 marijuana smokers Goode interviewed about half had tried LSD. Those who had tried it usually had had only one or two experiences. For this

---

[114] Goode, "Multiple Drug Use," p. 55.

[115] *Marihuana*, p. 52.

[116] Howard S. Becker, "Becoming a Marijuana User," in Becker, *Outsiders* (Glencoe, Ill.: Free Press, 1963), p. 49.

[117] *Marihuana*, p. 64.

[118] Goode, "Multiple Drug Use," p. 62.

[119] Ibid., pp. 57–58.

group LSD was not a drug of frequent use. The dropoff after the first experience with LSD is probably more precipitous than that for any other drug in use. "There was typically little desire to continue beyond the experimental first few instances."[120] Goode says that experimentation with LSD is a mutual component, with heavy marijuana use, of many drug-using subcultures. In the group there is a certain degree of prestige in having tried a wide range and a large number of drugs.[121] Overall, two thirds of Goode's respondents (young, white, urban, and high education) had taken at least one drug other than marijuana or hashish on at least one occasion. However, heroin had been tried by only 13 percent of the sample, and within that group extremely limited use was more common than repeated use.[122]

Most people who stop using marijuana do so because of a loss of interest. Often the effect has lost its novelty and may have even become boring. Less common reasons for stopping are "fear of legal hazards, social pressure and concerns over physical and mental drug effects." By comparison those who continue to use marijuana often turn away from the more traditional adult-oriented reward systems and intensify their peer group identification. "The meaning of marijuana use by this peer group emphasizes the ideological character of usage. In contrast to the infrequent type of user, these individuals seem to build their self-identity around the marijuana-using peer group."[123]

There has been some evidence that the marijuana-users' subculture overlaps with other subcultures. For example, there has long been an overlap between being a jazz musician and using marijuana. In the early days of jazz, around the beginning of the present century in New Orleans, the stimulant most widely used was alcohol. It has been suggested that the aggressive and loud behavior to which alcohol traditionally leads is reflected in the aggressive and loud Dixieland jazz. But in the 1930s the stimulant most frequently used began to be marijuana. During that period jazz was increasingly rejected by the broader society, and as a result many musicians grew more alienated. Winick points out that after World War II the use of heroin became more and more common. Its effect is to make the user detached and "cool," which is also a description of much of the jazz of the post–World War II period.[124] It seems clear that drugs have been a part of the experimental music subcultures and continue to be today.

There are also studies which suggest that drug use may be a part of

---

[120] Ibid., p. 52.

[121] Ibid., p. 60.

[122] Ibid., p. 54.

[123] *Marihuana*, pp. 53–54.

[124] Charles Winick, "The Use of Drugs by Jazz Musicians," in William A Rushing, *Deviant Behavior and Social Process* (Chicago: Rand McNally, 1969), p. 336.

delinquent subculture patterns. Various studies have indicated that a close relationship exists between drug use and participation in delinquent gangs in the types of neighborhoods in which both would be found and the kind of group context in which both often occur. This is not to say that gangs and drug use are inevitably related. Many boys who become users of "hard" drugs are less involved in the gang and its activities than are other members.[125] This distinction makes sense when it is kept in mind that taking marijuana is usually a group activity, while hard drugs are more often used individually and in private.

We conclude by pointing out that the use of drugs is becoming more and more common but that they are used in a continued setting of conflict. Certainly the idea of mystical experiences that result from drug use is not readily acceptable in the United States. A part of the Western cultural belief is that man is a self-determining force who attempts to control his world by the power of conscious effort and will. Within this framework nothing could be more foreign than the belief in spiritual or psychological growth through the use of drugs. A drugged person is by definition "dimmed in consciousness, fogged in judgement, and deprived of will."[126] In fact the basic belief that drugs might be used to enhance one's experience is so contrary to our dominant values that if a new drug came along that delivered all the mystical experiences with no ill effects it would be rejected. Such may already be the case with marijuana, which is probably the softest drug, yet is the most savagely attacked of the psychedelics.[127]

This general view that America sees the results of drugs negatively is important, because anything that provides ecstasy, visions, or even happiness and contentment without regard to one's material position poses a real social threat. On economic grounds alone it may be intolerable to many that anyone should receive those satisfactions without having earned them as a reward from society. "If anyone, after an injection or a pill costing a few pennies, were able to sit back and let the world go hang, where would we all be?"[128] This also helps to explain why many believe that all drugs *must* be dangerous and that what they do to the individual is not pleasant but painful.

But what may be most important in drug use in the United States in the future is the generational conflict. The older generation usually lumps all drugs together as equally harmful and undesirable. The younger generation often knows that some drugs are dangerous and others

---

[125] James F. Short, *Gang Delinquency and Delinquent Subcultures* (New York: Harper and Row, 1968), p. 108.

[126] Alan Watts, "Psychedelic and Religious Experience," *California Law Review*, January 1968, p. 74.

[127] Weakland, "Hippies," pp. 360–61.

[128] Laurie, *Drugs*, p. 46.

relatively harmless. Younger people are also not too influenced by an older generation that criticizes some of the drugs they use, especially marijuana, when they know that the older generation is using more dangerous things—barbiturates, tobacco, and alcohol. It would appear that in the years ahead there may be a somewhat more tolerant view of at least marijuana among the younger generation.

BIBLIOGRAPHY

Agar, Michael, *Ripping and Running: A Formal Ethnography of Urban Heroin Addicts*. New York: Seminar Press, 1973.

Bernstein, Arnold, and Henry L. Lennard, "The American Way of Drugging," *Society*, May 1973, pp. 14–25.

Blum, Richard H., *Society and Drugs*. San Francisco: Jossey-Bass, 1969.

Clark, June S., et al., "Marriage and Methadone: Spouse Behavior Patterns of Addicts Maintained on Methadone," *Journal of Marriage and the Family*, August 1972, pp. 496–502.

DeLong, James, "The Methadone Habit," *New York Times Magazine*, March 16, 1975, pp. 16, 78, 80, 86, 90, 92-93.

Fort, Joel, "Social Problems of Drug Use and Drug Policies," *California Law Review*, January 1968, pp. 17–28.

Goode, Erich, *Marijuana*. Chicago: Aldine, 1969.

Laurie, Peter, *Drugs: Medical, Psychological, and Social Facts*. Baltimore: Penguin Books, 1967.

Marijuana: A Signal of Misunderstanding, The Official Report of the National Commission on Marijuana and Drug Abuse. New York: New American Library, 1972.

Non-Medical Use of Drugs; Interim Report of the Canadian Government's Commission of Inquiry. Middlesex, England: Penguin Books, 1971.

Nowlis, Helen H., *Drugs on the College Campus*. New York: Anchor Books, 1969.

Snyder, Solomon H., *Uses of Marijuana*. New York: Oxford University Press, 1971.

Young, Warren, and Joseph Hixson, *LSD on Campus*. New York: Dell, 1966.

chapter eight

Suicide

T he act of taking one's own life is probably the most private and personal of all human events. However, while the act of suicide is a very
private event the processes leading up to it are highly social. The study of
suicide illustrates the fact that human behavior, regardless of its personal
dimension, is related to interaction with other people. Therefore, the
suicide of the individual cannot be understood in isolation from the social
dimension of his background. The unique social nature of human beings
means that only humans can will their own deaths and kill themselves.[1]

In many respects the act of suicide can be seen as the ultimate form of
social deviance. With rare exceptions the belief in maintaining one's life
at all costs has been common to all societies. In the past this was even
explained within the assumed biological context of "instinct"—the
instinct for self-preservation. This instinct implies that all persons would
do everything in their power to resist death. Yet, there have always been
many exceptions. The so-called instinct for self-preservation really reflects
the view of the common yet very strong social norms against ending one's
life. In fact, to commit suicide is to deviate from possibly the most
powerful of all social norms.

There is no more dramatic way to express contempt and rejection for
social norms and values than to renounce membership in the society that
holds them to be so important. In this sense suicide may be more than
simply a means of escaping from the undesired social context; the victim
may also expect others to see the act as a condemnation of the social
environment. As a result, in some social situations suicide may be a means
of undermining authority by clearly showing that certain laws or official
political actions are seen as worse than death. "Hence the suicides of

[1] Erwin Stengel, *Suicide and Attempted Suicide* (Middlesex, England: Pelican Books,
1969), p. 13.

210

Buddhist monks as protests against political regimes in South Vietnam received worldwide attention."[2]

It is highly probably that there have been instances of suicide since the beginning of mankind. There is no period in history without records of suicide. Going back to the early religious traditions of the Western world, neither the Old nor the New Testament explicitly forbids suicide. This changed, and the Christian church in the Middle Ages condemned suicide as a form of murder; St. Augustine denounced it as a crime under all circumstances.[3]

The highly negative views toward suicide have been carried down over the years in Western societies. For example, as recently as 1823 a London suicide was buried at a crossroads in Chelsea with a stake through his body, "and right up to 1961, in England and Wales, survivors of a suicide attempt were liable to criminal prosecution."[4] The United States has generally not taken a harsh view toward suicide. Only in Massachusetts, long before the incorporation of the Bill of Rights into the Constitution was there ever a law prohibiting Christian burial for the suicide. That early statute (1660) required that suicides be buried by a highway and that a wagonload of stones be placed on the grave as a mark of infamy. "The practice became obsolete, and it was finally repealed in 1823 as being out of keeping with the American ideal."[5]

The nature and the rituals of suicide have varied a great deal in different societies. Institutionalized suicides have flourished in nonliterate and non-Western societies. For example, widows of high rank among certain Central Africans and Melanesians were buried alive with their husbands. The Natchez of North America and the Maori of New Zealand strangled widows. Sacrificial suicide existed in some cultures of the past. "Many suicides in Greece and Rome were semi-institutional; others personal. There were honor suicides, misery suicides, suicides of affection, sacrificial or patriotic suicides, and the suicides of exhibitionists. Honor suicides constituted a highly respectable motivation."[6]

In the Western world the attitudes toward suicide have changed greatly over the years. The past attitudes of retaliation and abhorrence have given way to the common belief that anyone who tries to take his own life must be either sick or in great distress, and in need of medical and social assistance.[7] As with most of the areas of deviance discussed in this book, the causal explanations of suicide have moved from sin to mental illness.

---

[2] Jack Gibbs, *Suicide* (New York: Harper and Row, 1968), p. 45.

[3] Stengel, *Suicide*, p. 68.

[4] Ibid., p. 5

[5] Austin L. Porterfield, "The Problem of Suicide," in Gibbs, *Suicide*, p. 53.

[6] Ibid., p. 37.

[7] Stengel, *Suicide*, p. 5.

Meaning of suicide. No one can experience his own death. Death is the end of life, and the individual can only experience the process of dying up to his last conscious moment. Suicide is not the act of death itself, but rather the events that lead to death. This means that there can be confusion as to whether the causes that lead to death do or do not imply suicide. As Porterfield points out, if "one kills himself, we record it as a suicide; if he tortures another person until the other person kills him, we call it homicide; but if he tortures some animal into killing him, we call it an accident. In each case, however, the dead man may have had a suicidal intent."[8]

There are other problems in defining what is meant by suicide. If one starts from the assumption that suicide is essentially a social rather than a naturally defined form of behavior, then its actual definition becomes problematic and will vary over time among societies as well as within societies. Some arbitrary assumptions are made about suicide so as to provide a setting for the discussion that follows. It is assumed that when an individual commits suicide he has ended his life in some conscious and deliberate manner. By "conscious" it is meant that he is aware of what he is doing and by "deliberate," that he performs actions which bring about his death. It is obvious that both consciousness and deliberateness are matters of degree. But it is hard to imagine a suicide in which there is no evidence of these two dimensions.

Not only is the definition of suicide often unclear, but this is also true of legal definitions and legal reactions to it. Gibbs has pointed out that in the United States and in most urbanized countries the normative evaluation of suicide is now uncertain. "It has become legally 'permissive' in that officials no longer take any retaliatory steps (e.g., confiscation of the victim's property), but society is not clearly permissive in the extra-legal sphere. Generally, it appears to be still socially disapproved, or at least viewed as undesirable; but the normative evaluation is neither uniform nor categorical."[9] The belief also often exists that the victim has disgraced himself and his closest family members. While this belief is less prevalent now than in the past it certainly has not disappeared.

Religion has long had a dominant role in defining suicide and in determining society's reaction to it. Down through the centuries the traditional Catholic teaching as represented by Augustine and Aquinas was that a person receives life from God to use but not to dispense with. Hence, that person may not destroy it. Among the three major religions in the United States only the Jews have no specific moral prohibitions against suicide. Nor do Jews place much emphasis on the hereafter or heaven and hell. Yet, they are still strongly restrained and show low

---

[8] Porterfield, "Suicide," p. 33.

[9] Gibbs, *Suicide*, pp. 2-3.

suicide rates. Later in the chapter there will be a discussion of religious involvement as related to suicide rates.

Suicide rates. The rates of suicide vary widely for different countries. For example, countries with relatively low rates are Australia, with 14.9 per 100,000, and the United States, with 11.1 per 100,000. High rates are found in Hungary, with 29.8 per 100,000, and in West Berlin, with 41.3 per 100,000.[10] One problem is that the accuracy of the rates reported by various countries are often highly suspect. For example, the Republic of Ireland reports 1.8 suicides per 100,000 population. But in Roman Catholic and Moslem countries a verdict of suicide is often a disgrace for the deceased and his family, and is avoided if at all possible. "This is why the very low suicide rates of the Republic of Ireland and Egypt are suspect. In many countries the methods of registration leave very much to be desired."[11]

It has been estimated that in the United States during the 20th century there will be a total of 2 million suicides.[12] There are about 25,000 suicides each year, and possibly 7 or 8 attempts for each one that is completed. It is estimated that about 2 million persons now alive in the United States have attempted suicide. Suicide has been listed among the first ten causes of death and, at some ages, among the first three. There also appear to be wide geographic variations. For example, Nevada's rate was 22.8 per 100,000 as compared to Rhode Island's rate of 6.3 per 100,000. The western part of the United States has a substantially higher rate of suicide than does the southern or the northern areas.[13]

As suggested, the rates can only be taken as crude measures of the frequency of suicide, since many biases enter into their computation as well as into the identification of suicides. One problem is that there is no way of knowing how many accidents resulting in death are really suicides. For example, a middle-aged man who hits a tree head on while driving a car may have done so deliberately, as may a person who seems to have accidentally fallen from a high place. It is highly probable that if a death can be attributed to causes other than suicide that will be done. Douglas has pointed out that the more integrated the deceased person is into his local community, "the more the doctors, coroners, or other officials responsible for deciding what the cause of death is will be favorably influenced consciously or subconsciously, by the preferences of the deceased and his significant others."[14]

One authority suggests that the actual suicide rates in the United States

---

[10] Stengel, *Suicide*, p. 21.

[11] Ibid., p. 23.

[12] Porterfield, "Suicide," p. 53.

[13] Sanford Labovitz, "Variations in Suicide Rates," in Gibbs, *Suicide*, pp. 61–62.

[14] Jack O. Douglas, *The Social Meanings of Suicide* (Princeton, N.J.: Princeton University Press, 1967), p. 213.

may be higher than the official rates by from one fourth to one third. He points out that the official rates are largely derived from coroners' reports, which are sometimes inconclusive even in cases where the medical evidence for suicide is adequate.[15] This estimate of the underestimation of rates refers to coroners' decisions only. If one adds the number of suicides that are in general attributed to other causes there is no knowing how much a given suicide rate is underestimated.

Labovitz has suggested that there are four general reasons to question the reliability of official statistics on suicide. First, wherever there is social and/or legal disapproval of suicide the official statistics are probably understated. This is usually because the victim and the relatives may have attempted to conceal evidence that the death was really a suicide. Second, a suicide may be difficult to distinguish from an accident or a homicide. Third, physicians and coroners usually make the official decision as to the cause of death, and their definitions of suicide vary. Fourth, the characteristics of individuals in a census may not be consistent with those found on death records.[16]

A study of coroners in Great Britain illustrates some of the influences that may affect whether or not a death is diagnosed as suicide. The study found that certain ways of dying appeared to be regarded by coroners as almost certain indicators that a death was not a suicide. For example, deaths through highway accidents were very unlikely to be classed as suicides.[17] The study also pointed out that given the fact that coroners' courts are public and that inquests provide a steady flow of copy for local and even national news media, the role of the coroner in "maintaining and sometimes changing shared definitions of suicidal situations attains a crucial importance; for they can be seen as defining for their society what kind of behavior constitutes a suicide for a particular point in time."[18]

Variations in suicide rates. Different countries show great variations in suicide rates by sex. The range of female suicide rates runs from 1.0 per 100,000 in Costa Rica to 19.0 per 100,000 in Japan. In Austria, Finland, Hungary, and Switzerland the male suicide rate exceeds the female rate by over 20 per 100,000, while in the Netherlands, Iceland, and Costa Rica the difference is under 5 per 100,000. However, the female rates in Japan and Australia exceed the male rates found in several countries. In the United States suicide rates are much higher for men than for women.[19]

---

[15] Stengel, *Suicide*, p. 23.

[16] Labovitz, "Suicide Rates," pp. 58–59.

[17] J. Maxwell Atkinson, "Social Reaction to Suicide: The Role of Coroners' Definitions," in Stanley Cohen, *Images of Deviancy* (Middlesex, England: Penguin Books, 1971), p. 176.

[18] Ibid., p. 186.

[19] Labovitz, "Suicide Rates," p. 63.

One belief that has emerged in the United States from the romantic complex related to love and its greater significance for women is that women show higher suicide rates over unrequited love. Here prevalent beliefs may in some instances function as self-fulfilling prophecies. That is, more women may attempt suicide because more women than men are socialized to the belief that suicide is an answer for a failure in love. Douglas points out that this is probably a major reason for the almost universal finding that "women attempt suicide far more than men in Western society and that the peak of female attempted suicide is in the 20s when lover trouble is most socially credible."[20]

Another belief, also a part of the romantic heritage, is that couples confronted with unhappy or unfulfilled love affairs commit suicide together. Actually the proportion of unhappy lovers among couples who commit suicide together is very small. Couples who do commit suicide together are often physically ill and childless. Although the notes that are left behind usually indicate that the decision was evenly shared the initiative generally appears to come from one member of the pair, and sometimes a great deal of persuasion has to be used. "There are certain typical constellations; the initiator may suffer from depressive illness which has a notoriously depressing effect on those living with him; or both may be old and sick; or two people may have been caught in an extramarital entanglement."[21] However, mutual suicides are not common in the United States.

Even though more women *attempt* suicide the rate of successful suicide attempts is much higher for men. In all regions of the United States, among both whites and nonwhites, males have higher rates of suicide than do females. However, geographically there is considerable variation in the rates for both sexes. Because of the variations it is very difficult to generalize about sexual differences in suicide rates. "Witness, as a case in point, that white females in the West have a higher rate than non-white males in the South."[22]

There also appear to be differences in the social interpretation attached to suicides for males and for females. In general the view in the United States is that when men commit suicide it is because of extrafamilial "strains." By contrast female suicides are often perceived as being caused by intrafamilial "strains." "When a female commits a suicidal action, then, her significant others, especially her husband, who is seen as more responsible (i.e., more the cause) of her actions than anyone else, have a much greater incentive in this respect than a female in the same situation to attempt to conceal this suicidal action."[23] This

[20] Douglas, *Suicide*, p. 221.

[21] Stengel, *Suicide*, p. 45.

[22] Labovitz, "Suicide Rates," p. 63.

[23] Douglas, *Suicide*, p. 215.

might mean that the husband destroys a suicide note or conveys to others that the cause of death was natural. Also, the fact that the woman's suicide is more apt to occur in the home means that the husband has greater control over its public disclosure.

Some general social variables are related to suicide rates for women. Their rates of suicide increase with age, regardless of marital status. However, married women appear to commit suicide about twice as often as single women, regardless of age. It has also been found that divorced women have higher mean annual rates of suicide than do widowed women.[24]

An interest has long existed in suicide rates in the United States as related to rural-urban living patterns. Since the early days of sociology it has been commonly assumed that urban areas were more impersonal and alienated than rural areas and would therefore have higher suicide rates. However, there may be biases that make the relative rates of urban suicides appear higher than they should. Douglas argues that it is plausible to assume that the official statistical procedures of urban areas are more efficient than those of rural areas and that as a result the official statistics tend to be strongly biased in "the direction of showing a much lower suicide rate for the rural areas relative to urban areas."[25] Added to this may also be the factor that in rural areas there is often social pressure not to report a death as suicide because the deceased is known to the investigators and to the local community. By contrast officials dealing with a death in a large city would rarely know anything about the deceased person. The impersonality of the city often leads to a more objective assessment of the cause of death.

There are also seasonal variations in suicide rates. What is most striking is that the rates do not reach their peaks in autumn and winter when nature would usually be most depressing. They are highest in spring and early summer when the environment is most attractive and most people feel that life is worthwhile. "The incidence of suicide gradually increases from January, reaches its peak in May or June, and starts to decline in early July."[26] It may be that for some the splendor of spring and summer makes their own lives appear that much more dismal and that this helps account for the higher suicide rates.

As suggested earlier, an examination of social variables is very important because suicide occurs within a social context. All the data clearly indicate that suicide is an interpersonal social experience. Rushing makes three observations about what he sees as the interpersonal sequence that leads to suicide. First, before committing suicide many communicate

----

[24] Jesus Rico Velasco and Lisbeth Mynko, "Suicide and Marital Status: A Changing Relationship," *Journal of Marriage and the Family*, May 1973, p. 243.

[25] Douglas, *Suicide*, p. 36.

their intention to others. Second, suicides are often preceded by disruptions and problems in the victims' social relations. Third, various deviant actions (including economic failure) that normally result in ostracism and social rejection are common in the personal history of suicides.[27] The significance of the social dimension of suicide is also reflected in the fact that social isolation is the common denominator of a number of factors correlated with a high suicide rate. With these observations in mind we look at other social variables.

There is some evidence of a relationship between suicide rates and social class. In his study of suicide in Florida, Bock found that the suicide rates for men at the lowest social class level were nearly twice as high as those for men at the middle- and upper-class levels. "This relationship was explained by the fact that lower class individuals were less likely to be married, to have relatives in the community, or to belong to community organizations."[28]

As mentioned earlier, religious values have long had an influence on suicide. Around the world the suicide rates among Catholics in predominantly Protestant countries have usually been found to be below the national average. The same also applies to Orthodox Jews and to Moslems. Religious devoutness rather than a specific religious faith often appears to be decisive. However, this variable is not always associated with a low suicide rate. "It is true that some Roman Catholic countries, such as the Republic of Ireland, Spain, and Italy have very low suicide rates, but France, Austria, and Hungary, three solidly Roman Catholic countries, have high suicide rates, Austria and Hungary being among the top five in the world."[29]

In the United States the rates of suicide vary by religion. They tend to be highest for Protestants, next highest for Catholics, and lowest for Jews. However, the rate for any religious group varies greatly from time to time and from place to place. But variations in suicide rates among religious groups should always be treated with great caution because of the many biases in the reporting of suicides.

Another variable that shows some relationship to suicide rates is family background. The broken home background has often been found to be associated with various personal and social problems. One study found that 50 percent of the persons who had completed suicide and 64 percent of the persons who had attempted suicide came from broken homes. The incidence of the death of a parent was higher for the *completed* suicide group and was the most common cause of the broken home for that group. By contrast the most common cause of the broken home for those

---

[27] William A. Rushing, "Individual Behavior and Suicide," in Gibbs, *Suicide*, p. 107.

[28] Wilbur E. Bock, "Aging and Suicide: The Significance of Marital, Kinship, and Alternative Relations," *Family Coordinator*, January 1972, p. 77.

[29] Stengel, *Suicide*, p. 27.

who had *attempted* suicide was divorce. "Almost half of those who had come from broken homes in the completed suicide group had lost both parents; whereas, nearly two thirds of those who had broken homes in the attempted suicide group had lost both parents."[30]

Mental health and suicide. It is logical to assume that mental health problems related to extreme depression, anxiety, and so on would sometimes lead to suicide. One study found that in general the suicidal patient in a neuropsychiatric hospital seemed to be more seriously ill, with the illness showing more acute phases and greater extremes in behavior. "The suicidal patients tended to receive the more serious psychiatric diagnoses, such as schizophrenia and manic-depressive psychosis, while the controls received pre-diagnoses of neurotic disorders."[31]

In his survey of the research data related to suicide Stengel came to the conclusion that depressive illness, or melancholia, is the mental disorder with the highest suicide risk. The main symptoms are severe depression with deep pessimism, a feeling of futility and worthlessness, and a tendency to excessive guilt feelings and self-reproach.[32]

In some cases of suicide there is a linkage to mental illness and alcoholism. For example, some people who are prone to depression and therefore to suicide tend to resort to alcohol because it provides temporary stimulation. As discussed in Chapter 6, alcohol is in most instances a depressant. But because it often reduces inhibitions and self-control it may release suicidal tendencies. "This is why so many people take alcohol before committing or attempting suicide, even if they are not in the habit of drinking to excess."[33]

In any discussion of mental health problems and suicide the question arises of whether or not the act of suicide in itself signifies that there is a mental health problem. In general the clinical approach to suicide allows for the possibility that a person committing a suicidal act is free from mental disorder. However, it certainly seems reasonable to assume that suicide is a highly deviant act because whatever the circumstances the average individual would not react to them by committing suicide. There is also some evidence that rational processes, reflected in self-awareness and self-perception of one's problems and their possible resolutions, are related to suicide. This is reflected in the fact that persons less able to function with rational complexity, namely, the mentally subnormal, have a much lower suicide rate.

---

[30] Theodore L. Dorpat, Joan K. Jackson, and Herbert S. Ripley, "Broken Homes and Attempted and Completed Suicides," in Gibbs, *Suicide*, p. 176.

[31] Norman L. Farberow, Edwin S. Schneiderman, and Charles Neuringer, "Case History and Hospitalization Factors in Suicides of Neuropsychiatric Hospital Patients," in Gibbs, *Suicide*, p. 60.

[33] Ibid., p. 64.

College students.   College students are more apt to commit suicide than are nonstudents. However, the rates vary greatly among institutions and even among various groups of students within a given institution. The higher suicide rates of college students may be due to the strains that are associated with a sense of failure as a student. But studies also show that the suicide rates of students are linked to other social variables. There are more suicides and suicide attempts among students from broken homes and from families with higher levels of education.[34] The higher rates for students from better-educated homes may reflect a feeling of being unable to meet their parents' high expectations.

There may also be biases in the reporting of student suicides. Possible biases among coroners were found in Great Britain. It was pointed out that as coroners become more aware of the view that students are especially suicide prone they will be more likely to look for evidence of suicide when a student dies. The more suicide verdicts the coroners bring in on student deaths, the more papers experts will write on the subject. "Both the verdicts and the academic papers may then be transmitted to the rest of society via the media, with the result that the definition of students as special suicide risks will become more firmly established and more widely shared."[35]

The elderly.   Age is the social variable most closely linked to suicide. Higher suicide rates among the elderly are probably characteristic of most cultures. For example, recent statistics show that suicides committed by elderly people accounted for three fourths of all voluntary deaths in France. A 1960 report of the World Health Organization showed that the highest rates of male suicide occurred at age 70 and over in Great Britain, France, Italy, Belgium, Holland, Portugal, Spain, Switzerland, and Australia. The maximum rate for women came ten years earlier and was far lower.[36]

In the United States the average age of suicides is in the late 50s. One effect on the suicide rate among older people is better medical care, enabling more chronically-ill people to live longer. Many people who in the past would have died through "natural" causes may choose to end the lives that medical science has prolonged. In this way more scientific medicine and better medical care have tended to increase the suicide rate among the elderly.

Another way to illustrate the high rates of suicide among the elderly is to show how overrepresented they are in the total suicide population. That is, the elderly comprise about 10 percent of the total population but about 25 percent of reported suicides. The tendency to suicide is

---

[34] Graham B. Blaine, Jr., and Ledar Carmen, "Causal Factors in Suicidal Attempts by Male and Female College Students," *American Journal of Psychiatry,* 125 (1968), p. 836.

[35] Atkinson, "Reactions to Suicide," p. 187.

[36] Simone de Beauvoir, *Old Age* (Great Britain: Cox and Wyman, 1972), pp. 275–76.

especially high among white males, whose suicide rate steadily increases with advancing age. Suicide rates for white females reach a peak at about age 65. Nonwhite persons display less distinct patterns of suicide. "Twenty million elderly individuals living in the United States could conceivably contribute more than 5,000 or 6,000 suicides during the year."[37]

The elderly individual with the greatest suicide rate is the widower. Such men are more apt to commit suicide not just because they lost their marriage partner but also because they are isolated from kin, friends, neighbors, and formal organizations. By contrast the elderly widow is more likely to be closely supported by relatives because the maintenance of kin networks has depended more on females than on males. "Moreover, the elderly widow is more likely to maintain memberships in formal organizations and to continue to participate in these and other meaningful associations. Widowhood, in old age, particularly among males, is therefore characterized by unhappiness, low morale, mental disorders, high death rates, and high suicide rates."[38]

Bock's study of suicide among the elderly in Florida disclosed various kinds of relationships that tended to reinforce one another and to help prevent suicide. He found that marriage alone was often not enough and that the effectiveness of marriage in preventing suicide was greatly increased by involvement in other social groups. "Thus, married males who had no relatives in the county or who belonged to no organizations displayed a suicide rate higher than the married males who had these other kinds of social bonds."[39]

Finally, some discussion about the economic cost of suicide to society is in order. Many areas of social deviance are seen as draining money from the economy. However, suicide does not appear to be an economic problem. In fact most insurance companies regard suicide as a natural risk. "Despite some striking cases, suicide is not now a serious financial problem to the life insurance companies of the United States."[40]

Attempted suicides. Thus far our attention has focused mostly on variables related to those who commit suicide. In this section some of the variables related to those who attempt suicide are discussed. There are both similarities and differences between those who commit suicide and those who try but are not successful.

It is probable that most people feel at some time that they have a "reason" for wanting to commit suicide. Gibbs reports that it is not surprising that four fifths of the young adults replying to questionnaires indicated that at some time they had wished for death.[41] Yet, only a very

---

[37] Bock, "Aging and Suicide," p. 71.
[38] Ibid., p. 73.
[39] Ibid., p. 75.
[40] Stengel, *Suicide*, p. 73.
[41] Gibbs, *Suicide*, p. 4.

small part of those who have felt that death would be desirable ever attempt to bring it about.

There is no reliable way to gather statistics on all those who attempt suicide because often the would-be suicide is the only person who knows about the attempt. In many cases where others discover and stop the suicide attempt they will not report the fact to the authorities. Therefore, suicide attempts must be discussed with caution.

One estimate is that the number of suicide attempts is six to ten times that of actual suicides. The evidence also indicates that women are more apt to attempt suicide than are men while more men than women actually carry out suicide. However, the rates of suicide for women have increased greatly in recent years while those for men have not. This fits the fact that women's achievement of equality will be reflected in all kinds of areas—both desirable and undesirable.

One common belief is that the difference between those who complete suicide attempts and those who don't is a matter of determination to die. However, much of the research does not bear this out. Many suicide attempts and quite a few suicides are carried out in a "I don't care whether I live or die" mood rather than with a clear and unambiguous determination to end life.[42] Often the success or failure of a suicide attempt may be due to chance rather than motivation.

There has long been an interest in whether or not suicides can be predicted. Often those who are close to the person who committed suicide may feel that they should have been aware of its coming. Generally, when a suicide occurs it comes as a shock to relatives and others close to the person. But when they are interviewed later they often say that the suicidal intention had been expressed directly or indirectly well in advance of the act. "Some psychiatrists reported that 60 to 75 percent of their patients who had committed suicide had given a warning to somebody, though rarely to their doctors. The notion, therefore, that people who threaten suicide do not carry it out is a dangerous error."[43]

Many factors come together in the determination to commit suicide. One set of factors is related to the suicide's ability to convince himself that death will eliminate or reduce his problems. Often the decision to commit suicide results in a state of peace and calm immediately preceding the suicidal act. In some instances a strong religious belief can contribute to suicide. This is especially true if the person is able to take a religiously optimistic outlook toward the hereafter.

Suicide notes. It is probable that only a small number of all people who commit suicide leave a written message behind. In general the purpose of such notes is to elicit certain kinds of emotional responses from survivors close to the victim. Often the suicides ask for forgiveness. Study

---

[42] Stengel, *Suicide*, p. 82.
[43] Ibid., p. 43.

of suicide notes indicates a strong preoccupation with other people and an urge to influence and communicate. However, there is no evidence that suicide notes are more truthful than other communications made under emotional stress.[44]

From the perspective of the coroner trying to establish the cause of death the suicide note is highly important. However, many suicides do not leave notes, and often those who do have their notes destroyed. Atkinson reports that according to one police officer who had encountered many suicides, the notes often end up in fires long before the law arrives on the scene. The destruction of a suicide note would be the first step taken by anyone wishing to conceal a suicide.[45]

Methods of suicide.   Men and women differ in the methods they use in committing suicide. By far the most common method for men is firearms or explosives. This is almost four times as common as the next most frequently used method, hanging and strangulation. By contrast the most common means of suicide used by women are analgesics and narcotics; firearms and explosives rank second. For both men and women there has been a decrease in recent years in the use of hanging and strangulation and an increase in the use of analgesics and narcotics.[46] However, there can be severe biases in reporting the causes of suicide. For example, shootings and hangings are unduly prominent because they are the two methods most difficult to conceal or distort.

As suggested earlier, there may be guilt among those who survive, so that confronted with a suicide the survivors may feel that they could and should have prevented the suicide.[47] In some instances this may be the feeling that the victim wanted to create. If the survivors feel that the suicide was caused by some kind of problem they search their lives to determine their own part in the creation of that problem. Henslin found that the major areas of guilt were concerned with "(1) not being aware of the suicidal intent, (2) feeling they should have been able to prevent the suicide, (3) feeling that perhaps they had done something to cause the suicide, and (4) noncausal acts that were regretted."[48]

Many persons close to those who commit suicide are able to escape from any feelings of guilt, regardless of how they acted in actuality or in the opinion of others. Henslin found that certain factors were related to the absence of guilt feelings. A person showed little guilt if he defined other persons or impersonal factors as being the causes of the suicide or if he was able to define the suicide as inevitable or in positive terms.[49]

---

[44] Ibid., p. 44.

[45] Atkinson, "Reaction to Suicide," p. 175.

[46] Stengel, *Suicide*, p. 40.

[47] Gibbs, *Suicide*, p. 4.

[48] James M. Henslin, "Guilt and Guilt Neutralization: Response and Adjustment to Suicide," in Jack O. Douglas, *Deviance and Respectability* (New York: Basic Books, 1970), p. 200.

[49] Ibid., p. 222.

Theories of suicide. Psychoanalytic theory has long had a view of suicide based on Freud's observations about the "death instinct." This view argues that in all people there is a propensity for self-destruction and that this propensity is balanced against the life wish. Under various circumstances the death wish comes to predominate over the life wish, and suicide is the result. However, the theory doesn't really specify the conditions under which the death wish will come to predominate over the life wish.

Psychiatry does not have a general theory of suicide, although psychiatric case studies have yielded insights. The theoretical problem is related to mental illness. As pointed out earlier, not all suicides are mentally ill, and it is doubtful that all suicide victims have shown signs of intense emotional or mental disturbance. Often suicides are carried out in an extremely rational manner. "To be sure most investigators argue that suicide is the act of a mentally deranged person even though there are no other signs of psychopathology. But to make suicide an act of mental disorder by definition means any statement linking suicide and mental illness is a tautology."[50]

Sociological theory has had a longtime interest in the study of suicide. As Douglas points out, the theoretical treatment of suicide is one of the few classical subjects in sociology. Historically the subject was of great importance in the establishment of sociology as an independent academic discipline. This was a direct result of the French sociologist Emile Durkheim's work *Suicide.*[51] "To this day Durkheim's *Suicide* has dominated, with only a few important exceptions, the sociological works on suicide and much of all sociological methodology."[52]

The main focus of Durkheim's theory was that social facts must be studied as realities external to the individual. This placed stress on the social dimension of human nature as distinct from the psychological dimension. Durkheim conceptualized three types of suicide. The first was *egoistic* suicide, in which a person's strong individualism weakened the controls of society and thereby reduced his immunity against the suicidal inclination. This type of suicide was the result of the person's lack of concern for the community and inadequate involvement with it. The second was *altruistic* suicide. This type covered people over whom society had too strong a hold and who had too little individualism. They would be given to suicide because of excessive altruism and a sense of duty. This type was not very common and included the old, the ill, and women who followed their husbands into death. The third type was *anomic* suicide. If society failed to control and regulate the behavior of individuals suicide became more frequent. Anomic suicides occurred in

---

[50] Walter T. Martin, "Theories of Variation in the Suicide Rate," in Gibbs, *Suicide*, pp. 92–93.

[51] Emile Durkheim, *Suicide: A Study in Sociology* (Glencoe, Ill: Free Press, 1951).

[52] Douglas, *Suicide*, p. xii.

societies with a decline both in religious values and in marital and family bonds. This decline caused disturbances of the collective organizations, which in turn reduced the individual's immunity against suicidal tendencies. As a result anomic suicide would be less frequent in strict and rigid societies because the person would be more socially controlled.

Durkheim knew that individual states of mind were a factor in every case of suicide, but he felt justified in the hypothesis that those individual states were derived from collective states of mind. His major emphasis was on the forces of cohesion and consensus. Suicide varies inversely with the degree of integration of social groups, such as families, religious groups, age groups, corporate groups, and so on.[53]

Douglas has argued that since Durkheim most theorists of suicide have been assuming that the culture of the populations they have studied are basically the same or at least that any differences are not significant for an explanation of suicide. "The most important contribution of the works of sociologists on suicide has been the sociological perspective itself; the insistence on seeing suicidal actions as in some way the result of *social* factors."[54]

Gibbs suggests that from the sociological research two propositions can be made about suicide. First, the greater the incidence of disrupted social relations in a population the higher the suicide rate of that population will be. Second, all suicide victims have experienced a set of disrupted social relations that are not found in the history of nonvictims.[55]

As suggested earlier, suicide is a unique type of deviant behavior. It is distinctive in that the usual methods of social control to prevent deviant acts, such as fines and imprisonment, are not and cannot be effective in stopping individuals from ending their own lives. There have been some recent attempts to set up agencies to prevent suicide. Since 1950 various suicide prevention centers have been established in the United States. Probably the best known of these is one located in Los Angeles. The purposes of suicide prevention centers are to identify the potential suicides in an area, to refer them to sources of insight and encouragement, and to maintain a staff of persons who can answer around-the-clock telephone calls from persons who are allegedly contemplating suicide.[56] How successful such centers have been is very difficult to determine.

In summary, suicide represents deviation from what is possibly the most powerful of all social norms, that of maintaining life. Going against that norm is uncommon. A number of social variables related to those who go against the norm and choose suicide have been examined. Forms

---

[53] Porterfield, "Suicide," p. 52.

[54] Douglas, *Suicide*, p. 158.

[55] Gibbs, *Suicide*, p. 17.

[56] Porterfield, "Suicide," p. 56.

of deviance other than suicide represent degrees of deviation, and the deviant individuals continue to function within the social norms at least part of the time. However, suicide represents a complete rejection of society.

BIBLIOGRAPHY

Atkinson, J. Maxwell, "Societal Reaction to Suicide: The Role of Coroners' Definitions," in Stanley Cohen, *Images of Deviance* (Middlesex, England: Penguin Books, 1971), pp. 165–91.

Bock, E. Wilbur, "Aging and Suicide: The Significance of Marital Kinship and Alternative Relations," *Family Coordinator*, January 1972, pp. 71–79.

Douglas, Jack D., *The Social Meanings of Suicide*. Princeton, N.J.: Princeton University Press, 1967.

Gibbs, Jack, *Suicide*. New York: Harper and Row, 1968.

Henslin, James M., "Guilt and Guilt Neutralization: Response and Adjustment to Suicide," in Jack O. Douglas, *Deviance and Respectability* (New York: Basic Books, 1970), pp. 192–228.

Velasco, Jesus Rico, and Lizbeth Mynko, "Suicide and Marital Status: A Changing Relationship?" *Journal of Marriage and the Family*, May 1973, pp. 239–44.

Stengel, Erwin, *Suicide and Attempted Suicide*. Middlesex, England: Pelican Books, 1969.

chapter nine

Prostitution

No area of deviance has had more written about it than prostitution. If it is true that prostitution is the "oldest profession," then man has been interested in it since the beginning of time. Thousands of books have been written about prostitution, but only some aspects of the subject can be discussed here. There has been and there continues to be disagreement about what makes a person a prostitute. For example, some have even argued that a woman who exchanges sex in marriage for material gains is basically a prostitute. However, we will define prostitution as the vocation of selling sex outside of marriage. This would mean that an unmarried woman who is given gifts for sexual activities would not be a prostitute so long as that is not her occupational way of life.

We will briefly look at the historical background of prostitution. In most societies, past and present, at least some prostitution has been acceptable and often encouraged. In almost all human societies men have been the definers of acceptable behavior. Men have traditionally defined themselves as needing sexual outlets on the basis of the belief that they were very different from women in their sexual needs. Their assumption was that they needed outlets not only when they were unmarried but also after marriage because they had greater needs than their wives could be expected to satisfy. This means that in many societies in the Western world men not only defined prostitution as something for their own needs but also as a means to help protect their "good" women. Broader social factors also influenced the high prevalence of prostitution over time. Kingsley Davis has argued that the rates of prostitution increase when there are barriers to men's sexual freedom. He says that if the age of marriage is high and sexual outlets are quite restricted the rate of

[1] Kingsley Davis, "The Sociology of Prostitution," *American Sociology Review*, October 1973, pp. 746–55.

226

prostitution will be high.[1] This is the opposite of the situation in the United States today, where the ages at marriage are low and the opportunities for sexual outlets outside of marriage are great. As we shall see, this has had a great influence on the amount and nature of the prostitution that exists in the United States today.

In the United States it is generally believed that prostitution goes completely against moral and religious beliefs. However, this has not always been true, and there are many historical references to permissive and encouraging views taken by religion toward prostitution. In some Eastern religions prostitution was a basic part of the religion itself and sometimes involved sacred prostititutes. Henriques has pointed out that to the Western mind the association of sexual intercourse with the worship of the supernatural is at best blasphemous and at worst obscene and degrading. Many other cultures have not viewed sexual intercourse in this way. "Among the Ancient Greeks, for example, copulation itself was at times regarded as an act of worship. But it is in those societies where prostitution becomes an essential part of the worship of the gods that the most powerful expression of the union of sexuality and religion is to be found."[2] None of the major Western religions have gone so far as to incorporate prostitution into their dogma, but many have accepted it at least on occasion. At the beginning of the Middle Ages Saint Augustine believed prostitution to be essential. Saint Thomas Aquinas wrote that prostitution was a necessary evil that prevented seductions and rapes. However, as Western religions became increasingly concerned with "sins of the flesh" the restrictions on all types of sexual expression became greater.

Cultural variation is seen in the early influence of religion on sex in general and on prostitution in particular during the early colonial days in America. In the settlements of the South religious control was less stringent than among the Puritans, and it appears that prostitution was much more common there than it was in the North. Yet, even with the strong Puritan restrictions, some areas in New England believed it necessary to introduce legislation against fornicators, bawdyhouses, and "nightwalkers." "And around the time of the revolution, prostitutes were making their way across the ocean to marry the colonists."[3] In the northern states indentured servants had very few rights and were often at the disposal of their masters sexually. The same was also true for the black female slaves in the South. Therefore, many of the wealthier men had free access to sexual partners, while lower-class men often turned to prostitutes. It would appear that prostitution in the early days in the American colonies was primarily lower-class oriented.

---

[2] Fernando Henriques, *Prostitution and Society* (New York: Grove Press, 1962), p. 21.

[3] Harry Benjamin and R. E. L. Masters, *Prostitution and Morality* (New York: Julian Press, 1964), pp. 21-22.

In time prostitution became much more varied in the United States and there developed a level of prostitution aimed at the middle-class and upper middle-class market. It has been suggested that the last half of the 19th century and the early part of the 20th could be called the golden age of the brothel in the United States.[4] That period was also the Victorian era, during which women were divided into clear-cut categories of good or bad. It was the time when the double-standard view of sex held by men reached its peak. And many men believed that when they visited brothels they were not only meeting their own needs but were also being considerate of the good women in their lives. They believed that by directing their powerful, uncontrolled sexual needs at prostitutes they were saving their wives from distasteful functions. Also, a visit to the brothel often satisfied much more than just sexual needs. It was an evening of drinking, dining, cardplaying, and masculine company—to be capped off by going off with one of the girls. On this point Kinsey wrote that his male interviewees of the older generations explained how they visited houses of prostitution not only for sex "but on sightseeing trips and in social groups as well. They were more often involved in the non-sexual activities that occurred in the established houses, such as drinking, gambling, etc. Present day prostitution is more often a matter of dealing with an individual girl who operates on her own."[5]

During the late 19th and early 20th century the distinction between "good" and "bad" women was also reflected in the way prostitutes clearly stood out from other women. They not only lived in red-light districts but they were set apart from middle-class women by their flamboyant clothes, their hairstyles, the wearing of cosmetics, and their use of tobacco, alcohol, and profanity. "The social cleavage between the 'good' and 'bad' women was not only sharp but could be quickly determined by cultural insignia."[6] All of this has changed, and today, as Lemert goes on to point out, the prostitute looks no different than other women, "so that to separate her from the society matron, the debutante, or the college girl in a hotel lobby is an almost impossible task."[7]

Not until about the time of World War I did any real opposition to prostitution develop in the United States. At that time the opposition was based not so much on moral grounds as on an increasing venereal disease rate associated with prostitution. This was seen as threatening to the war effort, and therefore patriotism joined moralism in opposing prostitution. However, many houses of prostitution did survive World War I and did

---

[4] Ibid., p. 76.

[5] Alfred C. Kinsey et al., *Sexual Behavior in the Human Male* (Philadelphia: Saunders 1948), pp. 603-4.

[6] Edwin M. Lemert, "Prostitution," in Edward Sagarin and Donel E. MacNamara, *Problems of Sex Behavior* (New York: Crowell, 1968), p. 82.

[7] Ibid., p. 83.

not succumb to the forces of antiprostitution until early in World War II.[8] During World War II prostitution developed around military bases, but it was often not based in brothels but on the individual level. Today houses of prostitution are uncommon in most parts of the country. They are most apt to be found in the South, where the double standard of sex is strongest.

In the United States today prostitution is almost totally illegal. All of the states except one prohibit it. Prostitution is about the only crime in the penal law in which two people agree to do something illegal and yet only one, the female partner, is subject to arrest. A recent New York statute made the male client also guilty in an act of female prostitution, but it is not enforced and it may be disregarded.[9]

There has been one exception to the legal bans on prostitution among the states. In the state of Nevada prostitution has been accepted as a way of life since the early mining camp days. At present it is legal in 15 of Nevada's 17 counties. There are about 40 licensed brothels in Nevada, and they do a total annual business placed at between $3 million and $5 million. In 1970 it was estimated that the prostitutes earned an average of $500 a week, out of which they paid about $200 in room and board.[10] It was estimated that in 1973 about 300 women were working in the legal houses. However, far more common in Nevada and elsewhere are the free lancers who work either for themselves or through a pimp—many of them for $100 per customer.[11]

Throughout the United States, with the exception of the counties in Nevada, all prostitution is prohibited and all prostitutes are defined as criminals. The day-to-day practice of prostitution is controlled primarily through laws passed by various state legislatures, "which stalwartly resist federal government proposals for uniform legislation in this area, with the result that the prostitution laws differ drastically from state to state."[12] In most states persons who are associated with prostitutes in a business way, such as procurers, pimps, and madams, fall under the laws. As mentioned above, to be a prostitute is against the law in all states except Nevada, although 27 states do not mention prostitution *specifically* but legally categorize it as some type of vagrancy. Maximum penalties seldom go beyond a one-year prison term and in many cases do not exceed six months. In only eight states in the United States is there a statute specifying any punishment for the customer of the prostitute, or making his participation in illegal coitus a crime.

---

[8] Benjamin and Masters, *Prostitution*, p. 86.

[9] Kate Millett, "Prostitution: A Quartet for Female Voices," in Vivian Gornick and Barbara K. Moran.*Woman in Sexist Society* (New York: Signet Books, 1972), p. 79.

[10] *Newsweek*, March 9, 1970, p. 81.

[11] *Newsweek*, Feb. 12, 1973, p. 48.

[12] *Newsweek*, March 9, 1970, p. 87.

Most countries of the world, including the United States, subscribe to the United Nations International Human Rights Convention of 1957 with reference to the suppression of prostitution. Implementation of that agreement attempts to reduce the exploitation of women, their registration as prostitutes by police or other agencies, and the practice of living on their earnings as prostitutes. It is doubtful that this agreement has had any real influence in reducing prostitution.

It is necessary to say something briefly about male prostitution. Male prostitutes may be of two types—homosexual and heterosexual. The homosexual male prostitute has been by far the most common over time and still is. Homosexual temple prostitutes existed among the Hebrews and in India. There were boy prostitutes in the early civilizations of Egypt, Persia, Greece, Rome, China, and Japan. In ancient Athens, as well as in ancient harbor towns, there were brothels in which boys and young men were available either alone or with girls. The Greek attitude toward male prostitution was ambivalent. The brothels were well patronized, and the patron didn't feel that he was an object of scorn, as is often true for modern men who turn to female prostitutes. "The Greeks did not, however, have unreserved admiration for the boy prostitutes, because they regarded homosexuality not merely in terms of physical passion, but also in terms of love."[13]

It is also known that homosexual prostitution was quite common in Renaissance Italy and 18th century France. There is probably more male prostitution in the United States today than ever before. This is in part a reflection of the greater openness of male homosexuals who seek out young sex partners. These sex partners do not consider themselves to be homosexual and are often members of juvenile gangs.

Gagnon and Simon observe that the male prostitute plays many of the same roles for the male homosexual as does the female prostitute for her clientele. But the roles take on additional complexity because the male prostitute faces a client population that has a number of subcultural dimensions different from those of the female prostitute's heterosexual clients. Gagnon and Simon further point out certain aspects of male prostitution arise specifically from the manner in which male homosexual preferences are organized within the homosexual subculture. One major difference is that the female prostitute is paid so her customer can have an orgasm. But in nearly all cases the male prostitute is paid for his orgasm. "Therefore, unlike the female prostitute, the male prostitute must have sufficient sexual arousal from the contact to become erect and have orgasm."[14]

---

[13] Wainwright Churchill, *Homosexual Behavior among Males* (New York: Hawthorn Books, 1967), p. 131.

[14] John Gagnon and William Simon, *Sexual Conduct: The Social Sources of Human Sexuality* (Chicago: Aldine, 1973), p. 166.

Male heterosexual prostitutes in the United States have always been rare. This is especially true when the definition of prostitution as a vocation is applied. Some young men are "kept" by older women, but they are much closer to a "mistress" role than to that of a prostitute. There are stories in American folklore, probably developed by men, about men who are so good that women seek them out and pay them for their sexual services. But these stories appear to be based on wishful thinking rather than actual fact.

We next look at what is known about the number of prostitutes and their customers in the United States today. There is evidence to suggest that since the end of World War II the number of prostitutes and the number of their clients have not changed to any great extent. "On the contrary, what seems to have occurred is a decline in the frequency with which men patronize prostitutes."[15] This suggests that many men still visit prostitutes on some occasions, but that they turn to prostitutes much less often because there are more opportunities for sex with women who are not prostitutes. It seems probable that today's younger adult generation is turning much less to prostitutes. This would certainly be expected on the basis of the increased sexual freedom among the younger generation. A study of college students around the country found that only 4 percent had had experience with a prostitute.[16] A recent nationwide study found that only 3 percent of the single men aged 15 to 24 had had contact with prostitutes during the previous year (1972). The author suggests that the use of prostitutes by young single males is no more than half what it was in the 1940s and possibly much less.[17]

Once again we must turn to the Kinsey data as the best source of information on the use of prostitutes by American men. Kinsey found that more than two thirds of the white male population in his sample had had some experience with prostitutes. Most of them had had those relations no more than once or twice a year. Prostitution provided about one tenth of the male's total premarital coital experience.[18] The Kinsey data showed clear differences by social class in the use of prostitutes. The contacts were most common among the lower-class men. "Between 16 and 20, males of grade school level have intercourse with prostitutes 9 times as often, and males of the high school level have it more than 4 times as often as males of the college level."[19] This distinction no doubt continues to be true today, with lower-class males turning to prostitutes most often.

Historically men have turned to prostitutes for a variety of reasons. We suggest five general groupings of motives or reasons for which men seek

[15] T. C. Esselstyn, "Prostitution in the United States," *The Annals*, March 1968, p. 127.

[16] Vance Packard, *The Sexual Wilderness* (New York: McKay, 1968), p. 164.

[17] Morton Hunt, "Sexual Behavior in the 1970s," *Playboy*, October 1973, p. 88.

[18] Kinsey, *Human Male*, p. 599.

[19] Ibid., p. 601.

out this kind of sexual relief. For any given man the reasons may operate singly or in various combinations.

1. *Avoid competition.* Some men are unable, or believe they are unable, to compete for women. This may be because they are shy or emotionally very insecure. Some may have severe physical or mental handicaps. In some cases they may be too old. The prostitute provides them with a sexual outlet without risk of rejection.

2. *Impersonal sex.* Some men want to avoid any interpersonal involvement with women. They can pay the prostitute for their sexual relations and feel no personal or social obligation to her. This also means that they are free of the fear of getting a woman pregnant and being held responsible.

3. *Sexual variations.* Some husbands feel that their sexual relationships with their wives are too restricted. It may be that the wives refuse to engage in certain types of sexual activities or that the husbands don't want to perform such acts with their wives. As a result some of these men turn to prostitutes for such sexual activities as oral-genital sex or anal intercourse.

4. *Sexual peculiarities.* Some men have sadistic or masochistic needs or are addicted to a variety of fetishes. Their needs are very difficult to satisfy without payment. Depending on how bizarre or acute their desires are they may even have trouble finding prostitutes to satisfy these needs. Many prostitutes will not engage in various sexual behaviors. For such men it may be difficult to find sexual outlets among nonprostitutes.

5. *Uncomplicated sex.* Some men want to relax with women under circumstances in which the ordinary conventions are removed. They want sex uncomplicated by explanation or by worry about the partner. They know that an evening with a prostitute will end without commitment on their part.

Gagnon and Simon suggest that the middle-class male who turns to prostitutes is often more complex and characterized by more ambivalence than is his non-middle-class counterpart. Novelty among females and their sexual techniques is involved, as is the lack of responsibility for the consequences of sexual contact. But prostitutes also offer sexual contact that frees the middle-class male from time-consuming, conventional buildups to coitus and leaves him free for other pursuits. "The frequency of contacts with prostitutes by males at conventions and in other situations that are separated from the home suggests the loosening of social controls that is necessary for such contacts to take place."[20]

PROSTITUTION IN THE UNITED STATES TODAY

In the United States today there is no great social concern with

---

[20] Gagnon and Simon, *Sexual Conduct*, 231.

prostitution. This is not to say that prostitution is accepted, but rather that society has lost most of its moral indignation over prostitution and thus its inclination to strongly condemn prostitution or attempt to do something about it. Society appears to become concerned today when prostitution is linked with some other social problem. For example, there will often be a campaign to reduce prostitution because it is believed to contribute to an increase in venereal disease rates, or after some public outrage when call girls are linked with shady business practices or political manipulations. It appears common for the American public to link prostitution with criminality and shady business practices, yet prostitution's closest link to institutions is probably with legitimate, respected businesses.

As suggested, there is often public concern over the relationship between prostitution and venereal disease. The extent to which prostitution is practiced in a given culture will be reflected in prostitution's contribution to venereal disease. For example, it is estimated that in recent years in France prostitutes have accounted for 25 to 35 percent of all venereal infections. But in the United States prostitutes are estimated to be responsible for between 5 to 15 percent of all infections.[21] The relationship between venereal disease and prostitution is further discussed in Chapter 10.

Prostitution often continues to elicit concerned public reaction when it is associated with young men in the military forces. During the history of mankind prostitution has always been closely linked with armies. Up until recent times the armies of the world were almost always accompanied by prostitutes who did the cooking and the laundry, as well as took care of soldiers' sexual needs. In the United States the armed forces have traditionally treated sex with hypocrisy. There is usually an attempt to control the soldier's sexual life as much as possible, but at the same time to keep what is not controlled absolutely quiet. The soldier is told to live a virtuous sex-free life, but at the same time is officially taught how to use various methods of prophylaxis. The common argument by the military that prostitution must be controlled because of venereal disease is a questionable one. A study conducted during World War II found that a very small proportion of infections in the army were due to professional prostitutes (6 percent); 80 percent were due to amateurs; and a surprising 14 percent were marital in origin.[22]

Of course, many military leaders know that it would be much better to have military control over prostitution, and historically military leaders have often suggested this. It was suggested, for example, by the top army medical officer in Vietnam. General David T. Thomas said, "If the military were permitted to run houses of prostitution as part of the Post

---

[21] R. S. Morton, *Venereal Diseases* (Middlesex, England: Penguin Books, 1972), p. 123.

[22] Benjamin and Masters, *Prostitution*, pp. 52–3.

Exchange system we could cut venereal disease down to a very, very low figure merely by being able to supervise the operation, if not all the way, at least from the time the soldier goes into the room and from the time he comes out."[23] But his suggestion, as has been the case many times before in the United States, was met with indignation and ridicule. Benjamin and Masters point out that parents often react with the desire to see their sons in the army protected from temptation and seem to believe that if there were no prostitutes there would be no sex. Parents often hold the armed forces responsible for their sons. Yet, even with the military there appears to be less indignation about prostitution than there was only a few years ago. Many moralists prefer not to be confronted with the problem of prostitution for the military because then they wouldn't have to react to it. It's when they read a statement like General Thomas's that they feel they must react, and then hypocrisy becomes preferable to honesty.

What is the nature of prostitution in the United States today? For the most part the old houses of prostitution are gone and the occupation is less complex and organized. In the old days a madam might run a house with 20 women, and that represented a complex small business. Today prostitutes work alone or in small groups and have much more control over their career than they did in the past. Writers have described many different categories of prostitutes as they exist today, but for the purpose of discussion the role of prostitutes is divided into two general categories. One is the "street" or "bar" girl. These girls usually sell themselves directly and in person on the marketplace. That is, they are seen and picked out by the customer. The enactment of the sale by the street girl, in contrast with the call girl, is highly visible and is public evidence of deviance. Clothing, speech, gestures, stance, and other symbols announce the identity of street girl to both clients and authorities.[24]

The second type of prostitute is the "call" girl, who usually makes her first contacts with a customer *without* his actually seeing her. This may be through referral by a pimp or another call girl. These distinctions are not always clear cut and not always appropriate. For example, in some cases a street girl will have a customer brought to her by her pimp, and the customer will of course not see her until he arrives. In other cases a call girl will work certain cocktail lounges and be picked up there. Another general distinction is that the street girl usually has lower middle-class or lower-class customers. while the call girl has a middle-class and upper middle-class clientele. It is also generally true that call

[23] *Washington Post*, October 23, 1969.

[24] Nanette J. Davis, "The Prostitute: Developing a Deviant Identity," in James M. Henslin, *Studies in the Sociology of Sex* (New York: Appleton-Century-Crofts, 1971), pp. 321-22.

girls are more attractive, better educated, and make far more money than do street girls. Our primary concern in this chapter is with the call girl.

The rise of the modern call girl came about with the decline of the old madam type of prostitution. The call girl era also appeared to usher in a period when prostitution was more and more an individual undertaking rather than an occupation practiced in close association with others. "The ubiquity of the motel is believed to facilitate prostitution as well as other forms of extramarital sex experience."[25] Less organization to prostitution may also be a result of the lessened present concern with prostitution.

The status of the call girl is determined by her attractiveness, financial standing, dress, apartment, manners, and the state in which she keeps her pimp. Her status is also reflected in how she views other prostitutes. Greenwald points out that call girls have more scorn for streetwalkers than does the most puritanical reformer. "They will avoid bars and restaurants that are patronized by girls who, they feel, have inferior status as professionals or whom they consider amateurs."[26] As with any professional the prostitute takes pride in being very good, and her success can be measured against what she sees as the failures of the street girls.

Even when a call girl works a bar or cocktail lounge she does so in a manner different from that of the street girl. In many large cities certain cocktail lounges are known to be the hangouts of call girls. In those places solicitation is not made directly by the girl, as is usually true for the lower-class street girls. Rather, the call girl sits at the bar and drinks by herself. Many times she will be approached by men who may or may not know that she is a prostitute. If a man is trying to pick her up she quickly lets him know that it will cost money because she doesn't want to waste her time on noncustomers. Many of the cocktail lounges encourage the call girls to work there because it is good for business. Sometimes the bartender or the bar manager will introduce a potential client who is not too adventurous.[27] Greenwald found that the women who worked in the cocktail lounges usually started work about four in the afternoon to get the men who stopped in on their way home from the office, and usually continued to work until two or three in the morning.[28] But the most successful call girls never enter a bar to work and make all their arrangements by telephone. Some, like lawyers, are on retainers to various business firms. This means that they will be available whenever they are

---

[25] Esselstyn, "Prostitution," p. 127.

[26] Harold Greenwald, "The Social and Professional Life of the Call Girl," in Simon Dinitz, Russell R. Dynes, and Alfred C. Clarke, *Deviance* (New York: Oxford University Press, 1969), p. 407.

[27] Ibid., p. 405.

[28] Ibid., p. 406.

needed. But this level of prostitution is carefully concealed, and little is actually known about it.

Entering prostitution

As suggested earlier in the chapter, there has been a great deal of speculation as to the causes of prostitution as a social institution, and many attempts have been made to explain why girls become prostitutes. Generally the causal explanations have followed the same patterns as those for attempts to explain such areas of deviance as homosexuality, delinquency, drug use, and so forth. That is, it used to be assumed that women became prostitutes because they were sinful, but this shifted to their being defined as "sick" in some way. When the cause for becoming a prostitute was seen as sin the treatment was punishment. But with the causal view becoming "sickness," the way of handling prostitution was seen to be through treatment. It has almost always been assumed that becoming a prostitute was repugnant to the female and that she became one *only* because of some forces against her normal will or desires. In other words the assumption has almost always been that no woman in her right mind and with freedom of choice would enter prostitution. In the United States, as in many other countries, it is commonly believed that many women become prostitutes against their wills. This is a part of the "white slave" myth, which explains the prostitute as a woman who was innocent and was lured under false pretenses, drugs, or force. The myth says that these women were held captive in houses of prostitution and were beaten into submission by madams and pimps. It was believed that they were constantly moved from city to city, or even from country to country, and that eventually they would be sent to a Near Eastern country never to be heard of again. As Lemert points out, many prostitutes went along with the "white slave" myth. They often found that the story inspired sympathy and discounted their own responsibility.[29] But there is little evidence that many women have ever been forced through white slavery into prostitution.

In the United States several theories have been developed to explain why women become prostitutes. One theory tries to psychiatrically explain prostitution on the basis of a Freudian model. Within that framework the prostitute is often described as masochistic or as having an infantile mentality. She is described as being unable to form mature interpersonal relationships and as being emotionally dangerous to the male.[30] A more psychological point of view argues that prostitution is caused by various kinds of childhood experiences. Greenwald says that the prostitutes he studied had "early family experiences of parental

---

[29] Lemert, "Prostitution," p. 84.

[30] James H. Bryan, "Apprenticeships in Prostitution," *Social Problems*, Winter 1965, p. 287.

conflict, neglect, and rejection. They also had rewarding sexual experiences with older men. These experiences led the women to see sex as a commodity to barter for personal gain."[31] There is also a social interpretation of the causes of prostitution. This view sees the prostitute as a victim of her environment or as a person with little or no control over her destiny.

Whatever they are, the causes of entering prostitution are probably very similar to the causes of becoming an airline stewardess or a nurse, in part because, like those occupations, prostitution has been one of the few open almost exclusively to women. Benjamin and Masters have suggested several reasons why a woman might become a prostitute.

1. The economic rewards of prostitution are usually far greater than those of many other occupations.
2. The opportunity exists for adventure in what is seen by some as a world of glamour.
3. For some women the work is attractively easy and undisciplined. So long as they are young and attractive they don't have to put out much effort to make a good living.
4. A small minority of prostitutes are probably so highly sexed that they enjoy many of their sexual activities.[32]

Actually there is a great deal of speculating and theorizing about why women become prostitutes, with little in the way of empirical data. However, one recent study shows that force of any kind is *not* a common cause of entering prostitution. Gebhard found in his study of 127 white female prostitutes that only 4 percent could be said to have been forced into prostitution. And even in those few cases there were alternative choices. "The female who says her husband or boyfriend forced her to become a prostitute is really saying she chose prostitution rather than lose her mate and possibly experience a beating.[33]

It appears that the problems most prostitutes encounter center on their affectional relations rather than on moral guilt about their way of life. The notion that prostitutes go through life upset because of guilt feelings about their sexual morality is an exaggeration. In fact it may be that some women who have less need for emotional commitment as well as fewer moral restrictions are drawn to prostitution. Lemert has suggested that prostitution may draw women who are emotionally more self-sufficient than others.[34]

On the basis of their research, Gagnon and Simon have suggested that

---

[31] Greenwald, "Call Girl," p. 406.

[32] Benjamin and Masters, *Prostitution*, pp. 93-94.

[33] Paul H. Gebhard, "Misconceptions about Female Prostitution," *Medical Aspects of Human Sexuality*, March 1969, p. 28.

[34] Lemert, "Prostitution," p. 105.

a sense of detachment from the family or community often emerges prior to entry into prostitution. That detachment is reflected in geographic mobility, lack of contact with the family, and disordered heterosexual relationships or a disordered marriage. To the extent that entry into prostitution is a time-specific trauma, "it is seen more frequently among females with no earlier sexual conditioning by various sexual contacts with a number of men, who maintain relations with conventional others, or who perceive of themselves within the narrow range of 'good girls gone wrong.'"[35]

The reasons given by prostitutes for entering that profession have very often been discounted or defined as rationalizations. But it would appear that the insights that prostitutes can give about their own occupational choice are as important to consider as other interpretations. Most women say that they become prostitutes for very practical reasons. The occupation pays well, the work is reasonably pleasant, and they have a fair degree of independence and a chance of meeting a client they can marry.[36] Gebhard found that almost 90 percent of the prostitutes in his sample listed money as their prime motivation. He also reported that two thirds of the prostitutes said that they had no regrets whatsoever about entering the occupation.[37] Money is important in another way. In nearly all professions, one must begin by gaining experience and knowledge, and hope that over the years one's income will increase. But with prostitution most often just the opposite occurs. The woman can usually earn big money very soon after starting. This is because even though she may be inexperienced in both sexual and interpersonal techniques her novelty on the market gives her an advantage over her more experienced and better-known competitors. "It seems quite likely that the new girl, irrespective of her particular physical and mental qualities, has considerable drawing power because she provides new sexual experience to the customer. Early success and financial reward may well provide considerable incentive to continue in the occupation."[38]

It is a measure of the strength of the moral norms against prostitution that so many women after seeing the economic rewards of becoming a prostitute as against filling a low-paying clerical job will still take the clerical job. The very fact that almost all women with the lowest income potential never consider becoming prostitutes suggests the continuing strong moral taboos. If the moral controls are weakening, then it could be predicted that in the future more women would consider prostitution as a real occupational possibility. But the very forces that might allow more

---

[35] Gagnon and Simon, *Sexual Conduct*, p. 226.
[36] Esselstyn, "Prostitution," p. 30.
[37] Gebhard, "Misconceptions," p. 29.
[38] Bryan, "Prostitution," p. 295.

women to consider prostitution are based on the same greater sexual liberality for the female which makes the need for prostitutes decrease.

Many women drift into prostitution. For example, after a woman has been involved in quasi-prostitution for a while, her activity makes her self-definition as a prostitute inescapable. "A waitress who has been taken on dates by customers from the restaurant where she works and given entertainment or gifts in return for sexual favors may suddenly perceive the bargaining features of the relationships and decide to formalize them through a prostitute's role in order to improve what frequently is a bad bargain from her point of view."[39] In other cases a woman may become a prostitute because she is defined as such. This may occur if she is arrested and convicted on the formal charge of commercial vice. For example, if she has a venereal disease she may be given segregated treatment in a clinic along with prostitutes and then see herself as such because of her involvement in those settings. These are situations primarily of the lower-class prostitute and are much less apt to cause the call girl to enter the profession.

In American society there continues to be strong resistance to any suggestion that prostitution may be a rational occupational choice for some women. Women who become prostitutes are constantly defined within the "sick" or "manipulated" categories, and this strips them of any occupational self-determination. This theme cuts across many other areas of deviant behavior. The delinquent, the drug user, the homosexual, for example, are also often seen as "pawns" in society. To a great extent this is a reflection of the fact that society cannot accept the notion that what it considers to be deviance is not accepted as such by all. To recognize this would undercut the universal quality of society's notions of wrong behavior—something that many who live in a world of moral universals cannot accept. As suggested, the definers of many forms of deviance insist on a world of total conformity to their values as their basic goal.

PROSTITUTION AS A SUBCULTURE

As is the case in most areas of deviance, some prostitutes function essentially as individuals while many others function as part of a subculture. In this section our interest is with the subcultural setting of prostitution. Gagnon and Simon believe that most of the sexual events that may be defined as prostitution are carried out within a setting that may be seen as subcultural. They suggest that the subcultural world "includes as its elements specialized knowledge, language, and relationships with other persons. Being 'in the life' involves existing inside a prostitute's occupational culture. Most prostitutes exist in social networks consisting of other prostitutes and allied occupational and social

---

[39] Lemert, "Prostitution," p. 99.

roles (e.g., pimps, steerers, the police, customers, etc.)."[40] The subculture also has historical beliefs or a particular folklore that gives it a dimension of time. It has been suggested that no other deviant subculture has developed a greater collection of myths and beliefs. "The folklore of prostitution largely concerns the manner in which women become prostitutes, the type of life they lead, and the inevitable culmination of their lives in demoralization, disease, and early death."[41]

Highly important to the folklore of any deviant group is the belief in becoming successful, and in the subculture of prostitution this belief is reflected in stories about prostitutes who have been successful in escaping it. Among prostitutes it is common to tell stories about women who have married well-known politicians or businessmen. There are also many stories about movie actresses who were once "in the game." Not only do prostitutes like to talk about women who have left prostitution and become respectable, but they "also seem to treasure the stories of those who descended from respectability to join their ranks."[42] This contributes to the myth that under the right circumstances no woman would be immune to becoming a prostitute. The fact that most of the stories are about prostitutes who have escaped and become successful in the "straight" world seems to indicate that for most prostitutes the subcultural world is one they would like to leave—at least under some conditions.

Not only do prostitutes have their folklore, but there are also many myths about prostitutes. One myth sees the prostitute as a person with a "heart of gold" who is an easy "touch" and gives most of her money away. There is also an opposite myth that the prostitute hates men and is a cold-blooded businesswoman. The first myth is probably based on the notion that prostitutes give help to the poor families they often come from. Added to this is the fact that they often give up much of their earnings to their pimps. Most prostitutes are probably cold-blooded in that sex is their business and that they usually want no emotional involvement with their customers. This approach by the prostitute is smart from both an interpersonal and a business perspective. Bryan writes, however, that the assumption that "all whores hate men" was not supported by his study of prostitutes.[43]

Another common belief about prostitutes is that they are almost all heavy users of drugs. This belief has been supported by the fact that a number of prostitutes have been found to use drugs. However, in many, if not most, of these cases the women are not primarily oriented toward

[40] John H. Gagnon and William Simon, *Sexual Deviance* (New York: Harper and Row, 1967), p. 10.

[41] Lemert, "Prostitution," p. 83.

[42] T. Hirschi, "The Professional Prostitute," in William A. Rushing, *Deviant Behavior and Social Process* (Chicago: Rand McNally, 1969), p. 201.

[43] Bryan, "Prostitution," p. 292.

prostitution but rather toward using prostitution to satisfy the role demands of being a drug addict. In other words the deviant occupation of prostitute is the means to achieve the deviant end of drug use.[44] In his sample of subculturally oriented prostitutes Gebhard found that only 4 percent were ever addicted to "hard" drugs and that another 5 percent had experimented with drugs without becoming addicted.[45]

An important aspect of the prostitute subculture centers on the roles and norms directly related to the practice of prostitution. It is the occupational factor that gives the prostitute's way of life its significance. As with most deviant subcultures, it is this significance which makes the behavior deviant, in this case the profession of prostitution. What about the occupational recruitment of prostitutes? When and under what conditions do women become prostitutes?

On the basis of her research Davis has suggested that there are several routes by which a woman enters a career of prostitution. The chief of these are: "(1) response to peer group expectations, (2) involvement in a pimp-manager relationship, and (3) adolescent rebellion."[46]

It has been suggested that there are two modal age groupings when women usually enter prostitution. The first period, roughly between the ages of 18 and 22, is a high entrance age because the young woman finds that she is valuable on the market and is offered good money. Probably a minority of the women who become prostitutes enter prostitution during the second period, after the age of 25. It is probable that many of the women who become prostitutes at the older ages do so as a means of satisfying other deviant ends—that is, they are women who are on drugs or are alcoholics. There is also evidence that black prostitutes start much younger than do whites (from three to five years younger).[47] This has probably been true because black women have had fewer economic opportunities and because they are less controlled by the traditional sexual morality. There also appears to be an age difference for entrance by types of prostitutes. The street girl, who usually has less education than the call girl, probably starts at a much younger age. This means that a young street prostitute might be 17 while a young call girl might be 21. But even though the call girl may be older when she starts she can generally practice her profession with success much longer than the street girl because she is better able to maintain her attractiveness.

There appears to be some relationship between early sexual experience and prostitution. Among the 30 prostitutes studied by Davis the average age at first coitus was 13.6, and 19 of the prostitutes had had sexual intercourse by age 13. She found a number of variables related to those

---

[44] Lemert, "Prostitution," pp. 105–6.

[45] Gebhard, "Misconceptions," pp. 28-29.

[46] Davis, "Prostitution," p. 306.

[47] Benjamin and Masters, *Prostitution*, p. 100.

characterized by "early sexuality." First, there were high levels of family permissiveness, which led to associations with older males at parties or through street pickups. This meant that often family controls were lacking or were inconsistent. Second, the peer group norms often encouraged early sexuality. Third, sexuality came to be associated with freedom (a movement away from a disliked family), or conversely, security (the certainty of male companionship).[48]

Street girls most often become prostitutes by drifting into the profession. As suggested, they often move from amateur to semiprofessional to professional status without very much conscious planning. Davis found that regardless of the age at which the young woman first experienced intercourse there then followed a *"drift or slide process from promiscuity to prostitution,* with the girl first prostituting herself in late adolescence (average, 17.3 years of age)."[49] Often street girls tie up with a pimp but are not a part of the prostitue subculture. By contrast many call girls do make a conscious choice about entering the profession and are introduced into it by becoming a part of the prostitute subculture. The discussion that follows is concerned with the woman who becomes a part of the call girl subculture.

The apprentice call girl doesn't have to learn a great deal before she starts to practice. She becomes trained by becoming a part of the subculture, "where she learns the trade through imitation as much as through explicit tutoring. The outstanding concern at this stage is the development of a sizable and lucrative clientele. The specific skills and values which are acquired during this period are rather simple and quickly learned."[50] Bryan also says that despite the call girls' protestations to the contrary and their involved folklore the art of being a prostitute is at least initially a low-level skill. "That is, it seems to be an occupation which requires little formal knowledge or practice for its successful pursuit and appears best categorized as an unskilled job."[51]

The apprentice prostitute receives little instruction on various sexual techniques, even though her previous sexual knowledge may have been quite limited. What instruction there is usually centers on having oral sex with the customer. The prostitute learns that in general oral sex is more efficient for her than coitus. This is because coitus gives the man some control over his orgasm, and he may therefore prolong the act. Besides coitus is seen as messy and necessitates the time for a douche. By contrast oral sex enables the the prostitute to control the man's orgasm and can bring it about much faster, and it is also seen as less messy. Oral sex is something the customer often wants, so it is necessary for the beginning

---

[48] Davis, "Prostitution," pp. 301-2.

[49] Ibid., p. 304.

[50] Bryan, "Prostitution," p. 295.

[51] Ibid., p. 296.

prostitute to learn some skills in this area. Bryan also suggests that during the training period there is also stress "not to experience sexual orgasms with the client, though this may be quite variable with the trainer."[52]

The structure of the apprenticeship period appears to be similar for most prostitutes. The beginner receives her training from either a pimp or an experienced call girl. "She serves her initial two to eight months of work under the trainer's supervision and often serves this period in the trainer's apartment. The trainer assumes responsibility for arranging contacts and negotiating the type and place of the sexual encounter."[53] Most important about the training period is not so much the learning of skills and techniques but rather the building of a clientele. "For referring the customer, the trainer receives 40 to 50 percent of the total price agreed upon in the contact negotiated by the trainer and the customer."[54]

Over time the call girl tries to build up her clientele. In time most call girls get their clients by individual referrals, usually over the telephone, and make their own arrangements for sexual contact. The men are usually repeat customers or men who have been recommended by previous customers. Ideally the call girl would like all of her business to be arranged beforehand, either by telephone or by having someone else set it up. Sometimes if business is slow the call girl may initiate calls. "She doesn't solicit in the usual sense of streetwalking, but she will call a number of men in an effort to drum up trade."[55] While call girls compete for business, they also develop some close personal relationships. And even in business there is often cooperation. Call girls who have more customers than they can handle will refer some to a friend. The friend will in turn refer some of her extra customers, or a fee-splitting arrangement may be worked out. Because the call girls are in a deviant subculture they know that they must to some extent rely on one another. This dependence may take the form of mutual aid. For example, if a girl is sick or in jail her friends will often try to keep as much of her practice as possible for her until she returns.[56] And, too, call girls often live together because this has personal as well as business advantages.

The subculture of the prostitute may be better understood by looking at some of the roles and their meanings. The major role that the prostitute must deal with is that of the customer, or "John." The customer is almost always seen as the source of income, the more the better, and that is the basic limit of how he is defined. Economic considerations govern almost all the kinds of behavior directed at him by the prostitute. The per-

---

[52] Ibid., p. 293.
[53] Ibid., p. 294.
[54] Ibid., p. 295.
[55] Greenwald, "Call Girl," p. 405.
[56] Hirschi, "Prostitute," p. 201.

spective of seeing the customer almost only in the economic sense is supported by the rationalizations that prostitutes develop with regard to him. Basically the prostitute sees the customer as corrupt. This becomes empirically confirmed for her when she sees the married man cheating on his wife, the moralist secretly betraying his publicly stated values, or the "John" trying to cheat the prostitute.[57] All of these rationalizations mean that the customer is not to be trusted and should be "taken" in every way possible. Generally once the agreement is reached the prostitute will, "like labor in any exploitative relationship, try to do the least she possibly can to earn it."[58]

It appears that, once learned, the structure of prostitute-client talk becomes very ritualistic and predictable, though it varies from one social level of customer to another and from one situation of prostitution to another. For example, the importance of the cash exchange is high for the lower-class customer while the sexual activities discussed are limited and the content of sexual talk small. "On the other hand, in contacts with middle-class males the price is set and not referred to again, the sexual interests may be wide, and there is a certain expectation to talk that transcends the immediate sexual character of the relationship."[59]

The call girl has a code with regard to her customers that is based on good business practices and not usually on any concern for the customer as a person. For example, the call girl will protect her customers' anonymity. If she runs into a customer in public she will give no sign of recognition unless he does so first. She will not steal from her customers and often will not let them overpay her if she thinks they are doing so because they are drunk. As Greenwald points out, a "professional call girl will make every effort to satisfy a client even if he has difficulties. When working with groups of men she will not reveal the inadequacies of one of the men to the others in the group, but will praise him."[60] It can be seen that these are good business practices for the call girl.

Earlier, some of the reasons why men seek out prostitutes were discussed, but some further elaboration is useful here in terms of how the customer views the prostitute. Frequently the "John" wants the woman to tell him how she became a prostitute. The prostitute often chooses from a wide repertoire in answering a customer. Her story may range from an "atrocity tale" of white slavery to the equivalent of the proverbial "just lucky, I guess." "The customer, for his part, often attempts to justify his presence to the prostitute. This too, in many instances, takes the form of a hard-luck story."[61] Often both the customer and the prostitute concoct stories to explain why they are together.

---

[57] Bryan, "Prostitution," p. 291.

[58] Millett, "Prostitution," p. 90.

[59] Gagnon and Simon, *Sexual Conduct*, p. 228.

[60] Greenwald, "Call Girl," p. 407.

[61] Hirschi, "Prostitute," 201.

Sometimes the prostitute is puzzled by the entire nature of the transaction because prostitution puts down not only women but also sex. On this point one prostitute comments, "Often I really couldn't understand the customer, couldn't understand what he *got* out of this, because I really felt I was giving nothing. I would think it would be humiliating to buy a person, to *have* to offer somebody money."[62]

Other roles important to the prostitute subculture are those of the "madam" and the "pimp." The madam was traditionally the woman whom the prostitute worked for. The madam hired and fired, made the rules, and watched over the activities of the women on the job. The madam was important when houses of prostitution were important. She ran the house and the women. She was a boss and had much less interpersonal importance to the prostitute than did fellow prostitutes or pimps.[63] It has been suggested that when the well-being of the prostitute is of primary concern the house system with a madam is best, because the house provided safety, supervision, and other security benefits such as not even the expensive call girl can always enjoy.[64] The madam was often a different type of person from most of her prostitutes. She was often more intelligent, but probably the most important difference was her strong ambition for material success. A number of autobiographical books have been written by ex-madams, and in these they always present themselves as kindhearted social work types who contributed to the preservation of God, family, and country. But the madam has little significance to prostitution today. She has been made obsolete by the less formal, more individual prostitution of the street girl and the call girl.

The role of the pimp brings about as much hostile reaction as that of the prostitute. Society views the pimp as even lower than the prostitute because he is seen as living off her earnings. He is seen not only as a parasite, but as a parasite of the most despicable type, one who feeds off the immoral earnings of a woman's body. In general the attitudes taken toward the pimp are based on his real functions. A pimp is basically a prostitute's lover ("man") to whom she contributes an important part of what she earns as a prostitute. He is also in some cases "her business manager, bodyguard, panderer, and drug connection; but his main function is psychosexual, and his role of lover and recipient of the prostitute's money defines him."[65] A pimp is generally not just a business agent or even just a friend; the relationship between pimp and prostitute is typically that of lovers.[66]

There have been many stories about the sexual relationships between prostitutes and their pimps. One common belief is that the prostitute is

---

[62] Millett, "Prostitution," p. 96.

[63] Hirschi, "Prostitute," p. 203.

[64] Benjamin and Masters, *Prostitution*, p. 240.

[65] Ibid., p. 215.

[66] Bryan, "Prostitution," p. 289.

incapable of reaching sexual satisfaction with any man and that the pimp uses her but that she gets little or nothing from the sexual relationship. However, it appears quite likely that the average prostitute achieves orgasm with her pimp at least as frequently as does a wife with her husband. "The attempt to establish frigidity, along with homosexuality, as a common cause of women becoming prostitutes is far-fetched and doctrinaire. When a prostitute is frigid and/or homosexual, the condition is almost always an *effect*—of intercourse too often engaged in, of disenchantment with the male, etc."[67]

The pimp is almost always heterosexual and masculine in appearance and actions, and he is probably as virile as the average man. His most outstanding characteristic is that he holds high attraction for certain types of women and along with this is able to manipulate and exploit those women to his economic advantage.[68] It has been argued that the pimp is a functional necessity for the prostitute because he watches over her. One writer suggests that the similarity of the pimp-prostitute relationship to the husband-wife relationship, with the *economic roles reversed*, is quite obvious.[69] The view has been advanced that, quite simply, the pimp is often most important to the prostitute as her "family" and that the prostitute is most important to the pimp as his meal ticket.[70]

It has been suggested that because most prostitutes and pimps come out of the lower middle and lower classes a lot of the behavior between them can be explained on social class grounds. This interpretation recognizes that social class equals tend to marry one another and may also establish nonmarital living relationships. Socially a man is a pimp if he lives with a woman he knows is a prostitute, when she contributes to their mutual expenses and he helps her find work. "It is not a case of the man 'creating' the prostitute, nor is it a case of the woman 'selecting' a pimp; her occupation makes them both what they are."[71] As suggested, people who live at the same social class level tend to associate with one another, and their behavior will often reflect their particular socialization experiences. Therefore, when a pimp physically beats up the prostitute he lives with, his behavior need not be a reflection of the pimp-prostitute relationship but may be seen as the lower-class way of dealing with a disagreement—the equivalent of a middle-class family argument.[72]

Because of the assumption that prostitutes hate men, it is commonly believed that many prostitutes are homosexuals. This is also sometimes seen as the reason why many prostitutes do not have pimps. There are

---

[67] Benjamin and Masters, *Prostitution*, p. 221.

[68] Ibid., p. 225.

[69] Hirschi, "Prostitute," p. 202.

[70] Benjamin and Masters, *Prostitution*, p. 227.

[71] Hirschi, "Prostitute," p. 202.

[72] Ibid.

several reasons to assume that prostitutes would have a higher potential for homosexuality than other women. First, since prostitutes are engaged in a variety of sexual behaviors some would be prone to experiment sexually. A second and related reason is that prostitutes are often called upon by customers to perform homosexual acts with one another. While these are usually faked, in some cases the pretended act might lead them to really try it. Third, some prostitutes do dislike men and seek out both interpersonal and sexual satisfactions from other women. Davis found that prostitutes who expressed strong negative feelings toward clients developed a preference for lesbian relationships. Homosexuality is facilitated by: "(1) frequent imprisonments, whereby lesbian contacts are made, (2) impersonal or degrading confrontations with clients, and (3) hustler norms which emphasize the rewards of female sex relationships."[73]

However, there are probably far fewer homosexual prostitutes than is commonly believed. Gebhard provides some data on this point in his study of prostitutes. He found that almost two thirds of his sample had had no homosexual experience whatsoever; "6 percent had incidental experience (i.e., less than 10 events), and 9 percent had homosexual activity only in conjunction with prostitution. This leaves only 24 percent of the prostitutes who had homosexual experience 10 times or more for pleasure rather than profit. Of these, only a few had extensive homosexual activity."[74] Gebhard suggests that prostitutes may so effectively compartmentalize their lives that being a prostitute does not seriously interfere with their heterosexual interests, "their orgasmic capacities, or their ability to form affectional relationships with men."[75]

In any subculture there are some general rules and self-role definitions. It has been pointed out that the form of deviance tells a great deal about the need for deviant group formation and role interaction. Important to some deviant groups is their instrumentality for the broader society. Through their organization subcultures may provide goods and services to meet the demands of others. Prostitution is a good illustration of such an instrumental relationship to the rest of society.[76] Therefore, its general patterns of conduct are important both for the internal needs of the subculture and for the relationships of the subculture to the broader society which it *must* deal with. This kind of deviant subculture is different from others because of its needs to maintain outside relationships. By contrast homosexual subcultures generally want to avoid any contact with the broader society because they have little to gain and a great deal to lose thereby.

---

[73] Davis, "Prostitution," p. 317.
[74] Gebhard, "Misconceptions," p. 30.
[75] Ibid.
[76] Lemert, "Prostitution," p. 47.

Because prostitution is geared to the outside world, prostitutes must make themselves as efficient as possible in dealing with it. For example, as is the case in most businesses the prostitute must make her hours as convenient as possible for the customer. This means that she usually works at night. She will usually set certain hours for business and not accept customers at other hours. However, her hours may be altered given changes in the market demand. For example, in many large cities, such as New York and London, there is a large noontime and early evening trade.[77]

Often the rules of relationships to the customer become internalized into self-role images that the prostitute uses to justify her behavior. For example, the general rule that one gets as much as possible out of a customer becomes a part of a rationalization that the customer is immoral and dishonest and therefore *should* be taken for as much as possible. This also contributes to the self-image that prostitution should not be stigmatized and that one should not look down upon oneself for being a prostitute. For many prostitutes this appears to be a necessary and therapeutic practice. Bryan suggests that these simple rules help "justify exploitation, sustain what cooperative behavior is necessary for occupational functioning, and reduce both public and personal stigma, real or potential, attached to the actor."[78]

The need for rules and self-image concepts is particularly important for prostitutes when they first enter the profession. The "naming process"—consciously recognizing oneself as a prostitute—is often a traumatic experience. Therefore, the rules and rationalizations provided by the subculture are very important. Often the beginning prostitute makes the transition as a result of both push and pull. She feels pushed out of the broader society because she sees it as a hostile or indifferent world. At that time the prostitute often indicates that she has previously associated with people who meant very little to her or that she has no friends or close family at all. Her violation of the general sexual values is rationalized in two basic ways: "(a) everyone is rotten. Hence, prostitutes are no worse than other people, and they are less hypocritical; (b) society doesn't really scorn prostitutes." But as the authors go on to point out, the rationalizations don't work completely because every prostitute they interviewed expressed some degree of guilt feeling about her activity.[79]

Several "pull" factors operate on beginning prostitutes. The most important may be that they see money and the material way of life as highly desirable. But once they are in the prostitute subculture they find

---

[77] Hirschi, "Prostitute," p. 200.

[78] James H. Bryan, "Occupational Ideologies and Individual Attitudes of Call Girls," *Social Problems*, Spring 1966, p. 444.

[79] Norman R. Jackman et al., "The Self-Image of the Prostitutes," *Sociological Quarterly*, Spring 1963, p. 159.

available rationalizations that help them to define their roles in a positive way. Many prostitutes believe that they serve important social functions because in meeting the wide and varied sexual needs of males they protect both individuals and social institutions. A part of the prostitutes' belief system is that marriages are more enduring because of prostitution. As Bryan describes it, "the positive self-images prostitutes have about themselves are that they serve as important psychotherapeutic agents, giving comfort, insight, and satisfaction to those men too embarrassed, lonely, or isolated to obtain interpersonal gratification in other ways."[80]

The roles and the rules of behavior within the prostitute subculture are constantly influenced by the fact that its sexual behavior is illegal. This means that the subculture must develop means for dealing with the legal pressures from the wider society. But often it is difficult for the subculture to know what to do because the controls directed at it vary widely over time. Like most areas of illegal deviance prostitution is not treated consistently by legal agencies. So there is always some insecurity and anxiety as to whether the laws will be applied at a given time. Moreover, prostitution in the big city is often accepted by the authorities. Frequently arrest and prosecution are gestures that are made to keep up the front of public morality. Basically the legal method of dealing with prostitution is simply a form of harassment, not a form of prevention or punishment.[81]

Sometimes the prostitute can pay off the legal authorities to leave her alone. Therefore, the prostitute is in a position to be exploited by the legal agencies as well as by those who know that she is susceptible to legal punishment or public exposure. "The prostitute's fear of the police is often as much a fear of the publicity or jail sentence which would reveal her occupation to friends and family as it is a fear of punishment."[82] The very fact that she is engaged in an illegal and "immoral" area means that she is open to exploitation by a variety of people. Because she must reveal herself as a prostitute to the customer, she is always gambling in the sense that the customer may create problems for her. A plainclothesman posing as a customer may entrap her on a charge of prostitution, or an actual customer may refuse to pay her, knowing that there is often little she can do. People around her in the work situation may also exploit her. For example, desk clerks or bellhops in hotels may exploit their knowledge of her identity by demanding money or by becoming nonpaying customers.

Attempts have often been made to legalize prostitution in the United States, but except in Nevada such efforts have not met with success. According to Millett the chief opposition to legitimization besides the police is not organized religion but rather powerful hotel interests which

---

[80] Bryan, "Prostitution," p. 443.

[81] Millett, "Prostitution," pp. 72–73.

[82] Hirschi, "Prostitute," p. 203.

see the prostitute's "patronage as insufficiently lucrative to outweigh the possible threat to the public image of the more expensive hotels affluent enough to dispense with her custom."[83]

Possibly the most important change that could be legally made would be to remove prostitution from the criminal code. "This would in no way increase the incidence or availability of female prostitution, but it would frustrate the exploitation of prostitutes by the two classes of men who are their chief predators, pimps and police."[84]

It does not seem likely that prostitution will ever disappear completely from American society. There will probably always be some persons who, even in the most permissive society, will be unable to get sexual partners because of age, mental or physical disabilities, or sexual aberrations. But it does appear logical to assume that prostitution in the United States will continue to decrease. All of the indicators are that sexual expression is becoming for many Americans less restricted to the monogamous structure of marriage and less dependent on an emotional and interpersonal commitment. That is, as more women see at least some aspects of their sex lives as recreational and are willing to participate within that context, men will have less reason to seek out the prostitute for recreational purposes.

There are two segments of society in which prostitution will probably continue to be important for some time. First, in the lower middle and lower social classes, where the double standard of sex continues to be strong, the traditional reasons for turning to prostitution will probably continue to prevail. Second, the world of big business will probably continue to use the call girl. This is an area about which there is very little reliable information but in which the high-priced call girl is clearly very important. But in general, it appears that the profession of prostitution is being greatly reduced by the increase in extramarital sexual freedom among women.

BIBLIOGRAPHY

Benjamin, Harry, and R. E. L. Masters, *Prostitution and Morality*. New York: Julian Press, 1964.

Bryan, James H., "Apprenticeships in Prostitution," *Social Problems*, Winter 1965, pp. 287-97.

Bryan, James H., "Occupational Ideologies and Individual Attitudes of Call Girls," *Social Problems*, Spring 1966, pp. 441-50.

Davis, Nanette J., "The Prostitute: Developing a Deviant Identity," in James M. Henslin, *Studies In the Sociology of Sex* (New York: Appleton-Century-Crofts, 1971), pp. 297–322.

---

[83] Millett, "Prostitution," pp. 71-72.
[84] Ibid., p. 70.

Esselstyn, T. C., "Prostitution in the United States," *The Annals*, March 1968, pp. 123-35.

Gagnon, John H., and William Simon, *Sexual Conduct: The Social Sources of Human Sexuality* (Chicago: Aldine, 1973).

Gebhard, Paul H., "Misconceptions about Female Prostitution," *Medical Aspects of Human Sexuality*, March 1969, pp. 24, 28-30.

Greenwald, Harold, *The Call Girl: A Social and Psychoanalytic Study*. New York: Ballantine Books, 1958.

Henriques, Fernando, *Prostitution and Society*. New York: Grove Press, 1962.

Hirschi, T., "The Professional Prostitute," *Berkeley Journal of Sociology*, 1962, pp. 33-49.

Jackman, Norman et al., "The Self-Image of the Prostitute," *The Sociological Quarterly*, Spring 1963, pp. 150-60.

Millett, Kate, "Prostitution: A Quartet for Female Voices," in Vivian Gornick and Barbara K. Moran, *Woman in Sexist Society* (New York: New American Library, 1972), pp. 60-125.

chapter ten

Venereal disease

The diagnosis and treatment of verereal disease is a medical problem. However, with few exceptions venereal disease occurs through interaction between two people. Venereal disease can be treated as social deviance because it carries a social stigma. Thus, one can see that the problem of venereal disease exists on two levels. The first level involves the medical aspect of curing the disease; the second involves the social settings in which the individual is infected by the disease and the ways in which the infected are perceived and responded to by the broader society once that society becomes aware of the stigma.

Some people have a personal or a vested interest in almost all the other types of deviance discussed in this book. That is, they want the deviance to continue so they can participate in it themselves, or they have something to gain from its continuation among others. However, with venereal disease such is not the case. It is hard to imagine anyone who would want to keep a venereal disease if he could rid himself of it without personal or social loss. Nor does it appear that any vested interests want to maintain high venereal disease rates for reasons of personal profit.

Venereal diseases often occur as side effects of some of the areas of social deviance discussed in this book. The substantive area that has most commonly been associated with venereal disease is prostitution, but venereal disease has also been seen as related in varying degrees to all kinds of sexual behavior. In general the more socially deviant the area of sexual behavior the greater the probability of venereal disease. The discussion that follows covers the types of venereal disease, their frequencies, and some of the related social variables.

There is some disagreement as to when the venereal diseases first began to plague human beings. It has been argued that syphilis is almost as old as humanity and has been present in most societies from the earliest times.

Another point of view is that syphilis was a disease of the Western hemisphere which the men who sailed with Columbus first introduced into Europe. Both contentions have certain bases of support, but there is no absolute proof one way or another.[1] Regardless of when or where syphilis first appeared, it was very common in Europe by the start of the 16th century. This led to great fear and to many attempts to isolate the infected. For example, an act was passed in Edinburgh, Scotland, ordering all the infected to gather together to be placed on an offshore island. Failure to comply was to be punished by branding on the cheek.[2]

There is also evidence that gonorrhea is a disease of great antiquity. In fact the word *gonorrhea* was coined by Galen in A.D.130. Also, according to biblical sources it appears that gonorrhea has plagued human beings from the earliest times.

The general concept of venereal disease has also been around a long time. It was first introduced by Jacques de Bethercourt in 1527. But from that time until about the beginning of the 19th century the term *venereal disease* was used in the singular because gonorrhea and syphilis were considered to be the same disease. The word *venereal* refers to the act of sexual intercourse or contact. However, venereal disease is not always transmitted sexually. Some children are born with syphilis, contracting the infection in the mother's womb. There have been reports of syphilis after transfusions of fresh blood and even after tattooing. It is also possible for babies to suffer gonococcal eye infection by contamination with their mother's discharge at birth. However, it is very doubtful that venereal disease can be spread by nonsexual contact, such as simple touching. Venereal disease has nothing to do with poverty, dirt, lack of sanitation, or personal hygiene per se. Venereal diseases cannot be self-engendered. "They do not arise spontaneously even in the most socially unacceptable places of people."[3]

While venereal disease is infectious and is transmitted by one person to another, contact with a carrier does not always lead to infection. It is estimated that one out of five persons who have sexual intercourse with a syphilitic person will be infected, and that for gonorrhea the risk is about one in three.

It is highly probable that venereal disease has been defined as undesirable in all societies. The reasons for so defining it have been physical, social, and moral. In the United States venereal disease is still generally considered to be a shameful condition, a moral as well as a physical degradation. In the past such ideas were held much more strongly than they are today. Many pious people believed that pain and suffering were

---

[1] William Brown et al., *Syphilis and Other Venereal Diseases* (Cambridge, Mass.: Harvard University Press, 1970), p. 1.

[2] R. S. Morton, *Venereal Diseases* (Middlesex, England: Penguin Books, 1972), p. 16.

[3] Ibid., p. 17.

the just retribution of transgression; and "since venereal disease was commonly associated with violations of sexual morality, its victims received little consideration."[4] Karen Jacobs suggests that the lack of cleanliness associated with venereal disease has made it even more taboo.[5] The fact that getting a venereal disease has nothing to do with cleanliness is beside the point. Since venereal disease has been defined as a "dirty" thing, getting it often makes the victim feel personally and socially dirty.

As in all areas of sexual behavior there are variations in the perceptions of venereal disease when related to men and women. Karen Jacobs points out that often men who contract venereal disease are seen as victims while women with venereal disease are often treated as criminals. Society assigns varying punishments to those who have venereal disease. For example, although the military assumes that many of its men will contract a venereal disease it does not punish those who do so. By contrast some states will not allow a woman who has had a venereal disease to hold certain jobs.[6]

In the past the social taboos against syphilis were so great that there was resistance to its official recognition as a problem. In 1908, for example, the U. S. Treasury Department rejected a Public Health Service request that it publish a pamphlet on venereal disease because "the matter contained in this bulletin is not in keeping with the dignity of the fiscal department of government."[7]

As will be discussed shortly, the rapid increase in venereal disease rates in recent years has led to a new social response. It is usually the young who have venereal disease, and this has led to some generational conflict. Many older people see the rising rates of venereal disease as related to the sexually free patterns of life they feel are common among the young. However, during and after World War II the older generation was responsible for a syphilis rate higher than today's and for an approximately equivalent gonorrhea rate.[8]

TYPES OF VENEREAL DISEASE

All told, about a dozen diseases can spread during sexual intercourse. Only three of these—gonorrhea, syphilis, and chancroid—are defined by law as venereal. But it should be mentioned that a high proportion of cases of two other common conditions are sexually transmitted. One of these conditions is nonspecific urethritis, a disease that affects the lining

---

[4] Ibid., p. 7.

[5] Karen Folger Jacobs, "Venereal Disease, War, Sexism and Racism," *Mademoiselle*, May 1972, p. 112.

[6] Ibid., p. 112.

[7] Brown, *Syphilis*, p. 36.

[8] American Social Health Association, "The V. D. Control Program," in Ann McCreary Juhasz, *Sexual Development and Behavior* (Homewood, Ill.: Dorsey Press, 1972), p. 338.

of the male urethra. The disease is characterized as nonspecific because no discernible bacterial, viral, protozoal, allergic, or chemical cause has been found to explain it. The second is trichomoniasis, a vaginal infection caused by protozoans.[9]

Our attention will be directed to two of the three types defined legally as venereal diseases—gonorrhea and syphilis. The third, chancroid, is an acute, painful, ulcerative condition of the genitals. It is most commonly found among men in tropical and subtropical areas.

Gonorrhea. This is by far the most common of the venereal diseases. It is an infection that begins in and is usually confined to the linings of the generative and urinary organs. In 1793 Benjamin Bell, of Edinburgh, separated the conditions of syphilis and gonorrhea. However, not until 1879 was the diagnosis of gonorrhea placed on a scientific basis. In that year the causal organism was first identified.

There are important differences between men and women in the symptoms and ease of diagnosis of gonorrhea. With few exceptions it is men who have the initial symptoms. Usually the first symptom a man notices is a burning sensation in the penis when he is passing water. Soon he will notice a continuous discharge of yellow pus from the urethra.

With women there are no symptoms during the early stages, and there will not be any until complications set in. This means that hundreds of thousands of symptomless infected females, "probably about one third of them prostitutes, form the great worldwide reservoir of infection."[10] It also means that unless specific tests are made there is no way for a woman to know whether or not she has gonorrhea. An added problem for the woman is that gonorrhea may spread through her body. For example, rectal gonorrhea may result from the spread of infected vaginal discharge or menstrual blood over the anus while the woman is asleep or defecating. Sometimes a woman may spread the infection with toilet paper when she wipes herself. In such instances the secretions, containing live germs, seep into and along the short canal into the rectum. The inflammation of the rectum is called proctitis, and it is fairly common. It is rarely a result of anal coitus.[11]

Over the years there have been many different attempts to treat gonorrhea. Until the middle of the 1930s the most common treatment was local washes or what were called curative vaccines or very weak antiseptics taken by mouth. In most cases these treatments didn't work. In the late 1930s, with the introduction of sulfonamides, gonorrhea treatment was placed on a scientific level. However, the success of the sulfa drugs was short-lived; in less than a decade the efficacy of those drugs had waned.[12]

---

[9] Morton, *Venereal Diseases*, p. 19.

[10] Ibid., p. 17.

[11] Ibid., p. 55.

[12] Ibid., p. 23.

At present there is no vaccine for gonorrhea and no immunity against repeated infections. Furthermore, the means of detection are often inadequate. In 1971 the best-known tests for detection were found to be only 60 percent effective.[13] The standard treatment since World War II has been penicillin, but the gonococcus is increasing its resistance to that, and larger and larger dosages are needed for a "cure."

While the consequences of gonorrhea are rarely fatal their cost to the individual can be great. For women a serious internal complication is inflammation of the Fallopian tubes. There is increasing evidence of harmful effects from gonorrhea. Its complications can produce kidney failure, arthritis, sterility, heart damage, and meningitis.

Syphilis.   For many centuries the causes of syphilis baffled medical science, but in 1905 it was demonstrated that *Treponema pallidum* was the organism causing it. In 1906 Wasserman, Bruck, and Neisser revolutionized the diagnosis of syphilis when they produced a complement fixation test that detected infection from analysis of specimens of blood or spinal fluid. "The year 1907 was a landmark in syphilology when Paul Ehrlich developed an arsenical treatment which he hoped would provide a cure for syphilis in a single injection."[14] The treatment did not prove very successful.

Although far less common than gonorrhea, syphilis is a far more dangerous disease. During the first few months or even years it is manifested as an infection of body surfaces, such as the skin and the lining of the mouth and throat. Even in the early stages it invades many if not all organs of the body. These stages are followed by a period, varying from 5 to 50 years, when the disease lies dormant in the body tissues or organs. In some cases syphilis manifests itself again in forms which may be disfiguring, chronically crippling, or deadly.[15]

Since syphilis spreads throughout the body and then, generally after five years at most, becomes completely symptomless, the carrier rarely has any idea that he has the infection. During the symptomless period syphilis is not contagious. However, if it is carried by a woman it is potentially transmissible to her children. Congenital syphilis is transmitted to the fetus by the mother. The father has no direct part in the transmission because the infection passes to the unborn child through the placenta. In general the more recent the mother's infection the more likely is the fetus to be affected. "Succeeding pregnancies in the same syphilitic woman tend to end more favorably, until in the late latent syphilis the chances are at least 5:1 that, even without maternal treatment, the child will be born healthy."[16] If the syphilitic condition of the mother is known, then an-

---

[13] Jacobs, "Venereal Disease," p. 70.

[14] Brown, *Syphilis*, p. 14.

[15] Morton, *Venereal Diseases*, p. 18.

[16] Ibid., p. 86.

tepartum therapy for syphilis can assure the birth of an uninfected child. There has been an increase in the reported rates of congenital syphilis for children under one year of age. The rate in 1962 was 8.1 percent, but by 1971 it had increased to 19.5 percent.[17]

As with gonorrhea, moisture is essential for the development of syphilis. Syphilis flourishes in such areas of the body as the mouth, the genitals, and the anal region. Syphilitic sores develop in places that are particularly vulnerable to infection. In some instances primary sores, sometimes called chancres, appear in various parts of the body. Often homosexual men will develop their primary lesion around the anus or inside the wall of the rectum.

The seriousness of syphilis is reflected in the great medical concern over the years to find a cure. In general, medical authorities have come to the belief that there is no natural or induced immunity to syphilis. This assumption has not been disproven, but considerable evidence has accumulated to suggest that some individuals have a high level of resistance. Clinical records throughout the United States contain case histories of people who have been exposed repeatedly to lesion syphilis but have not developed any clinical or serological signs of infection.[18]

At present syphilis can be cured in the early stages and its progress can be arrested in the later stages. But in all of its stages syphilis is capable of imitating many other diseases, and it is for this reason that, especially in efforts to resolve puzzling medical problems, a blood test for the disease is frequently included.

The most important medical event in the treatment of syphilis was the use of penicillin. While Alexander Fleming had observed the effect of penicillin on bacterial cultures in 1928 it was not until 1943 that "Dr. John Mahoney, working in a Public Health Service hospital on Staten Island, demonstrated the efficacy of the drug as therapy for syphilis. Penicillin was first made available to the Public Health Service in June 1944, for use in rapid treatment centers."[19] The cure rate with penicillin was very high. The cure rate with one course was put as high as 97 percent, and some specialists who wanted to cure all their patients in a short period of time gave more than one course. Follow-up blood tests are an essential part of the treatment, and these are usually given each month at first, and later at three-month intervals. For all those treated for syphilis a minimum follow-up of two years is essential.

In the 30-odd years since its introduction the success of the penicillin treatment has been greatly reduced. It is possible that the organism causing syphilis has built up a resistance to penicillin because so many people have been treated with the drug for various medical problems that

[17] American Social Health Association, "V. D. Control," p. 335.

[18] Brown, *Syphilis*, pp. 22–23.

[19] Ibid., p. 16.

the body builds up a resistance. In any case the dosage needed for the successful treatment of venereal disease has gone up drastically over the years. In the early days as little as 300,000 units of penicillin could be depended on to cure a case of gonorrhea. Now the United States Public Health Service recommends 2½ million units for men and twice that for women. Even among those treated with as massive a dosage as 6 million units, 44 percent were not cured. However, women given penicillin plus probenecid had a 100 percent cure rate. "Probenecid, now being employed with penicillin by more and more U.S. physicians, is a drug usually used to treat gout, but it is also valuable in delaying excretion of penicillin by the kidneys so the antibiotic remains in the body longer and has more chance to work."[20]

Both the personal and the social costs of syphilis have been very high to American society. The United States Public Health Service estimates the cost of maintaining the syphilitic blind to be $6 million per year and the cost of hospitalizing the syphilitic insane to be about $50 million per year. Even more costly and serious has been the death rate caused by syphilis. It has been estimated that in the United States since 1900 syphilis has taken the lives of 3 million babies and 1 million adults. It has been estimated that worldwide during the same period syphilis has taken the lives of about 100 million people.[21]

As mentioned earlier, the gonorrhea rates are higher than those for syphilis. The ratio is usually about three or four to one. However, there can be fairly wide variations among different societies. Morton has suggested that in societies where sexual freedom is growing and where sexual equality is increasing the ratio tends to decrease to about two cases of gonorrhea for every case of syphilis. He argues that the main reason for this is that syphilis is more generally acquired from a regular contact and that such contacts can be more readily traced.[22]

Venereal disease rates.   The upsurge in venereal disease is worldwide. In the mid-1960s the World Health Organization estimated that gonorrhea affected about 60 million people. Since then the number has gone well beyond that. The advent of penicillin in the 1940s lulled many people into the complacent belief that the venereal disease problem was well under control. Various figures indicate the recent worldwide spread. A United Nations report for 1967 estimated that there were 20 million to 50 million cases of syphilis in the world. But possibly the best indication of the high rates of venereal disease was the proportion of pregnant women found to have positive blood tests. These rates varied greatly. For example, in Pakistan the rate was 1 to 2 percent of all pregnant women;

---

[20] Lawrence Galton, "VD: Out of Control?" *Medical Aspects of Human Sexuality,* January 1972, p. 22.

[21] Ibid., p. 18.

[22] Morton, *Venereal Diseases,* p. 116.

in India, 2 to 15 percent; in Morocco, 14 to 30 percent; and in Ethiopia, 30 to 60 percent.[23] Gonorrhea also has universal distribution. The World Health Organization estimates that 65 million new cases of gonorrhea occur each year around the world. The transmission of the gonococcus is almost always through sexual intercourse, and human beings are the only reservoir and known host of the organism.

What is sociologically important is that the spread of venereal disease is highest in areas experiencing civil unrest, social change, and population mobility.[24] When the old social controls are greatly weakened, individuals have a greater number of temporary sexual contacts and therefore greater opportunities to receive and spread venereal diseases. The increase in transitory relationships also means that it is much more difficult to determine which persons are spreading the diseases and to bring them under treatment.

In the United States the changing rates in venereal disease have followed the patterns found in other parts of the world. By the mid-1950s the reported cases of syphilis had declined so greatly that many medical authorities regarded venereal disease as another conquered health problem. One consequence of this attitude was that federal funds to states were decreased, clinics were practically eliminated, and epidemiological follow-up was all but abandoned. From 1958 to 1967 a continuing rise brought the reported early infectious syphilis case rates to over three times the 1957 level.[25]

The estimates of the actual prevalence of venereal disease in the United States in 1970 ran from 2 to 6 million. This meant that from one out of 100 to one out of 33 Americans had a venereal disease. The Public Health Service estimates that in 1970 510,000 Americans had syphilis and at least 2 million Americans had gonorrhea.[26] Venereal disease rates vary greatly by age, but in general they can be said to be highest among young adults. For example, the syphilis rates are highest in the 20-24 age group. The same applies to gonorrhea, although the 15–19 age group also has a relatively high rate. The evidence is clear that syphilis is acquired almost exclusively during the young- and middle-adult years. In 1966 only 1 percent of the cases which occurred were for persons less than 15 years of age, and only 3 percent for persons past 50 years of age.[27]

The reported cases of gonorrhea increased by about 16 percent during 1970. It was estimated that more than 2 million cases were treated during that year, making gonorrhea by far the most common reportable com-

---

[23] Ibid., p. 41.

[24] American Social Health Association, "V. D. Control," p. 340.

[25] Brown, *Syphilis*, p. 40.

[26] Jacobs, "Venereal Disease," p. 112.

[27] Brown, *Syphilis*, p. 78.

municable disease in the United States. All over the country routine tests performed during prenatal examinations disclosed that one woman in 12 was infected with gonorrhea and was unaware of her infection. At some family planning clinics 10 percent of all women tested had asymmetrical gonorrhea, and gonorrhea was found in 12.5 percent of women admitted to prisons.[28] These rates refer only to defined and reported cases. An unknown number of cases escape detection and contribute to "the *silent reservoir of infection in females,* a phenomenon of the present pandemic. In the 20–24 age group, as many as 1 in 20 sexually active females may be suffering from gonorrhea and unaware of her infection."[29]

There is an increasing medical awareness that one of the major problems in the treatment of venereal diseases is the unknown carrier. One recent study found that many more men are unknown carriers of gonorrhea than had been previously believed to be the case. A major factor in the current gonorrhea pandemic is the failure of physicians to identify and treat symptomless male carriers. One reason for this is that the test used to detect gonorrhea is generally not a part of a routine medical examination. The failure to recognize the importance of symptomless infections in men has led to two misconceptions. The first is that gonorrhea is almost always symptomless in the female and symptomatic in the male. The second is that men get gonorrhea from women with chronic symptomless infections but that women get gonorrhea from men with incubating or symptomatic infections. "Although seldom verbalized, this misconception has served as a basis for public health practices and has led to an attitude that it is futile to trace male sexual contacts of women with gonorrhea, because the male will develop symptoms and seek treatment."[30]

One of the problems common to most of the areas of deviant behavior discussed in this book is that the extent to which a specific deviant category of individuals exists in a society cannot be accurately known, but only estimated. The unreported may result from the individual's conscious concealment of his deviant variable or from his unawareness of having it. Both of these factors operate with venereal disease rates. One estimate suggests that the reported venereal disease rates may represent no more than one fourth of the cases that actually occur. This may be because many people who seek treatment for a venereal disease do not become a part of the reported category. Many of the treated but unreported cases are handled by physicians in private practice. Often the physician will report some cases but not others because he is torn between his desire to protect the patient and his responsibility for the health of the

---

[28] Galton, "VD," p. 17.

[29] American Social Health Association, "V. D. Control," p. 333.

[30] Lawrence K. Altman, "Some Gonorrhea in Men Lacks Sign," *New York Times,* Jan. 20, 1974, p. 51.

community. It is probable that a great majority of physicians solve the problem by reporting some patients and remaining silent on others.[31] The physician is perhaps more inclined to report young single persons than older married persons. There is also a social class bias in the reporting because middle-class patients are usually treated by private physicians, who are less likely to report them, while lower-class patients usually seek treatment at public clinics, which almost always report them. Some experts believe that if all cases were known it would be seen that the present increase of venereal disease crosses all age and socioeconomic groups.[32] The low reporting rate of venereal disease by private physicians is reflected in the fact that they treat 80 percent of the cases but report only 17 percent of the overall reported total. "In effect, people who can afford to purchase private doctors' care buy anonymity from venereal statistics and control boards."[33]

In the past some studies were made of specific populations that provide more reliable measures about the frequency of venereal disease rates. This has been true for the military, where all members are given medical tests and where all with venereal diseases are reported. For example, a study of the physical examinations of servicemen during World War I indicated that at the time of induction 5.6 percent were infected with some type of venereal disease. Another 2 percent acquired infection while on active duty. "From those figures some authorities estimated that possibly 10 percent of the United States population was infected with at least one of the venereal diseases at the time of World War I."[34] In 1973 a study of 2,628 sexually active soldiers undergoing routine physical examinations found that 2.2 percent of them had gonorrhea.[35]

Legal aspects of venereal disease. To have a venereal disease is not in itself against the law. However, there are laws related to testing for venereal diseases. In 1935 Connecticut became the first state to require blood tests for both males and females to qualify for a marriage license. However, many of the states have required only the male to furnish proof of freedom from venereal diseases. And even today the state of Washington requires the male, but not the female, to submit an affidavit declaring "that such male is not affected with any contagious venereal disease." Kanowitz observes that the exemption is a subtle, albeit indirect, reflection of the law's acquiescence in separate standards of morality for male and female and that it should be changed to apply to women as well as men. "Though the particular problem is now limited to one state and has, therefore, lost its former vital significance, it continues

---

[31]Galton, "VD," p. 21.

[32] Jacobs, "Venereal Disease," p. 70.

[33] American Social Health Association, "V. D. Control," p. 337.

[34] Brown, *Syphilis*, p. 58.

[35] Altman, "Gonorrhea," p. 51.

to be of interest as another example of the American legal system's endorsement of society's double standard of sexual morality."[36]

Another important area of legal concern is the prenatal blood tests required for pregnant women. Rhode Island was the first state to enact this requirement, in 1938. Forty-two states now have laws requiring blood tests for women when pregnancy is diagnosed. However, many women do not get prenatal care nor do they do it before they are 16 weeks pregnant. As a result, regardless of the laws, there are still many syphilitic fetuses that are aborted before birth as well as many severely damaged syphilitic newborns.[37]

One important change in state laws has been the enactment of provisions allowing minors to give their own consent for venereal disease diagnosis and treatment. The number of states allowing this increased from 14 in 1968 to 30 in 1970. In the past many minors would not seek medical help because their parents had to be informed. The new laws encourage many minors to seek out medical help who would not have done so in the past.

Related social variables. The frequency of venereal disease is influenced by a number of social factors. As suggested earlier, rapid social change is related to increased rates. In general, venereal disease rates increase for those levels of society most characterized by social problems and certain types of social deviance. For example, high rates are associated with poverty and overcrowded living conditions as well as high rates of delinquency and crime, drunkenness, and attempted suicide. In this respect venereal disease is as much a social as a medical problem.

It also appears that particular types of social relationships are related to venereal disease rates. One study reports that three out of four contacts from whom venereal disease was received were either spouses or other persons with whom the afflicted persons had had multiple exposure. This is because increased exposure to a carrier increases the possibility of receiving infection. The same study found that exposure to a person of the same sex was responsible for about 15 percent of the infections. "Although the data is limited, exposure to the same sex occurred relatively much more often among contacts to infectious syphilis (occurring in 19 percent of the named contacts) than for gonorrhea (occurring in less than 6 percent of the named contacts)."[38] Morton says that few developments in the epidemiological field of venereal disease have been more striking than the growth of male homosexuality. He reports that at St. Mary's Hospital in London in the years 1954 to 1956 only 12 percent of early male syphilis cases occurred in homosexuals. By 1960 to 1963 the figure was 65 per-

[36] Leo Kanowitz, *Women and the Law* (Alburquerque: University of New Mexico Press, 1971), p. 15.

[37] Jacobs, "Venereal Disease," p. 69.

[38] American Social Health Association, "V. D. Control," p. 335.

cent.[39] In the United States half of all venereal diseases reported in New York City in 1964 occurred among male homosexuals.[40]

Other changes related to sexual behavior have also contributed to the increase in venereal disease. Most important has been the development of contraceptive techniques—for example, birth control drugs—that give no protection against venereal infection. In the past, when the condom was used much more extensively, there was less chance that the male would receive or spread venereal infection. The use of birth control drugs has also had other effects. For example, birth control pills make the woman more susceptible to venereal infection. One of their side effects is that the normal pH (acidity) of the vagina is neutralized, making it less resistant to infection. One medical estimate is that women not taking pills have a 40 percent chance of contracting gonorrhea from one exposure while women taking pills have an almost 100 percent chance.[41]

What are the possibilities for the future control of venereal diseases? Probably the most practical solution would be an antivenereal contraceptive. This would allow persons to protect themselves against both pregnancy and disease at the same time. Research is going on in this area. However, the concern over the problem of venereal disease doesn't seem to be great enough to bring about any concerted effort to solve it. In general those who state great public concern do so for moral rather than medical reasons. Churchill asks why, if venereal disease is indeed regarded as a serious threat to the health of the world, there has not been a crash program to develop and to dispense adequate methods of immunization. "One suspects that neither cure nor prevention is the real issue in the minds of a great many who raise a hue and a cry over venereal disease and that moral rather than medical issues preoccupy these people."[42]

Churchill goes on to suggest that if as much money were appropriated for syphilis research as went into poliomyelitis in 1965 a vaccine could be found within a few years.[43] The present programs to educate the public about venereal diseases and to provide inexpensive treatment are costly and generally not very effective. As mentioned at the start of the chapter, venereal disease is an area of deviance that almost all would agree should be eliminated. However, it has not yet been defined as a severe enough problem either in this country or on an international scale to justify the outlays in time, effort, and money that are necessary to bring about a solution.

---

[39] Morton, *Veneral Diseases*, p. 131.

[40] Jacobs, "Venereal Disease," p. 112.

[41] Ibid., p. 120.

[42] Wainwright Churchill, *Homosexual Behavior among Males* (New York: Hawthorn Books, 1967), p. 30.

[43] Ibid., p. 30.

BIBLIOGRAPHY

American Social Health Association, "The V.D. Control Program," in Ann McCreary Juhasz, *Sexual Development and Behavior* (Homewood, Ill.: Dorsey Press, 1973), pp. 332–41.

Brown, William J., et al., *Syphilis and Other Veneral Diseases.* Cambridge, Mass.: Harvard University Press, 1970.

Galton, Lawrence, "VD: Out of Control?" *Medical Aspects of Human Sexuality*, January 1972, pp. 17–24.

Jacobs, Karen Folger, "Venereal Disease, War, Sexism, and Racism," *Mademoiselle*, May 1972, pp. 69–70, 112–14.

Morton, R. S., *Venereal Diseases*, 2d ed. Middlesex, England: Penguin Books, 1972.

chapter eleven

Male homosexuality

In the area of sexual deviance an interest in homosexuality has long existed. In recent years in the United States there has been an increasing amount of public awareness and reaction. For the most part interest has centered on the male homosexual, and he will be the center of attention in this chapter. In the next chapter our focus will be on the female homosexual. Women are treated separately. Male and female homosexuality differ in many respects. Our first concern in this chapter will be to look briefly at male homosexuality from a historical and cross-cultural perspective.

In antiquity homosexuality was widely prevalent in most countries of the eastern Mediterranean, and to this day it is more prevalent there than in other parts of the Western world. Homosexuality was common among the early Greeks, perhaps because their cultural values about beauty resulted in the idealization of the slim body of the young man. But with the rise of Christianity homosexuality became more and more tabooed. As the years went on the homosexual was seen increasingly as the ultimate in depravity and excessive self-abuse. During the Dark Ages and the Middle Ages homosexuality was thought to be a supernatural state of mind. It was attributed to possession by devils, and the cure was exorcism by bell, book, and candle.

Until well through the 17th century in England no special role was given to the homosexual, but toward the end of the 17th century the belief developed that homosexuality was a condition characterizing certain persons and not others.[1] In other words, being a homosexual was seen as a broad social role rather than as simply a sexual act. It was a fairly complex role, built around the homosexual's desire and activity,

---

[1] Mary McIntosh, "The Homosexual Role," *Social Problems*, Fall 1968, p. 188.

and this appears to be the way homosexuality is viewed in most of the Western world today, even though countries do vary in their definitions of homosexuals. A majority of European countries do not prohibit homosexual acts between consenting adults.

In the United States the frontier way of life isolated men from women for long periods of time. Under those conditions many men turned to one another for sexual satisfaction and homosexuality was often taken for granted. Homosexuality also appears to have been common among the soldiers of both the North and the South during the Civil War, "and there are accounts of male prostitutes who followed the armies."[2]

A look at cross-cultural views about male homosexuality provides a picture of differential social treatment. In general it has been found that among mammals there is some homosexual activity, sometimes to the point of ejaculation. This has been found to be true of both wild and domesticated animals. However, it is rare to find individual mammals which show an exclusive pattern of homosexual behavior. Ford and Beach in their cross-cultural comparisons found that in 64 percent of the human societies where information was available homosexual activities of some kind were considered normal and socially acceptable for at least certain members of the community.[3] A cross-cultural survey of American Indian cultures showed that over half of 225 groups accepted homosexuality while about a fourth rejected it.[4] Homosexuality has caused anxiety and disapproval in many cultures, but a majority of cultures have provided for some approved means of homosexual outlet and have "attempted to *regulate* rather than to *suppress* homosexual behavior." However, in no society has exclusive homosexuality been required of any substantial part of the population. Wherever homosexuality is required or expected of all males in a community it coexists with heterosexuality.[5]

To say that various cultures accept homosexuality doesn't necessarily mean that they practice it. Nor does the report of no homosexuality in a society actually mean that none exists. For example, of the 76 cultures studied by Ford and Beach, 37 percent reported homosexual activities on the part of adults to be totally absent, rare, or carried on only in secrecy. "It is expected, however, that the estimate would run considerably below actual incidence, since this form of sexual expression is condemned in these societies."[6] Also, in societies where adult homosexuality is said to be rare specific social pressures are directed against it. These range from the sanction of ridicule to the death penalty.

[2] Wainwright Churchill, *Homosexual Behavior among Males* (New York: Hawthorn Books, 1967), p. 57.

[3] Clellan S. Ford, and Frank A. Beach, *Patterns of Sexual Behavior* (New York: Harper, 1952), p. 130.

[4] Wardell B. Pomeroy, "Homosexuality," in Ralph A. Weltge, *The Same Sex: An Appraisal of Homosexuality* (Philadelphia: Pilgram Press, 1969), p. 4.

[5] Churchill, *Homosexual Behavior*, p. 72.

[6] Ford and Beach, *Sexual Behavior*, p. 129.

Many societies have fallen between the extremes of permissiveness and restrictiveness in dealing with homosexuality. In actual fact many societies have been permissive informally while being restrictive formally. There is evidence that in societies where homosexuality is highly restricted persons turn to either homosexuality *or* heterosexuality, but that in societies where there are no strong social sanctions against homosexuality the activities of the males are less apt to be either homosexual or heterosexual and more often a combination of the two.[7] It must also be recognized that cultures are rarely consistent in their definitions of homosexuality, but are very often characterized by internal disagreements. In other words, in any given society there are different people with different views of homosexuality. For example, homosexuals see their activity as a legitimate minority practice while psychologists see it as a type of illness (but often with an implied plea for tolerance, as well as treatment), and law enforcement agencies see it as a crime.[8]

Legal views

The American laws about homosexuality come out of the same background as do most American laws about sexual behavior. They come from the English common law, with strong religious moral overtones. For the purposes of the legal discussion homosexual behavior is defined as sexual behavior between two persons of the same sex. This sexual behavior can consist of simple touching, kissing, petting, stroking the genitalia, oral-genital contact, and anal intercourse (for the male). This definition will be used for the time being, although later in the chapter there will be a further discussion about the definition of homosexuality.

None of the 50 states defines homosexuality as a crime per se; "the diverse limitations imposed by the states are aimed at punishing the acts employed by homosexuals to achieve sexual gratifications."[9] While it is no crime to be a homosexual, most of the states do have laws against homosexual acts between adults and minors, among adults, and in private as well as in public. "The homosexual, in other words, has no legal outlet for the kind of sex life to which he is drawn; his only alternative to law-breaking is abstinence."[10] Many laws are passed to protect persons or property against the invasion of others. But this does not appear to be the case with regard to the laws against homosexuality. Such laws are passed not to protect persons or property against the "dangers" of

---

[7] Pomeroy, "Homosexuality," p. 6.

[8] William Petersen and David Matza, *Social Controversy* (Belmont, Calif.: Wadsworth, 1963), p. 5.

[9] "The Consenting Adult Homosexual and the Law," *UCLA Law Review*, University of California at Los Angeles, March 1966, p. 658.

[10] Edwin M. Schur, *Crimes without Victims: Deviant Behavior and Public Policy* (Englewood Cliffs, N.J.: Prentice-Hall, 1965), p.77.

adult homosexual activity but rather to enforce the cultural taboos against homosexuality. One writer argues that the laws represent an effort to enforce a morality rooted in religion that is no longer appropriate.[11] However, this is not to say that a definite majority of Americans no longer believe that homosexuality is "bad" and no longer believe that it should be controlled. Most Americans *do* take a negative view, but this doesn't affect the logic of the legal position one way or another. That is, the people of a country may support a point of view that has no logical or rational basis—and they often do.

Given the laws against homosexual activity, how restrictive or harsh are the legal controls? In theory the laws are very harsh. For example, a number of states provide a maximum penalty of ten or more years in prison for some homosexual offenses. The penalties range from a maximum of one year in New York for a crime against nature with a person over 18 years of age where consent was given, to life imprisonment for the same situation in Nevada. Four states provide a five-year *maximum* for sodomy, while four other states provide a five-year *minimum* for the same charge. Not only do the penalties vary widely by states, but there is also a wide variation in how homosexual crimes are defined. For example, some states use the term *sodomy*, others *crimes against nature*, and still others *buggery*. This also means that the state courts define the same types of homosexuality in different ways and mete out different kinds of punishment. For example, some states have defined these laws as applying only to intercourse per anus (the common-law meaning of sodomy), while other states have held the laws to include fellatio. Twenty states have sodomy laws which have been framed to enlarge the common-law definition.[12] Furthermore, in some states an individual may receive the same penalty for a single homosexual experience that he would receive in other states for a continuous record of homosexual experience. All of this means that the laws are confused, and therefore their application varies widely over time, by location, and by who is doing the applying. This leaves a great deal of discretion not only to the courts but also to the police.

Actually, in an overwhelming majority of the cases in which homosexuality occurs there is no way in which they could be brought to legal attention. And even if there were, in most situations the legal authorities would do nothing about it. In most situations homosexuality involves the consent of the participants, and therefore there is no victim who can complain to the legal authorities. While in theory the punishments for homosexual activity are harsh, in reality they do not constitute a strong threat to the average practicing homosexual. Schur points out

---

[11] Gilbert M. Cantor, "The Need for Homosexual Law Reform," in Weltge, *Same Sex*, p. 88.

[12] Ibid., p. 85.

that here, as with abortion, there is the problem of obtaining evidence. "Because there is a willing exchange of services involved, there is no complainant; except, occasionally, in instances when force has been used, and indecent assault on a homosexual has been made, or a blatant display has taken place."[13]

The legal controls over deviance are applied on two levels. One is the level of abstraction as presented through the formal legal codes and laws and interpreted through the courts, and the other is the use and application of the laws by the police. As suggested, there is confusion in the formal laws with regard to homosexuality and confusion in how the courts interpret those laws. This means, as is often the case with legal confusion and changing legal views, that the police make many interpretations in applying the laws. The police know what range of legal possibilities they have, and they can choose within that range on the basis of a number of factors they see as important. Furthermore, laws may or may not be applied because of a lack of police manpower, because of the belief that police efforts are needed elsewhere, or because the police feel that homosexuality is not an area of great importance and so leave it alone. It is also true that the police sometimes use homosexuals as informants and will therefore leave those homosexuals alone. In general the police do not bother homosexuals unless they define them as constituting a public nuisance. A legal study in Los Angeles found that even when the police knew that homosexuals were cohabiting they usually would not initiate any action. In part that was a practical decision because the law was unenforceable in private situations, since it was almost impossible to arrest persons for private homosexual activity without exceeding search and seizure limitations.[14] Generally the police leave homosexuals alone if they are in private or in clubs unless there are complaints of soliciting or lewd conduct. Actually, as we shall see, decorum is common to the places frequented by middle-class and upper middle-class homosexuals. In Washington, D.C., male homosexual arrests totaled 496 in 1960 but only 69 in 1968. "Today, sodomy is becoming as rare a charge as heresy; a lesser charge like disorderly conduct or loitering is customarily substituted."[15]

In many cities it has been a common practice for the police to use "entrapment" methods to apprehend homosexuals. There has often been disagreement between the police and the homosexual as to what constitutes "entrapment." The police have generally argued that it is only entrapment if the decoy policeman makes a clear and unequivocal solicitation of the person and arrests the person when he agrees. But most homosexuals consider it to be entrapment if the decoy uses any dress,

---

[13] Schur, *Crimes without Victims*, p. 79.

[14] "Consenting Adult," p. 689.

[15] *Washington Post*, October 25, 1969.

gestures, or language that lure the homosexual in any way into a solicitation. However, the trend in many large cities has been for the police to give up almost all entrapment methods. The New York police publicly announced abandonment of their entrapment procedures, and this was reflected in a decline in arrests of homosexuals from about 800 in 1965 to about 80 in 1969.[16] The "hands off" policy toward the homosexual often reflects the views of political leaders but not the feelings of the policemen. Policemen often reserve a special contempt for deviants; cases of unprovoked homosexual beatings are a part of the record of most large police departments.

The police have always been responsible for determining who gets arrested as having committed a homosexual act. Legally both persons engaging in the homosexual act, whether sodomy or oral intercourse, are guilty. But the police often arrest only the active person. The police tend to see the man who performs the sex act as "queer," while they often see the man who receives the sex act as unfortunate but as having an understandable tendency toward sexual opportunity. To the police the crux of the matter is that the man who brings the other man to orgasm is the "real" homosexual while the man who is brought to orgasm is not. "To put it another way, the policeman may feel that seeking an orgasm is not really blameworthy even in a homosexual situation, but that being interested in bringing another male to orgasm is unmitigated perversion. We have interviewed many men who disapproved of homosexuality and hotly denied homosexual activity, but freely admitted that they had been brought to orgasm by other males."[17]

On the basis of an examination of 550 white males interviewed by Kinsey between 1940 and 1956, Gagnon and Simon say that most homosexuals cope fairly well, "and even particularly well, when we consider the historical period involved and the stigmatized, and in fact criminal nature of their sexual interests. Of this group, between 75 and 80 percent reported having had no trouble with the police."[18]

According to the UCLA *Law Review* study on homosexuality three basic types of people are picked up by the police for being involved in homosexual acts. The first type is the "cruiser," a confirmed homosexual who very often moves compulsively from bar to bar, or who hangs out around public restrooms, aggressively seeking a number of sexual partners. The second type is the homosexual who hangs out around homosexual gathering places and accepts solicitations, but does not himself actively solicit partners. The third type is the "situational" of-

---

[16] *Newsweek*, Oct. 27, 1969.

[17] Paul H. Gebbard, et al., *Sex Offenders* (New York: Harper and Row, 1965), pp. 324-25.

[18] John H. Gagnon and William Simon, *Sexual Conduct: The Social Sources of Human Sexuality* (Chicago: Aldine, 1973), p. 138.

fender, who is usually the passive partner in oral sex, who is approached
by the "cruiser," and who accepts "or is induced to make a solicitation for
various nonhomosexually motivated reasons including sexual deviation,
intoxication, curiosity, or thrill-seeking, and the hope of robbing the
'cruiser.' For instance, sailors on shore leave exhibit a tendency towards
'situational' violations."[19]

As suggested, there have been recent attempts to liberalize the laws
about homosexuality. In 1973 eight states (Illinois, Connecticut,
Colorado, Oregon, Ohio, North Dakota, Delaware, and Hawaii) had
done away with their penalties against private sexual relationships, both
homosexual and heterosexual, between consenting adults. In some states
various discriminations are maintained. For example, Kansas has reduced
sodomy penalties for homosexual adults from felonies to misdemeanors
but allows heterosexuals, married or unmarried, to perform oral or anal
sex without any legal restraint. "Delaware and Texas appear to be
moving in the same direction. The *very same acts* would thus be legal for
heterosexuals, but illegal for homosexuals."[20]

Other states have attempted to enact more liberal laws with regard to
sexual freedom, but for the most part they have not been successful. It
appears quite possible that more states will accept new sexual laws. All of
the laws that have been presented in the various states have been very
much concerned with the protection of specific societal interests. The
concern has been: (1) that all people be free from any kinds of sexual
aggressions; (2) that children be carefully protected from any sexual
exploitation; and (3) that people be insulated from any public displays of
a sexual nature.[21]

One must be careful about suggesting that there is any strong trend in
the United States in the direction of more liberal laws about sexual
behavior in general and homosexuality in particular. The sodomy laws
are indicative of the possible legal trends with regard to homosexuality.
In the period from 1951 to 1965 Arizona, California, New Hampshire,
New Jersey, and Wyoming increased their penalties against sodomy.
During the same period Arkansas, Colorado, Georgia, Illinois, Nevada,
North Dakota, New York, Oregon, and Wisconsin lessened their
penalties.[22] These changes do *not* indicate any very strong liberal trend
with regard to homosexuality. One common fear is that if the laws were
liberalized there would be a sharp increase in homosexuality. Gagnon
and Simon have suggested that greater tolerance of homosexuality
through the reform of sex laws would not increase the incidence of

---

[19] "Consenting Adult," p. 690.

[20] Del Martin and Phyllis Lyon, *Lesbian Women* (New York: Bantam Books, 1972), p.
43.

[21] "Consenting Adult," p. 668.

[22] Cantor, "Homosexual Law," p. 83.

homosexuality even if it encouraged those males who had not, due to fear of the law, engaged in homosexual contact to enter into such relationships. "At the same time, there may be a countertendency. The lowering of sanctions and the decrease in stigma may reduce the barrier between the homosexual and heterosexual world, and this may allow some persons in the homosexual world to develop an interest in heterosexual adjustments."[23]

The best available data on the extent of homosexuality in American society still come from the Kinsey study. That study found that about 10 percent of all American men had had fairly extensive experiences with homosexuality. However, only about 4 percent of the total male population had had an extensive adult commitment to homosexuality.[24] Studies indicate that the incidence of homosexual behavior is high and continues to increase with age among single men, while among married men it is low and decreases slightly with age. If the Kinsey 4 percent figure still holds true then it may be extrapolated that between 2 and 3 million men are exclusively homosexual in the United States today. This should be taken as only a crude estimate because the actual figure cannot be known. But what is important is that homosexuality is the exclusive sexual pattern followed by a large minority of American men.

"CAUSES" OF HOMOSEXUALITY

It is doubtful whether any other area of human deviance has been subjected to as many attempts to explain its causes as has homosexuality. It appears that because homosexuality has been traditionally seen as so "abnormal" there has been a great need to explain it, in part so that "normal" sex can be more securely understood. Homosexuality has presented a challenge to the developing personal and social sciences of the past hundred years. There have been attempts to explain homosexuality by biologists, geneticists, physiologists, psychiatrists, psychoanalysts, psychologists, social psychologists, sociologists, and others. The body of literature in this area is so vast that it can only be very briefly mentioned here.

The beliefs about the causes of homosexuality have changed over the years. A hundred years ago, when homosexuality was seen as a vice, it was attributed to depravity, excessive "self-abuse," satiation, and the hedonistic search for new sensations. The cure at that time was public censure and private penance. "Seventy years ago, when homosexuality was regarded as a form of moral and neurological degeneracy, the cause

---

[23] John H. Gagnon and William Simon, "Sexual Deviance in Contemporary America," *The Annals*, March 1968, pp. 116–17.

[24] Alfred C. Kinsey, Wardell B. Pomeroy, and Clyde E. Martin, *Sexual Behavior in the Human Male* (Philadelphia: Saunders, 1949), p. 640.

was attributed to the 'bad seed' of one's ancestors, and there was no cure because it is impossible to reverse heredity."[25]

The attempts to explain the "causes" of homosexuality may be placed into three general groupings: medical, psychological, and social. In earlier days homosexuality was seen as sinful and evil behavior. Later it was viewed as moral degeneracy. But neither of those approaches is now given serious consideration.

Medical explanations

Under this heading we may briefly consider several medical approaches. For example, there has long been an attempt to explain homosexuality on the grounds of inborn characteristics; that is, the person is seen as having been born with traits or forces that would make him become a homosexual. However, no research of any significance supports this approach. Another medical approach has been in terms of hormone treatments for believed deficiencies. But almost uniformly hormonal studies have failed to find any differences between homosexual and heterosexual individuals, as have various studies of body structure, genital anatomy, and brain injuries. "Studies showing any positive findings in these areas have been poorly done, have had too few subjects or a poor selection of subjects, or have been contradicted by other studies."[26] In recent years there has developed a small body of research indicating that hormonal inbalance may be involved in the explanation of at least some homosexuality. "But there are many questions still to be answered about the role of hormones in homosexuality."[27]

The more common medical approach to homosexuality is reflected in the tendency to label it as a "disease" or an "illness." This is in part a reflection of a trend in society to apply the concept of illness to many personal and social problems. The view that homosexuality is a disease implies several consequences. "The first is that those in whom the condition exists are sick persons and should therefore be regarded as medical problems and consequently as primarily a medical responsibility. The second is that sickness implies irresponsibility, or at least diminished responsibility."[28] It has been argued that homosexuality does not fit the criterion of using symptoms to determine whether a disease exists because in many cases it is the only symptom and the person is healthy in all other respects. There are cases where psychiatric abnormalities do occur, and

---

[25] Churchill, *Homosexual Behavior*, p. 89.

[26] Pomeroy, "Homosexuality," p. 12.

[27] Robert E. Gould, "What We Don't Know about Homosexuality," *New York Times Magazine*, February 24, 1974, p. 58.

[28] "Wolfenden Committee," in Edward Sagarin and Donel E. MacNamara, *Problems of Sex Behavior* (New York: Crowell, 1968) pp. 115–16.

if, "as has been suggested, they occur with greater frequency in the homosexual, this may be because they are products of the strain and conflict brought about by the homosexual condition and not because they are causal factors."[29] It appears that the disease approach does little to explain the causes of homosexuality and contributes little to understanding homosexuality.

Psychiatric explanations

Probably the best-known theories about the causes of homosexuality have been developed by psychiatrists. This is particularly true of the psychoanalytic theories, which assert that homosexuality is a form of mental sickness. The psychoanalytic approach is to try to affect the causes of the "sickness" in the homosexual or to help him accept his "sickness" and live with it. In any sociological attempt to understand the causes of homosexuality the psychoanalytic approach is of very little value.

Psychiatry has played a major role in defining how the homosexual is viewed both by society in general and by those interested in seeking professional "treatment." During the 20th century psychiatry has been the major force in stereotyping the homosexual. Under the guise of a value-free medical model many psychiatrists have translated the rhetoric of religion into the rhetoric of mental illness. Defining homosexuals as mentally ill has often served only to degrade the homosexual as inferior to the heterosexual because health (heterosexuality) is better than illness (homosexuality).[30]

Psychiatrists have almost always assumed that heterosexuality is best. They have considered both homosexuality and bisexuality to be unhealthy and have usually maintained that anyone who desires bisexual activity is basically homosexual. However, some psychiatrists are abandoning this approach. For example, one argues that if there were no social restrictions on sexual object choice most human beings would be functioning bisexuals. "Indeed, if all taboos were lifted, pathology might well consist of exclusive interest in one sex, regardless of which sex one chooses."[31]

One of the basic problems with psychiatrists' generalizations about behavior is the biased nature of their samples. The basic question is how psychiatrists who see only a small number of disturbed homosexuals can reach conclusions about all homosexuals, the vast majority of whom do not come in for treatment. "The few studies that have compared non-patient homosexuals and nonpatient heterosexuals have not borne out the

---

[29] Ibid., p. 117.

[30] Barry M. Dank, "The Homosexual," in Patricia Keith-Spiegel and Don Spiegel, *Outsiders USA* (San Francisco: Rinehart Press, 1973), p. 227.

[31] Gould, "Homosexuality," p. 63.

theory that homosexuals are sick or even different, except for sexual preferences."[32]

Another psychological approach to the causes of homosexuality sees early childhood experiences as the crucial causal setting. Theories based on this approach attempt to relate homosexuality to the child's early experiences with his family. Some researchers stress "undue attachment to the mother, others emphasize unsatisfactory relations with the father, while still others seem to have evidence that both are of equal importance."[33] Another limitation of this approach is that it depends on the individual's recall of childhood experiences and requires him to submit evidence not only about himself but also about his parents. To illustrate this limitation Simon and Gagnon point out that recent research in child-rearing practices indicates "that two years after the major events of childrearing, weaning, and toilet training mothers fail to recall accurately their previous conduct."[34] If this is true for adults then how much trust can be given to an adult's recall of his childhood after a far greater span of years?

Given the general assumption that homosexuality is undesirable the psychiatric approach has traditionally been to try to eliminate it. The psychiatrist has sought to reverse the patient's homosexuality and to bring his sex life into conformity with conventional, heterosexual norms. Evidence of successful conversion therapies has not been produced. "Although there have been numerous claims of success by therapists, those claims are not supported by systematic scientific research."[35] More often than not, after "successful" therapy the individuals either revert to their homosexual activities or "in robotlike fashion and with a supercilious air akin to that often found among religious converts, they function as 'heterosexuals.' In neither case, however, do they usually convey the slightest impression of ease, happiness, naturalness, or contentment."[36]

There is some evidence of changing views about homosexuality among psychiatrists. In 1973 the American Psychoanalytic Association's board of trustees voted unanimously to remove homosexuality from the category of mental illness. The new official definition uses the term *sexual orientation disturbance* for "individuals who are disturbed by, in conflict with, or wish to change, their sexual orientation." The trustees hasten to add that "the diagnostic category is distinguished from homosexuality, which by itself does not necessarily constitute a psychiatric disorder."[37] The impact

---

[32] Ibid., p. 59.

[33] Eva Bene, "On the Genesis of Male Homosexuality," in William A. Rushing, *Deviant Behavior and Social Process* (Chicago: Rand McNally 1969), p. 164.

[34] William Simon and John H. Gagnon, "Homosexuality: The Formulation of a Sociological Perspective," *Journal of Health and Social Behavior*, September 1967, p. 178.

[35] Dank, "Homosexual," p. 291.

[36] Churchill, *Homosexual Behavior*, p. 252.

[37] Gould, "Homosexuality," p. 13.

this change will have on the ways in which psychoanalysts actually treat homosexuals and on the extent to which homosexuals trust psychoanalysts and seek out help will probably not be great.

What is important is that many homosexuals are involved in satisfying and meaningful social relationships that serve to make their world orderly, intelligible, and integrated. A homosexual subculture (discussed later in the chapter) serves the individual homosexual well in many ways, though it "makes him less reachable by conventional therapies and social agencies when he suffers from problems, whether or not those problems are associated with his homosexual preferences."[38]

Social explanations

There is a psychological assumption that social theories of homosexuality make. This assumption is that there is nothing innate in the sex drive of the individual other than the need for tension release. Therefore, the objects toward which the sex drive is directed are a result of social learning. "Young male mammals who have not been previously conditioned will react to any sufficient sexual stimuli, whether these are autoerotic, heteroerotic, or homoerotic in character, and moreover may become conditioned to any of these stimuli."[39] Consequently homosexuality, like heterosexuality, is learned through one's social experiences with regard to the sex drive. This means that there is no "natural" sexual pattern, but rather there are sexual patterns that one learns in order to satisfy the drive. Whatever the causes for the direction by which one seeks to satisfy the drive, it is satisfied within a dynamic social setting that may variously reinforce or undercut that direction over time. For example, a boy may be pushed socially because he is of slight body build and not able to compete successfully in the world of sports. But social conditions are inevitable, and many may contribute in varying ways to a trend already started, or may even help to start a trend.

One writer has argued that not until the sociologist sees homosexuals as representing a social category, rather than a medical or a psychiatric one, will we begin to ask the "right questions about the specific content of the homosexual role and the organization and functions of homosexual groups."[40] This approach recognizes that the sexual inclinations of the committed homosexual are a part of a continuing role and not simply a series of specific sexual activities. The role of the homosexual is not peculiar to himself, but is shared with other homosexuals. As will be discussed in detail, the very nature of their particular deviance draws homosexuals into interaction with one another.[41] It has been pointed out

[38] Gagnon and Simon, *Sexual Conduct*, p. 164.

[39] Churchill, *Homosexual Behavior*, p. 95.

[40] McIntosh, "Homosexual Role," p. 192.

[41] Schur, *Crimes without Victims*, p. 85.

that the homosexual's sexual object choice has dominated and controlled the views about him and led to the assumption that his sexual choice determines all other aspects of his life. "This prepossessing concern on the part of nonhomosexuals with the purely sexual aspect of the homosexual's life is something we would not allow to occur if we were interested in the heterosexual."[42] Of course, homosexuals vary widely in the degree to which their sexual commitment is the major focus for organizing their lives.

The view of homosexuality as a social role implies a "naming process" for both the homosexual and for others who define him as such. As McIntosh has pointed out, the "naming process"—the social labeling of deviants—operates as a means of social control in two ways. First, it provides a clear-cut and recognized dividing line between permissible and impermissible behavior. Second, it helps to segregate the deviants from others and thus restricts their practices and rationalizations to relatively confined groups.[43] Often the deviant sees his social role as a condition which he cannot control. Given this view, the homosexual often sees his homosexual role as justified because he cannot move back into the heterosexual world completely. But it is suggested that the homosexual should be seen as playing a social role rather than as having a condition.[44]

What can be said sociologically about the causes of homosexuality? The concern with the basic causes of homosexuality may be overdone. Even if the causes could be distinguished, that knowledge would have limited application to influencing or even understanding the *development* of homosexuality. This is true because often the reason for starting to move toward some form of deviant behavior has little to do with the influences that occur once the start is made. For example, the initial reason for taking drugs may have little relevance to the developing patterns that change the drug user into a drug addict. There is a tendency to think of causes as discrete and set in time rather than as diffuse and changing over time. The research data on homosexuality clearly show it to be a complex phenomenon not only in its manifestations in individual and social experience and behavior but also "in its determination by psychodynamics, biological, cultural, situational, and structural variables. An 'either-or' position with respect to any one of these variables simply does not account for the extraordinary diversity of the phenomena to be accounted for."[45] There also appears to be general agreement among experts as to two aspects of homosexuality: first, that there exists in some people a homosexual propensity that varies quantitatively in dif-

---

[42] Simon and Gagnon, "Homosexuality," p. 179.

[43] McIntosh, "Homosexual Role," p. 183.

[44] Ibid., p. 184.

[45] Evelyn Hooker, "Male Homosexuals and Their 'Worlds,'" in Judd Marmor, *Sexual Inversion* (New York: Basic Books, 1965), p. 86.

ferent individuals and can also vary quantitatively in the same person at different stages in his life cycle; and second, that this propensity can influence behavior in several ways, some of which are not clearly sexual, although exactly how much and in what ways are matters for disagreement and dispute among experts.[46]

In what is probably the best sociological study of male homosexuality Dank provides data on the age of homosexual identity development. Based on a sample of 386 self-identified male homosexuals the study shows that the median age for homosexual identity development was 25. For the total sample the age distribution was: "12 percent between ages eight and fourteen; about 35 percent ages fifteen and nineteen; about 31 percent ages twenty and twenty-four; and about 22 percent age 25 or older."[47]

There is a need to question some of the assumptions made about the causes of homosexuality and the directions that homosexuality takes, because often the discovery of homosexuality in a person is taken as clear evidence that major psychopathology exists. "When the heterosexual meets these minimum definitions of mental health, he is exculpated; the homosexual—no matter how good his adjustment in nonsexual areas of life—remains suspect."[48] The image of the homosexual often presented to society is that of the homosexuals the medical practictioner encounters, and these are almost always people with severe problems. On this point Pomeroy, a practicing psychologist, has said that if his concept of homosexuality were based on what he has seen in his practice he would also think of it as an illness. "I have seen no homosexual man or woman in that practice who wasn't troubled, emotionally upset, or neurotic. On the other hand, if my concept of marriage in the United States were based on my practice, I would have to conclude that marriages are all fraught with strife and conflict, and that heterosexuality is an illness,"[49]

Sociologically the most fruitful approach to the study of homosexuality may center on the notion of social roles. Some roles which have as a basic part the nature of one's sexual inclination also include far more than that. Simon and Gagnon have been the major figures in the attempts to develop a sociology of homosexuality. They feel that the problem of finding out how people become homosexual requires an adequate theory of how they become heterosexual and that the patterns of adult homosexuality are dependent on the social structures and values that surround the homosexual after he becomes such.[50] Therefore, in the next section our concern will be with the development and significance of the homosexual subculture.

---

[46] "Wolfenden Committee," p. 113.

[47] Dank, "Homosexual," p. 275.

[48] Simon and Gagnon, "Homosexuality," p. 180.

[49] Pomeroy, "Homosexuality," p. 13.

[50] Simon and Gagnon, "Homosexuality," p. 179.

THE HOMOSEXUAL SUBCULTURE

The homosexual subculture is found in the large cities of the United States. There are undoubtedly some variations among the different cities with regard to the size and complexity of the subculture. But there are patterns that are common to all cities, and those are the focus of interest in this section. One of the problems in trying to study a deviant subculture is that so much of it is hidden, not only from the broader society but often even from many of the deviants themselves. Hooker has compared the homosexual subculture to an iceberg because the visible aspects of the subculture are only a small part of the whole and an understanding of the hidden aspects is fundamental to an understanding of the whole. She writes that the broad world of homosexuality includes men who have "longstanding living relationships with other homosexual men and who rarely, if ever, go to bars or other public establishments because of their sexually predatory and competitive character."[51] In other words many homosexuals are isolates. For the most part they will not be a part of the discussion in this section because little is known about them and they are not a part of the homosexual subculture.

The homosexual subculture or the gay community is not a unitary, cohesive group, since homosexuals come from very diverse social backgrounds. Dank and Warren have each studied what they refer to as gay communities. (Their concept of community is essentially the same as the concept of subculture.) Both researchers found that while homosexuals have a common sexual identification, that does not eliminate their economic, political, religious, ethnic, and educational differences. "Gay life styles are the product of both the individual's own unique social background and personality, and the nature of his interaction with other homosexuals."[52] Warren found these variables to be related to types of homosexual relationships. She observes that short-term relationships were based on different criteria than were long-term relationships. "Gay men select their lovers according to general rules of ethnic, racial, age, and class similarity, although there are exceptions. The short-term sexual relationship, on the other hand, is based more on strictly sexual preferences."[53]

What does the homosexual subculture mean in the broadest sense? The subculture implies a continuing group of individuals who share some significant activity and begin to develop a sense of a bounded group possessing special norms and a particular argot. These individuals engage in various social activities that reinforce a feeling of identity and provide a way of institutionalizing the experience, wisdom, and mythology of the

---

[51] Hooker, "Male Homosexual," pp. 100–101.

[52] Dank, "Homosexual," p. 279.

[53] Carol A. Warren, *Identity and Community in the Gay World* (New York: Wiley, 1974), p. 75.

collectivity.[54] As Hooker explains, it is within the context of the subculture in relation to the broader society that homosexuals are able to develop working solutions to problems of sexual performance and psychological gender which cannot be understood in the perspective of the heterosexual world.[55]

Of course, all deviant subcultures represent structures built around that which makes their members deviant. The deviance becomes a highly significant role for the individual. This is similar to the complex of activities that are built around the person's other major roles such as sex role, his occupational role, or his role as a family member. But for the deviant, as well as for others who know him as a deviant, the role of deviance may transcend all other roles in importance. Therefore, a consequence of the deviant commitment to homosexuality is its major importance in the organization of the homosexual's overall life-style. The homosexual may organize his "friendship, leisure time, and occupational adjustments around the homosexual community and around homosexual friends."[56] The subculture becomes a socialization setting not only for the new homosexual but also for those who have been in it for a while. Once individuals enter that life their personal and social identities as homosexuals are continually being defined through their interaction with one another. Of course, different people are involved in different degrees within the subculture and are therefore differentially influenced by it.

However great the homosexual's degree of involvement in the subculture, it must always be recognized that that involvement is only one important influence on his life-style. The subculture presents one set of variables, which interact with many other variables, "such as personality dynamics and structure, personal appearance (including body build, gesture, demeanor), age, and occupation, to produce these attitudes, self-concepts, and behavior. Most accounts of gender identity and sex roles in male homosexuals focus on personality traits and psychodynamics, and ignore the important contribution of the shared perspectives of homosexual subcultures."[57] While the stress here is on the subculture's influence on the homosexual it must be kept in mind that other forces of varying strength are also influencing and shaping his behavior.

It is useful to look at some of the patterns of community life that Warren discovered in her study. She found that for many male homosexuals their homes were very important. While the younger men

[54] William Simon and John H. Gagnon, "Femininity in the Lesbian Community," *Social Problems*, Fall 1967, p. 217.

[55] Evelyn Hooker, "An Empirical Study of Some Relations between Sexual Patterns and Gender Identity in Male Homosexuals," in John Money, *Sex Research: New Developments* (New York: Holt, Rinehart and Winston, 1965), p. 26.

[56] Gagnon and Simon, "Sexual Deviance," p. 116.

[57] Hooker, "Male Homosexuals," pp. 44–45.

did a lot of their socializing in the gay bars, the older men entertained far more in their homes, which became an ever-greater focus of attention. "The younger men claim that the older men drift into this pattern because they are no longer able to compete sexually in the marketplace of the gay bar, but the older men say it is because home entertainment is more intimate and rewarding."[58]

When a homosexual is having a party at his home, clear structural roles are filled by the guests and the host. The host has the obligation to provide the liquor that will enable the guests to relax and engage in conversation. The guests have an obligation to carry on sociable conversation. "Sociable talk is not heavy nor is it intimate; heaviness suggests an overcommitment to the self, whereas intimacy suggests an overcommitment to the other, and neither is suitable for sociability."[59] Generally the men don't look for sexual partners at such parties. Because the aim of the parties is sociability any sexual searching must be done subtly.

But the most important point that Warren makes about sociability in the homosexual community is that it is deadly serious. As she points out, the traditional Protestant ethic viewed play as both trivial and secondary to the world of work. "Gay sociability, however, is work. It symbolizes both the centrality of leisure and playful nihilation of the straight world and all its seriousness."[60]

Evelyn Hooker's research provides an indication of the various types of homosexuals that will be encountered in an analysis of subcultures. She suggests three general social levels of homosexual types that generally *will not* be a part of the subcultural setting: (1), closely knit cliques formed around pairs of homosexually "married" persons or around singles, many of whom are married to women; (2), larger groups with one or more loose clique structures as a central group along with a number of peripheral members; and (3), loose networks of friends who may meet once in a while at various parties.[61]

Warren found some people who were willing to accept a homosexual identity but not a gay world (or homosexual subculture) identity. In general this was because they held critical attitudes toward the subculture. "Some men regard the gay community as too isolated from the rest of the world; others, like gay liberationists, regard it as too secretive. Still others see it as culturally inproverished and intellectually arid, and some do not like the stigma attached to membership."[62]

---

[58] Warren, *Gay World*, p. 29.

[59] Ibid., p. 47.

[60] Ibid., p. 65.

[61] Evelyn Hooker, "The Homosexual Community," in John H. Gagnon and William Simon, *Sexual Deviance* (New York: Harper and Row, 1967), p. 180.

[62] Warren, *Gay World*, p. 158.

Because a special sexual choice sets homosexuals apart it is important to look more specifically at the direction the sexual activity takes. That is, there is a need to examine the range of homosexuality both as a sexual act and as a sexual role. One basic distinction that is made is between the bisexual and the homosexual. Bisexuals are persons who have both homosexual and heterosexual experiences. Some persons are bisexuals because they believe that the sexual act is the thing that one does and that the gender of the partner doesn't really matter. The sexual experience, not the sexual partner, is what matters. But other bisexuals may be caught in conflict because they are bothered by their inability to make a clear choice to go one way or another. Many of these seek out the homosexual subculture because they see it as providing them with a rationale for their homosexual inclinations.

In an extensive study of male homosexuals Weinberg and Williams reported that 56 percent said that they had engaged in sexual relations with a female. But only 11 percent reported doing so within the 6 months prior to completing the questionnaire. Of that same group 50 percent reported having had homosexual relations about once a week or more while 24 percent reported having had homosexual relations once a month.[63]

Warren found that often men who defined themselves as bisexuals were excluded from the sociable gay world, although they might be welcomed as bed partners. Bisexuality as a self-definition is regarded both as an instance of bad faith and as an exhibition of a lack of commitment to the gay community. "The gay see the bisexuals as copping out from the polar choice gays see as the core of their lives."[64]

The term *homosexual* as it is used here refers to persons who have made an overwhelming personal commitment for some time to sexual partners of the same sex. This means that they are homosexual regardless of the sexual roles that they choose to play during homosexual activity. Traditionally the role of homosexual was seen as applying only to those who played the female role. The old terms of *active and passive* partners or *masculine and feminine* roles are no longer applicable to many homosexuals. "Instead, the variety and form of the sexual acts between pair members, the distribution of tasks performed and the character of their performance do not permit us to make such a differentiation."[65]

There are a few women in the subcultural world of the male homosexual. These women may be homosexual or heterosexual. Their involvement in the subculture seems to serve functions for both the men and themselves. The men mention such advantages as having women as

---

[63] Martin S. Weinberg and Colin J. Williams, *Male Homosexuals* (New York: Oxford University Press, 1974), pp. 99–100.

[64] Ibid., p. 135.

[65] Hooker, "Male Homosexuals," p. 102.

decorative objects at gay parties. "The heterosexual women, many of whom are divorced and some of whom are middle-aged, get attention from the gay community without commitment or sexual threat."[66]

The stereotype of the homosexual continues to be one of a highly effeminate male. He is seen as a person who deliberately acts like, and uses, the speech patterns and gestures of women. "Blatant displays of effeminacy are viewed with scorn by many male homosexuals; similarly, in some cases it may be an exaggerated display of masculinity that makes one man an object of sexual desire for another."[67] Dank says that if there is any consensus on any subject in the male homosexual world it is that masculinity is better then femininity. The norm is that one should be masculine and not a "sissy."[68] When effeminacy is found in the homosexual male it is probably not due to measurable differences from other males in physical characteristics, but rather to the use of the voice, facial gestures, walk, gait, manner of wearing the hair, and other characteristics.[69]

Not only is there effeminacy among some male homosexuals, but there is also an exaggerated masculinity among others. Some male homosexuals act excessively male and almost caricature the image of masculinity. To further confuse the picture there are, as Pomeroy has pointed out, "false positives"—"people whose mannerisms, vocal inflection, or way of dress suggests homosexuality even though they have no homosexual tendencies."[70] Pomeroy goes on to say that the relationship between effeminacy and homosexuality is very elusive. For example, "overt homosexual contact was probably more common among the cowboys and the Indian fighters of the west in the 19th century than among any other single group of males in our century."[71]

Furthermore, it is often difficult, if not impossible, to distinguish the homosexual from the heterosexual by psychological tests. Evelyn Hooker presented a group of judges, selected on the basis of their clinical expertise, with the results of three widely used clinical projective tests that had been given to homosexuals and heterosexuals. The judges were able to distinguish the homosexuals from the heterosexuals on no better than a chance level.[72] The evidence clearly shows that one cannot accurately define the homosexual as a distinguishable type either in appearance or in personality, at least on the basis of present psychological tests.

---

[66] Ibid., p. 81.

[67] Schur, *Crimes without Victims*, p. 69.

[68] Dank, "Homosexual," p. 283.

[69] Donald W. Cory, "Homosexuality," in Albert Ellis and Albert Abarbanel, *Encyclopedia of Sexual Behavior* (New York: Hawthorn Books, 1961), p. 488.

[70] Pomeroy, "Homosexuality," p.11.

[71] Ibid.

[72] Cited in Naomi Weisstein, "Women as Nigger," *Psychology Today*, October 1969, p. 22.

If homosexuals cannot be clearly distinguished on the basis of appearance, they can be distinguished by the type of sexual activity they engage in. In the broadest sense homosexuality refers to any kind of sexual activity that occurs between members of the same sex. However, the two basic types of homosexual activity are oral and anal sexual relations. Many homosexuals view sodomy (anal sex) with revulsion because it is very painful initially and becomes pleasurable only after considerable conditioning. One researcher estimates that only about 20 percent of all homosexuals engage in sodomy as recipients.[73] Bancroft has suggested that the social prejudice against anal intercourse may have been intensified by the association of sodomy with witchcraft. The term *sodomy* has been applied to both homosexual and heterosexual anal intercourse and sodomy was once seen as a way in which witches had communion with the devil, who used his forked penis to commit sodomy and fornication at the same time. "The failure to discriminate between sodomy and homosexuality persists in the English law to this day."[74]

So oral sex is the overwhelming activity of male homosexuals. It used to be believed that only the effeminate homosexual used his mouth in providing oral sex while the masculine role partner received oral sex but never gave it. In fact, many, if not most, homosexuals do have a preference for one way or the other *but* are often willing to be either the passive or active partner in oral sex depending on the partner's desires. It also appears that the beginning and younger male homosexuals most often have oral sex performed on them but that as homosexuals get older they will often turn to performing oral sex on a partner. This shift over time is reflected in an old homosexual belief that "today's trade is tomorrow's competition." However, who does what in the sex act is not a clear indicator of the broader sex roles played among homosexuals.

One of the characteristics of the homosexual subculture is a high degree of sexual promiscuity. Hoffman writes that "since the sexual relationships in gay life tend to be transitory, the sexually active homosexual constantly needs new partners in order to obtain a reasonable amount of sexual satisfaction."[75] The amount of promiscuity makes it very difficult to estimate the number of sex partners of the adult male homosexual. Many homosexuals estimate that they have had hundreds of sex partners, and some even place their estimates in the thousands. In his sample of adult male homosexuals Gebhard found that two thirds had had over 75 sex partners. He points out that part of the reason for the large numbers is that some homosexuals are as interested in sexual activity for its own sake as in achieving orgasm. In fact they are sometimes more

---

[73] Clifford Allen, "Sexual Perversions," in Ellis and Abarbanel, *Sexual Behavior*, p. 804.

[74] John Bancroft, *Deviant Sexual Behavior: Modification and Assessment* (Clarendon Press, 1974), p. 8.

[75] Martin Hoffman, *The Gay World* (New York: Bantam Books, 1968), p. 42.

interested in the former. "This is particularly true of the homosexual who is desirous of fellating other males. In one evening he may tally more sexual partners than many purely heterosexual males may accumulate in a lifetime."[76]

Some general distinctions concerning the nature of the sexual relationship are made within the subculture. The "one-night stand" is probably the most common type of homosexual relationship. However, this may take two forms, one of which is the "quickie," which may range from a few minutes to a few hours. In that situation the partners have probably never seen each other before and will usually never see each other again. In a second kind of one-night stand the partners spend the night or even a weekend together. By contrast an "affair" between homosexuals is a relationship that lasts for weeks or months.[77] These types of relationships are very similar to those found among many unmarried men and women.

As suggested, many sexual encounters between male homosexuals involve only a single encounter, after which they never see each other again. One study found that 60 percent of the respondents, sex partners were persons with whom they had had sex only one time. For about 40 percent of the respondents the longest homosexual affair had lasted less than a year.[78] Having so many different partners carries certain risks. The risks are particularly great when the partners are sought in public and semipublic locations. It was found that between a fourth and a third of the homosexual respondents reported having been robbed by a sexual partner.[79]

Mark Freedman argues that homosexual males are more comfortable engaging in group sex than are heterosexual males. He goes on to say that, in his opinion, group sex offers pleasures that are impossible for couples. Freedman cites a study by John Gigl, "who in 1970 investigated a sample of 680 gay men, and learned that 55 percent of them participated in group sex at least once a month. In contrast, two recent studies of heterosexual group sex showed that over three quarters of the men were unable to perform."[80]

"COMING OUT"

Highly important to any deviant subculture is what takes place when an individual enters and is accepted by the subculture. In the life cycle of

---

[76] Gebhard, *Sex Offenders*, p. 344.

[77] David Sonenschein, "The Ethnology of Male Homosexual Relations," *Journal of Sex Research*, May 1968, p. 77.

[78] Simon and Gagnon, "Homosexuality," p. 354.

[79] Ibid.

[80] Mark Freedman, "Homosexuals May Be Healthier than Straights," *Psychology Today*, March 1975, p. 31.

the individual this is a crucial "naming stage." Within the homosexual subculture this stage is referred to as "coming out"—presenting oneself as being homosexual at least to the extent of wanting to function at times within the subculture. "This process often involves a change in the symbolic meaning of the homosexual category for the homosexually oriented individual. What for him was previously a category for the mentally ill, perverts, etc., now becomes a socially acceptable category."[81]

So coming out is the point at which the person sees himself as a homosexual and makes his first exploration of the homosexual subculture. Hoffman says that walking into a homosexual bar for the first time is a momentous act in the life history of the person because in doing so he publicly identifies himself as a homosexual. "Of equal importance is the fact that it brings home to him the realization that there are many young men like himself and, thus, that he is a member of a community and not the isolate he had previously felt himself to be."[82]

When the homosexual first comes out his decision may release a great deal of sexual energy. During the initial period after coming out he may pursue sex quite indiscriminately and with great vigor and enthusiasm. At this time the young homosexual often throws himself totally into the homosexual life. He frequently wants to become totally involved because he is now part of a subculture in which he feels comfortable. Gagnon and Simon have suggested that this period resembles the honeymoon of the young married couple. That is, sexual intercourse is for the first time seen as legitimate and is therefore pursued with great energy. However, the high sexual involvement declines as demands are made on the young couple. "In these same terms, during the homosexual 'honeymoon' many individuals begin to learn ways of acting out homosexual object choice that involve homosexual gratification, but that are not necessarily directly sexual and do not involve the genitalia."[83] The same authors also suggest that during the coming out stage there is often a tendency to "act out" in public places in a somewhat effeminate manner. Many young males (between 18 and 25) go through a crisis of femininity. "Some, in a transistory fashion, wear female clothing, known in the homosexual argot as 'going in drag.' "[84] However, "the tendency is for this kind of behavior to be a transitional experiment for most homosexuals, an experiment that leaves vestiges of 'camp' behavior, but traces more often expressive of the character of the cultural life of the homosexual community than of some overriding need of individual homosexuals."[85]

While coming out implies an entrance into the homosexual subculture

---

[81] Dank, "Homosexual," p. 275.

[82] Hoffman, *Gay World*, p. 14.

[83] Gagnon and Simon, *Sexual Conduct*, p. 356.

[84] Simon and Gagnon, "Homosexuality," p. 182.

[85] Simon and Gagnon, "Homosexuality," p. 147.

it also implies leaving the straight world behind to some extent. This carries with it certain risks for the homosexual. It may endanger his livelihood or his professional career. But if he is able to escape those dangers his coming out may have positive effects on his relationship with the broader society. For example, it may absolve him from failure to assume the responsibilities of marriage and parenthood, and it is a way of fending off painful involvements in heterosexual affairs.[86] Once the individual has made the move and is accepted as a part of the homosexual subculture he may find himself a functioning member with a number of shared values and behavior patterns. One area of values in the subculture centers on love and the establishment of extended homosexual relationships.

There are a variety of ways in which the homosexual male can structure his relationships to the homosexual world. These range from rapid, impersonal sex in public restrooms to political activism on behalf of the homophile movement. "Other combinations of sexual and social desires can produce 'one-night' stands, affairs, nonsexual friendships, and homosexual 'marriages.' "[87]

Probably most homosexuals desire love and permanent relationships. If these values do not seem too important to the homosexual when he is young they take on increasing importance as he gets older. Most homosexuals distinguish sex and love relationships from friendship. They usually try to keep sex separate from their friendships. Many homosexuals have friends with whom they have never attempted to have sex, as well as friends who were once sexual partners. Sonenschein also found that while "genital relations between friends were extremely rare, sex play was very common."[88] There is sexual kidding but not actual sexual activity.

It is often said that the homosexual is like anyone else except that he chooses a sex object of the same sex. He is said to be like heterosexuals in wanting long-lasting and monogamous relationships based on love. The homosexual recognizes that many of his relationships do not come close to approximating this ideal of love and permanency. This, he may argue, is no different from the contrast between the ideal and the reality in the heterosexual world. He often sees that world as one in which every husband cheats, there is a high level of wife-swapping, and the only thing that holds marriages is the social pressure of children.[89] This view helps the homosexual in his rationalization that his world isn't very different from that of the heterosexual.

---

[86] Edwin M. Lemert, *Human Deviance, Social Problems, and Social Control* (Englewood Cliffs, N.J.: Prentice-Hall, 1967), p. 48.

[87] Weinberg and Williams, *Male Homosexuals*, pp. 10–11.

[88] Sonenschein, "Homosexual Relations," p. 73.

[89] Edward Sagarin, *Odd Man In: Societies of Deviants in America* (Chicago: Quadrangle 1969), p. 99.

Gebhard found that deep emotional involvements were commonly reported among homosexuals. In his sample 81 percent said that they had loved another male, and 63 percent had loved more than one male.[90] As suggested, finding a permanent partner was a goal of many homosexuals. The proportion who pursued this goal increased after "aging" set in (about age 30), when finding a steady mate became a significant concern.[91] As the homosexual's competitive ability on the sexual market decreases a more permanent relationship becomes even more desirable to him.

Some homosexuals set up fairly permanent relationships and define themselves as "married." Sonenschein's study details the characteristics of homosexual "marriages." 1. There was usually some sort of ritual, and in most cases it was an imitation of the heterosexual marriage ceremony. 2. Some symbols of the marriage ceremony were used, such as wedding rings. 3. There was a tendency to dichotomize social roles. Sometimes a feminine partner stayed home and a masculine partner went to work. But this was not a typical pattern and described a special type of "marriage."[92] In most cases the division of labor in terms of household duties was based on personal choice rather than masculine or feminine role differences.[93]

Most attempts to develop a homosexual marriage based on the heterosexual model run into difficulties. The elements which generally strengthen the ties in male-female marriages are absent. There are no legal or religious bonds, no manifestations of society's approval, and no legally enforceable mutual property protection. Since homosexuals do not have children, their emotional relationships are more focused and consequently more fragmentary. "The only bind in the gay marriage is 'spouse-to-spouse' and *not* the multiple emotional affective binds that are often found in heterosexual marriages."[94]

It is clear that an increasing number of homosexual couples want to legitimate their relationships. In one recent case, *Baker* v. *Nelson* (Minnesota, 1972), one such couple challenged the restrictions on homosexual marriages, arguing that "the right to marry without regard to the sex of the parties is a fundamental right of all persons and that restricting marriage to only couples of the opposite sex is irrational and invidiously discriminatory." The court disagreed, affirming the traditional position that marriage "is the state of union between persons of the opposite sex."[95]

---

[90] Gebhard, *Sex Offenders*, p. 347.

[91] Sonenschein, "Homosexual Relations," p. 80.

[92] Ibid., p.81.

[93] Ibid., p. 75.

[94] Dank, "Homosexual," p. 280.

[95] Lenore J. Weitzman, "Legal Regulation of Marriage: Tradition and Change," *California Law Review*, July-September, 1974, p. 1235.

eleven/Male homosexuality 289

Probably the first legal religious marriage in the United States between two persons of the same sex was performed in Los Angeles in 1970. The ceremony was conducted under a provision of California law that allows a common-law liaison to be formalized by a religious ceremony and a church certificate of marriage. Under these circumstances "the law does not require that the couple obtain a marriage license, the church certificate being sufficient to prove the legality of the marriage."[96]

The homosexual bar

Important to any subculture are the settings in which the members meet and interact with one another. Such settings may also take on a symbolic meaning for the deviant because entering them signifies to him that he is among his own kind and that he may be open and relatively free in filling his deviant role. Probably the most important subcultural setting for the homosexual is the bar. It has been suggested that the bar provides a natural setting for the homosexual community because most of the homosexual's involvement in his subculture occurs during his leisure time, and the bar provides the setting for free time sociability. It has also generally been true that because homosexuals are subject to legal and police pressures they need gathering places which are mobile and can open, close, and open again without great loss or difficulty. However, it should be stressed that a minority of all practicing homosexuals turn to bars. Nevertheless, the homosexual bar is important because it is visible and tells us something about general patterns of interaction in the homosexual subculture.

It is quite probable that most large cities not only in the United States, but throughout the Western world, have homosexual bars. The number of such bars and their freedom from legal intervention vary greatly. For example, in Europe the city of Amsterdam is informally known as the homosexual capital. This is because Amsterdam not only has many homosexual bars and other homosexual gathering places, but also because it takes a generally permissive view toward homosexuality. This has proved to be an economically profitable point of view for that city. In the United States the most permissive city with regard to homosexual bars and other homosexual activities is probably San Francisco. This is a part of that city's longtime permissive attitude toward sexual matters in general, which is also manifested in its acceptance of erotic movies, nude dancers, and so forth.

In the various cities the homosexual bars tend to cluster in certain areas. This is in part because their clientele often like to move from one bar to another during the course of an evening. Hooker found that in Los Angeles the clusters of homosexual bars are typically situated in the

---

[96] Martin and Lyon, *Lesbian Woman*, p. 105.

following areas: "residential sections with heavy concentrations of homosexuals; beaches or other places of homosexual group recreation or leisure-time activity; public entertainment districts—theaters and so forth; and areas of high tolerance and relative permissiveness toward other forms of deviant behavior."[97] Some indication of how many homosexual bars there are in cities can be obtained from the figures for San Francisco and Los Angeles County. In the middle 1960s more than 30 bars in San Francisco catered to an exclusively homosexual clientele. In the late 1960s it was estimated that at least 35 bars in Los Angeles County catered exclusively to homosexual customers.[98] At a few bars heterosexual customers come in to "watch" the homosexuals. The homosexuals (and sometimes they put on an act) in those bars are in effect the floor show or entertainment that draws the straight crowd. However, this is not the kind of bar the homosexual wants to frequent as a part of his subcultural involvement.

In some cities there also appear to be a wide range of homosexual bars that are differentiated by type of clientele. A study in Los Angeles found a variety of homosexual bars, such as the S&M (sadists and masochists) clubs and the "makeout" bars. Often the owner of a bar cultivates a specific type of homosexual customer and takes steps to keep others out. "One bar owner stated that on rare occasions when nonhomosexuals try to enter, he will either ask them to leave, or serve warm beer, or turn off the heating system. Further, if homosexuals who are not regular customers try to enter, they will be ostracized by those present. Thus most homosexual bars are quasi-private clubs which create no risk of outraging the public."[99] In most cities the general policy of the alcoholic beverage commissions and the police departments is one of tolerance. In Los Angeles this is true as long as the owners do not allow overt homosexual activities to take place on their premises. In general the authorities feel that the mere congregation of homosexuals at a bar is not enough to justify any action. But it has been found that the policies of police departments toward harassment of homosexual bars do vary, with larger communities appearing to be more tolerant than smaller communities.[100]

Homosexuals do not congregate in just any homosexual bar; rather, they seek out bars whose atmosphere allows them to feel at ease. Therefore, the successful operation of a homosexual bar calls for skill on the part of the operator. "It requires a knowledge of the tastes and behavior of homosexual clientele and the ability to create the kind of atmosphere that will attract them in large numbers, as well as the ability

---

[97] Hooker, "Male Homosexuals," p. 95.
[98] "Consenting Adult," p. 689.
[99] Ibid., pp. 689–90.
[100] Ibid., p. 730.

to control behavior within limits to which law enforcement officers, passing as ordinary clientele, cannot legally object."[101] The successful bar begins to take on an atmosphere of its own. This is reflected in the reappearance of the same faces several nights of a week. "Every bar has its cluster of friends who gather to exchange gossip, to look over the new faces, and to spend social evenings in an atmosphere congenial to them, where the protective mask of the day may be dropped."[102]

The most important function of the homosexual bar is that it serves as a "flesh market." In this respect it is very much like the swingers' "socials" discussed in an earlier chapter. On a given evening two persons may meet and make arrangements to get together later in the evening for sexual purposes, or may exchange information that will enable them to get together at some future date. Hoffman writes that men go to bars for the purpose of finding sexual partners, "and if this function were not served by the bar there would be no gay bars, for, although homosexuals also go there to drink and socialize, the search for sexual experience is in some sense the core of the interaction in the bar."[103] While the "flesh market" aspect of the homosexual bars may be their basic reason for existence they do perform other important functions for the homosexual. They are also centers where friends can meet and exchange news about the homosexual world. Hoffman suggests that the sexual function of the homosexual bar is illustrated by the way the patrons sit. He says that in a heterosexual bar the patrons' interests are focused on one another as they sit in pairs or small groups. But in a homosexual bar the patrons sitting at the bar usually face away from the bar and look toward the other people in the room and toward the door as they watch for possible sex partners.[104]

Besides the homosexual bars there are other gathering points for homosexuals. These are locations in which some subcultural interaction may take place, but which more specifically provide a setting for sexual exchanges. Among these gathering points are the public baths found in most large cities. Here the persons are stripped and are judged on their physical attributes. The baths function as homosexual gathering places for male homosexuals because of the strong tendency among some male homosexuals to be highly promiscuous. It is difficult to imagine female homosexuals developing a similar kind of sexual gathering place. Many of the men who go to the baths will feel disappointed if they have only one sexual experience during a visit. Hoffman writes that he interviewed a young man at one of the baths who "preferred to take the receptor role in anal intercourse and had 48 sexual contacts in one evening, simply by going into his room, leaving the door open, lying on his belly and letting

---

[101] Hooker, "Male Homosexuals," p. 96.

[102] Ibid., p. 98.

[103] Hoffman, *Gay World*, p. 51.

[104] Ibid., pp. 53–54.

48 men in succession sodomize him."[105] This is an illustration of the ultimate in purely physical sexual interaction.

Much more common than the use of baths is the use of public restrooms for sexual contact. In the jargon of the homosexual subculture these are referred to as "tearooms." Public restrooms are used because those who know can easily recognize which are suitable settings for their purposes. "Drives and walks that separate a public toilet from the rest of the park are almost certain guidelines to deviant sex. The ideal setting for homosexual activity is a 'tearoom' situated on an island of grass with roads close by on every side."[106] The tearooms, like the baths, represent settings in which the most impersonal sex takes place. Throughout most of the sexual encounters in the public restroom nothing is said. "One may spend many hours in these buildings and witness dozens of sexual acts without hearing a word. The mechanism of silence goes beyond satisfying the demand for privacy. Like all other characteristics of the tearoom setting, it serves to guarantee anonymity, to assure the impersonality of the sexual liaison."[107] In the homosexual subculture the restroom serves a highly specialized function—a setting for the sex act. Within the specialized setting of the tearoom there are really only two roles. One person performs the sex act, and the other receives it. The person who performs the sex act is the one who is usually a homosexual. This man often wants a large number of sexual experiences, and he may fellate 10 or 15 men a day. The men who come to the tearooms so that the sex act can be performed on them are called "trade" in the homosexual sub-culture. Many of these men are known as regulars and stop in the restroom almost every day on the way to or from work. Humpheys found that only a small percentage of the homosexuals who hang out in bars are also found in the restrooms. "The so-called closet queens and other types make up the vast majority of those who engage in homosexual acts—and these are the persons most attracted to tearoom encounters."[108]

Most of the men who seek homosexual release in the tearooms appear to be seeking nothing more than physical sexual release. "They want a form of orgasm-producing action that is less lonely than masturbation and less involving than a love relationship."[109] But with no verbal exchange it is hard to see that these kinds of sexual activities are any more personal than masturbation. In fact the trade's code of behavior is reflected in the absence of friendship groups among those who come to the restrooms. They come in alone, seek out the sexual outlet, and avoid conversation with one another. Impersonality is the keynote of tearoom sex.

---

[105] Ibid., p. 48.

[106] Laud Humphreys, "Tearoom Trade: Impersonal Sex in Public Places," *Trans-Action*, January 1970, p. 12.

[107] Ibid., p. 13.

[108] Ibid.

[109] Ibid., p. 18.

Humpheys found that those who sought out sexual release in the public restrooms were uniformly lonely and isolated and were unsuccessful in marriage or work. "En route from the din of factories to the clamor of children, they slip off the freeways for a few minutes of impersonal sex in a toilet stall."[110] While the marriages of these men were nothing special Humphreys did not find that they were especially unstable. Nor did it appear that any of the wives were aware of their husbands' secret sexual activity.[111] Very few of the trade think of themselves as homosexual— certainly not as long as they are receiving the sex—although as some get older they will be givers in the sex act and may then define themselves as homosexual. It should also be noted that tearoom homosexuality is risky because it is responsible for a majority of the arrests for homosexual offenses in the United States.

There is a related type of social situation in which homosexuals find their sexual partners. In this situation boys, usually members of delinquent gangs, are paid by homosexuals to serve as sexual partners. These boys are often hustlers or prostitutes in the sense that they sell their sexual services. Very often older and less attractive homosexuals may have to seek out the hustler if they want a sexual partner. It may also be that "married homosexuals from out of town and ultrasecretive homosexuals who seek the ultimate in anonymity may also be among the hustler's customers."[112]

In a study of delinquents and homosexuals, Albert Reiss found that the boys functioned as members of gangs and that their gang involvement set the patterns for their behavior with homosexuals. The boys could let themselves be used by homosexuals but could under no circumstances show any sexual or personal concern for the homosexuals. The boys did not define themselves as homosexuals. They defined homosexuality not on the basis of homosexual behavior but rather on the basis of participation in the homosexual role. "The reaction of the larger society in defining the *behavior* as homosexual is unimportant in their own self-definition. What is important to them is the reaction of their peers to violation of peer group norms which define roles in the peer-queer transaction."[113]

Aging

Of all the personal factors that might worry the homosexual probably none is more psychologically upsetting for many than aging. Because such great importance is attached to appearing youthful and attractive in order to compete successfully the homosexual often worries about losing

---

[110] Ibid.

[111] Ibid., p. 17.

[112] Schur, *Crimes without Victims*, p. 90.

[113] Albert J. Reiss, "The Social Integration of Queers and Peers," in Howard Becker, *The Other Side* (New York: Free Press, 1964), p. 207.

his youth. In some of the subcultures aging may occur at around age 30, and men past that age may be seen as "senior citizens." It is very common for the homosexual to try to postpone getting old by imitating the young. One observer writes that the middle-aged homosexual lets grow long "what is left of his hair, wears beads, body shirts, western vests, and peace emblems, studies the head's manner of movement and speech, and goes right on getting high on alcohol, because he considers drugs unsafe."[114]

Gagnon and Simon have suggested that aging is a life-cycle crisis that the homosexual shares with the heterosexual in our youth-oriented society. They point out that while American society in general places an extremely high emphasis on youth, the homosexual community places an even greater stress. But the homosexual has fewer resources with which to meet the crisis of aging than does the heterosexual. "For the heterosexual there are his children whose careers assure a sense of the future and a wife whose sexual availability cushions the shock of declining sexual attractiveness. In addition, the crisis of aging comes later to the heterosexual, at an age when his sexual powers have declined and expectations concerning his sexuality are considerably lower."[115]

As suggested, when the homosexual gets older and becomes less desirable on the sexual market it may be necessary for him to pay for his sexual partners. When the older homosexual can afford it he may have a "kept" boy or young man. This person is "kept" in the role of "mistress," and his interest in the relationship is usually materialistic. His involvement with his older partner tends to be superficial and exploitative.[116] Sonenschein found that young men who were being kept by older homosexuals tended to have limited involvement in the homosexual subculture. This was due to the older man's fear that his "boy" would be stolen from him and "to the fact that the other members of the group held a rather low opinion of such a relationship and the individuals involved in it. The 'kept boy' however apparently served a social function to his 'keeper' in that the older homosexual liked to occasionally 'show off' his partner and the manner which he could 'keep' him to the rest of the community."[117]

Communication in the subculture

As mentioned, the homosexual subculture provides the setting for passing along information and gossip of importance to the community. Also, the direction that language and communication takes contributes to

---

[114] Tom Burke, "The New Homosexuality," *Esquire*, December 1969, p. 308.

[115] Gagnon and Simon, *Sexual Conduct*, p. 357.

[116] Sonenschein, "Homosexual Relations," p. 75.

[117] Ibid., p. 76.

the subculture's solidarity and helps to dramatize for the members their adherence to homosexual values. "Thus, the gossip about sex, the adoption and exaggeration of feminine behavior, and the affectation of speech represent ways of affirming that homosexuality is frankly accepted and has the collective support of the group."[118] One measure of the effectiveness of communication within a subculture is how fast the subculture can transmit information. Hoffman points out that a characteristic of the homosexual subculture is that news travels very fast and that information as to streets, public parks, and restrooms where homosexual contacts may be found is rapidly circulated among the members of the subculture.[119]

As with all subcultures, that of homosexuality has developed a specialized jargon. Homosexuals have borrowed words from the subcultures of jazz, criminals, drug users, and so forth, but have also coined some of their own words. These words refer to homosexual roles, values, and activities. While the homosexual jargon contributes to subcultural cohesiveness it is above all communicative. It centers on social and sexual relationships rather than on the sex act itself. "To illustrate this: when, in the subject group, homosexuals talked about sex it was for the most part in the context of *who* had sex with *whom* and *why* that particular relationship might or might not have taken place; it was, in other words, talk about sexual *partners* rather than sexual outlets."[120]

In many instances the deviant subculture adopts some of the derogatory terms used by the broader society as a part of its own vocabulary. For example, it is not just the straight world that uses such terms as "deviant," "sick," and "pervert" to describe those they feel are outside the social norms. Homosexuals often use these and similar terms in a parallel way. Warren reports that in the community she studied homosexuals defined other homosexuals as transsexuals, transvestites, pedophiles, and "other trash."[121]

Sonenschein found that a small number of the homosexuals he studied imitated female speech patterns. This was done in several ways. First, an attempt was made to imitate the sound of female conversation. This generally involved copying inflectional and stress patterns, but rarely the stereotyped lisp. Second, use was made of what are often thought of as feminine adjectives—words like *darling* and *lovely* and phrases like *terribly sweet*. Third, feminine familiars like *honey* and *darling* as well as pronouns like *she* and *her* were used both as terms of address and in

---

[118] Maurice Leznoff and William A. Westley, "The Homosexual Community," in Gagnon and Simon, *Sexual Deviance*, p. 187.

[119] Hoffman, *Gay World*, p. 45.

[120] David Sonenschein, "The Homosexual's Language," *The Journal of Sex Research*, November 1969, p. 285.

[121] Warren, *Gay World*, p. 131.

references to males. Finally, masculine names were feminized. Harry became Harriet, and David became Daisy.[122]

Often the feminine stress among male homosexuals is a part of "camp" behavior. That is, the use of feminine names and pronouns describes behavior which is not serious but fun and a parody of femininity, without implying female gender or deviance for the participants. "These types of behavior include exaggerated gestures of the hand and body, a lisping style of speech, and, at the highest camp—drag, the caricaturing of female clothing, behavior and role."[123]

There are more subtle means of communicating among homosexuals. While it is not true that nonhomosexuals could pick out many homosexuals on sight, it is true that homosexuals can often recognize one another. This is not necessarily because of any physical or even dress characteristics. The signs are given and recognized when homosexuals are "cruising"—looking to pick up or be picked up. When cruising they make gestures which immediately identify them to each other. "A large part of cruising is done with the eyes, by means of searching looks of a prolonged nature and through the surveying of the other man's entire body. It is also done by lingering in the presence of the other person, and by glancing backward."[124] Or homosexuals may use signals that tell what they are interested in sexually. For example, foot tapping indicates a willingness to participate in oral copulation.[125]

Another area of homosexual behavior about which there is a great deal of speculation, but little empirical data, is the extent to which homosexuals dominate or are disproportionately represented in certain occupations. In fact, in recent years some have argued that there is a homosexual conspiracy to dominate the arts and other fields. There are undoubtedly a large number of homosexuals in many artistic occupations such as classical music, the theater, and interior decorating. This may occur because the individual who selects such occupations finds himself defined as "different" because of his choice. For example, a boy who develops a strong interest in ballet at an early age will often have difficulty in developing a strong masculine self-image. But whatever the reasons there do appear to be a high number of homosexuals in certain occupations. It may be that once homosexuals are in certain fields they have a tendency to recruit and encourage others who are sexually like themselves. This is similar to the ethnic or religious favoritism found in some occupations. But it seems doubtful that there is a homosexual conspiracy because whatever homosexuals create or sell does go for the most part to a heterosexual

---

[122] Sonenschein, "Homosexual's Language," p. 283.
[123] Warren, *Gay World*, pp. 105–6.
[124] Hoffman, *Gay World*, p. 45.
[125] "Consenting Adult," p. 692.

market. That market may be influenced, but could hardly be manipulated, by an organized homosexual conspiracy.

All subcultures are characterized by a high level of conformity, and this conformity is often manifested in such areas as dress styles and other material goods. That is, there develops an "in" knowledge as to what is really right in dress, places to eat, books to read, and so forth. In some of the larger cities businesses have developed that are patronized primarily by the homosexual because of the influence of his subcultural values. Helmer has pointed out that in New York City there are a number of such clothing stores, restaurants, barber shops, tailors, and even some stationery shops "who carry a line of greeting cards for 'gay' occasions." He also says that "some homosexuals feel enough group loyalty to patronize mainly those establishments considered 'gay,' usually because of their employees, but others are indifferent to the point of calling them 'fruitstands.'"[126] In general the homosexuals who most strongly identify with the subculture are the ones most apt to support the business outlets run by and/or for homosexuals.

One theme of this book has been that deviant activities and subcultures frequently overlap. There has often been speculation that the homosexual way of life has a high overlap with those patterns of attitudes and behavior associated with the use of drugs. It is suggested by one writer that most homosexuals under the age of 40 frequently use marijuana and occasionally use "acid." It is also suggested that drug use is very common among homosexuals in their early and mid-20s because it was a part of their growing up experience, but that they used more than their heterosexual peers because drug use annoyed heterosexual adults. "Their heterosexual fellow heads, after all, though properly alienated, did maintain one important allegiance with the system: heterosexuality."[127]

Timothy Leary and other spokesmen of the drug movement have stated that LSD cures homosexuality. There has been some suggestion that LSD does appear to bring about in many homosexuals a new, if somewhat ill-defined and subordinate, interest in the opposite sex.[128] The present-day homosexual seems to be more secretive about his drug use than about his sexual interests. This suggests that being caught for drug use is now more dangerous than being caught for homosexuality. Of course, the punishments are much more severe for drug use than for homosexuality. In general one would expect deviants to be more willing than nondeviants to try other areas of deviance. The very fact of being a part of one deviant pattern makes one experienced in the ways of deviance.

---

[126] William J. Helmer, "New York's 'Middle-Class' Homosexuals," *Harper's*, March 1963, p. 87.

[127] Burke, "New Homosexuality," p. 308.

[128] Ibid., p. 312.

In summary, what can be said about the homosexual subculture? Basically it provides a social setting in which the deviant may find others like himself both for sexual contacts and social reassurance. Because the subculture is the only setting in which the homosexual feels he can be himself he often develops a deep emotional involvement which contributes to his willingness to accept the controls of the subculture. The regularity with which he seeks out subculture members is a clear indication of his dependence.[129] As suggested, there are divisions within the homosexual subculture, and a basic division, already alluded to, is the division into secret and overt groups. The secret groups are based on small, loosely knit cliques. Interaction within the cliques is frequent, and clique members generally meet in one another's homes. By contrast overt homosexuals gather in cohesive social groups which become the major force in their lives. Their activities in the straight world are seen as peripheral, and are often empty of any meaning for them.[130] The subculture may vary widely in the significance that it has for a given homosexual over time.

The militant homosexual

Militancy is usually based in the subculture because that is the source of organizational structure and force. However, some homosexuals have been involved in the new militancy in various ways that are only partly related to the homosexual subculture. But basic to the new homosexual militancy is some organization. This is necessary so that homosexuals can present their case collectively and not as isolated individuals. Up until recent years almost all homosexuals in the United States were extremely secretive, and the last thing they wanted was any kind of public exposure. As a result they had no way of presenting organized resistance to the forces against them in the broader society.

Among homosexuals the militant movement is usually known as the "homophile" movement. Sagarin has pointed out that no group so large in number and so completely stigmatized has remained unorganized so long.[131] No homophile organization appeared in America until after World War II. He suggests that several factors inhibited earlier organizing among homosexuals. First, before World War II the attitude in the United States was negative to social change with regard to sex and particularly with regard to homosexuality. Second, the concealment of the homosexual encouraged him *not* to organize. Third, there was no

---

[129] Leznoff and Westley, "Homosexual Community," p. 186.

[130] Ibid., p. 193.

[131] Sagarin, *Odd Man In*, p. 79.

structure for the exchange of ideas and values which could lead to an organization. Finally, there were no leaders primarily because those who had the intellectual respect that might allow them to be leaders had the most to lose by giving up their anonymity.[132]

But these restrictions changed in many respects, and the greater sexual permissiveness of society created a climate that made possible the emergence of the homophile organizations. The generally new attitudes toward sex meant that even the highly tabooed area of homosexuality could be discussed. The 1960s saw the discussion of homosexuality even in the most conservative of mass media—television. At the present time there are homosexual groups which conduct programs to educate the public to a better understanding and tolerance of homosexuality; for example, the Mattachine Society, which was founded in 1950 in Los Angeles, has as its aim promoting the acceptance of homosexuality by American society. By 1969 there were about 150 known formal and structured voluntary associations that could be called a part of the homophile movement. There were also many small clubs on the periphery of the movement.[133]

The one thing all the homosexual groups have in common is the willingness of their membership to identify themselves as homosexual and to seek an end to social discrimination against the homosexual. These aims are reflected in the slogans: "Out of the closets and into the streets" and "Gay is good" and in the general revolutionary rhetoric of the militant young.[134]

Originally the homosexual organizations were not militant. Their early functions were seen as educating the broader population and counseling homosexuals. In the 1950s counseling was the main focus of action, and this continues to be a major function even in a more militant age. The militant homosexuals, like other deviant groups, have taken the black revolution as their model. As with all militant groups, there is controversy within the ranks of the homosexuals as to the best methods for achieving their ends. Some argue for revolutionary action while others argue for peaceful protests. But what is important is that homosexual militancy has taken to the streets on some occasions. There have been public protests against police raids on homosexual bars as well as against sodomy laws. In Greenwich Village 500 homophiles yelled "Gay power to gay people" and threw firebombs and bricks at police.[135] According to estimates by the mass media on June 28, 1970, between 5,000 and 10,000 homosexuals marched up Sixth Avenue to Central Park in New York City. They were

[132] Ibid., p. 81.
[133] Ibid., p. 87.
[134] Weinberg and Williams, *Male Homosexuals*, p. 28.
[135] *Washington Post*, Oct. 25, 1969.

proclaiming their pride and solidarity and protesting laws that made homosexual acts between consenting adults illegal.[136] It seems reasonable to expect that this new openness and militancy will continue in the future. "And many homosexuals, whether organized or not, have an enhanced feeling of self-worth from knowing there are homophile spokesmen, groups as well as pickets, in front of the White House."[137]

Also basic to the homophile movement is the changing concept that the homosexual has about himself. The homosexual organizations try to bolster their members' feelings that they are "as good as anybody else"—which means "as *well* as anybody else." [138] The groups argue that homosexuality is neither a sickness nor a mental disturbance and that talking about cures is therefore irrelevant. "Anyone who suggests cure, according to Mattachine leaders, must be a charlatan or a quack."[139] For them the slogan might be "Gay is good" in the same way that "Black is beautiful." This is also seen in the belief that "cure" is irrelevant. One homophile spokesman remarked that he did not see "the NAACP and CORE worrying about which chromosome and gene produces a black skin, or about the possibility of bleaching a Negro." [140]

Many homosexuals are not in agreement with the methods of the gay liberation movement. This is because of very basic differences over exposure of identity. Where the gay liberationists are overt in their gay identity the general homosexual community is covert. And Warren found that while the gay liberationists are politically radical and in general sympathy with oppressed groups the secret community of male homosexuals tends to be either apolitical or fairly conservative.[141]

Exactly what is the position of the new militant homosexual groups? The old question of the 1950s was "Why are we what we are?" But this has given way to the assertion "Here we are, now let's take it from there." In other words the argument of the homophiles is that they don't want rehabilitation, or cure, or acceptance of homosexuals as "persons" in distinction from their sex "acts." The militant homosexual wants to be accepted in society not in spite of his homosexuality but together with it. "And he wants himself and his homosexuality, and other homosexuals and their homosexuality, not merely to be tolerated, but to be positive values as worthy contributors to the social order and as a worthy way of

[136] Sidney Abbott and Barbara Love, "Is Women's Liberation a Lesbian Plot?" in Vivian Gornick and Barbara K. Moran,*Woman in Sexist Society* (New York: Signet Books, 1972), p. 616.

[137] Sagarin, *Odd Man In*, p. 345.

[138] Ibid., p. 103.

[139] Ibid.

[140] Ibid., p. 104.

[141] Warren, *Gay World*, p. 109.

[142] Foster Gunnison, Jr., "The Homophile Movement in America," in Weltge, *Same Sex*, p. 128.

life."[142] It would appear that his chances of getting this in the near future are very slight.

THE HOMOSEXUAL SUBCULTURE IN THE BROADER SOCIETY

In this last section we will look in more detail at how the broader society views the homosexual. The focus thus far has been primarily from the perspective of the homosexual in his own subcultural setting. Here we will look at some other aspects of the homosexual in terms of the broader society, both from his perspective and from that of the broader society. Also our interest is primarily in the homosexual in general with little special interpretation given to the small militant minority.

It is important to keep in mind that the role of homosexual often submerges all the other roles a person may fill. All of the homosexual's acts, like those of most significantly labeled persons, are interpreted through the framework of his deviance. "Thus the creative activity of the playwright or painter who happens to be homosexual is interpreted through the fact or rumor of his homosexuality rather than in terms of the artistic roles and conventions of the particular art form in which he works."[143]

Probably few, if any, homosexuals are able to so immerse themselves in the homosexual subculture as to cut themselves off from the broader society. Being members of the homosexual subculture does not remove homosexuals from the social influences of society. Even if the role of homosexual becomes the major role for some persons in the subculture, it is not the only one. Such persons will probably have to interact or be defined according to broader society in some significant areas of their nonsexual behavior. "For instance, the Negro homosexual is a Negro as well as a homosexual; the homosexual lawyer cannot restrict his behavior and identity to that which centers on his sexual orientation."[144] But probably most homosexuals feel that they must hide their homosexuality on many if not most occasions, and this builds in a strain in making sure that they are filling the proper role in a given social situation. We will look at some of the different pressures on the homosexual that exist in various social settings of the broader society.

As mentioned at the start of the chapter, engaging in homosexual acts is against the law, and there is always the danger of getting caught. The greater the success of the homosexual in the "straight" community the greater his anxiety about getting caught. The fact that his homosexual secret is "criminal" means that any exposure may lead to legal consequences—and this increases his personal anxieties. Although most

---

[143] Gagnon and Simon, *Sexual Conduct*, p. 133.
[144] Sagarin, *Odd Man In*, pp. 91-92.

homosexuals are able to avoid exposure, the potential for exposure is always there.

Weinberg and Williams provide some evidence on the homosexual's willingness to let his sexual preference be known. Thirty percent of their respondents reported trying to hide their homosexuality from *all* heterosexuals; 20 percent said that they tried to hide it from a few heterosexuals or none; and about one fifth of their sample could be considered overt homosexuals.[145] As to social interactions, about half was with other homosexuals, and only a small number said that they socialized only with other homosexuals. "Sixteen percent state that they are not really known among homosexuals, and an additional 29 percent that they are not part of any homosexual group. While 30 percent attend homosexual bars and clubs once a week or more, 34 percent never or almost never attend." [146]

In recent years there has been some concern with the homosexual from a combined legal and medical perspective. That concern has centered on the possibility of his being a high carrier of venereal diseases. Up until the late 1950s there were no standard reports on male-to-male transmissions of venereal disease. In fact, the American Social Health Association, which accumulates such data from 120 health departments each year, did not request that information until 1967. However, as early as 1955 there had been scattered reports which indicated an increasing spread of syphilis by homosexuals. One recent finding showed that only 7 percent of male patients with gonorrhea admitted to homosexual contact as compared to 57 percent of male patients with syphilis. "There would appear to be no logical reason why the percent of homosexuals should be so much lower among patients with gonorrhea than with syphilis.[147] One reason why venereal disease rates are higher among homosexuals is that their sexual contact rates are twice as high as those of heterosexual patients. This is, homosexuals averaged twice as many sexual contacts as did heterosexual males. Trice found that venereal diseases are usually spread by homosexuals who prefer anal intercourse. Another study concluded that "syphilitic infection is most likely to occur in the male homosexual in the age group 15 to 29, who is apt to be highly promiscuous, and whose sexual preference is anal sodomy."[148]

Another important area of interaction between the homosexual and the broader society is interaction with his family. Simon and Gagnon found that between one fifth and one fourth of the exclusive homosexuals

---

[145] Weinberg and Williams, *Male Homosexuals*, p. 98.

[146] Ibid., p. 99.

[147] E. Randolph Trice, "Venereal Disease and Homosexuality" *Medical Aspects of Human Sexuality*, January 1969, p. 70.

[148] Ibid., p. 71.

they studied reported difficulties of orientation with their families.[149] However, many homosexuals do maintain close relationships with their families. There is no strong evidence that the proportion of homosexuals for whom relatives are significant differs from that of heterosexuals. "The important differences rest in the way the relationships are managed and, again, the consequences they have for other aspects of life."[150] This means that when the homosexual is around his family, he must often be careful not to give cues at to his sexual preference and way of life. Simmons reports one homosexual respondent as saying, "When I was home watching television with my folks, I'd catch myself saying, 'that's a good looking guy.' "[151] Of course, many parents do know about their son's homosexuality, and their reactions range from total acceptance to total rejection.

How do the institutions of religion, government, and the military treat the homosexual? In recent years some religious groups have accepted the homosexual, but for the most part organized religion has rejected him. A part of the reason for the rejection of homosexuality by religion may be that religious groups have often had to deal with it in their own ranks. When a lay person is found to be a homosexual it usually means silent shunning, and if a clergyman is found to be a homosexual it means a transfer to a different location. But given the changing nature of some religious groups—their increasing concern with personal and social problems—there will probably be a liberalizing of many church policies with regard to homosexuality. But the changes will probably come from a few of the leaders and not from the more conservative congregations. One recent change was a resolution advocating equal rights for women and homosexuals, passed in March 1975 by the governing board of the National Council of Churches. At the same time the board made it clear that the stand did not imply that homosexuals should be eligible to serve as ministers.[152]

The possible conflict between their protests and their religious convictions has sometimes been a problem for the religious homosexual. Weinberg and Williams found that many religious homosexuals reinterpret religion as not violated by homosexuality. Among the most religious such an interpretation helps neutralize the negative psychological effects. "Thus, we found that some psychological problems are correlated with the perception that homosexuality violates religion, but this relationship holds only among the most religious respondents."[153]

San Francisco passed in 1972 the first civil rights legislation for homo-

[149] Simon and Gagnon, "Homosexuality," p. 180.

[150] Gagnon and Simon, *Sexual conduct*, p. 360.

[151] J. L. Simmons, *Deviants*, (Berkeley, Calif.: March 7, 1975, p. 11.

[152] *New York Times*, March 7, 1975, p. 11.

[153] Weinberg and Williams, *Male Homosexuals*, p. 256.

sexuals. By a vote of ten to one the Board of Supervisors expanded the city's job discrimination ordinance to include prohibitions against discrimination on the basis of sex or sexual orientation by companies doing business with the city. [154]

The federal government has long had a policy of not hiring homosexuals as well as a policy of getting rid of homosexuals discovered after hiring. This has been done on the ground that the homosexual is a security risk because he would be subject to blackmail and other forms of extortion. A chairman of the Civil Service Commission has said that a person who proclaims publicly that he engages in homosexual activities would not be suitable for federal employment. However, the same chairman went on to say that homosexual tendencies alone were not sufficient cause for denial of employment. "In other words, It's all right to have homosexual tendencies but it isn't all right to exercise them, even in private with consenting adults."[155] However, the liberalizing influence has been affecting federal employment policies. The Federal Appeals Court in Washington, D.C., recently declared that a government agency could not dismiss a homosexual employee without first proving that his homosexuality would significantly influence the efficiency of the agency's operations. In 1971 one United States District Court ordered the defense department to restore security clearances to two declared homosexuals. The court ruled that the Bill of Rights prohibited the government from subjecting homosexuals to "probing personal questions." Furthermore, the government could not withhold security clearance for refusal to answer such questions."[156]

Finally, one United States institution that has always taken a highly repressive view toward homosexuality is the military, although historically armies have not only tolerated homosexuality but have on occasion encouraged it. It is possible that the strongly repressive policies of the American military establishment are an overreaction to the homosexual permissiveness of the military in other societies.

The rates of homosexuality in the armed forces are difficult to estimate. One study of the army shows that from 1960 to 1967 only 8 out of every 10,000 soldiers were discharged for reasons of homosexuality. Of course, this number represents only those homosexuals whom the Army found out about and processed for discharge.[157] A study of homosexuals who had been in the military services found that only about one fifth of

[154] Martin and Lyon, *Lesbian Woman*, p. 228.

[155] Lewis I. Maddocks, "The Law and the Church versus the Homosexual," in Weltge, *Same Sex*, p. 101.

[156] Martin and Lyon, *Lesbian Woman*, p. 216.

[157] William M. Sheppe, "The Problem of Homosexuality in the Armed Forces," *Medical Aspects of Human Sexuality*, October 1969, p. 72.

them reported difficulties during their military experience.[158] Apparently a definite majority of homosexuals are able to complete their military careers without being in trouble on that score.

Sheppe noted that there had been a sharp decline in the number of official separations for homosexuality since 1966. However, some qualified observers suggest that the decline may have been directly related to a concurrent rise over that period in the rates of drug abuse as grounds for separation. In the Armed Forces the investigation and control of drug use have required a great deal of manpower "which might otherwise have been expended in ferreting out homosexuals. There is also far less stigma attached to separations based on drug abuse than to separations based on homosexuality." [159]

The hostile view that the military takes toward homosexuals is reflected in the procedures it uses when one is brought to its attention. The individual is abruptly removed from duty, told that he is a security risk until proved otherwise, and subjected to intensive interrogation. "In the course of the matter, it may be implied that the charges against him are airtight, but that such unpleasantness, including court-martial and possible imprisonment, may be avoided if the individual will only cooperate."[160] This also shows that under the present military regulations homosexuality is not seen primarily as a medical matter but rather as a legal offense, proscribed and punishable under the Uniform Code of Military Justice. The present policy is that if it is established that a person has had homosexual activities with a consenting adult in private he is given an undesirable discharge. This makes him ineligible for any GI benefits.

In this last section we have been considering some institutional responses to homosexuality. What about general public opinion? Even the medical profession is far from unanimous in its acceptance of more permissive views toward the homosexual. In a recent sample of doctors 68 percent agreed that discreet homosexual acts between consenting adults should be permitted without legal restrictions, while the rest felt they should not. This is a much more liberal position than that of the general public. A Harris poll reported that 63 percent of the nation considered homosexuals "harmful to American life." Respondents in a study of traits attributed to the male homosexual found them: "sexually abnormal," 72 percent; "perverted," 52 percent; "mentally ill," 40 percent; and "maladjusted," 40 percent.[161] In a 1970 study based on a nationwide

---

[158] Simon and Gagnon, *Sexual Conduct*, p. 180.
[159] Sheppe, "Homosexuality in Armed Forces," p. 73.
[160] Ibid., p. 81.
[161] Simmons, *Deviants*, p. 29.

random sample two thirds of the respondents regarded homosexuality as "very much obscene and vulgar," and less than 8 percent endorsed the view that homosexuality was not at all obscene and vulgar. Substantial majorities of the respondents agreed that homosexuals should be allowed to work as artists, beauticians, florists, and musicians, but almost equally substantial majorities did not believe that they should be permitted to engage in occupations of influence and authority. "Three quarters would deny to a homosexual the right to be a minister, a school teacher, or a judge, and two thirds would bar the homosexual from medical practices and government service."[162] As pointed out earlier in this chapter, the role of the homosexual far transcends sexual choice. In the same way the broader world's view of the total person is influenced by the knowledge that he is a homosexual. The way in which all his roles are seen is colored by his homosexuality. However, there are many variations among groups in the United States in their treatment of homosexuals, and often the homosexual seeks out an environment where he runs into the least amount of discrimination. This may be in terms of occupational choice, a city to live in, or a place to go on vacation. As suggested, the most permissive city for the homosexual is probably San Francisco, and that city probably has more homosexuals per capita than any other city.

But even if public opinion in general is not becoming significantly more permissive with regard to the homosexual some changes are taking place. For example, in San Francisco if a homosexual feels he is receiving undue police harassment he is encouraged to go to the police department's community relations division, which will usually straighten the matter out. And recently the State Liquor Authority of New York lifted its traditional ban on homosexual bars, and various state courts decided that "intrasexual" dancing, touching, and even kissing were not necessarily disorderly so long as they refrained from touching one another upon primary sex organs.[163] Finally, in late 1969 the National Institute of Mental Health recommended the repeal of laws against private homosexual acts between consenting adults and a reassessment of bans by employers against hiring homosexuals. Yet, this recommendation came at the same time that a CBS poll found that two thirds of all Americans regarded homosexuals with "disgust, discomfort or fear."[164]

The future of the homosexual in America is difficult to predict. This is because there is such a wide gulf between some professional belief and argument for greater tolerance and freedom and the prevailing feeling of contempt and disgust found among most Americans. If the homosexual, through his subcultural support and strength, chooses to become increasingly militant for his rights one of two things will probably happen.

---

[162] See Weinberg and Williams, *Male Homosexuals*, p. 21.

[163] Burke, "New Homosexuality," p. 308.

[164] *Washington Post*, October 25, 1969.

He might be able to make the general population more tolerant of his sexual choice. But more likely, if he becomes militant he will antagonize more "middle Americans" and find the resistance to him even greater. Whichever course is taken the homosexual subculture will continue to have great importance and will probably become the rallying point for an even greater proportion of homosexuals.

BIBLIOGRAPHY

Churchill, Wainwright, *Homosexual Behavior among Males*. New York: Hawthorn Books, 1967.

Dank, Barry M., "The Homosexual," in Patricia Keith-Spiegel and Don Spiegel, *Outsiders USA*. San Francisco: Rinehart Press, 1973, pp. 267-97.

Freedman, Mark, "Homosexuals May Be Healthier Than Straights," *Psychology Today*, March 1975, pp. 28, 30-32.

Gagnon, John H., and William Simon, *Sexual Conduct: The Social Sources of Human Sexuality*. Chicago: Aldine, 1973.

Gould, Robert E., "What We Don't Know about Homosexuality," *New York Times Magazine*, Feb. 24, 1974, pp. 13, 51, 54, 56, 58, 62.

Hoffman, Martin, *The Gay World*. New York: Bantam Books, 1968.

Hooker, Evelyn, "Male Homosexuals and Their 'Worlds,' " in Judd Marmor, *Sexual Inversion*. New York: Basic Books, 1965, pp. 83-107.

Humpheys, Laud, "Tearoom Trade: Impersonal Sex in Public Places," *Trans-Action*, January 1970, pp. 11-25.

McIntosh, Mary, "The Homosexual Role," *Social Problems*, Fall 1968, pp. 182-92.

Sagarin, Edward, *Odd Man In: Societies of Deviants in America*. Chicago; Quadrangle, 1969.

Simon, William, and John H. Gagnon, "Homosexuality: The Formulation of a Sociological Perspective," *Journal of Health and Social Behavior*, September, 1967, pp. 177-85.

Sonenschein, David, "The Ethnology of Male Homosexual Relationships," *Journal of Sex Research*, May 1968, pp. 69-83.

"The Consenting Adult Homosexual and the Law," *UCLA Law Review*, University of California at Los Angeles, March 1966.

Warren, Carol A. B., *Identity and Community in the Gay World*. New York: Wiley, 1974.

Weinberg, Martin S., and Colin J. Williams, *Male Homosexuals*. New York: Oxford University Press, 1974.

Weltge, Ralph A., ed., *The Same Sex: An Appraisal of Homosexuality*. Philadelphia: Pilgram Press, 1969.

chapter twelve

Female homosexuality

The emergence in the United States of an increasing awareness of the male homosexual was discussed in Chapter 11. It was also suggested that often strong negative feelings are directed at the male homosexual by the general public. By contrast, when the female homosexual (or lesbian) is mentioned there is often vague, almost puzzled, reaction by many people. That is, people are aware that such women exist but have never come in contact with them, so their awareness is abstract and not based on experience. Also, by contrast with the male homosexual relatively little has been written about the lesbian and she has rarely been presented through the mass media. So for most Americans the level of knowledge as well as the level of experience is low.

This chapter will be shorter than Chapter 11 because there has been less research and less speculation concerning the female homosexual. However, we believe that the female homosexual should be discussed and analyzed separately from the male homosexual because, even though there are some similarities among homosexuals of both sexes, the differences are probably greater than the similarities. The basic similarity is that both male and female homosexuals choose members of their own sex as sex partners. But once that is recognized the similarities are generally not very great. Basically the male homosexual is a male and the female homosexual is a female in terms of the basic roles by which others see them and they see themselves. And the choice of a same-sex partner generally does not significantly change these basic roles for either men or women. It will also be seen that within the homosexual setting males are more apt to develop and depend on subcultural involvement than are females. That is, the social context of being a homosexual is more complex and developed for the male than for the female. In the discussion ahead some contrasts will be drawn between the patterns of male and female

308

homosexuals. This should contribute to a better understanding not only of homosexual variations but also of basic sex-role differences in the United States.

HISTORICAL BACKGROUND

While there are many historical references to male homosexuality there are relatively few references to female homosexuality. The Talmud of the ancient Hebrews regarded the practice of lesbianism as a trivial obscenity, and the woman's punishment was that her marriage ceremony could not be performed by a priest. There is some evidence that lesbianism was common in the harems of Egypt and India, where women were herded together and often saw no men other than the husband they shared. Each wife was expected to wait her turn to be sexually satisfied by the shared husband. But many may have turned to one another for sexual release. It may have been that the husband knew of the homosexuality but was willing to overlook it rather than to have his wives' sexual frustration create problems for him.

The first real advocate of female homosexuality in the Western world was Sappho, who lived in the 6th century B.C. She was born and lived most of her adult life on the island of Lesbos. Sappho had several affairs with men and was the mother of one child. She was one of the first persons to argue for the rights of women. Sappho appears to have fallen in love with many of her female students, and she wrote sensuous poems for them. Those poems later won her great respect, and she came to be known among Greeks as the Tenth Muse. Basically the belief that developed on Lesbos was that the admiration of beauty could not be separated from sex, and as a result many women took sexual delight in one another.[1] The word *lesbian* has become a universal generic term for the female homosexual.

During the medieval period as sexual repression became an important part of religion homosexuality was also condemned. The medieval church found homosexuality sinful for both men and women, but the male homosexual was obligated to perform penance longer. There have been many periods in many European countries during which some female homosexuality was practiced. For example, lesbianism was fashionable in the court of Marie Antoinette, although whether she participated is not known for sure.

Given the high repression of all forms of sexual behavior in the early days of the American colonies there is little evidence that lesbianism existed at that time and if it did it must have been very well hidden. In the early written records of the United States there is little reference to

---

[1] Richard Lewisohn, *A History of Sexual Customs* (New York: Harper, 1958), p. 60.

female homosexuality. In fact, in American literature, the female homosexual is ignored throughout the 19th century except possibly for some suggestion in the novels of Oliver Wendell Holmes. Lesbianism appears "for the first time in American literature in explicit fashion in the expatriate writing of Henry James and Gertrude Stein."[2] Up until very recently the lesbian was rarely presented in novels. The few times she was written about she was either presented as an erotic symbol for the satisfaction of the male reader or presented sympathetically as a highly romantic and mysterious figure.

Given the limited historical references to the female homosexual, what is known about her on the cross-cultural level? Ford and Beach found that in only 22 percent of the cultures they studied was there any specific information about female homosexuality. In only a few of those cultures was there evidence concerning the nature of the homosexual practices involved.[3] They also point out that in most societies female homosexuality is given much less attention than is male homosexuality. Ford and Beach found that frequently some substitute for a penis is employed, as it also may be in solitary masturbation. They go on to write that "among the Dahomeans, the common practice of homosexuality on the part of women is believed to be a cause of frigidity in marriage. Interestingly, the Haitians put it just the other way; the frigid woman who cannot please her husband seeks another woman as a sex partner."[4] Pomeroy points out that among American Indian cultures 53 percent accepted male homosexuality while only 17 percent accepted female homosexuality.[5] However, there appears to be only one primitive society, the Mohave Indians of the southwestern United States, for which there were records of exclusive homosexual patterns among the females. That group was also the only one for which there were reports that female homosexuality was openly sanctioned.[6] However, it should not be assumed that biological gender differences account for the fact that female homosexuality has been much less common than male homosexuality among primitive groups as well as in literate cultures. The difference has been due to the social roles that women have traditionally played and the means by which they have been personally and socially controlled in their sexual experiences. These points will be further elaborated in the discussion ahead.

---

[2] Donald W. Cory, *The Lesbian in America* (New York: Citadel Press, 1964), p. 48.

[3] Clellan S. Ford and Frank A. Beach, *Patterns of Sexual Behavior* (New York: Harper, 1952), p. 133.

[4] Ibid.

[5] Wardell B. Pomeroy, "Homosexuality," in Ralph W. Weltge, *The Same Sex: An Appraisal of Homosexuality* (Philadelphia: Pilgram Books, 1969), p. 4.

[6] Alfred C. Kinsey et al., *Sexual Behavior in the Human Female* (Philadelphia: Saunders, 1953), p. 451.

LEGAL ASPECTS

The laws that exist with reference to the female homosexual are much simpler and less restrictive than those that exist for the male homosexual. Basically the reason is that in most societies homosexuality among men has been seen as far more threatening in both scope and complexity. It is also important that with few exceptions the legal controls over sexual behavior developed in all societies have been the work of men. In many respects the laws about sexual behavior have been aimed at protecting their interests. For example, in prostitution the male customer is usually protected. In extramarital relationships the woman has more to lose and is more severely condemned than the man. Few laws have been directed against the lesbian because men have rarely ever seen her as a threat. When men have thought about her they have always felt superior to the lesbian and have seen no need to legally constrain her.

Much of the American legal system came from the common law of England, and it can be seen that the English legal view of the female homosexual is close to that found in the United States. At no time in England was homosexual behavior between women prohibited by law. This has probably been a reflection of the relative unimportance of women in society. When the criminal law of England was recently reformed to allow private homosexual relations between consenting adults, lesbians were never taken into consideration because there were no laws against them in the first place.[7] In fact the Wolfenden Report, upon which the reforms were based, found no case in which a female had been convicted in Great Britain of an act with another female which exhibited "the libidinous features that characterize sexual acts between males."[8]

In many states the sex laws don't apply to lesbians, but in some states the laws for female homosexuals are similar to those for the male homosexual. For example, in New York State it is not illegal to be a female homosexual, but it is illegal to perform a homosexual act. Yet, rarely do the women run into the law because most homosexual arrests are made for public behavior. Lesbians are rarely "cruisers" and don't hang around public toilets, where the majority of male arrests are made. According to Kinsey, from 1696 until 1952 there was not a single case on record in the United States of a sustained conviction of a female for homosexual activity. Kinsey also found that of his total sample of several hundred women who had had homosexual experience only three had had minor difficulties and only one had had serious difficulties with the police.[9]

---

[7] Martin Hoffman, *The Gay World* (New York: Bantam Books, 1968), p. 174.

[8] *The Wolfenden Report* (New York: Lancer Books, 1964), p. 76.

[9] Kinsey, *Human Female*, p. 484.

For the most part the police do not consider lesbians as a threat because lesbians keep to themselves, are not as promiscuous as male homosexuals, and rarely solicit others. The UCLA study in Los Angeles found that "decoy enforcement is considered too degrading for policewomen. However, entertainment licenses have been revoked as the result of observation of lewd conduct in lesbian bars by male undercover officers."[10] The same study goes on to say that the police view lesbians as much less aggressive than male homosexuals. Their behavior is much less conspicuous than that of male homosexuals and less likely to offend the public. Thus, "there are a minimal number of complaints concerning female activity."[11] However, the police seem to have been picking up more female homosexuals in recent years. In New York City the police have picked up women for "loitering," a charge applied "for soliciting another for the purpose of engaging in deviate sexual intercourse." Ten women were picked up on this charge in 1968, but a total of 49 women and 69 men have been apprehended on the same charge during the first nine months of 1969.[12] These arrests are probably the most militant lesbians, who are insisting on their rights in all areas, including that of soliciting sex partners if they choose to do so. In a recent study of active lesbians in Philadelphia one fourth said that they had been arrested by the police, but usually on a drug or solicitation charge. Twenty percent said that they had experienced physical aggression from the police. But some of these women were a part of other militant and deviant subcultures, and therefore their encounters with the police were often not simply a result of lesbian activities. The women may be lesbians, political militants, female militants, and so forth, and may come into contact with the police in various roles or combinations of roles.

Joanne Long recently conducted a study of several lesbian bars in a large city. Over a period of two years she spent several hundred hours in these bars as a participant-observer. She comments that throughout her research the police never raided or made any arrests in the lesbian bars. "Also in contrast to male gay bars, the presence of plainclothes vice squad officers did not occur. One reason why the lesbian bar is subject to less legal surveillance is because it is not a setting for sexual transactions."[13]

In the discussion ahead some references will be made to the Philadelphia study mentioned above. Although the sample was only 40 lesbians the study is included because there is so little empirical data and because the findings will possibly contribute to some better understanding. The 40 lesbians were interviewed mostly in lesbian bars, and all openly

---

[10] "The Consenting Adult Homosexual and the Law, *UCLA Law Review*, March 1966, p. 693.

[11] Ibid., p. 740.

[12] Enid Nemy, "The Woman Homosexual: More Assertive, Less Willing to Hide," *New York Times*, Nov. 17, 1969, p. 61.

[13] Joanne Long, "The Lesbian Bar—A Public Institution," unpublished paper, 1975.

defined themselves as having at least some homosexual interest. Their average age was 25, and three fourths of them had never married. The women were also well educated, one third of them having graduated from college. This group was basically quite militant and open about its homosexuality.

The point has been made that there are fewer female homosexuals than male homosexuals. In a study done in the 1920s of 1,200 unmarried female college graduates who had been out of college for at least 5 years, about half indicated that they had experienced intense emotional relations with another woman. About half of that number had participated in overt physical practices. However, while the figure is not given, it is probable that only a small percentage of the women had had sexual experience to the point of orgasm with another woman.[14] The Kinsey study found that at the time of marriage 5 percent of the women had had at least one sexual experience to orgasm with another woman.[15] As would be expected, the homosexual experiences of women vary by marital status. Homosexual outlets were employed by 0 percent of the married women, 2 percent of the postmarried women, and 19 percent of the single women.[16] Kinsey also found some variations by education among women having homosexual experience. By education the percentages of women who had had homosexual experience to orgasm were: grade school, 6 percent; high school, 5 percent; and college, 10 percent. [17]

It is hard to estimate with any accuracy the frequency of male homosexuality, and even harder to estimate the frequency of female homosexuality. Most lesbianism is hidden because it is less physical and less overt. The differences also contribute to a misconception shared by many that female homosexuality is less common than it is in fact, and that makes estimating the rates even more difficult. There are several other reasons for underestimating the number of lesbians. One, an effeminate male is usually associated with homosexuality, whether or not he is a monosexual. But masculine women are not usually defined as homosexual. Therefore, the defining of visual characteristics varies for men and women. Two, male homosexuals are much more apt to gather in public places, and the public is therefore more aware of them than it is of the lesbians it rarely sees. Three, the male is promiscuous and seeks out his sexual partners openly and aggressively—ways that are rare for the lesbian. He is therefore seen in his sexually seeking role. Finally, male homosexuals are more open and aggressive and are therefore given much more publicity in the newspapers.[18]

---

[14] K. B. Davis, *Factors in the Sex Life of Twenty-Two Hundred Women* (New York: Harper, 1929).

[15] Kinsey, *Human Female*, p. 488.

[16] Ibid., p. 562.

[17] Ibid., p. 488.

[18] Cory, *Lesbian in America*, p. 88.

A rough estimate of the number of married women who have had some homosexual experience since the age of 18 can be from the responses of over 100,000 readers of *Redbook* to an extensive questionnaire on sexual behavior. In that study, which the writer constructed, a subsample of the responses of 18,347 women was analyzed. The *Redbook* respondents are biased in the direction of being higher educated and of willingness to answer the questionnaire. Of the respondents 11 percent said that they had had a homosexual experience since the age of 18. For a majority this had happened only once, and 60 percent described their homosexual experience as unpleasant or repulsive.[19]

CAUSES

Most theories about homosexuality have been developed to explain the male homosexual. Often such theories are applied to the female homosexual as a kind of afterthought. The basic assumptions of the medical, psychological, and social theories were discussed in Chapter 11. The failure to study female homosexuality is not due only to the fact that fewer lesbians turn to psychiatry for therapy. The truth is that psychiatric studies almost invariably emphasize male behavior. This is another reflection of society's traditional view that what men do is more important that what women do.[20] However, some lesbians believe that their sexual orientation is a problem that should be taken to the psychiatrist. Of the women in the Philadelphia sample 42 percent had received some psychological help. There is probably a strong desire by most lesbians to understand their sexual orientation. Most recognize that their behavior is deviant, and that having some explanation for it is important to themselves and to others. For example, if the lesbian accepts the belief that she was born a homosexual, then that relieves her and her parents of any responsibility for what she is or for doing anything about it.

One study characterizes as sexist the belief that women who are dissatisfied with the traditional feminine roles of wife and mother are by definition sick and need to be cured. "It is, in fact, the very fallacy that, in the past, allowed psychotherapists to do many of their female clients more harm than good. The interpretation is doubly hazardous to lesbians, insulting not only their homosexuality, but their womanhood as well."[21] The study also points out that the well-meaning therapist is often stymied by the paucity of practical or theoretical literature concerning the lesbian and especially the mentally healthy lesbian. The lack of nonjudgmental material is said to have had a great deal to do with the

[19] Robert R. Bell, unpublished material.

[20] Robert E. Gould, "What We Don't Know about Homosexuality," *New York Times Magazine*, Feb. 24, 1974, p. 59.

[21] Janet S. Chafetz, Patricia Sampson, Paula Beck and Joyce West. "A Study of Homosexual Women," *Social Work*, November, 1964, p. 716.

failure of the helping professions to be supportive of lesbians. "Furthermore, many members of the helping professions continue to speak in terms of curing the lesbian of her current sexual preference. Such treatment of the lesbian can create rather than solve problems."[22]

Mark Freedman, clinical psychologist, states that his research on lesbians shows them to score higher than a control group in autonomy, spontaneity, orientation toward the present (as opposed to obsession with the past or anticipation of the future), and sensitivity to their own needs and feelings. Another study comparing lesbians with a control group found the lesbians to be more independent, resilient, bohemian, and self-sufficient. Still another study, quoted by Freedman, found that lesbians scored higher than the controls on both goal direction and self-acceptance.[23]

A common belief about the causes of lesbianism is that older women seduce innocent younger girls. But Gagnon and Simon found in their study of lesbians that seduction by older women was not mentioned as an experience. They suggest that the real social importance of the image of the older seducer is that it provides a basis for many popular explanations of what "causes" homosexuality and thus serves the function of reducing the sense of guilt and shame.[24] The belief is seen as making the lesbian a victim of circumstances over which she has no real choice.

It seems probable that most lesbians follow a pattern of growing up similar to that of most heterosexual girls. The notion that "extreme" or "special" socialization causes homosexuality is not substantiated by the available research. All the women that Gagnon and Simon studied reported some heterosexual dating and mild sex play during their high school years. "Only two carried it to the extent of intercourse, although a larger number indicated that they had experimented with heterosexual coitus after homosexual experiences."[25] It appears that by high school age many young homosexuals, both male and female, are aware of schoolmates like themselves. Love reports that homosexuals in Philadelphia say there are cliques of "gay boys and gay girls in every school in the city and intercommunication among them. Even if no one else knows they are there, the youngsters involved do."[26]

Simon and Gagnon have provided the best sociological explanation for the development of female homosexuality. They argue that in most cases the female homosexual follows a conventional pattern in developing her

---

[22] Ibid., p. 722.

[23] Mark Freedman, "Homosexuals May Be Healthier than Straights," *Psychology Today*, March 1975, p. 30.

[24] John H. Gagnon and William Simon, *Sexual Deviance* (New York: Harper and Row, 1967), p. 255.

[25] Ibid., pp. 259-60.

[26] Nancy Love, "The Invisible Sorority," *Philadelphia Magazine*, November 1967, p. 69.

involvement with sexuality. They go on to say that the organizing event in the development of male sexuality is puberty, while the organizing event for females is the period of romantic involvement that culminates in marriage for most. For females the "discovery" of love relations precedes the "discovery" of sexuality while the reverse is generally true for males. "The discovery of their homosexuality usually occurred very late in adolescence, often even in the years of young adulthood, and the actual commencement of overt sexual behavior frequently came at a late stage of an intense emotional involvement."[27] What Simon and Gagnon are saying in part is that for women training in love comes before training in sexuality. And for most women, including most lesbians, the pursuit of sexual gratification is something distinct from emotional or rational involvement and is not particularly attractive; "indeed, for many it may be impossible."[28]

The above argument suggests that in one sense the female homosexual should be defined somewhat differently than the male homosexual. They both choose sex partners of the same sex, but there are often differences in what is wanted from and with the partner. The male most always wants the partner primarily for sexual activity, while this is frequently much less true for the female. This is not to argue that the lesbian doesn't have a strong sexual interest, but rather that her sexual interest is a part of an interpersonal interest. A lesbian, then, is a woman who feels a strong and recurring need to have sexual relations with another woman within an interpersonal context.

The idea has often been presented that all humans are potential homosexuals. This idea assumes that under certain conditions most persons would turn to homosexuality regardless of their negative socialization. If the idea is valid it might be more appropriate for women than for men because homosexuality is less threatening to women's basic self-image. The idea recognizes that in certain social situations homosexuality may be manifested. The situations are not seen as causes, but rather as providing "conditions, learning patterns, and justifications differentially favorable to the occurrence of homosexual contacts and self-concepts."[29] One good illustration of this is the prison "turnout" who enters into homosexual activities while in prison but gives them up on leaving that setting. In a setting such as the prison women are more likely to enter into homosexual involvements. Giallombardo, in her study of women in prison, suggests that the ease with which women may demonstrate acts of affection, both verbally and physically, toward

---

[27] Gagnon and Simon, *Sexual Deviance*, p. 251.

[28] William Simon and John H. Gagnon, "Femininity in the Lesbian Community,"*Social Problems*, Fall 1967, p. 214.

[29] Charles H. McCaghy and James K. Skipper, Jr., "Lesbian Behavior as an Adaptation to the Occupation of Stripping," *Social Problems*, Fall 1969, p. 263.

members of the same sex "may provide a *predisposition* to widespread homosexuality and its ready acceptance under the extreme conditions of isolation in the prison settings."[30]

An isolated environmental setting, such as the prison, with its high rates of homosexuality also develops rationales that help new members make the transition. Another study of a woman's prison points out that a folklore develops that is intended to justify and encourage the new inmates' homosexual adaption to prison life.[31] A part of the rationale is that the sexual adaption is temporary and brought about *only* because of the isolated conditions. So those women who turn out in prison "define themselves as *bisexual,* and they expect to return to heterosexual relationships upon release.[32] Often the women find it easier to accept homosexuality because they see it as a part of an affectional relationship they need. "The overriding need of a majority of female prisoners is to establish an affectional relationship which brings in prison, as it does in the community, love, interpersonal support, security, and social status. The need promotes homosexuality as the predominant compensatory response to the pains of imprisonment."[33]

While far more males than females turn to homosexuality in society this does not appear to be true in prisons. The evidence suggests that a greater proportion of women than men have homosexual experiences while in prison. This would appear to be evidence for the hypothesis that women are less threatened by homosexuality than are men and find it easier to accept, at least temporarily. If the hypothesis is correct one would expect the same greater tendency for homosexuality in other situations where one sex is isolated. At present there is no evidence from other sex-segregated instituitions that might be applied to this hypothesis.

As is true for many other areas of deviance there can be problems for lesbians when they define themselves as deviant. The self-naming process for the female homosexual sometimes leads to fear and anxiety. Martin and Lyon have suggested that every lesbian must face an identity crisis. This occurs during that period of life when she is at odds with the society in which she lives. Martin and Lyon report a discussion involving 20 lesbians between the ages of 25 and 32 in which it was revealed that only two had not attempted suicide when they were teenagers.[34] Fear plays a big part in the life of most lesbians, and often the fear is justified. "Lesbians

---

[30] Rose Giallombardo, "Social Roles in a Prison for Women," *Social Problems,* Winter 1966, p. 286.

[31] David A. Ward and Gene Kassebaum, "Homosexuality in a Prison for Women," *Social Problems,* Fall 1964, p. 168.

[32] Ibid., p. 176.

[33] Ibid.

[34] Del Martin and Phyllis Lyon, *Lesbian Woman* (New York: Bantam Books, 1972), p. 27.

are subjected to reprisals from all quarters of society: friends, family, employers, police and government."[35]

In general, the causes of female homosexuality, like those of male homosexuality, are seen as complex and varied. As Sawyer points out, homosexuals are coming to be viewed as people who emerge as special kinds of social beings because of their intrinsic motivations, individual adaptations, and childhood conflicts. But along with this the homosexual is also coming to be viewed as a product of the total and ongoing environment, which includes the family, "peer groups, various legal and societal penalties and sanctions, and subcultural expectations, all of which help to shape the homosexual as he exists in American society." [36] And as is the case with the male homosexual there is little reason to believe that the strongly committed female homosexual is very often going to be totally reoriented from complete homosexuality to complete heterosexuality. There seems little likelihood of any "cure" for female homosexuality in the sense of changing the nature and the object of the lesbian's sexual desires.

THE LESBIAN SUBCULTURE

As suggested earlier, the subculture is much less important for female homosexuals than it is for male homosexuals. The main reason for this difference is the women's greater desire for privacy. In general the women are much less aggressive in all ways than are the men. However, for some women the lesbian subculture does exist and does have meaning, and therefore it is important to examine what is known about it. In this section our concern is with the subculture in general, but we will also discuss two specific groups of lesbians that have been studied. One is a group of lower-class black women, and the other a group of strippers. These studies refer to specialized groups within the homosexual subculture, but they are of interest in what they tell about the group themselves as well as for the general insights they provide into female homosexuality.

What can be said in a general way about the lesbian subculture? For the individuals who participate in it, the subculture serves a number of functions. First, it provides a means for making sexual contacts as well as for expediting those contacts, though it is nowhere the "flesh market" of the male homosexual subculture. However, physical appearance does play a part in the interaction within the lesbian bar. For example, considerable emphasis is placed on youth, and the younger lesbians are often critical of the appearance of older lesbians. Joanne Long reports

---

[35] Ibid., p. 205.

[36] Ethel Sawyer, "The Impact of the Surrounding Lower-Class Subculture on Female Homosexual Adaptations," *Society for the Study of Social Problems*, San Francisco, Calif., August 1967, p. 2.

that on many occasions young lesbians referred to the one bar that attracted older lesbians as the "wrinkle room." She reports that it is fairly common for attractive women to pair off with unattractive ones. But some of the most unattractive lesbians, especially those who are obese, are often forced to settle for unattractive lovers because they are rejected by the other women. "In general, however, physical attractiveness is not as important in the lesbian subculture as in the heterosexual society.[37]

The pickup procedures in lesbian bars are different from those found in male homosexual bars. Typically the women engage in conversations and look at each other rather than scanning the barroom. There is not the pervasive cruising and looking in the lesbian bar that are so common in the male gay bar. In the lesbian bars women with their dates or lovers are closed to pickups. However, all others can be defined as open to a bar pickup, and any lesbian can initiate a pass. Usually pickups begin with an exchange of glances, known as "cruising." A woman will periodically focus her eyes on another woman, "sometimes undressing her with her eye movement. The recipient will return or hold sustained eye contact with the woman if she is interested. Sometimes nothing further develops because neither of the women is aggressive enough to make a formal advance."[38]

The lesbian subculture also provides a source of social support. It is a place where the lesbian can express her feelings or describe her experiences because she is interacting with others like herself. The subculture also "includes a language and an ideology which provides each individual lesbian with already developed attitudes that help her resist the societal claim that she is diseased, depraved, or shameful."[39] It can be seen that these ends of the lesbian subculture are basically no different than those of the male homosexual subculture, rather, the difference is one of degree, with the subculture generally being less important to lesbians than to male homosexuals.

The importance of the lesbian subculture to its members has been shown by Chafetz and her colleagues. They asked their lesbian respondents whom they would turn to in six different situations—the death of someone close, dismissal or promotion at work, as companion for a vacation, during an illness, for entertainment, or for "killing time," The responses point overwhelmingly to the gay community. "About half the sample group said they would turn to a gay lover, and the second most frequent response was to a gay friend who was not a lover, less than 10 percent would go to their family, and only slightly more than 10 percent to a straight friend."[40]

---

[37] Long, "Lesbian Bar."

[38] Ibid.

[39] Gagnon and Simon, *Sexual Deviance*, p. 262.

[40] Chafetz, "Homosexual Women," p. 721.

There is some overlap between the male and female subcultures. Warren found that the homosexual women who were a part of the male homosexual subculture she studied were women who often did not fit into the lesbian subculture. This may have been because they were professionals, because they preferred more traditionally "feminine" dress than the norm for the lesbian subculture, or because they preferred the company of men. "Many of the women state the gay men are polite and gentlemanly, and reinforce their femininity."[41] Sonenschein found that lesbians shared only infrequently in male group activities, that the homosexual subculture was in fact a male subculture. He says that the lesbians shared a number of terms used by male homosexuals such as *gay* and *butch*, and that the word *fluff* (a very feminine lesbian) was their only unique term. [42] In the larger cities, however, there does appear to be a distinct lesbian subculture that sometimes overlaps with that of the male but is in no real sense dependent on it. Lesbians are probably more influenced by male homosexuals than are male homosexuals by lesbians. Simon and Gagnon suggest another important difference between the two subcultures. They argue that for the males the primary subcultural emphasis is placed on the facilitation of sexual activity while for the females it is placed in the socialization process.[43]

Reasons have been suggested for the lesser involvement of women in the homosexual subculture. One is that the woman who makes a commitment to homosexuality is not as removed or as alienated from conventional society as is the man. Her sexual choice and her patterns for pursuing it are less recognized and recognizable to the broader society. A second reason is that the forces of repression that result in differences between males and females during the ages when sexual activity is initiated may also help the female to handle subsequent sexual restrictions more easily than the male is able to. "More females than males should therefore be able to resist quasi-public homosexual behavior which increases the risks of disclosure; further, lesbians should be better able to resist relations that involve sexual exchange without any emotional investment."[44]

All of the lesbians whom Gagnon and Simon interviewed in their study were a part of a subculture to at least some degree, but they concluded that most lesbians avoid such participation. As suggested, the lesbian may have less need. Gagnon and Simon point out that the "lesbian may mask her sexual deviance behind a socially prepared asexuality. Not all

[41] Carol A. B. Warren, *Identity and Community in the Gay World* (New York: Wiley, 1974), p. 81.

[42] David Sonenschein, "The Homosexual's Language," *Journal of Sex Research*, November 1969, p. 288.

[43] Simon and Gagnon, "Lesbian Community," p. 219.

[44] Ibid.

categories of women in our society are necessarily defined as sexually active, as, for example the spinster."[45] American society is more permissive toward the interaction of women than toward that of men, and this tells us a great deal about why male and female homosexuals are differentially treated. Basically, unmarried females, unlike unmarried males, may live together, they may kiss and touch each other affectionately, and they may seek each other's company without attracting any undue notice.[46]

The bar is for the lesbian, as for the male homosexual, the main public center of the subculture. But there are far fewer bars for female homosexuals than for male homosexuals. The UCLA study found that in Los Angeles out of 15 homosexual bars 12 were for male homosexuals and 3 for female homosexuals.[47] The bars are different in other ways; for example, there is not much "cruising" in the lesbian bars. One study suggests that the bar is a good place to meet, but that lesbians often do not leave together the first time they meet.[48] A recent description of one of the most popular and expensive lesbian bars in New York City points out a notable absence of "drag dykes"—women who imitate men in their dress and manner. In that bar the girls gather, young and middle-aged, white and black, miniskirted and pantsuited. The women talk, drink, and dance, usually with arms around each other's waists or necks.[49]

In her study of lesbian bars Joanne Long says that they provide anonymity and protection from the outside world. The management and often the patrons take measures to keep heterosexuals out. They may keep them out by telling them there is a private party that night. If heterosexuals do get in the regular patrons sometimes attempt to get rid of them by staring at them. In general the measures are successful, and the bars serve as private retreats where the women can be among their own kind and at ease in their lesbian role. But even among the lesbians in the bars there is a high degree of anonymity. The women usually do not furnish such personal information as addresses, occupations, and places of employment. "So great is the need for anonymity that it is common for women to become acquainted, converse nightly and never learn each other's last name."[50]

Finding a lesbian bar doesn't mean instant success in finding an acceptable partner. Most of the lesbian bars serve a repeat clientele, people who already know one another and who tend to come in couples or in

---

[45] Gagnon and Simon, *Sexual Deviance*, p. 262.

[46] John H. Gagnon and William Simon, "Sexual Deviance in Contemporary America," *The Annals*, March 1968, p. 118.

[47] "Consenting Adult," p. 740.

[48] Love, "Invisible Sorority," p. 67.

[49] Nemy, "Woman Homosexual," p. 61.

[50] Long, "Lesbian Bar."

groups. "They may eye a stranger suspiciously, wondering if she really knows what kind of place she is in. And if she is shy it may take a visiting lesbian a few visits to become acquainted."[51] Not all male homosexuals spend time in homosexual bars, and the same holds true for female homosexuals. It would seem logical to speculate that an even smaller percentage of female homosexuals than of male homosexuals even frequent gay bars and that the older the members of both groups the less they visit the bars.

What roles do lesbians play? As the above description suggests, they are much less strong than male homosexuals, and the stereotype of the masculine lesbian is as far from reality as is the stereotype of the ef-feminate male homosexual. The masculine-appearing lesbians, often called "dykes" or "butches," are women who usually wear masculine-styled clothing and have some male mannerisms. They are fairly easy to identify as homosexuals, but they imitate men only to a degree. What the terms imply is that the lesbian *dyke* and *butch* in some observable way appears like a male. This may be not only through dress and mannerisms but also through body stance, speech, or vocabulary. By contrast the "femme" is a homosexual who appears as feminine as does the average heterosexual woman. She does not look "different."

In the lesbian bars the butch role is the most common. Because there are more butches than femmes some butches must adapt to the unequal distribution and turn femme if they want to maintain that distinct role in their relationships. But in general these distinct roles are played most often by older and working-class women. Long comments that over the two-year period she studied the lesbian bars the distinctiveness of roles was reduced, and that can probably be explained by the efforts of the women's liberation movement to minimize masculine-feminine role differences.[52] On the same point Martin and Lyon observe, "We have watched the decline of the butch-femme concept of relationship for sixteen years. It has been a gradual decline—the stereotype has not yet vanished."[53]

The stereotype of the lesbian also tends to define her as being a "counterfeit man." But the only thing that most lesbians share with men is the gender of the object of their sexual desires. The same point may be made about the stereotype that defines the male homosexual as being like a woman. The mannerisms peculiar to the lesbian are less distinguishable than those of the male homosexual. For example, fewer behavior gestures and signs indicate homosexuality on the part of females than on the part of males. Also, "camp behavior"—behavior seen as both outrageous and

[51] Martin and Lyon, *Lesbian Woman*, p. 133.
[52] Long, "Lesbian Bar."
[53] Martin and Lyon, *Lesbian Woman*, p. 81.

outraging—appears to be essentially a product of the male homosexual community. There is very little visible avant-gardism in the lesbian community.[54] This would suggest that female homosexuals may be basically more conservative than male homosexuals in their patterns of behavior. And this of course tends to be a general characteristic of male and female differences with regard to sexual expression in any kind of social setting.

As with male homosexuals, the "passive" and "active" roles of female homosexuals have been exaggerated. The stereotype has been that the "active" sex partner who performs the sex is the "dyke" while the "passive" partner who receives sexual stimulation is the "femme." But often lesbians do not define themselves with such simplicity. In the Philadelphia sample half of the female homosexuals defined themselves as "gay" and half as "bisexual." The distinction appeared to be that the "gay" women had completely rejected men as sex partners while the "bisexual" women had *almost* completely rejected men.

It appears that a large proportion of lesbians have had some heterosexual experiences. Martin and Lyon comment that at least three fourths of the lesbians they knew had had heterosexual intercourse more than once. These experiences took place within a marriage situation, while dating, as experiments conducted out of curiosity, or as tests of sexual identity. "For the majority of those women the experience was good, erotically; that is, orgasm was achieved and there was a pleasurable feeling. But there was not the emotional involvement which was present in the lesbian sexual relationship."[55] Joanne Long found that among the women she studied it was a "cardinal sin" to have sexual relations with a man. "Bisexual women are generally rejected in the lesbian subculture. Men are given almost no place in the lesbian world and are seen in all ways as intruders."[56]

The lesbians in the Philadelphia sample were asked how, in a permanent relationship with another woman, they preferred to participate sexually. Eighteen percent said "an active role," 21 percent "a passive role," and 61 percent "both about equally." Most of the lesbians went on to say that while they might have a slight sexual preference the situation and the desires of the partner more often determined whether they were sexually passive or active. Many lesbians reject the active-passive distinction as appropriate only for heterosexual activity. Lesbians often see their sex activity as not involving anything like a masculine role. A part of this belief is reflected in the argument that one woman can better understand what will sexually satisfy another woman. The argument goes

---

[54] Simon and Gagnon, "Lesbian Community," p. 216.

[55] Martin and Lyon, *Lesbian Woman*, p. 88.

[56] Long, "Lesbian Bar."

on to say that lesbianism is based on a knowledge and intimacy between two women that make it significantly different from anything that can occur between a man and a woman. In fact this is often the major argument when one woman is trying to persuade another to have sexual relations with her.

Another characteristic of lesbians that distinguishes them from male homosexuals is that they are much less promiscuous. The Kinsey data show that of single females who had had homosexual experience half had had it with only a single partner. Twenty percent had had it with two partners. Only 29 percent had had three or more partners in their homosexual relations, and only 4 percent had had more than 10 partners. So the female homosexual record contrasts sharply with that of the male. "Of the males in the sample who had homosexual experiences, a high proportion had it with several persons, and 22 percent had it with more than 10 partners."[57] This distinction between the promiscuity of male and female homosexuals reflects a general sexual difference and not just a homosexual one. That is, heterosexual males who engage in premarital, extramarital, and postmarital coitus have a greater number of partners than do heterosexual females who are also experienced in these areas. To put it another way, males are more promiscuous than females, regardless of the sexual object.

The women in the Philadelphia sample were asked several questions about their type of sexual involvement. Half of them said that they had had no "one-night stands" in the past year. Lest one might think that a low level of promiscuousness is inherent in the female it might be noted that 12 percent of the women in the sample had had "one-night stands" with more than 50 different partners in the previous year. For many lesbians, as for male homosexuals or even sexually active unmarried men and women, there is often regret over past sexual experiences. However, there doesn't appear to be any evidence that lesbians are particularly regretful of their sexual choice. Kinsey found that of the lesbians with the most extensive homosexual experience 71 percent said they had "no regrets."[58]

There appears to be little question that lesbians in general have a high desire for permanent relationships. This is a pattern generally common to women, regardless of the type of sexual partner. The lesbian, like the heterosexual female, places a higher stress on interpersonal involvement than on sexual outlet. As a result homosexual relationships between females tend to be more effective, to take place under more stable conditions, and to be viewed in terms of a total relationship. Men are far more likely to see homosexuality simply as a means of sexual gratification

---

[57] Kinsey, *Human Female*, p. 458.
[58] Ibid., p. 477.

and as a casual impersonal act. Joanne Long found that the over-whelming emphasis among lesbians was to meet new women in the hope of developing permanent relationships rather than simply of obtaining sex. Many women go to the lesbian bars in the hope of finding a lover. Since there is so much pressure among the women to find mates the lesbian bar might be called a "mate market." This is in sharp contrast to the male homosexual bar which is much more a "sexual market."[59]

However, many lesbians are not able to establish relationships that last for any great length of time. In the Philadelphia sample 70 percent of the lesbians said that they had had at least one satisfying relationship during the past two years. This doesn't mean that all relationships are satisfying, because only 44 percent said that they had been "very satisfied" with any of their relationships over the past two years. But they nevertheless continued to search for good relationships. Gagnon and Simon report in their study that almost all of the women they interviewed defined themselves as "women who wanted to become emotionally and sexually attached to another woman who would, in turn, respond to them as women."[60] They go on to point out that what often seems to be involved is a kind of 19th century commitment to romantic values. "Their aspirations were fundamentally those embodied in 'the American dream': a comfortable home, an interesting job, access to enjoyable leisure ac-tivity, and above all, a sustaining and loving partner."[61]

The ideal of a permanent monogamous relationship is not shared by all lesbians. This appears to be especially true among some of the younger lesbians, who, like their heterosexual counterparts, are protesting the validity of a permanent paired relationship. As with many young heterosexuals, these lesbians feel free to play the field and enter into an affair with another woman without the thought that it will or should last forever. "Communes are forming among lesbians, non-monogamous relationships are being experimented with. Sexual freedom indeed seems possible in certain circumstances. In all these experiments, the desire is for the freedom to choose alternative life styles."[62]

In Chapter 11 it was suggested that aging was crucial for the male homosexual in many ways, including an increasing desire for more durable relationships. It appears that aging is less traumatic for the lesbian because she doesn't operate in a setting as competitive as that of the male homosexual. There is some irony in the fact that in a society in which the decline in physical attractiveness that comes with aging is generally more crucial to and resisted more by women the reverse may be true among female homosexuals. This difference is also explained in part

---

[59] Long, "Lesbian Bar."

[60] Gagnon and Simon, *Sexual Deviance*, p. 265.

[61] Ibid., p. 275.

[62] Martin and Lyon, *Lesbian Woman*, p. 120.

by the greater stress homosexual females place on interpersonal factors. In general it would appear that aging is easier for the female homosexual to handle psychologically than it is for the male homosexual.

One crude measure of the importance of the subculture is the extent to which lesbians choose their friends from within that setting. It is in the area of friendships that the male and female homosexual subcultures most often overlap. Gagnon and Simon found that almost all the lesbians they interviewed "included some male homosexuals among their friends; for some of the lesbians male homosexuals constituted their only close male friends."[63] In the Philadelphia sample 85 percent of the lesbians said that they had some good friends who were "straight," but in most cases they were referring to "straight" female friends. The "straight" male is not usually a friend because he is usually seen as competitive. The homosexual male is not only not competitive but is often seen as understanding because of the similarity of his position in society. Often the lesbian in interacting in the "straight" world needs a male companion, and the male homosexual can meet this need without demands or expectations by either. The extreme illustration of this is the marriage of a female homosexual to a male homosexual as a means of social convenience and with no sexual involvement between them.

As with the male homosexual, there is often some risk for the female homosexual in having "straights" of the same sex as friends. That is, there may be a desire on the lesbian's part, and possibly an attempt, to have sexual relations with the "straight" woman. There are also some risks in establishing friendships with other lesbians. As pointed out, the population from which the individual lesbian is likely to select her friends is the same population from which she is likely to choose her sex partners. "As a result, most discussions of friendship were filled with a sense of anticipated impermanence."[64] Therefore, for many lesbians impermanence may be a characteristic of both sexual relationships and friendships.

One area in which there is a great difference between male and female homosexuals is with regard to children. Many lesbians not only want children but have them. Often lesbians will have children from a marriage and keep them after divorce. A woman would have to be quite openly homosexual before the court would refuse to give her custody of the child, because children are almost always placed with the mother. Actually there is no law against placing a child with lesbians, and any refusal by the courts probably would be on the ground of a poor moral atmosphere in the home. There has been some pressure in recent years to allow lesbian couples to adopt children. It is doubtful whether this will

---

[63] Gagnon and Simon, *Sexual Deviance*, p. 273.
[64] Ibid.

occur where the women openly state that they are lesbians. However, there have been moves in some places to allow single women to adopt, and this will enable lesbians who do not identify themselves as such to adopt children. It would also appear that lesbians who have children to take care of find it somewhat easier to adjust to the "aging" process.

Unlike the situation of male homosexuals, no occupations are stereotyped as being lesbian occupations. About the only prediction that might be made is that lesbians would be found more commonly in those occupations in which women are isolated from men through physical separation or other restrictions against heterosexual interaction. There is one occupation, however, in which female homosexuals appear to be overrepresented. Before examining that occupation it should be stressed that occupations are important to lesbians because they are not dependent on males as breadwinners. Lesbians appear to be more seriously committed to work than are most women, and one reflection of this is that they tend to have relatively stable work histories.[65] Martin and Lyon believe that most lesbians make it a practice to keep their private lives completely separate from their work, even though they may be aware of the presence of other lesbians where they work. "Consequently most lesbians observe an unspoken moral code of not exposing one another, a sort of mutually protective loyalty pact."[66] In the Philadelphia sample 60 percent of the lesbians defined their jobs as "rewarding" while the rest defined them as simply "a way of earning a living." And 70 percent of the lesbians said that they had to hide the fact that they were "gay" in their work situations. About a fourth said that they would be fired if this were found out, but only 6 percent had actually ever been fired. The dangers and the rates of job loss for being homosexual are much higher for men. It would appear that the occupation is another means of helping the lesbian adjust to being sexually different from other women.

THE STRIPPER

An interesting study on the relationship between occupation and lesbian practices has been conducted with strippers in burlesque theatres. McCaghy and Skipper asked the 35 strippers whom they interviewed to estimate the proportion of strippers who had homosexual contacts. The estimates of the proportion who were currently at least bisexual in their contacts mostly fell within the 50 to 75 percent range. McCaghy and Skipper also found that 26 percent of their respondents had engaged in homosexuality although they did not ask for that information or have prior evidence of the respondents' involvement.[67] The two sociologists

[65] Ibid., p. 270.
[66] Martin and Lyon, *Lesbian Woman*, p. 94.
[67] McCaghy and Skipper, "Lesbian Behavior," p. 265.

suggest that several social factors operating within the setting of "stripping" as an occupation help to explain the high rates of lesbianism.

One factor is the isolation of the strippers from effective social relationships. Many of the strippers were not able to maintain any permanent social relationships, such as marriages or close friendships. Beyond whatever personal limitations the strippers may have had there were also severe restrictions based on the nature of the occupation. The strippers on tour spent only one week in each city and worked every day of the week, with their workday starting in the early afternoon and not ending until late at night. So one of their universal complaints was the loneliness they constantly encountered. This meant that they had to turn to each other for friendships. However, loneliness was not necessarily conducive to homosexuality because the strippers were not only isolated from men but also from women, other than the ones in their troupe. "But strippers find that contacts with males are not only limited but often highly unsatisfactory in content, and homosexuality can become an increasingly attractive alternative."[68]

A second factor that contributes to the homosexuality of strippers is their disillusionment with men. They often see their male customers as "dirty" and want nothing to do with them. When they do develop lasting relationships with men "chances are good that they will result in another embittering experience."[69] This is very similar to the pattern of relationships that prostitutes often have with men. Therefore, limited contacts with men along with the strippers' wariness tend to sharply hold down their sexual activity. So the opportunity for a warm and close relationship without the hazards the male brings to such a relationship becomes attractive. McCaghy and Skipper stress that pressures placed on the stripper toward lesbian practices should not be overdone. More important, they feel, is the fact that opportunities for homosexuality take place in an atmosphere of permissiveness toward sexual behavior. The strippers did not see sexual behavior as being right or wrong by any universal standard, and many of them "firmly expressed their view that lesbianism and prostitution are easily as common among women outside the occupation as among strippers."[70]

What appears to be the case is that the strippers see themselves as in a situation where lesbianism becomes acceptable. The chances are that if they could be in a situation with a greater probability of more satisfying relationships with men they would give up their lesbian relationships. This is very similar to what happens to women when they are in prison; there lesbianism is seen as an acceptable adjustment based on

---

[68] Ibid., p. 266.
[69] Ibid., p. 267.
[70] Ibid., p. 269.

psychological needs and special social crcumstances. What this also suggests is that women are more tolerant and accepting of sexual deviance than are men, at least under certain circumstances. McCaghy and Skipper's study is of value not only in pointing out the importance of the situation as a determining factor in sexual deviance for women, but also in indicating how situational adaptations differ between men and women.

BLACK LOWER CLASS

A second study that gives some insights into lesbianism will also be discussed briefly. Ethel Sawyer has studied the impact of the black lower-class subculture on female homosexual roles. Her subjects were a group of black lesbians between 17 and 34 years of age. They were involved in a subculture that centered on bars, taverns, and nightclubs that catered to homosexuals who made little or no effort to conceal their deviance from the larger society.[71]

Sawyer analyzes the two basic roles that existed within the homosexual subculture. The women were designated as "studs" or as "fish." The studs are female homosexuals who fill both socially and sexually a role modeled after that of the male in the broader society. The fish are those who take on the feminine role. Sawyer points out that the roles are more than just labels because they carry with them "matters of appropriate dress, mannerisms and behavior, domestic responsibility, attitudes toward homosexuality, the larger society and toward oneself which accompany each of the roles and which serve to distinguish them. These roles are complementary, i.e., a stud and a fish make a homosexual couple."[72]

Sawyer suggests that the term *stud* probably had its origins with the male animal and notes that it was applied to black male slaves who were used to breed slave children. The term connotes virility and sexual prowess, and is commonly used in the black lower class by one male in referring to another. Often the stud in the lesbian subculture is referred to as a "stud broad" to make a gender distinction.[73] The use of the term *fish* in place of *femme*, the term commonly used among lesbians, is of interest. The term *fish* may come from several sources. In some prisons, the term designates a new prisoner, and often the fish is someone who is entering lesbianism for the first time. However, Sawyer suggests that the term may have a more direct sexual connotation, deriving its meaning from the nature of the smell which is often believed to come from the female sexual organs. She suggests that this interpretation takes

---

[71] Sawyer, "Female Homosexual," p. 3.

[72] Ibid., p. 5.

[73] Ibid., p. 6.

on importance when it is examined in the context of two other points of concern important to the lesbian subculture. One is its almost "obsessive and compulsive" concern with cleanliness in the sexual area. The other centers on oral-genital contact and the stigma that goes with it. Sawyer found that although oral-genital contact was widespread and generally accepted, there was still a good deal of ambivalence surrounding the activity. "One 'gives head' for instance to those who are clean, one takes a bath and has her mate do so before indulging in mouth-genital activity."[74]

As mentioned, the stud role includes far more than simply the direction of participation in the sexual act. Ideologically the stud is the "aggressor, the provider and the protector," and Sawyer says that one often hears this cliche uttered by both studs and fish in the subculture. In theory the role of the stud closely approximates that of the male in the broader society. Even many of the double-standard values of society have been adopted. The studs have one-night stands, and go out on the town while the fish remain at home; the studs drink large amounts of alcohol while the fish are expected to drink in moderation; "and studs are the ones who may at any point 'let their hair down' while fish are to always exhibit the most 'ladylike' conduct."[75] Often the employment record and economic responsibility of the stud are no different from those of the male in the black lower-class subculture. Like some black lower-class males, some employed studs do not support their fish. Often the stud uses the male models of "hipster" or "stud on the corner" as a prototype for her behavior. As a result studs "are sometimes inclined to view fish in an instrumental and exploitative fashion, and often cast them into roles of persons from whom they may gain favors, particularly along monetary lines."[76]

Sawyer was also interested in the relationships of the studs and fish to their own children. She found that studs who had children of their own were more likely to take care of them financially than they were to take care of the children of their fish. But often the studs were capable of developing strong emotional ties to the children of their mates. And in most cases the studs did not hesitate to show their feelings for the children. "It is not an uncommon sight to see a stud wheeling the baby carriage of another's child or walk into a home and observe the stud caring for a baby or engaged in play activities with children of their mates."[77] Sawyer's study is important not only in itself but also because it provides a picture of an attempt by lesbians to develop different patterns under special social circumstances—those of the black lower-class sub-

---

[74] Ibid., pp. 6–7.
[75] Ibid., pp. 9–10.
[76] Ibid., p. 12.
[77] Ibid., p. 19.

culture. It may also be seen as another illustration of women's use of and ability to deal with homosexuality where it has some value to them. It is hard to imagine men being able to make the same kind of adaptive use of homosexuality in a similar social situation.

We conclude this chapter by looking a little more at the relationship of lesbianism to the broader society. As already indicated, the female homosexual probably has fewer problems with the broader society than does the male homosexual. Gagnon and Simon point out that the female homosexual "is probably better integrated than the male homosexual into conventional relationships such as the family of origin, work, religion, and conventional leisure time pursuits."[78]

Like the male homosexuals, but to a much lesser extent, lesbians have developed militant organizations to push for what they believe to be their rights. The largest lesbian organization, the Daughters of Bilitis, was founded in 1955. It derives its name from some 19th century song lyrics that glorified lesbian love. The organization has its headquarters in San Francisco, and in 1969 there were four official and five probationary chapters. The organization's purpose is to explore changing some laws that are believed to discriminate against the lesbian, but it also maintains social clubs where some counseling takes place. The organization is generally known by its initials, DOB, and it has a few honorary male members whom it calls Sons of Bilitis, or SOB's.[79]

Abbott and Love argue that the radical lesbian is no longer ashamed of her commitment to a lesbian way of life and she has come to realize that most of her problems are due to social repression rather than to unhealthy traits in her personality.[80] They point out that the homosexual movement is different from most other social movements because of the ease of concealment. "As a social movement fighting for acceptance, lesbians and male homosexuals will have to find a way to mobilize the many homosexuals who still feel they cannot afford to 'come out' in the open."[81]

The new militancy of some lesbians is not so much a result of their feeling that discrimination against them has been increasing as that they should do something about the wrongs they feel they have long suffered. There is also some evidence of overlap between the militant lesbians and some factions of the militant women's liberation movement. This should not be surprising because the female homosexual is a member of two minority groups—she is a woman and a homosexual. There is hyper-

---

[78] Gagnon and Simon, "Sexual Deviance," p. 118.

[79] Edward Sagarin, *Odd Man in: Societies of Deviants in America* (Chicago: Quadrangle 1969), p. 89.

[80] Sidney Abbott and Barbara Love, "Is Women's Liberation a Lesbian Plot?" in Vivian Gornick and Barbara K. Moran, *Woman in Sexist Society* (New York: Signet Books, 1971), p. 606.

[81] Ibid., p. 613.

sensitivity in the woman's liberation movement to the charge of lesbianism. The existence of a few militant lesbians within the movement once prompted one of the leaders, Betty Friedan, to complain about the "lavender menace" that was threatening to warp the image of women's rights. Regardless of the relationship it seems likely that the aggressiveness of the female homosexual will increase in the near future.[82]

In general Chafetz and her colleagues point out that though lesbians are less threatened than their male counterparts they have also been less understood and supported. However, they note that this may be changing. "In response to the question of whether the women's liberation movement has helped or hurt them, 80 percent of the lesbians agreed it had helped."[83]

One of the greatest problems for the lesbian appears to be with her family. Of the Philadelphia sample of lesbians 50 percent said that their parents knew they were homosexual, and 21 percent said that their parents absolutely did not know. Almost half of the respondents said that fear that their parents would find out about them had been a source of concern to them. Gagnon and Simon found that frequently parents suspected or even knew that their daughters were lesbians, but decided to ignore the possibility.[84] However, it is probably much easier for a parent not to recognize or to ignore a daughter's being a homosexual than a son's.

It seems quite likely that in the future lesbianism, if not more common, is going to be much more open. This would seem to be an inevitable part of women's achieving greater equality. As women attain rights to sexual expression closer to those of the male, those rights are going to be directed in a number of different directions. As society moves toward a single sex standard for both males and females the consequences will cut across all areas of sexual expression. Therefore, women will have greater equality both heterosexually and homosexually.

BIBLIOGRAPHY

Abbott, Sidney, and Barbara Love, "Is Women's Liberation a Lesbian Plot?" in Vivian Gornick and Barbara K. Moran, *Women in Sexist Society* (New York: Signet Books, 1971), pp. 601–21.

Cory, Donald W., *The Lesbian in America*. New York: Citadel Press, 1964.

Gagnon, John H., and William Simon, *Sexual Deviance*. New York: Harper and Row, 1967.

---

[82] Susan Brownmiller, "Sisterhood Is Powerful," *New York Times Magazine*, March 15, 1970, p. 140.

[83] Chefetz, "Homosexual Women," p. 719.

[84] Gagnon and Simon, *Sexual Deviance*, p. 268.

McCaghy, Charles H., and James K. Skipper, Jr., "Lesbian Behavior as an Adaptation to the Occupation of Stripping," *Social Problems*, Fall 1969, pp. 262–70.

Martin, Del, and Phyllis Lyon, *Lesbian Women*. New York: Bantam Books, 1972.

Nemy, Enid, "The Woman Homosexual: More Assertive, Less Willing to Hide," *New York Times*, Nov. 17, 1969, p. 61.

Sawyer, Ethel, "The Impact of the Surrounding Lower-Class Subculture on Female Homosexual Adaptations," *Society for the Study of Social Problems*, San Francisco, Calif., August 1967, pp. 1–23.

Simon, William, and John H. Gagnon, "Femininity in the Lesbian Community," *Social Problems*, Fall 1967, pp. 212–21.

chapter thirteen

Delinquent subcultures

There is a vast body of literature about the many different aspects of juvenile delinquency. Therefore, any attempt to deal with the topic in a single chapter must be highly limited. The intention here is to present a brief discussion of delinquency primarily as it relates to the concept of a deviant subculture. This means that such areas as individual deviance, where the young person commits an illegal act by himself and without the direct influence of age peers, will not be considered here.

The concern with delinquency is probably about as old as mankind. This is because all societies have recognized that certain kinds of behavior are wrong because they are defined as harmful at least to some. Out of this protective view emerged the social concern with criminal norms and laws, and various means for protecting the innocent and punishing or trying to change the guilty. But there probably also developed early in the history of mankind the recognition that not all persons who did wrong things could be defined and treated in the same way. Over the centuries one variation related to the age of the individual wrongdoer, while others were related to his mental competence as determined by either mental ability or mental illness. The problem of age and individual responsibility has been confused by the transitional years between childhood and adulthood. In some primitive societies this was not a problem because they defined a person as a child, with few rights and obligations, until he reached a certain age and then defined him as an adult if he passed the tests to which he was subjected at that time. In the United States it is the pattern that a child up until 10 or 12 years of age is defined as prerational in that he is not usually held responsible for his actions. For example, if an 8-year-old child kills someone he is not held responsible for his action. In most situations by age 18 the individual is held responsible for what he does (assuming mental competence and in some cases an absence of mitigating circumstances). During the period of adolescence the individual is only partly responsible. Juvenile courts as well as various types of detention centers have been set up to work with those whose behavior is based on only partial individual responsibility.

Sociologically any study of the delinquent must start with the recognition that he is, in effect, a "second-class citizen" because he has only partial rights in society. And most adolescents, whether delinquent or nondelinquent, often seek adult status with all the rights and privileges they see as going with that status. The adolescent, being neither child nor adult, and having no clearly defined roles available to him in the overall culture, has created a loose cultural system to provide some role meanings for his adolescence. This means that there are certain conflict points with the dominant adult cultural system. And the inconsistency of adult definitions of adolescent behavior has also contributed to the emergence of subcultural values. The very fact that the adult views the adolescent with indecision as to appropriate behavior means that the adolescent is treated one way on one occasion and a different way on another. Since the adolescent often desires decisiveness and some precision in role definitions, he may try to create his own roles. When he does, he often demands a high degree of conformity by other adolescents as "proof" of the rightness of his definitions. There is a certain irony here in that many adolescents think of themselves as social deviants. What they fail to realize is that their adolescent groups deviate from the adult world, but that the requirements for conformity within their subcultures are extremely strong. And this level of subcultural conformity is just as powerful for delinquent subcultures as it is for nondelinquent ones.

Over space and time the behavior of adolescents has varied widely, as has the definition of that behavior. And some of the features of delinquency that are so pervasive in the United States and that have come to be taken for granted as inherent in the idea of delinquency may be absent in other cultures. It is probable that delinquent subcultures have different stresses in different societies and that those stresses could be related to differences in the various social systems of which the subcultures are a part. This also helps to emphasize the point that there is nothing inherent in an activity that makes it delinquent. Furthermore, our own society's definition of delinquency has varied over time. For example, school truancy was at one time defined as a more serious form of delinquency than is the case today. Or one of the most common types of delinquency today—the stealing of automobiles—did not exist 50 years ago.

But whatever specific acts are defined as delinquent the general concept has probably been close to universal. "In every society known to us, a certain number of minors have also been transgressors. And, when troubled by the delinquency in their midst, members of every society have sought to account for that phenomenon. The threat posed by 'ungovernable youth' has provoked a multitude of reactions and led to a variety of explanations."[1] Few areas of human behavior have been more extensively studied than that of delinquency. Part of the reason for this is that personal alarm competes with the economic cost. "In a culture where the cash nexus has much to do with shaping morals, 'experts' feel heavy pressure to find a remedy, cut the loss, declare war on crime and stamp it out. Moral and financial accounts are to be settled simultaneously."[2]

As a result of the vast amount of research, almost every social variable believed to have negative consequences has been linked to delinquency. In one sense the concern about delinquency becomes a rallying point around which one may aim at a variety of assumed causes. This means that often attention is directed at delinquency not so much because it is a problem in itself as because it is seen as the result of other problems of deviance that various groups are concerned about. For example, one may study the relationship of delinquency to broken homes because the delinquency is seen as further proof that broken homes are bad and the broken home is the area of deviance where the concern rests. This approach may also be found in studies attempting to causally link delinquency to poverty, racial conflict, and so forth.

Since our concern in this chapter is primarily with collective rather than individual juvenile delinquency, our interest is in delinquency as it refers to gang or subcultural forms. From the sociological point of view the interest is not in the individual delinquent and what he does but rather in the overall delinquent group, which implies that the collectivity has some qualities beyond the mere sum of the individuals involved. This means that the sociological view is different from the legal one, because in the legal approach of the Western world the weight of legal responsibility is on the individual actor and not on the collectivity as a whole.[3]

One major difficulty in any study of delinquency is trying to bring together the various legal meanings. The laws in the different states are very general and often quite vague. For example, in the state of Illinois a delinquent is described as "an 'incorrigible' growing up in 'idleness,' 'loitering' in the streets at night without a proper excuse, or guilty of 'indecent' or 'lascivious' conduct. New Mexico, as another example, exceeds Illinois in vagueness by making 'habitual' infraction a necessary condition for the definition of delinquency."[4] Furthermore, delinquency is not simply crimes committed by juveniles, because the statutes are so

---

[1] Bernard Rosenberg and Harry Silverstein, *The Varieties of Delinquent Experience* (Waltham, Mass.: Blaisdell, 1969), p. 3.

[2] Ibid., p. 4.

[3] Hans Sebald, *Adolescence: A Sociological Analysis* (New York: Appleton-Century-Crofts, 1968), pp. 354–55.

[4] Ibid., p. 352.

broad that they allow juvenile authorities to assume control over all types of adolescents engaged in all kinds of misbehavior. In some cases the laws empower the juvenile court to take jurisdiction of adolescents who show vague conditions, such as "immorality," as well as of those who are involved in specific areas of midconduct.

It seems clear that most adolescents at some time commit delinquent acts but are not officially defined as delinquents. In a 1967 national survey of youth 88 percent of the teenagers in the sample confessed to having committed at least one chargeable offense in the three years prior to the interview. It is clear that if the authorities were omniscient and zealous a large majority of American teenagers would be labeled juvenile delinquents. But less than 3 percent of the sample were detected by the police, only 22 percent had had any contact with the police, and less than 2 percent had ever been under judicial consideration.[5] Thirteen percent of the boys and 3 percent of the girls reported being apprehended by the police for some delinquent act during the three-year period.[6]

To be defined as an official delinquent is the result of social judgments, in most cases made by the police. The individual becomes "a delinquent because someone in authority has defined him as one, often on the basis of the public face he has presented to officials rather than of the kind of offense he has committed."[7] This suggests that most adolescents are at some time behavioral delinquents, but whether they become labeled as such is determined by legal agency decisions. There are many agencies in addition to the police that contribute to defining some youths as delinquents. In fact those who do the defining contribute to many confusions because many different conceptions are held by the police, social workers, psychiatrists, psychologists, sociologists, judges, and so forth. These different perspectives may lead to redefinitions of an adolescent as "disturbed" rather than "wild" or "insecure" and "in need of love" rather than of strong discipline and "a kick where it hurts." "The behavior of a youth, therefore, may not be as critical in such cases as the interpretations which are placed upon it by others."[8] What is important is that there are a number of different vested interests with different views of delinquents and how they should be treated. This can lead to confusion for the adolescent as well as the broader society.

Regardless of the variety of vested interests the real source for defining

---

[5] J. R. Williams and Martin Gold, "From Delinquent Behavior to Official Delinquency," *Social Problems*, Fall 1972, p. 213.

[6] Ibid., p. 219.

[7] Irving Piliavin and Scott Briar, "Police Encounters with Juveniles," in Earl Rubington and Martin S. Weinberg, *Deviance: The Interactionist Perspective* (New York: Macmillan, 1968), p. 145.

[8] Aaron V. Cicourel and John I. Kitsuse, "The Social Organization of the High School and Deviant Adolescent Careers," in Rubington and Weinberg, *Deviance*, p. 132.

most delinquents is the police. The police come upon adolescents doing something that is against the law, and they must decide whether the lawbreaking youth should be treated as a "bad one" needing court attention or as a "good kid" who needs only a strong talking-to. Other agencies may enter if the police define him as needing the attention of the court. For example, "someone must decide whether a youth should be sent to a training school or placed on probation. Someone must judge whether a training-school inmate should be turned loose on parole this week, next month, or at some other time."[9]

As Williams and Gold point out, a line is drawn between delinquent behavior and official delinquency. "Delinquent behavior is norm violating behavior of a juvenile which, if detected by an appropriate authority, would expose the actor to legally prescribed sanctions. Official delinquency is the identification of and response to a delinquent behavior by the police and courts."[10]

When the police respond to delinquent actions they are usually responding as more than just policemen. They are often responding as individuals who have strong moral values about what they feel to be right adolescent behavior. Because many police come out of lower middle-class backgrounds they usually believe that the adolescent should be seen and not heard, and this in itself may decide whether or not an arrest takes place. In general the police tend to see the adolescents they come in contact with as being of two general types. First, there are those they see as "good kids" who do not usually cause any trouble, and second, there are the "troublemakers," who constitute most of the adolescent groups the police have contact with. The police may even make further distinctions. For example, among the good kids they may distinguish between the "quiet, studious kids who never cause any trouble" and the "good kids who cut up a little and need to be warned." The police may also make a distinction between two types of "troublemakers." One type is described as "wild kids who need a good kick in the ass," and the other as "real no-good punks" headed for criminal careers.[11]

Gusfield has observed that juveniles apprehended by the police received more lenient treatment, including dismissal, if they appeared contrite and remorseful about their violations than if they did not. "This difference in the posture of the deviant accounted for much of the differential treatment favoring middle-class 'youngsters' as against lower-class 'delinquents.'"[12]

---

[9] Peter G. Garabedian and Don C. Gibbons, *Becoming Delinquent* (Chicago: Aldine, 1970), p. 4.

[10] Williams and Gold, "Delinquent Behavior," p. 210.

[11] Cicourel and Kitsuse, "Deviant Adolescent," p. 141.

[12] Joseph R. Gusfield, "Moral Passage: The Symbolic Process in Public Designations of Deviance," *Social Problems*, Fall 1967, p. 179.

A number of other factors determine how the police will react to potential delinquents and how they will treat them. It has been suggested that other than the previous record of the youth the most important factor is his behavior toward the police. In the opinion of policemen themselves the demeanor of apprehended juveniles was a major determinant of their decisions in about half of the juvenile cases they processed.[13] The actual cues that the police used to decide the demeanor of the juvenile were quite simple. When juveniles were contrite about their wrongs, respectful to the policemen, and fearful of the sanctions that might be employed against them they were usually seen by the police as basically law-abiding or at least "salvageable." By contrast youthful offenders who were fractious, obdurate, or who appeared nonchalant in their encounters with patrolmen were likely to be viewed as "would-be tough guys" or "punks" who deserved the most severe sanction: arrest.[14]

The animosity that police officers tended to show toward recalcitrant or aloof offenders appeared to come from two sources. The first was moral indignation that the juveniles appeared to be self-righteous and indifferent about their transgressions. The second was the feeling that the youths did not accord the respect that the police believed they deserved. Because the police saw themselves as honestly and impartially performing a vital function that deserved respect from the community they often attributed the lack of respect shown them by the juveniles to the latter's immorality.[15]

There is evidence that many police respond to adolescents in terms of stereotypes. For example, compared to other youths, blacks and other boys whose appearance matches the delinquent stereotypes are more often stopped and interrogated by policemen. This often occurs even when there is no evidence that an offense has been committed. Also, when arrested, boys fitting the sterotypes are usually given more severe dispositions for the same violations than those who do not fit the stereotypes.[16] Therefore, becoming a delinquent, like becoming a criminal, often depends on factors that may have little or nothing to do with the illegal act itself.

How much delinquency?

If one tried to estimate how many young people engage in acts that could be defined as delinquent the number would be extremely high. In fact "self-report studies reveal that perhaps 90 percent of all young people have committed at least one act for which they could have been brought to

---

[13] Piliavin and Briar, "Police Encounters," p. 141.
[14] Ibid., p. 142.
[15] Ibid., p. 143.
[16] Ibid.

juvenile court."[17] So while it seems that nearly all youngsters engage in acts of misconduct, only about 3 percent of all juvenile court-eligible children (between 7 and 18 years of age) ever get into the juvenile court each year while about double that percentage come to the attention of the police. Most of those who are officially processed by the police and the courts are working-class children who have engaged in serious and repetitive acts of law breaking.[18]

During the 1960s the number, as well as the percentage, of adolescents defined as delinquent showed a substantial increase. For example, in 1960 about 14 percent of all urban offenders were in their teens, but by 1965 this had increased to 21 percent. Actually most crimes, wherever they are committed, are committed by boys and young men. About one in every six male youths is referred to juvenile court in connection with a delinquent act (excluding traffic offenses) before his 18th birthday. "Arrest rates are highest for persons aged 15 through 17, next highest for those 18 through 20, dropping off quite directly with increase in age."[19] Put another way, in the period between 1960 and 1965 the teenage population in the United States increased by 17 percent but its rate of delinquency increased by 54 percent. More specifically, there was an extremely sharp increase in delinquency in the suburban areas during the 1960s. Adolescents made up 32 percent of all criminals in the suburban areas as compared to 21 percent in the urban and 19 percent in the rural areas.[20]

The high rates of juvenile delinquency are costly to society because of the necessary detention and treatment procedures. For example, in the 1960s a daily average of around 63,000 youths was incarcerated in juvenile institutions in the United States. Another group of roughly 300,000 were under supervision in community programs through probation and parole. The institutionalized delinquents required approximately 32,000 employees to process and supervise them, while another 10,000 individuals were employed as community correctional agents.[21] It can be seen that just the sheer size of delinquency makes it a costly and complex social problem.

DELINQUENT SUBCULTURES

Given the long and intense interest of sociologists in juvenile delinquency, it is not surprising that many sociological theories have been developed to try to explain the phenomenon. Only the main points of

---

[17] Sebald, *Adolescence*, p. 357.

[18] Garabedian and Gibbons, *Becoming Delinquent*, p. 3.

[19] Sebald, *Adolescence*, p. 363.

[20] Ibid., p. 364.

[21] Garabedian and Gibbons, *Becoming Delinquent*, p. 3.

some of these theories can be considered here. All of the theories see delinquency as part of a group process.

The earliest sociological theories of delinquency came out of attempts to explain the characteristics and the spatial distribution of gangs in cities. "These, in turn, were related to research and speculation concerning structural and growth processes of cities and the influence of different, and sometimes conflicting, cultures in the American melting pot."[22] Ever since the publication of Shaw's famous studies many American sociologists have argued that the most serious forms of male juvenile delinquency "can be described as distinctively subcultural phenomena, manifestations of a deviant peer-group tradition, or way of life."[23] During the same general period Thrasher's work on gangs had a great influence. In essence Thrasher saw the delinquent subculture as the way of life that would be developed as a group became a gang. Bordua suggests that the most important difference between Thrasher and some of the more recent theoreticians of delinquency was that Thrasher saw crime and delinquency as being attractive to the boy and being a good boy as dull. "They were attractive because one could be a hero in a fight. Fun, profit, glory, and freedom is a combination hard to beat, particularly for the inadequate conventional institutions that formed the competition."[24]

Albert Cohen

In recent years the most influential sociological theory about delinquency has come from Cohen.[25] In his study Cohen examined what he called a delinquent subculture, which he saw as a system of beliefs and values brought about through the process of verbal interaction among young men in similar circumstances. Their circumstances were alike by virtue of their like positions in the social system, and the subculture constituted a solution to problems of adjustment for which the established culture provided no satisfactory solutions. The problems were for the most part problems of status and self-respect which arose among working-class children because of their inability to meet the standards and expectations of the established culture. "The delinquent subculture, with its characteristics of non-utilitarianism, malice, and negativism,

---

[22] James F. Short, Jr., *Gang Delinquency and Delinquent Subcultures* (New York: Harper and Row, 1968), p. 133.

[23] Paul Lerman, "Argot, Symbolic Deviance and Subcultural Delinquency," *American Sociological Review*, April 1967, p. 209.

[24] David J. Bordua, "Delinquent Subcultures: Sociological Interpretations of Gang Delinquency," in William A. Rushing, *Deviant Behavior and Social Process* (Chicago: Rand McNally, 1969), pp. 27–78.

[25] Albert K. Cohen, *Delinquent Boys: The Culture of the Gang* (Glencoe, Ill.: Free Press, 1955).

provides an alternative status system and justifies, for those who participate in it, hostility and aggression against the source of their status frustration."[26] Basically Cohen argued that many working-class boys were forced to develop the delinquent subculture as a way of recouping the self-esteem destroyed by the dominating institutions of the middle class. Rather than concentrate on the gang and its development over time, "Cohen's theory focuses on the way of life of the gang—the delinquent subculture."[27]

Richard A. Cloward and Lloyd E. Ohlin

The theory of Cloward and Ohlin is similar to that of Cohen except that they see a variation in types of delinquent subcultures.[28] They argue that all delinquent subcultures emerge because individuals have limited access to legitimate opportunities. Given limited access, specific types of delinquent subcultures result from variations in the means of *illegitimate* opportunity available to lower-class boys. According to Cloward and Ohlin some communities are characterized by politically protected organized crime, and in that setting there exists the fullest access to illegitimate opportunity. In that setting, they argue, a *criminal* type of delinquent subculture will predominate. They go on to suggest that in lower-class areas where there is an absence of both illegitimate and legitimate opportunity two other types of delinquent subculture may be expected to develop. One is the *conflict* type of street gang, and this includes boys who are frustrated in their aspirations for big money and who have no effective access to illegitimate opportunity and therefore shift their status goals to being street fighters. The second is the *"retreatist* type of gang which includes boys for whom illegitimate opportunity is similarly unavailable. But unable to use violence because of subjective inhibition, they resort to drug use as they seek status in groups for which the cultivation of inner experience constitutes a dominant value."[29]

Walter Miller

Miller argues that gang delinquency is most directly influenced by the lower-class community itself.[30] He says that there is a long-established, distinctly patterned lower-class cultural tradition with an integrity of its

[26] Albert K. Cohen and James F. Short, Jr., "Research in Delinquent Subcultures," *Journal of Social Issues*, 14 (1958), p. 20.

[27] Bordua, "Delinquent Subcultures," p. 28.

[28] Richard A. Cloward and Lloyd E. Ohlin, *Delinquency and Opportunity* (New York: Macmillan 1960).

[29] Solomon Kobrin et al., "Criteria of Status among Street Groups," in Short, *Gang Delinquency*, p. 180.

[30] Walter Miller, "Lower-Class Culture as a Generating Milieu of Gang Delinquency," *Journal of Social Issues*, 14 (1958), pp. 3–19.

own rather than a delinquent subculture which has arisen through conflict with middle-class culture and is oriented to the deliberate violation of middle-class norms. Miller sees the lower-class culture as coming from the shaking-down processes of immigration, internal migration, and vertical mobility. "Several population and cultural streams feed this process, but primarily, lower class culture represents the emerging common adaptation of unsuccessful immigrants and Negroes."[31] Miller sees the focal concerns of lower-class subculture as trouble, toughness, smartness, excitement, fate, and autonomy.

Miller argues that participation in lower-class street gangs produces delinquency in several ways. First, as with Cloward and Ohlin's illegitimate means, many cultural practices are made up essentially of elements in the overall pattern of the lower class which automatically violate specific legal norms. Second, where alternative means to similar ends are available, illegal means often provide a greater and more immediate return for a smaller investment of energy than do legal means. Third, the expected responses to a variety of situations often occurring in the lower-class culture involve the performing of illegal acts.[32] The adolescent street gang also provides the boy with mechanisms for dealing with girls as well as for fitting him into the all-male activity of which he will be a part as an adult. So Miller emphasizes the wide range of activities of a nondelinquent nature that gang members engage in—because of the desire to be "real men."[33] Miller's view differs from the others primarily in stressing that the subculture of the delinquent boys comes from the broader lower class and in viewing what delinquents do as not being significantly different.

Lewis Yablonsky

In his writings Yablonsky has reacted against the view of delinquent subcultures with their assumed structures and functions.[34] He suggests that one way to view human collectivities is on a continuum of organization characteristics. At one extreme of the continuum would be a highly organized, cohesive, functioning collection of individuals making up a group. At the other extreme would be a mob of individuals characterized by anonymity and disturbed leadership, motivated by emotion, and in some situations representing a destructive collectivity within the inclusive social system.[35] He goes on to argue that midway along the continuum are collectivities that are neither groups nor mobs.

---

[31] Bordua, "Delinquent Subcultures," p. 31.

[32] Ibid., p. 32.

[33] Miller, "Gang Delinquency," pp. 3–19.

[34] Lewis Yablonsky, "The Delinquent Gang as a Near-Group," *Social Problems*, Fall 1959, pp. 108–17; reprinted in Rubington and Weinberg, *Deviance*, pp. 225–34.

[35] Ibid., pp. 225–26.

These he calls "near-groups," and they are characterized by "(1) diffuse role definition, (2) limited cohesion, (3) impermanence, (4) minimal consensus of norms, (5) shifting membership, (6) disturbed leadership, and (7) limited definition of membership expectations. These factors characterize the near-group's 'normal' structure."[36]

Yablonsky applied his concept of the near-group to the study of gang battles in New York City. He argues that the press, public, police, social workers, and others project group conceptions into near-group activities. In their treatment of the aggregates as gangs they attribute to them subcultural characteristics that may not exist in reality. Yablonsky says that most of the young men at the scene of gang wars were actually participating in a kind of mob action. "Most had no real concept of belonging to any gang or group; however, they were interested in a situation which might be exciting and possibly a channel for expressing some of their aggressions and hostilities."[37]

It is suggested by Yablonsky that to approach a gang as a group, when it is not, tends to give it a structure that did not formerly exist. He says that the gang worker's usual set of notions about gangs existing as groups includes some of the following distortions: "(1) the gang has a measurable number of members, (2) membership is defined, (3) the role of members is specified, (4) there is a consensus of understood gang norms among gang members, and (5) gang leadership is clear and entails a flow of authority and direction of action."[38] So Yablonsky's contribution to the theory of delinquent subcultures is to caution against attributing subcultural characteristics to delinquency simply because it is shared activity.

David Matza

Matza also recognizes that subculture is the central idea of the dominant sociological view of delinquency.[39] He suggests that the sociological theorists have a remarkably similar picture of the delinquent. That is, they see the individual as committed to delinquency because of his membership in a subculture that requires the breaking of laws. "The sociological delinquent is trapped by the accident of membership, just as his predecessors were trapped by the accident of hereditary defect or emotional disturbance. The delinquent has come a long way under the auspices of positive criminology. He has been transformed from a defective to a defector."[40]

---

[36] Ibid., p. 226.

[37] Ibid., p. 227.

[38] Ibid., p. 230.

[39] David Matza, *Delinquency and Drift* (New York: Wiley, 1964).

[40] Ibid., p. 21.

Matza goes on to suggest that the subculture of delinquency is a delicately balanced set of precepts doubly dependent on extenuating circumstances. Both performing and abstaining from delinquent acts are approved only under certain conditions. Matza is saying that the delinquent subculture is really of two minds regarding delinquent actions, one which allows members to gain prestige by behaving illegally and another which shows the impact of conventional precepts of legal conformity.[41] His thesis is that even in the situation of company the commitment to delinquency is a misconception—first of delinquents and later of the sociologists who study them. "Instead, there is a system of shared misunderstandings, based on miscues, which leads delinquents to believe that all others situated in their company are committed to their misdeeds."[42] Matza believes that the subculture of delinquency is more dependent on and integrated into the conventional society than are most other deviant subcultures. Therefore, he says that the key to the analysis of the subculture of delinquency may be its high degree of integration into the wider society rather than its slight differentiation.[43]

A basic part of Matza's theory is the concept of neutralization. The concept suggests that modern legal systems recognize the conditions under which misdeeds may not be penally sanctioned, and that these conditions may be unknowingly duplicated, distorted, and extended in customary beliefs. So the delinquent's neutralization proceeds along the lines of the negation of responsibility, "the sense of injustice, the assertion of tort, and the primacy of custom."[44] The theory of neutralization is also an explicit denial of Cohen's thesis of a delinquent subculture. The neutralization view suggests that most delinquents are not following a different or subcultural set of norms. Rather, they are basically adhering to the conventional norms while accepting many justifications for deviance. Matza also introduces the concept of "subterranean values" to show that the values behind a large portion of juvenile delinquency are far less deviant than is commonly indicated. Subterranean analysis requires the exploration of connections between local deviant traditions in a subculture and a variety of traditions in conventional society. "Subterranean tradition may be defined by specification of key points along the range of support. It is deviant, which is to say that it is publicly denounced by authorized spokesmen. However, the tradition is viewed with ambivalence in the privacy of contemplation and in intimate publics by most conventional citizens."[45] The subterranean values are close to the old code of conduct for "gentlemen of leisure." There is high emphasis on

---

[41] Ibid., p. 40.
[42] Ibid., p. 59.
[43] Ibid., p. 60.
[44] Ibid., p. 61.
[45] Ibid., p. 64.

daring and adventure, the rejection of disciplined work and labor, a desire to obtain things of luxury and prestige through the show of masculinity. "It is only the form of expression that differs—the form being labeled 'delinquent.' In essence, it is not the values that are deviant but only the forms of expressing them."[46]

The various theories presented disagree as to whether or not a subculture exists, and those that accept its existence disagree about how the subculture develops its basic structure and what its values are. When one looks at the various theories it seems that the delinquents discussed by Cohen, Miller, and Matza were, in varying degrees, clearly recognizable as having once been children. By contrast Cloward and Ohlin's delinquents seem to suddenly appear on the scene sometime in adolescence and to look at the world and discover that there is little in it for them.[47] Bordua in his summary of delinquent theories suggests that in general it does not seem much like fun any more to be a delinquent. He says that Thrasher's boys enjoyed being chased by the police, shooting dice, skipping school, rolling drunks but that though Miller's boys do appear to have a little fun somehow they seem generally desperate. "Cohen's boys and Cloward and Ohlin's boys are driven by grim economic and psychic necessity into rebellion. It seems peculiar that modern analysis has stopped assuming that 'evil' can be fun and sees gang delinquency as arising only when boys are driven away from 'good.'"[48] Before examining in further detail the elements many researchers see as basic to delinquent subcultures it is necessary to look at some social variables that are commonly thought to be related to delinquency.

Family

As mentioned earlier, many attempts have been made to associate delinquency with family factors. The most common variable studied has been that of the broken home. In part this has been a reflection of the "sacred" view of the family, which assumes that any disturbance of the family leads to all kinds of problems for the children. Often in the past the purpose of such studies has been more to make a moral point than to shed any objective light on the relationship. However, in recent years there have been some studies that show relationships between delinquency and the broken home.

Chilton and Markle found that proportionately more children who come into contact with police agencies as well as juvenile courts on delinquency charges live in disrupted families than do children in the

---

[46] Sebald, *Adolescence*, p. 372.

[47] Bordua, "Delinquent Subcultures," p. 35.

[48] Ibid., p. 37.

general population. "In addition, the study suggests that children charged with more serious misconduct more often come from incomplete families than children charged with less serious delinquency."[49]

Studies also show relationships between how parents treat their children and the probability of delinquency. Jensen found that "the neutral or isolated child is more likely to be a delinquent than the child who is loved by and attached to his parents even when delinquent patterns 'outside the home' are scarce or absent."[50] Viewing the relationship from another perspective is the finding that the parents of delinquent boys are more sanctioning of antisocial behavior than are the parents of nondelinquent boys. In this study mothers of delinquent boys were seen by their sons as highly sanctioning. The mothers sanctioned delinquency by their antisocial expectations, their insistent discipline, and a cold hostile attitude. "Fathers sanctioned delinquency by their insistent discipline, and by serving as antisocial models."[51]

Foster and his co-workers found that the delinquent youths they interviewed did not feel that their contact with a law enforcement agency had resulted in any significant social liability in terms of interpersonal relationships. They did not perceive any negative effects whatever on the attitudes of their friends toward them. The boys felt that their parents had relatively fixed opinions of them that were developed before they got into trouble. "The parents appear to expect their boys to get into trouble. Likewise, the parents who consider their children basically good continue to believe so despite what happened with the police."[52]

Religion

Religious values and institutions have traditionally been seen as the antithesis of all kinds of "badness"—including delinquency. A part of the American stereotype sees the boy who goes to church and participates in religious activities as a good boy. Frequently various types of religious therapy and orientation have been used as means for dealing with delinquency. Yet, it is also clear that often those who get in trouble also appear to be religiously active. Therefore, the question of the relationship between religious involvement and delinquent behavior may be raised.

A recent study of high school students found that those who often

[49] Roland J. Chilton and Gerald E. Markle, "Family Disruption, Delinquent Conduct, and the Effect of Subclassification," *American Sociological Review*, February 1972, p. 98.

[50] Gary F. Jensen, "Parents, Peers, and Delinquent Action: A Test of Differential Association Perspective," *American Journal of Sociology*, November 1972, p. 244.

[51] Curt Gallenkamp, "Parents and Their Delinquent Sons," *Dissertation Abstracts* 29 (1968), p. 3085.

[52] Jack Donald Foster, Simon Dinitz, and Walter C. Reckless, "Perceptions of Stigma Following Public Intervention for Delinquent Behavior," *Social Problems*, Fall 1972, p. 204.

attended church were slightly more likely than infrequent attenders to express respect for the police, and were slightly less likely to agree that law violation was all right if you didn't get caught.[53] But this study also found that students who believed in the devil and in a life after death were just as likely to commit delinquent acts as were students who did not hold these beliefs. And students who attended church every week were just as likely to commit delinquent acts as were students who attended church rarely or not at all.[54] The authors conclude that the church is "irrelevant to delinquency because it fails to instill in its members love for their neighbors and because belief in the possibility of pleasure and pain in another world cannot now, and perhaps never could, compete with the pleasures and pains of everyday life."[55] This study is a good indication that the positive effects of religion on decreased delinquent behavior have been exaggerated.

Schools

The high school years are the years in which delinquency is most apt to occur. The high school is crucial if for no other reason than that it has control over the adolescent for so many hours of the day. It brings the young together for functions that extend far beyond those of the formal school system. Undoubtedly a great deal of delinquency either occurs in the school or is planned there. Furthermore, various types of delinquent acts are specifically related to the school, for example, truancy and school vandalism. And other, more general delinquent acts, such as assault, intimidation, shakedowns, rapes, and so forth, often occur within the school.

Almost all high schools operate on the basis of such middle-class values as deferred gratification, interpersonal courtesy, respect for the individual and property, and hard work. But for many high school students those values are of no importance, and they are in high school only because they must remain there until they are old enough to legally quit. For many of these young people the attractions of life are outside the school. Studying so as to get a good job is not even a part of the real world many young boys know. What is prestigeful and important to them are the lower-class values of toughness and immediate, hedonistic pleasures. Therefore, for many lower-class boys, both black and white, the future world implied in the high school system is meaningless and seems to stand in the way of the immediate pleasures and status symbols that are important to them. In most cases it is lower-class students whom the school

---

[53] Trovis Hirschi and Rodney Stark, "Hellfire and Delinquency," *Social Problems*, Fall 1969, p. 207.

[54] Ibid., p. 211.

[55] Ibid., p. 213.

defines as troublemakers because from the school's point of view they go against the school's values and norms most often.

Those students who are defined as delinquent by the schools are also defined as such by the police. In fact, when the police officially define a student as delinquent the school often defines him the same way and at the same time. The "official" delinquent is seen by the school as "disruptive" and as being bad for its reputation. So contacts between the adolescent, the police, and the school will have major significance for the adolescent's career as a delinquent within the school system.[56]

Another way in which the school sees itself as combating delinquency is through athletic programs. The assumption seems to be that physical prowess and high energy can be channeled from delinquent acts into organized athletics. And one study did find that there were fewer delinquents among athletes than among nonathletes. The study found that the association was most marked among boys who were blue-collar low achievers; that is, boys who came out of the lower middle class and were not successful in school often became either delinquents or athletes. There is a possibility that athletics attracts the most conforming types of boys. "Stated differently, the negative relationship between athletic participation and delinquency may not be the result of the deterrent influence of athletics at all, but rather to selection of conformers into the athletic program."[57] Organized sports in the United States not only places great stress on *conformity* but also tends to stress conservative, traditional values. The players are constantly told that what matters is the team's winning and not the individual performance. But they learn that one gains far more by being a star on a mediocre team than by being a mediocre player on a great team. Athletes will usually accept extremely authoritarian control by the coaches not only over their athletic activities but often over many other aspects of their lives. Given these considerations, it may be that those boys who choose sports over a delinquent career may have qualities that allow them to be severely controlled and regimented.

Social class

For the most part the discussion in this chapter has centered on delinquency in the lower middle and lower classes. Most of the studies of the past, as reflected in the various subculture theories, have seen delinquency as rooted primarily in the lower class. In recent years there has emerged a strong awareness that delinquency in the middle class is much greater than has generally been recognized. But to say this is not

---

[56] Cicourel and Kitsuse, "Deviant Adolescent," p. 131.

[57] Walter E. Schafer, "Participating in Interscholastics and Delinquency: A Preliminary Study," *Social Problems*, Summer 1969, p. 47.

the same as to say that delinquency is as high in the middle class as it is in the lower class. One obvious reason is that the middle-class young person has less need for delinquency because he has many more material possessions; for example, he is more apt to have legal access to a car.

Patterns of delinquency differ by social class. Generally in the middle class there are less involved expressions of delinquent patterns, and these are probably less deeply rooted than the delinquent patterns of the lower class. For example, for some middle-class adolescents the delinquency patterns in school may include such activities as vandalism, truancy, drug experimentation, and disruptive behavior. These behavior patterns are not subcultural in the strict sense "since they are often done by the individual in isolated fashion. They can be called 'normative' because they are common offenses, relatively accepted by the peers, and under certain circumstances even expected and respected by peers."[58] One of the most important differences between lower-class and middle-class delinquency is that the lower-class boy is more apt to engage in activities that will contribute to his sense of manliness and adult status.

One study of lower-class and middle-class delinquents shows some of the differences in their values and behavior patterns. It was found that lower-class boys defined themselves as tougher, more powerful, fiercer, more fearless, and more dangerous than middle-class boys. By contrast the middle-class delinquents conceived of themselves as being more loyal, cleverer, smarter, and smoother.[59] From an overall perspective it appears that the two classes differed chiefly in that significantly more lower-class delinquents felt themselves to be "loyal and daring comrades."[60]

Another important difference between the two groups was the frequency with which their members committed reported and unreported robberies and assaults. Of the lower-class delinquents, 84 percent had committed one such offense as compared to only 28 percent of the middle-class delinquents. Also, more of the lower-class boys used weapons, and more of them advocated "stomping." A greater proportion of the lower-class boys regularly carried weapons on their persons.[61] All of these differences reflect a greater involvement in physical aggression among lower-class delinquents.

The two groups of delinquents also differed with regard to their sexual expression. This difference was tied into their different views of masculinity as reflected in their treatment of adolescent girls. "Toughness, callousness, and physical prowess appeared to be dominant

---

[58] Sebald, *Adolescence*, p. 356.

[59] Leon F. Fannin and Marshall B. Clinard, "Differences in the Conception of Self as a Male among Lower and Middle Class Delinquents," in Edmund W. Vas, *Middle-Class Juvenile Delinquency* (New York: Harper and Row, 1967), p. 106.

[60] Ibid., p. 107.

[61] Ibid., pp. 108–9.

for the lower class, while sophistication, dexterity, and verbal manipulation seemed prominent for the middle class."[62] Dating was seen by the lower-class boys as the means to the end of sexual intercourse while the middle-class boys often saw dating as an end in itself involving the fun element of going out. "For the lower class boy, sexual intercourse was to be achieved by the raw force of his masculinity; he would not 'seduce' his date so much as he would 'conquer' her."[63]

Regardless of the social class level of delinquents most of them grow up and leave their delinquency behind. They "settle down, marry, go to work, repudiate criminal careers and no more (nor less) seriously violate laws than most of the rest of us."[64] It is important that delinquency, unlike many other forms of deviance, is restricted to an age range. While one might become a homosexual, a drug addict, an alcoholic, and so forth during adolescence and remain that type of deviant for the rest of his life, he cannot remain a delinquent. When he reaches his early adult years he can enter the straight world or the deviant one of criminality. It may be that some of the forces that make delinquency attractive to some adolescents are the very forces that contribute to their wanting to leave the delinquent subculture. As suggested, the delinquent subculture often gives the boy the sense of being an adult—something he very much wants. But when he becomes an adult he no longer needs the subculture for that status and in fact may find that continuing in it will cost him something in his newly achieved adult recognition.

DELINQUENT SUBCULTURE

Despite the considerable disagreement as to the extent and meaning of the delinquent subculture, it is still useful to describe the subculture in a general way. Here we define a delinquent subculture as consisting of a system of values, norms, and beliefs that influence the behavior of its members so that some significant part of this behavior goes contrary to the modes of behavior generally defined as right and proper by the broader culture. David Matza has suggested that the subculture of delinquency "is a synthesis between convention and crime, and that the behavior of many juveniles, some more than others, is influenced but not constrained by it."[65]

Cohen and Short have argued that there are five types of male delinquent subcultures. The first is the *parent male subculture*. This is the subculture that Cohen describes in his work. It has been described as

---

[62] Ibid., p. 110.
[63] Ibid.
[64] Rosenberg and Silverstein, *Delinquent Experience*, p. 116.
[65] Matza, *Delinquency and Drift*, pp. 47-48.

stressing such values as short-run hedonism and group autonomy and it is believed to be the most common type of delinquent subculture in the United States. Cohen and Short suggest that it is basically a working-class subculture. The second is the *conflict-oriented subculture.* This is the subculture characteristic of large gangs that may have memberships running into the hundreds. Size makes this subculture different from the parent male subculture, which consists of small gangs and cliques. The conflict-oriented subculture has a territory or "turf" which it defends. The status of the gang is dependent on its toughness. In its other activities it is like the parent male subculture, for example, in drinking, sex, gambling, stealing, and vandalism, which are prominent activities. The third is the *drug-addict subculture.* The addict wants no part of the violent forms of delinquency and prefers the income-producing forms of delinquency which are necessary to support his drug habit. So the addict subculture, in contrast to the parent male and conflict groups, is utilitarian, but this utilitarianism is in support of, and a precondition for, the addict way of life. The fourth is the *semiprofessional thief subculture.* This seems to characterize persons who in their young years become robbers and burglars. The first stage of this sequence describes what is called the parent subculture. But most participants seem to drop out or taper off at around the age of 16 or 17. Finally, there is the *middle-class delinquent subculture.* Cohen and Short assume that subculture arises in response to problems of adjustment that are characteristic products of middle-class life. They further suggest that this subculture will underplay the qualities of malice and violence and that it will more often emphasize the deliberate courting of danger and the sophisticated approach to roles centering on sex, liquor, drugs, and automobiles.[66]

Short has suggested that it is important to distinguish between gangs and subcultures. He points out that most subcultures embrace more than one gang and that what happens in any gang may be more than the values of the particular subculture which binds it together, the point being that most gangs have a dimension that goes beyond the subcultural limits. For example, the character of gangs that are involved in conflict depends to a great extent on their relationships with other conflict gangs—as either allies or enemies—and their reputations among those gangs. [67] All of these gangs are a part of the delinquent subculture, but each possesses qualities that make it different from the others. Two gangs may be subculturally alike in every significant way, but the very fact that they are different gangs may be the most crucial factor because this may force them to fight each other or work out some accommodation.

As the various theories of delinquency suggest, there is disagreement

[66] Cohen and Short, "Delinquent Subcultures," pp. 24–28.
[67] Short, *Gang Delinquency,* p. 9.

about the strength of ties in delinquent subcultures. It would seem that different groups will vary widely in the strength of their ties and that a given subcultural group may vary widely over time. For example, if a gang is threatened by other gangs then the strength of its ties may be very great because of the need for protection, but these ties may be relaxed during peacetime. It has been argued that internal strengths have less impact among gangs than among most subcultural groups. This argument suggests that gang cohesiveness derives from and is perpetuated by forces mostly external to the gang.[68] This view would be supported if threats by other gangs, the police, and so forth led to greater cohesiveness. But it might also be that in certain cases external pressure will splinter the subculture. For example, if the police exert strong pressure on a gang some members may feel that the police will leave them alone if they remain apart from the gang. The strength of the subcultural controls over the individual members will be determined by the internal needs that are felt to be met by the group and the external forces that may either splinter the group or bring it together.

There is a common belief, probably helped along by movies and television, that gangs each have a few strong leaders. A part of the same belief is that the leader is very powerful and that his followers will do what he wants when he wants. This is clearly an exaggeration because while there are powerful gang leaders most of the time, the delinquent gang operates without leadership because none is needed. For example, the many hours spent standing on a street corner don't call for leadership. During these long periods other roles filled by members may be given more attention, for example, those of the comedian, the storyteller, and so forth.

But there are times in the life of a gang when leadership does become important, and it is therefore useful to look at some variables associated with gang leaders. Yablonsky argues that at the center of the gang are the most psychologically disturbed members—the leaders. He says that it is these individuals who need the gang the most. So it is the coterie of disturbed leaders who make up the core of the gang and give it its cohesive force. In a gang of about 30 members there may be about 5 members who provide the leadership.[69] There is generally no desire to be a leader when the person feels no sense of importance about the group he is part of. Assuming that he has the abilities needed to be a leader, he must also have the motivations. Yablonsky points out that leadership in the gang may be assumed by almost any member who emotionally needs the power of being a leader at a given time. "It is not necessary to have

---

[68] Malcom W. Klein and Lois Y. Crawford, "Groups, Gangs, and Cohesiveness," in Short, *Gang Delinquency*, p. 259.

[69] Yablonsky, "Delinquent Gang," p. 230.

his leadership role ratified by his constituents."[70] Probably in most gangs the aspiring leader must also show that he is physically or mentally tough enough to qualify for the possible roles of a leader.

All subcultures are basically defined through their relationship to the broader society. The various theories of delinquent subcultures recognize that how delinquents think and behave collectively is based to a great extent on how the broader society defines them and how they *think* the broader society defines them. But one cannot say that the relationship between the subculture and the broader society is simply one of disagreement. Actually the relationship is subtle, complex, and sometimes devious. This is because the subculture exists within a cultural setting which affects it and which it, in turn, affects. Matza suggests that when it is kept in mind that the conventional culture is complex and many-sided then the relationship of the subculture to it can be seen as highly complex and frequently changing.[71]

Members of the delinquent subculture, like those of most subcultures, probably look at the broader world's treatment of them with a sense of injustice. This is based on their perspective of the legal and police systems. "The role played by the sense of injustice is to weaken the bind of law and thus ready the way for the immediate condition of neutralization—the negation of intent. Neutralization enables drift. It is the process by which we are freed from the moral bind of law."[72] What Matza argues is that the delinquent subculture's reaction to the legal system is not one of ignorance but rather one of antagonism.

Matza suggests that the subculture of delinquency is not highly committed to delinquency. He argues that if there were a high commitment to delinquency there would be much less shame or guilt upon apprehension. In this delinquents differ from the members of other deviant subcultures; for example, the homosexual or the professional thief may be angry when he is arrested, but he is not often ashamed. Such deviants are most apt to respond to apprehension with indignation, a sense of martyrdom, and fear of the consequences.[73] Many delinquents agree that someone should be apprehended and punished, but not themselves. "Thus, the indignation of the delinquent differs from that of, say, a nationalist rebel. The delinquent's is a *wrongful* indignation."[74] The delinquents' view of the law also reflects this perspective because they direct their antagonism at the officials who run the system. Therefore, their antagonism takes the form of a jaundiced view of of-

---

[70] Ibid., p. 232.
[71] Matza, *Delinquency and Drift*, pp. 37–38.
[72] Ibid., p. 176.
[73] Ibid., p. 40.
[74] Ibid., pp. 40–41.

ficials, "a view which holds that their primary function is not the administration of justice but the perpetuation of injustice."[75]

The members of the delinquent subculture spend time together and engage in some activities together. Most delinquent gangs when they are together may be doing little or nothing— talking, playing cards, and so forth—but for many of them being together is important even if their activity is limited. When the gang members engage in illegal behavior they generally do it together. Estimates based on official statistics suggest that somewhere between 70 and 90 percent of adolescent crimes are committed by two or more individuals. What is important is that the main reason for defining delinquency as a subculture is shared behavior.

As suggested, the most important value of the delinquent subculture is manliness. So being an adult through specific acts of manly prowess is a prime concern of subcultural delinquents. Therefore, the primary goal is a system of behavior that almost incidentally permits and encourages criminal acts, but essentially pursues gratification deriving from the license of precocious manhood.[76] Often those acts which define the adolescent as delinquent may have been pursued not for their own sake, but rather for the end of achieving manliness within the delinquent subculture.

The most common means of expressing manliness in the delinquent subcultural setting is through fighting. A boy's reputation can be won or lost in a fight. The common code is that a boy does not walk away from a fight, and often the preliminaries are governed by an elaborately plotted choreography. "You do not provoke the fight; against all reason, you are trapped into it. Beyond a certain point, not to fight is to be chicken, and there is no talking or finessing your way out. Honor calls for a duel with friend, foe or stranger."[77] Often it is only necessary for a boy to fight a few times to prove himself, and if word of his prowess spreads he may then be able to ride on his reputation.

Closely related to fighting is the delinquent boy's involvement with girls as a status-giving factor. It may be that fighting over a girl to win her admiration may or may not cause his stock to rise with her; however, "it will almost certainly reinforce his self-esteem and his social standing in a community where fisticuffs, well mastered, is a vehicle for elevation into manhood."[78] For boys in delinquent gangs sexual activity usually starts at a very young age. Initially girls are seen primarily as objects for sexual play, and it is not until the boys are 17 or 18 that they show girls anything resembling respect. Often the boys' sexual involvement is not on an inter-

---

[75] Ibid., pp. 101-2.
[76] Ibid., p. 168.
[77] Ibid., p. 166.
[78] Ibid., p. 86.

personal, pair level, but rather a number of boys with one or more girls. This often occurs as a "gang bang," in which a number of boys have sexual intercourse with one girl. It also appears that there are periods when the boys in some gangs have little sexual contact with girls. This is because often the boys will use a girl sexually only if she becomes available. Usually after a gang gets a girl there may be a week or so of intensified sexuality, after which the girl will disappear. Then the boys enter their involuntary celibacy until another willing girl comes along.[79]

FEMALE DELINQUENCY

There has been very little research into female delinquency as compared to the studies made of male delinquency. This has been true because there has been much less interest in female delinquency and because female delinquency is believed to be a minor problem as compared to male delinquency. In part this view is justified, because the number of male delinquents is far greater than that of female delinquents. In recent years the ratio of boys to girls appearing in juvenile courts has been about five to one. However, sex ratios vary by different types of delinquency. Boys tend overwhelmingly to be arrested on charges involving stealing and mischief of one sort or another, "while girls are typically brought before the court for *sex offenses* and for *'running away,'* *'incorrigibility,'* and *'delinquent tendencies,'* which are often euphemisms for problems of sex behavior."[80] This means that most of the girls who are defined as delinquent are so defined because of their moral behavior rather than for legal reasons. For most of them their wrong is that they are sexually promiscuous by society's moral standards.

There seems to be some evidence that when girls are a part of a delinquent subculture they are in a male subculture. When this happens a girl is largely dependent for her status on the male with whom she is identified. However, in some instances delinquent girls do develop a separate subcultural group. This may be for the purpose of sexual activities, drug addiction, or as counterparts of the male hoodlum gang.[81] In general, Short suggests, when girls are involved in delinquent subcultures their activities are as varied as those of any male member. He points out that the participation of girls in drug-use subcultures is extensive. He found that drug-using girls seem especially caught up in a vicious cycle of unsatisfactory interpersonal relations. But even the nondrug users "appear to be swept along by limited social and other abilities, and experience which limits opportunities to acquire those skills

[79] Rosenberg and Silverstein, *Delinquent Experience*, p. 75.
[80] Cohen and Short, "Delinquent Subcultures," p. 86.
[81] Sebald, *Adolescence*, pp. 355–56.

or to exercise them is acquired."[82] Girls in the lower class generally have low status in social activities important to males because this is a reflection of a male-dominant view of the sexes. So the girl in the delinquent male gang has a second-class membership and has little direct influence on activities defined as important by the male members. Cohen has argued that the subculture of the male delinquent gangs is really inappropriate for the adjustment problems of lower-class girls. This is because at best it is "irrelevant to the vindication of the girl's status as a girl, and at worst because it positively threatens her in that status in consequence of its strongly masculine symbolic function."[83] It would appear that most girls who become a part of the male delinquent gangs do so because they are willing to accept second-class membership. It would also seem that when delinquent girls so violate the norms of society it is not because of ignorance of or hostility to the norms. Rather they are motivated toward deviance because they want to maintain status within the subculture.

One researcher suggests that one important difference between the delinquent female and her male counterpart is related to the extent to which girls possess resources that they may manipulate for their own ends in the adult world. "Specifically, adolescent females are more than capable of competing successfully with adult females through the use of promise of sexual rewards."[84] The adolescent boy has little of value, whether morally or legally acceptable, to the broader society. But what the adolescent girl has is prized by many adults, though legally and morally prohibited. She is therefore in the position of being wanted, and knowing this she can negotiate other ends that are desirable to her.

At the same time the female has more freedom to pursue some activities that are not legally available to the male. For example, the adolescent female who is not old enough to drive can get an older male to take her places. By contrast the adolescent male restricted to his age peers may often steal a car. It may also be easier for the adolescent girl to drink illegally by being with an older male.[85] In general the adolescent girl has more social agencies helping her satisfy many of her needs than does the adolescent boy.

As indicated, almost all discussion of female delinquency stresses its sexual nature but says little about other aspects. There is little data on what the delinquency of the female delinquent actually consists of, other than that it usually involves sexual misconduct of some kind. Whatever

---

[82] Short, *Gang Delinquency*, p. 6.

[83] Cohen, *Delinquent Boys*, p. 143–44.

[84] Gerald Marwell, "Adolescent Powerlessness and Delinquent Behavior," in Rushing, *Deviant Behavior*, p. 43.

[85] Ibid., pp. 43–44.

other delinquent aspects of her life there might be are generally overlooked. But it does appear that sexual delinquency is often used by her as a form of bargaining and even social control. One important research question might be: If one put aside all female delinquency directly and indirectly related to sexual activity, what would be left? It might be that the findings would show that generally female delinquency is really sexual delinquency. If this is true then it is possible that the rates of female delinquency will decrease if the degree of premarital sexual freedom continues to increase and what is seen as sexual deviance continues to decrease. On the other hand, one might also speculate that as boys and girls become more alike in their behavior patterns more girls will become delinquents in areas usually associated with males, such as physical aggression, truancy, stealing, and so forth. This would be consistent with the argument that as females achieve greater equality with males this will be reflected in all areas including deviance and social problems.

BIBLIOGRAPHY

Bordua, David J., "Delinquent Subcultures: Sociological Interpretations of Gang Delinquency," *The Annals*, November 1961, pp. 119–36.

Chilton, Roland J., and Gerald E. Markle, "Family Disruption, Delinquent Conduct, and the Effect of Subclassification," *American Sociological Review*, February 1972, pp. 93–99.

Cloward, Richard A., and Lloyd E. Ohlin, *Delinquency and Opportunity*. New York: Macmillan, 1960.

Cohen, Albert K., *Delinquent Boys: The Culture of the Gang*. Glencoe, Ill.: Free Press, 1955.

Cohen, Albert K., and James F. Short, Jr., "Research in Delinquent Subcultures," *Journal of Social Issues*, 14 (1958), pp. 20–37.

Foster, Jack Donald, Simon Dinitz, and Walter C. Reckless, "Perceptions of Stigma Following Public Intervention for Delinquent Behavior," *Social Problems*, Fall 1972, pp. 202–9.

Garabedian, Peter G., and Don C. Gibbons, *Becoming Delinquent*. Chicago: Aldine, 1970.

Jenson, Gary F., "Parents, Peers and Delinquent Action: A Test of the Differential Association Perspective," *American Journal of Sociology*, November 1972, pp. 570–78.

Matza, David, *Delinquency and Drift*. New York: Wiley, 1964.

Miller, Walter, "Lower-Class Culture as a Generating Milieu of Gang Delinquency," *Journal of Social Issues*, 14 (1958), pp. 3–19.

Rosenberg, Bernard, and Harry Silverstein, *The Varieties of Delinquent Experience*. Waltham, Mass.: Blaisdell, 1969.

Short, James F., Jr., *Gang Delinquency and Delinquent Subcultures.* New York: Harper and Row, 1968.

Vaz, Edmund W., *Middle-Class Juvenile Delinquency.* New York: Harper and Row, 1967.

Williams, J. R., and Martin Gold, "From Delinquent Behavior to Official Delinquency," *Social Problems,* Fall 1972, pp. 209–29.

Yablonsky, Lewis, "The Delinquent Gang as a Near-Group," *Social Problems,* Fall 1959, pp. 108–17.

chapter fourteen

Prisons

Probably from the time people first felt a need to protect themselves from other people there has been some way of holding threatening individuals and controlling their behavior. This may have represented a more humane stage in man's development because he probably at first destroyed those he had reason to fear before they could destroy him. Over time man developed procedures for incarcerating his fellowman. And historically, as penal systems developed they had three major functions: custodial, coercive, and corrective. The *Digest* of Justinian established the principle of custodial care through the assertion that "a prison is for confinement, not for punishment." In the countries that followed Roman law the principle that imprisonment was not a legal punishment was dominant for about a thousand years. In early England the courts wanted to clear the jails rather than to fill them, and so the prisons of the Middle Ages were primarily concerned with simply holding prisoners while they waited for trial.

In England the earliest prisons were the common jails, and these were in theory the king's jails. During the medieval period the jails were not like those we are familiar with today. A jail might be a castle tower, a gatehouse, or a cellar. The first house of correction was set up in London in 1553. Its primary purpose was to make the offenders good citizens by subjecting them to the discipline of industry, education, and religious instruction. But during the 18th century these houses became more and more penal institutions and less and less concerned with corrective functions. This was essentially the tradition that was brought to the early settlements in America.

In the early prisons in America there were no barriers to communication among inmates. The prisoners were held in common areas, and no attention was paid to differences in age, sex, criminal history, or mental status. Over the years various prison reformers were shocked by the promiscuity, violence, and organized deviant behavior found in congregate prison systems. As a result they moved to institute a "separate system" of prisons. So in 1791, the Walnut Street Prison in Philadelphia, a prison containing 16 cells was built. The belief was that the use of cells would prevent the inmates from contaminating one another and that religious conversion leading to the individual's reformation would occur during the years of enforced meditation. Subsequently the congregate but silent system came to be the accepted type of prison design. Prisons using this system "contained industrial shops, dining halls, and large recreational yards in addition to individual cells. But whenever and wherever prisoners assembled strict silence was enforced."[1]

The development of types of prisons is largely determined by how a society views criminality and by how it believes the criminal should be treated. Over the past two centuries in the United States the societal reaction to criminality has been mainly punitive. Punishment for criminals has been pain or suffering which the state inflicted intentionally in the belief that it had some value. The programs that were developed to carry out the punitive reaction to crime were seen as correctional techniques. "Physical torture, social degradation, restriction of wealth, and restriction of freedom are among the programs used for inflicting pain on criminals. At present, the most popular techniques of this sort are restrictions on wealth (fines) and restrictions on liberty (imprisonment)."[2]

The prison, according to the conventional view, is like the mental institution in that it performs an integrating function for society. There are two principal aspects to the integrating function. First, the prison is expected to restore society to the state of equilibrium and harmony that existed before the crime was committed. This means that the undesirables of society are removed from society and segregated in the prison. Second, the prison is expected to help with social integration by reducing the occurrence of future crimes. This function is seen as taking place in two different ways. In the first place, the crime rates are believed to be held to a minimum through the deterrent effects of imprisonment and the fact that imprisoning men reinforces anticriminal values of the society. In the second place, imprisonment is expected to reduce crime rates by changing criminals into noncriminals.[3]

The isolating nature of the prison makes the inmates different in an important way from most other types of deviants. Most kinds of deviants,

---

[1] Richard A. Cloward, "Social Control in Prison," in Lawrence Hazebrigg, *Prisons within Society* (New York: Anchor Books, 1969), p. 85.

[2] Donald Cressey, "The Nature and Effectiveness of Correctional Techniques," in Hazebrigg, *Prisons*, p. 350.

[3] Ibid., p. 351.

such as alcoholics, are treated in groups for therapeutic reasons. However, prisons which are based on isolation and minimal communication between prisoners have been reluctant to recognize the possible therapeutic use of inmate groups. In this situation the punitive function of the prison makes the therapeutic one difficult if not impossible to pursue.

On the broadest level the prison may be seen as representing certain needs of society. In this sense the prison is a service organization, "supported by the community largely for the purpose of maintaining order and not for the production of any goods which yield the individual or the community an immediate ecomomic return. Like most other service organizations (such as mental hospitals and social agencies), the prison is a means of safeguarding other institutions of the society."[4] In general society thinks of the prison as performing an important function because the prison is protecting it against the dangerous threats of some of its members. It appears that the greater society's fear of a given deviance, the greater the autonomy given to those social agencies that stand between society and the deviance.

The prison itself is a fairly isolated social system. It can be seen as a caste system made up of those in control and those under control. This caste system is regarded as necessary by society. The prison is given autonomy because it does not compete with any other organization. That is, the prison justifies its existence by fulfilling a legal mandate, and this allows those who run it a great deal of latitude. Furthermore, the prison is generally protected from outside scrutiny. "Public cries for reform and shake-ups in the prison system are rarely, if ever, an immediate response to the day-to-day operation of the relatively static prison community, but are usually the work of outside interest groups."[5] In general there is little control by outside forces over what goes on within prisons.

From the point of view of most of those who run prisons this primary aim is to maintain order and control over the prisoners. Usually the most efficient way to achieve this is to keep the prisoners from influencing one another in any way that might disturb order. The belief is that this is best done by isolating the prisoners from one another as much as possible. So there are strong custodial exhortations to "go it alone" which are a part of a systematic attempt to reduce the frequency and saliency of interaction among prisoners. By this definition the model prisoner is the isolated prisoner who bothers no one.

In the earlier days physical violence was a common means of controlling prisoners, but under the influence of 19th century penal reform it

---

[4] George H. Grosser, "External Setting and Internal Relations of the Prison," in Hazebrigg, *Prisons*, p. 9.

[5] Ibid., p. 11.

was pretty much eliminated as a legitimate means of control. So except in certain cases, such as riots, assault, escape, and similar crises, the custodian could not take the life of, or otherwise do bodily injury to, an inmate.[6] However, as will be discussed later, violence is an important part of prison social control, but it is more often violence between prisoners than violence between guards and prisoners.

Along with punitive controls the prisons also have rewards that may be used to try to get the prisoners to accept their position with minimal problems for the prison authorities. There are two types of formal incentives. The first are incentives that provide for an early release from the prison. That is, if the prisoner behaves he may get parole and time off his sentence. The second are incentives that help make prison life a little more bearable. Such incentives include various degrees of freedom as well as the right to certain privileges.

Some prisons may control the inmate by the threat of sending him to more restrictive prisons. That is, a limited form of expulsion is sometimes employed in penal systems. As a result a difficult prisoner in a minimum security prison can be transferred to a medium or maximum security prison. However, when transfer is employed as a control mechanism "one institution's solution simply becomes another's dilemma. The deviant cannot be expelled from the system as a whole; somewhere, someone must come to terms with him."[7]

The guard

The guard in a total institution such as a prison or a mental hospital is the person concerned with the day-to-day operations of the institution. Often the philosophy or ideology of care and custody is seen by the guard as unimportant in light of the chores he must handle each day, but because the guard does serve as the representative of society and the prison administration he has a great deal of power. Sykes has suggested that the prison community may be best seen as resting in an uneasy balance between two hypothetical poles. "At one extreme all inmates would be constantly secured in solitary confinement; at the other, all inmates would roam freely within the limits set by the wall and its armed guards.[8] In reality, and varying among different prisons, the inmates have a limited degree of freedom, and this creates a wide variety of interaction patterns between the guards and the prisoners. As a result the guards and the inmates become involved in a complex pattern of social

---

[6] Cloward, "Control in Prison," p. 80.

[7] Ibid., p. 81.

[8] Gresham M. Sykes, "The Corruption of Authority and Rehabilitation," in William A. Rushing, *Deviant Behavior and Social Process* (Chicago: Rand McNally, 1969), p. 157.

relationships in which the authority of the guard is subject to a number of corrupting influences.[9]

Often the guard has an important choice to make, and that is the degree to which he will enforce the rules of the prison. Some guards in the cellblock may rigidly enforce all the rules in the belief that a minor violation of a regulation may be the beginning of a serious breach in the control system of the prison. Or, and this may occur more often, other guards may be lulled into forgetting about the possible dangers of their position.[10] Whichever pattern the guard follows, the need for some consistency is important, because with inconsistency the guard may be seen as playing favorites, and this can lead to increased problems from among the inmates.

It has been argued that the guard is often under pressure to try to achieve a smooth-running cellblock with the carrot rather than the stick. But this is not always easy because the rewards he can hand out are limited. Often the guard has a kind of future favor he wants from the inmates which may influence him to ease up on the enforcement of the prison regulations. This is that "many prisons have experienced a riot in which the tables are momentarily turned and the captives hold sway over their *quondam* captors."[11] And if that should ever happen the guard wants to be sure that the inmates will protect him.

In many prisons a lot of the minor chores that the guard is expected to perform each day can be turned over to inmates whom the guard comes to trust. When this occurs it represents an overlap of the formal system of the prison with the informal social system of the inmates. That is, the effectiveness with which inmates can handle the guards' chores is largely determined by the willingness of their fellow inmates to have them do so. And in general, so long as an inmate's first loyalty is to his fellow inmates, it is to their advantage to cooperate with him and to help keep him in a position of power.

In general the success of the prison system is highly questionable. That is, most of the "techniques" used in "correcting" criminals who are in prison have not been found to be either effective or ineffective and are only vaguely related to any reputable theory of behavior or criminality.[12] This will be seen as we examine in some detail the subcultural world of prisons. In the next sections we look at men's prisons, and in the last section we examine women's prisons.

MEN'S PRISONS

In general when a man enters prison he leaves behind one world and

---

[9] Ibid.

[10] Ibid.

[11] Ibid., p. 159.

[12] Cressey, "Correctional Techniques," p. 371.

enters another. This is certainly true in terms of physical separation in that his new world is physically confined and that all he can interact with must be found within the prison setting. As in the mental hospital, life is isolated. However, as we shall see, the prison subculture is very much affected by what goes on outside the prison and by what the inmates have brought with them in the way of values and behavior patterns. Most of the values and behavior patterns brought into the prison must be adapted to the special nature of the isolated, confining world of the prison. Out of this comes the subculture of the prison. First, we shall discuss the prison subculture in general, and then some of the variations within prison subcultures.

As indicated earlier, prisons are total institutions, and one effect of this life-style is that it allows only psychological means of "escape." As in all total institutions, many prisoners fantasize and daydream about the world outside. To the extent that they escape psychologically they are able to resist the socializing of the prison world. A person totally socialized to the prison subculture would concern himself very little with the outside world, but most inmates think of the prison as a temporary world. Because the subcultures of the prisons are very much influenced by values and behavior from outside the prison these subcultures serve as a means of preventing the prisoner from being totally socialized to a prison world. If one function of the prison is to socialize the inmates to the world of prisons to attain "corrective or therapeutic" orientations, that function is usually undercut by the close link of the inmate subculture to the outside world with its related values and patterns, which are the very values and patterns the formal institution of the prison is trying to alter.

But to say that a subculture develops in prisons is not to say that all inmates are a part of it in the same way and to the same degree. Very often inmates react to various situations simply as individuals even though this may create problems for them. This is in part due to a selective factor—that a number of men who are in prison are there primarily because they are not able or willing to conform to any extended set of social restrictions. So for some inmates there may be personal refusal or inability to conform to the formal demands of the prison or the informal demands of the inmate subculture. Of course, there are often high costs for inmates who fail to conform. "Those who dominate others are viewed with a mingled fear, hatred and envy; and the few who manage to retreat into solidarity may well be penalized in the struggle to evade the poverty-stricken existence—both material and immaterial—prescribed by the institution."[13]

The importance of the inmate subculture is recognized by most prison authorities, and the subculture is often tolerated and even encouraged because it is believed to help make the prison run more efficiently. This is

---

[13] Gresham Sykes, "The Pains of Imprisonment," in Norman Johnson et al., *The Sociology of Punishment and Correction* (New York: Wiley, 1962), p. 137.

because basically the prison operates not by force or even the threat of force, but because of the acceptance of rules on the part of most inmates and their willingness to adhere to those rules. "These rules are partly the official rules of the prison, partly the mores of the inmate culture developed by many generations of convicts to the official code."[14]

When the inmate comes into prison he may have to make some very severe adjustments to the restrictive and isolated world. The degree to which he must adjust may be related to his previous experiences with prisons. At any given time, of the persons entering a prison, a large proportion have been there before. In fact a number of inmates have been socialized to the world of the prison from a young age. This is true of the large number of adult criminals who spent time in institutions for juveniles. In many juvenile detention centers there exists a form or variation of the adult prison subculture. As a result some of the newcomers to prisons for adults are persons who have been oriented to the prison subculture and who "have found the utilitarian nature of this subculture acceptable."[15]

Role adaptions in prison and normative assimilation into the inmate subculture are interrelated. Whether or not the individual chooses a prosocial or antisocial role is clearly mediated by factors outside the inmate social system. It is especially important to recognize the powerful influence of previous prison experiences.[16] All new arrivals in prison are subjected to close scrutiny. Often, if a man is not a well-known returnee or has no friends who will define him as a "solid con" to other prisoners, he may be in serious trouble. An inmate who does not have such resources and who does not possess a sufficient level of prisonization to operate in an acceptable manner will often have to run a terrifying gauntlet of sexual "pressuring" from the other prisoners.[17]

During the period after one first enters prison the greatest personal problem may be adjusting to the isolation. In time many inmates become involved with others. Studies show that most of the role types found during the middle periods in prison are situations of involvement with others. "The tendency for inmates to become involved suggests that pressures toward involvement are stronger and more keenly felt at a period when they are further removed from the free community."[18] Garabedian goes on to suggest that the extent of inmate solidarity is

---

[14] Grosser, "External Setting," p. 18.

[15] John Irwin and Donald R. Cressey, "Thieves, Convicts and the Inmate Culture," in Howard S. Becker, ed., *The Other Side* (New York: Free Press, 1964), p. 233.

[16] Charles W. Thomas and Samuel C. Foster, "Prisonization in the Inmate Contra-culture," *Social Problems*, Fall 1972, p. 237.

[17] George Kirkham, "Homosexuality in Prison," in James M. Henslin, *Studies in the Sociology of Sex* (New York: Appleton-Century-Crofts, 1971), p. 341.

[18] Peter G. Garabedian, "Social Roles and Processes of Socialization in the Prison Community," *Social Problems*, Fall 1963, p. 151.

"likely to depend not on the number of right guys found in the prison population, but rather on the balance that exists between inmates located at the two extremes of the institutional career and those located in the middle periods of confinement."[19]

Closely related to the isolation the new inmate must cope with are the related problems of loss of freedom and material deprivation. Loss of freedom means that the inmate must give up the material services and goods that were his outside of prison. Along with this he also loses his heterosexual relationships, "personal autonomy, symbolic affirmation of his value as an individual, and a variety of other benefits which are more or less taken for granted in the free community."[20] In the broader society the individual often gets status from his material possessions. His status may be based on the kind of automobile he drives, the clothes he wears, and where he lives. But the material signs of personal status are for the most part removed when he enters prison. Because material possessions are often so much a part of a person's self-concept, stripping him of them may threaten the basic core of his personality. As a result, whatever the discomforts and irritations of the inmate's way of life, he must also carry the "additional burden of social definitions which equate his material deprivation with personal inadequacy."[21]

Because of the restriction of material symbols of success in the prison two kinds of adaption often occur. These also occur in other settings in which the individual must give up most of the material things that were important to him, for example, in mental institutions, or the military. One way in which the inmate attempts to adapt is to talk a great deal about what he had in the outside world. The inmate may tell about all the expensive clothes he owned and about the costly restaurants he went to. A lot of what he says may be fiction, but he often feels it very important to give the impression of having been successful when he was outside. A second way of adapting to the lack of material symbols is to place high importance on material goods which might be relatively unimportant in the outside world. For example, having enough cigarettes or reading material may be a measure of material success in a system where many do not have those things. In other words, possessing a few things that most others do not possess may contribute to the inmate's sense of individual identity and worth.

Another problem the inmate in prison must attempt to cope with is his aggression. Many prisoners who were aggressive outside of prison must curb their aggressions in prison if they are to avoid very severe consequences. Yet, when they do, the problem arises as to what prevents

---

[19] Ibid., p. 152.
[20] Sykes, "Rehabilitation," p. 132.
[21] Ibid., p. 133.

them from turning aggression inward against themselves. It has been suggested by Grosser that aggression becomes partly restrained and partly displaced, and projected, "both onto *rats* and other unreliable inmates and onto a variety of outgroups within and outside the walls, thus helping to sustain the hostile attitude of the inmate ingroups."[22] So one function of the prison subculture is to help provide the means for redirecting aggression. Sykes and Messinger have pointed out that if a group of prisoners develops a state of mutual antagonism then many of the problems of prison life will become even more acute. "On the other hand, as a population of prisoners moves in the direction of solidarity, as demanded by the inmate code, the pains of imprisonment become less severe. They cannot be eliminated, it is true, but their consequences at least can be partially neutralized."[23]

There is another way in which the external world influences the involvement of the inmate in the subculture, and that is the point in time he has reached in serving out his prison sentence. The prisoner's notion of time and his response to the world around him will usually vary with the length of time he still has to serve. And at any point in time the temporal frame of reference of various types of inmates can have various psychological and social meanings.[24] For example, one would expect that for most inmates the extent of conformity to the demands of the prison would be greater the nearer they are to the time of release.

The concept of "prisonization" has been suggested to describe the central impact of the prison on its inmates. Prisonization describes the socialization of the inmate to the subcultural systems of the prison. It is the process whereby the inmate is indoctrinated into those codes, norms, dogma, and myths which sustain a view of the prison and the outside world generally different from what the prison wants, at least to the extent of its wanting to rehabilitate the inmate. The core concept in prisonization is the inmate code or system of norms requiring loyalty to other inmates and opposition to the prison staff, who serve as representatives of a rejecting society beyond the walls.[25] Wheeler further suggests that no inmate can remain completely unprisonized. The very fact of being in prison means that the offender is exposed to certain general features of imprisonment. "These included acceptance of an inferior role and recognition that nothing is owed the environment for the supplementing of basic needs."[26]

---

[22] Grosser, "External Setting," p. 144.

[23] Gresham M. Sykes and Sheldon L. Messinger, "The Inmate Social System," in Rushing, *Deviant Behavior*, p. 135.

[24] Stanton Wheeler, "Socialization in Correctional Communities," in Rushing, *Deviant Behavior*, p. 145.

[25] Ibid., p. 144.

[26] Ibid.

Thomas and Foster point out that two models of prisonization—the deprivation model and the importation model—have provided the theoretical grounding for research on the determinants of the degree of prisonization. The *deprivation* model presents the inmate subculture as a closed social system. It views prisonization as an adaptive process which reduces the various "pains of imprisonment." Those who support the *importation* model do not question the assertion that the pressures and deprivation associated with imprisonment foster high levels of prisonization. They do, however, suggest the utility of a more inclusive model of the inmate subculture. "Specifically, the importation model implies that the antisocial content of the inmate normative system and the degree of assimilation into that system are influenced by factors external to the immediate situation in which the inmates find themselves."[27]

We now look in more detail at some of the general aspects of the prison subculture. Basically the inmate is faced with the need for physical, social, and psychological survival. He is helped in this by the basic value of endurance in the face of difficult conditions. This value is made available to the new inmate by the prison subculture. The subculture provides him with the means to attain some self-respect and some sense of independence. This can be achieved despite "prior criminality, present subjugation, and the free community's denial of the offender's moral worthiness. Significantly this path to virtue is recognized by the prison officials as well as the prisoners."[28] Some prisoners are able to survive with little help from the subculture, but most prisoners turn to their fellow inmates on at least a number of occasions.

In the prison subculture, as in most subcultures, there may be variation between an individual's stated acceptance of the values and his actual behavior. Studies have found that many of the inmates who deviate the most from the values and norms of the prison subculture are the most vocal in stating their commitment to them. "Much of the answer seems to lie in the fact that almost all inmates have an interest in maintaining cohesive behavior on the part of others, *regardless of the role they play themselves*, and vehement vocal support of the inmate code is a potent means to that end."[29] It would seem likely that those inmates who do the opposite, conform to the subcultural norms but talk against them, would find themselves in severe difficulty. Sykes and Messinger suggest that those inmates who are actively alienated from the other inmates but continue to give lip service to the subculture are like a manipulative priesthood, "savage in their expression of belief but corrupt in practice. In brief, a variety of motivational patterns underlies allegiance to the inmate

---

[27] Thomas and Foster, "Prisonization,".p. 231.
[28] Sykes and Messinger, "Inmate Social Systems," p. 135.
[29] Ibid., p. 136.

code, but few inmates can avoid the need to insist publicly on its observance, whatever the discrepancies in their action." [30]

It has been suggested that five basic tenets make up the inmate code to be found in most prison subcultures. The first is not to interfere with the interests of other inmates. This is based on the desire to serve the least amount of time and to do it as easily as possible. The second is to keep oneself under control and not do anything rash. This means that emotional conflicts should be minimized and that one should try to ignore the irritants of daily life. The third is that one should not exploit his fellow inmates. This means not taking advantage of others through force, fraud, or deceit. The fourth is that there are rules for self-maintenance; for example, the dictum "Don't weaken." This means developing the ability to withstand frustration or threatening situations without complaining. The last is that one should not give any prestige or respect to the guards or to the formal system for which they stand. "Guards are *hacks* or *screws* and are to be treated with constant suspicion and distrust."[31] These basic tenets are not always followed, and inmates may sometimes deviate without severe criticism or punishment by the subculture, but the tenets do provide a value system for most of the inmates most of the time.

We move from the general values and norms of the prison subculture to some of the roles that are commonly found in prisons. The various roles develop around a focal value or set of values, and the interrelationships between the various role sets are primary to the prison subculture. A number of different roles have been distinguished in the studies of prison life. One role is that of the "right guy." He is seen as the hero of the inmate subculture, and his role contributes to the meaning of the various villain roles. The deviants in the subculture are the "rat," the "gorilla," and the "merchant." What is important about the right guy is that he serves as a base line, however idealized or infrequent in reality, from which the inmate population can take its bearings.[32] A number of characteristics are attributed to the right guy. It is believed that he never interferes with other inmates who are attempting to manipulate the formal system. It is also believed that anyone who starts a fight with him had better be prepared to go all the way. If he gets anything extra he shares it with his friends. In his dealings with the prison officials he is clearly against them, although he doesn't do anything foolish. Even though he doesn't look for trouble with the officials he'll go the limit if they push him too far.[33] In short he possesses all the desirable qualities of the inmate as idealized by the inmate subculture.

---

[30] Ibid.
[31] Ibid., p. 131.
[32] Ibid., pp. 131–32.
[33] Ibid., p. 132.

The roles of the prison subculture are also seen in the interpersonal involvements among inmates. Clemmer suggests role variations on the basis of the degree of involvement with other inmates. The first is what he calls the complete "clique man." This refers to a man who is one of a group of three or more very close friends. These men share material goods as well as personal secrets and will accept punishment if necessary to help or support one another. The second is the "group man," who is friendly with a small group of men but does not completely subject himself to the wishes and acts of the group. He also mixes freely with other men and at least is friendly with them in a casual way. The third is the "semi-solitary" man. This kind of man is civil with other inmates but never becomes intimate with any of them, nor does he share with them in any way except the most casual. The fourth is the "complete-solitary" man. This kind of man keeps almost constantly to himself and shares nothing with any other inmates.[34] These roles represent a range from interpersonal commitment to individual isolation. Most inmates would define the first variation, that of the clique man, as the best way of doing time, while the prison authorities would most often prefer the fourth type, the complete-solitary man.

Another important role in the prison subculture is that of the various leaders. One study has found a number of characteristics that appear to be common to leaders in prisons. When compared to other inmates the leaders have served more years in prison, have longer sentences still to be served, are more frequently charged with the crimes of violence, and are more likely to be repeated offenders. The same study goes on to point out that more leaders than other inmates are diagnosed as homosexual, psychoneurotic, or psychopathic. "Finally, the institutional adjustments of leaders are marked by a significantly greater number of serious rule infractions, including escape, attempted escape, fighting and assault."[35] In other words leaders in prisons are those who deviate the most from what the formal system of the prison wants. The very fact that they are the most rebellious contributes to their being the leaders because this indicates their strength and their willingness to go against the formal prison.

The prison subculture and prisonization also have a strong influence on how inmates view their release from prison. Some inmates look forward to release with confidence. But others clearly have little to look forward to other than discrimination against "ex-cons," unemployment, and the many other secondary punishments that the larger society often imposes on them. Still other inmates look forward to release because they

---

[34] Donald Clemmer, "Informal Inmate Groups," in Johnson et al., *Punishment and Correction*, pp. 113–14.

[35] Clarence Schrag, "Leadership among Prison Inmates," in Johnson et al., *Punishment and Correction*, p. 118.

plan to continue their criminal careers. "In brief, postprison expectations may either encourage or discourage prisonization and its consequences."[36]

Still another important role in the inmate subculture is that which prisoners assign to the guards. Because the guard must interact with the prisoners he will generally be defined as a good or a bad guard, and the inmates constantly attempt to influence him. So good guards are those who often do not report infractions and who pass on forbidden information to the inmates in criticism of the higher authorities. This "corruption" of the guard's formal role is generally not due to bribery. There are a variety of pressures in American society to "be a decent guy," and the guard in prison is not immune to them. [37] In many ways the guard is probably closer to the inmate than to those who make policy decisions about the prison. Usually the inmates and the guards have similar social class backgrounds and therefore share many of the same values. Furthermore, some of the values they share go contrary to the formal requirements of the prison, and guards may be inclined to go with the values if they can do so without any great risk. However, it may be that some guards, even though they are from the same type of background as the inmates, are unsympathetic to them because they believe that the individual "badness" of the inmates takes precedence over any appeal to similarity of social class background.

The discussion thus far has been about a general prison subculture, but there has been some debate as to the possible existence of variations in prison. The argument for differences in prison subcultures is based on the contention that different subcultures have been brought into prison and that variations develop within the prison setting. It has been suggested that a great deal of the subcultural behavior of the prison is not peculiar to the prison at all. In reality, goes the argument, there is little real difference between the subculture of the criminal and that of the prison. "It seems rather obvious that the 'prison code'—don't inform on or exploit another inmate, don't lose your head, be weak, or be a sucker, etc.—is also part of a *criminal* code, existing outside prisons."[38] It may also be suggested that the prison subculture is close to that of another closed institution—the mental institution. So it may be the closed nature of the institution that leads to the similarities, rather than a specific approach to life and society.

It seems clear that one may visualize a prison subculture as we have described it, and that any distinctions one makes within the subculture do not discount the overall similarities. Two criminologists in a prison study

---

[36] Thomas and Foster, "Prisonization," p. 233.

[37] Sykes, "Rehabilitation," p. 158.

[38] Donald R. Cressey and John Irwin, "Thieves, Convicts and the Inmate Culture," *Social Problems*, Fall 1962, p. 145.

divided inmates into three rough groupings, and while all three were a part of an overall prison subculture, they did have some important differences. The three groupings represented somewhat different orientations and were referred to as the "thief," "prison," or "convict," and the "conventional" or "legitimate" subgroups.[39]

"Thief" subgroup. Basically the patterns of adjustment that these inmates make to prison are based on the criminal norms that exist outside the prison. The types who fall into this group are professional thieves and career criminals. For many of these people there are shared values which extend to criminals across the country with a high level of consistency. According to the values of this group, criminals should not betray each other to the police, but should be reliable, trustworthy, cool headed, and so forth. High status is also awarded to those who possess skill as thieves, "but to be just a successful thief is not enough. There must be solidness as well."[40] For the thief, imprisonment is one of the recurring problems which he must learn to deal with. It seems almost inevitable that he will be arrested from time to time, and the subgroup provides him with patterns for dealing with this problem. "Norms which apply to the prison situation and information on how to undergo the prison experience—how to do time 'standing on your head'—with the least suffering and in a minimum amount of time are prepared."[41] The thief subgroup values and information are developed and spread around in various prisons across the United States.

"Prison" or "convict" subgroup. This subgroup originates in the prisons. Its most central value is the utilitarian use of the prison setting. This means that the most manipulative inmates acquire the available wealth and the available positions of influence. This subgroup can be found wherever men are confined, "whether it be in city jails, state and federal prisons, army stockades, prisoner of war camps, concentration camps, or even mental hospitals. Such organizations are characterized by deprivations and limitations on freedom, and in them available wealth must be competed for by men supposedly on equal footing."[42] Irwin and Cressey suggest that the inmates in both the thief and the prison subgroups are conservative in that they want to preserve the status quo. However, their motivations are somewhat different. "The man oriented to the convict subculture is conservative because he has great stock in the existing order of things, while the man who is thief oriented leans toward conservatism because he knows how to do time and likes things to run smoothly with a minimum of friction."[43]

---

[39] Ibid., p. 148.

[40] Ibid., p. 146.

[41] Irwin and Cressey, "Inmate Culture," p. 231.

[42] Ibid.

[43] Ibid., p. 238.

"Conventional" or "legitimate" subgroup.   The inmates in this group
are not a part of the thief subculture before they enter prison and reject
the "convict" subculture after they enter prison. These men present few
problems for those who run the prisons and are generally seen as the
"ideal" type of inmate. They represent the largest percentage of inmates
in most prisons. They may enter various groups within prison, such as
religious groups or athletic teams, but they are primarily oriented to the
problem of achieving goals through the means that are approved in the
world outside the prison.

Sexual behavior

One area of behavior important to any understanding of the relationship among prisoners is that of sexual expression. In a world where
the men are cut off from all women they have the choice of no sexual expression, masturbation, or some kind of sexual contact with
other men. There has been some research with regard to the inmates who
abstain from sex or who use masturbation to meet their needs. Most of the
research has centered on various types of homosexual patterns found in
prison.

Many prisoners abstain from all types of sexual expression. Kirkham
found that successful self-imposed continence was usually associated with
a very short sentence and with strong beliefs against the "evilness" of both
masturbation and homosexuality. However, many prisoners do turn to
masturbation, and Kirkham argues that this is the sexual adaptation
made by the vast majority of men in prison. In a random sample study at
Soledad Prison in California he found that 81 percent agreed with the
statement "I think that masturbation is far more common in here than sex
acts between inmates."[44]

Chapter 11 was concerned with male homosexuality, and the reader
may wonder why male homosexuality in prisons is being treated again
here. There are two major reasons for this. First, in male prisons
homosexuality is generally not a matter of choice and usually refers to a
physical sexual act and not to a role filled by an individual. Second,
homosexuality in prison is often not sexually motivated but rather is a
consequence of power relationships between men. These two points will
become clear in the discussion ahead.

For the inmate who is shut off from women the problem is more than
simply being deprived of potential sex partners. The absence of women
removes the heterosexual meaning to a great deal that is important in the
male world. "Like most men, the inmate must search for his identity not
simply within himself but also in the picture of himself which he finds

---

[44] Kirkham, "Homosexuality in Prison," p. 330.

reflected in the eyes of others; and since a significant half of his audience is denied him, the inmate's image is in danger of becoming half complete."[45] The research clearly indicates that for most inmates the lack of interaction of all types with females is a very frustrating experience and one which weighs painfully on their minds. In prison there is constant reference to sexual matters. One common theme is the problem of sexual frustration, and another is the frequency of homosexuality in prison. Often the inmate is confronted with the possibility of homosexual resolution of his heterosexual frustrations—a possible resolution geared to physical release but often at the risk of psychological guilt and a questioning of his masculine self-image. "And if an inmate has in fact engaged in homosexual behavior within the walls, not as a continuation of a habitual pattern but as a rare act of sexual deviance under the intolerable pressure of mounting physical desire, the psychological on-slaught on his ego image will be particularly acute."[46]

With the elimination of women to help the man develop his male self-image he is forced to turn to other means. He may, for example, attempt to achieve masculine status through "toughness." This path is also found in situations outside of prison. For example, in some lower-class sub-cultures a man who cannot attain status through an occupation and whose involvement with women tends to be brief and not status-giving he may also turn to toughness as a means of achieving masculine status and recognition.

All of the related research indicates that homosexuality in male prisons is quite common. The two major roles related to homosexuality indicate the way in which it is viewed and how participating inmates are defined. In general the extent to which homosexual behavior is seen as being masculine or feminine appears to be the most important consideration and provides the setting for defining sexual perversion by the inmate population. One group are the "fags" and "punks." They are looked down upon because they are seen as having sacrificed their manhood. The second group are the "wolves," who are seen as making a temporary adjustment to the sexual tensions in the male prison. In general the behavior of the wolf is seen as consistent with the cultural definitions of the masculine role. In sexual acitvity it is the wolf who is performing the act on the fag or punk. That is, the wolf is active and the fag is passive in sexual relations.

Many males who engage in homosexual contacts do not become defined as homosexuals. The individual must fulfill two criteria in order to avoid becoming stigmatized. First, the homosexual act or acts must represent only a situational reaction to the deprivation of heterosexual

[45] Sykes, "Pains of Imprisonment," p. 134.
[46] Ibid.

intercourse. Second, they must involve a complete absence of emotion-
ality or effeminacy—both of which are regarded as signs of "weakness"
and "queerness." "An inmate who engages in homosexual activity must
present a convincing facade of toughness to escape being defined as a
homosexual."[47]

There are some further distinctions in the sexual roles played. The fag
is recognized by his exaggerated and feminine mannerisms. That is, he
generally pretends to be female in more than just the sex act. By contrast
the punk submits to the demands of the more aggressive homosexuals
without showing any other signs of femininity. He often fills the punk role
because he has no choice.

One "feminine" role played in male prisons is that of "queen." Queens
represent the smallest category of homosexualy involved inmates, but
they are the most readily observable because of their appearance and
mannerisms. Even though often subjected to ridicule by the inmate population, the queen actually enjoys the position of a scarce object of high
functional utility. "The queen's effeminacy thus often evokes a memory
and longing for females, a longing which sometimes leads otherwise
exclusively heterosexual men to seek sexual relief from the queen."[48]
Often the queen will enter a number of sexual prison liaisons which may
be best described as approaching serial monogamy.[49]

The stress on the wolf's masculinity is reinforced because many inmates
believe that his part in homosexuality implies absolutely nothing on his
part. He is seen as one who seeks out a partner to be used for the
mechanical act of achieving an orgasm. "Unmoved by love, indifferent to
the emotions of the partner he has coerced, bribed, or seduced into a
liaison, the *wolf* is often viewed as simply masturbating with another
person."[50] The fact that the wolf doesn't see his activity as homosexual
may be in part a reflection of a lower-class characteristic. Various studies
have shown that persons in the lower class do not define as homosexual
the person who plays the active role in the sexual act. This appears to be
much less true in the middle class. In other words, in the lower class being
homosexual depends on who does what in the sex act while in the middle
class being homosexual is more often based on any sexual experience with
a member of the same sex. To use the middle-class definition in the prison
situation would be to take away one of the few activities that is seen as
clearly masculine.

A study of homosexual rapes carried out in Philadelphia prisons and

----

[47] Kirkham, "Homosexuality in Prison," p. 331.

[48] Ibid., pp. 333–34.

[49] Ibid., p. 335.

[50] Gresham Sykes, "Argot Roles: Wolves, Punks, and Fags," in Johnson et al.,
Punishment and Correction, p. 139.

police vans shows that in prison homosexual rape can occur on *any* inmate if there are other inmates who choose to do so. All the men were potential rape victims, but some were quickly selected. For example, practically every slightly built young man sentenced by the court was sexually approached within a day or two after his admission to prison. "Many of these young men are repeatedly raped by gangs of inmates. Others, because of the threat of gang rape, seek protection by entering into a homosexual relationship with an individual tormentor."[51]

Those who committed the assaults did not think of themselves as homosexual or even as engaging in homosexual acts. But the most important finding in this study was that sexual release was not the primary reason for the sexual aggression. The primary goal of those who carried out the sexual aggression was the conquest and degradation of the victim. It was repeatedly found that aggressors used such language as "Fight or fuck," "We're going to take your manhood," "You'll have to give up some face," and "We're going to make a girl out of you."[52] Most of the aggressors were members of the prison subculture to whom most other avenues of asserting their masculinity were closed. "To them, job success, raising a family, and achieving the respect of other men socially have been largely beyond reach. Only sexual and physical prowess stands between them and a feeling of emasculation."[53] But what is so overpowering in the prison situation is that homosexual rape is an inevitable consequence for many men. Prison not only strips the inmates of most of the means of achieving a masculine status but may even destroy those few means that are still available in prison. That is, the repeatedly raped man loses any sense of masculinity through his lack of strength to resist and is forced into the female role in sexual activity. Such experiences are often so overwhelmingly destructive to the personality of the individual that he is completely stripped of any sense of masculinity.

In concluding this section on the male in prison it should be pointed out that prison experiences directly and indirectly influence a man long after he leaves prison. He is often placed on probation and subjected to close controls over his activities. He may also have trouble getting a job or may have to take a job lower in status than what he would have been able to obtain if he had not spent time in prison. His prison status is often continued because he is known as an "ex-convict." Like most other deviances that one leaves, having been a prisoner still carries some stigma. This is also true of the ex-mental patient, ex-alcoholic, ex-drug addict, and so forth. (About the only "ex" who gains prestige in American society is the "ex-communist.") Also, for many types of ex-deviants there

---

[51] Alan J. Davis, "Sexual Assaults in the Philadelphia Prison System and Sheriff's Vans," *Trans-Action*, December 1968, p. 9.

[52] Ibid., pp. 15–16.

[53] Ibid., p. 16.

are social organizations to help them adjust to the world. This is true for those who were on drugs or who were alcoholics. But all efforts to form organizations of ex-convicts have met with one serious obstacle, namely, the tradition that a prisoner discharged on parole is not allowed to associate with known criminals, which means, among others, ex-convicts. "So that while many officials countenance the self-help movement in *prison*, they oppose its continuations outside."[54]

WOMEN'S PRISONS

In this last section we look at prisons for women, and it will be seen that they are different in many important ways from prisons for men. Two excellent studies of women's prisons will be drawn on in the discussion that follows. The first was a study of a woman's prison in California, by Ward and Kassebaum,[55] and the second a study of a woman's federal prison located in West Virginia, by Giallombardo.[56] The findings of these two studies show remarkably high agreement.

Women entering prison are defined by those who work with them in a very different way than are new male inmates. The male criminal is usually seen as dangerous to society, but the woman is most often viewed as disgraced and dishonored and is often seen as pathetic. So the women who commit criminal acts are often regarded as erring and misguided persons who are in need of help rather than as dangerous criminals from whom society must be protected.[57] In the past, and still commonly today, the method of treatment for females in prison is to try to instill in them certain standards of sexual morality and to train them to fill the duties of mothers and homemakers. So traditionally women's prisons have tried to surround the prisoners with what were believed to be good influences: "small homelike residences, individual rooms, attractive clothing to develop self-respect, educational classes, and recreation. In addition, the view that criminal women were sinful and misguided had much to do with the development of a benevolent maternal orientation of the staff toward their charges."[58]

Physically the women's prisons are very different from those for men. The federal prison in West Virginia is approximately five hundred acres of farm, pasture, and woodlands enclosed with wire fences topped with barbed wire. The women live in cottages, each of which is operated as an independent unit with kitchen, dining room, living room, and library,

---

[54] Edward Sagarin, *Odd Man In: Societies of Deviants in America* (Chicago: Quadrangle, 1969), p. 166.

[55] David A. Ward and Gene G. Kassebaum, *Women's Prison* (Chicago: Aldine, 1965).

[56] Rose Giallombardo, *Society of Women* (New York: Wiley, 1966).

[57] Ibid., p. 7.

[58] Ibid., p. 8.

and with individual rooms for every inmate.[59] The state prison in California does not look like the traditional penitentiary either. There are no gun towers, no stone walls, no armed guards. The grounds are surrounded by a cyclone fence ten feet high and topped with accordian wire. The women live in dormitories, and most inmates live by themselves in rooms with curtained windows, bedspreads, rugs, and wooden doors.[60]

Almost any person put in prison and isolated from the outside world will find the adjustment difficult. But it seems a reasonable argument that the impact of imprisonment is more severe for women than for men because for them a socially isolated life is much more unusual. One concern that is particularly serious for women in prison is the severing of their ties with their children. "The male prisoner can serve time with the knowledge that, although the family may experience great difficulty while he is not the breadwinner, the wife can care for the children. The confined mother, however, loses her ability to fill what is, in our society, her most important role."[61] Far fewer men than women in prison are married, and far fewer who are parents feel any strong sense of concern for their children.

When women enter prison they do not become a part of an inmate subculture like that found in men's prisons. The traditional criminal values do not fit the women's prisons because those values are concerned with features of imprisonment that are relevant to men but are not usually relevant to women. "Women in our society are not prepared to 'play it cool,' 'to take it like a man,' to refrain from 'copping out' or to use force to fight for one's rights, if provoked,"[62] So the inmate code is usually met with indifference in the women's prisons. "This is not because the women are unexposed to criminal norms and values, but because the values embodied in the code reflect psychological needs and social roles of male prisoners."[63]

When women enter prison they react to the situation from several different perspectives. Most of them bring together several views and influences. First, they must respond to a situation that imposes deprivations and restrictions on them. Second, they may sometimes respond within the context of some preparation for that kind of life, that is, to the extent that they have internalized, to varying degrees, the values of delinquent subcultures and of prisoner codes. Third, they react as

---

[59] Ibid., p. 22.

[60] Ward and Kassebaum, *Woman's Prison*, p. 7.

[61] David A. Ward and Gene G. Kassebaum, "Homosexuality: A Mode of Adaptation in a Prison for Women," *Social Problems*, Fall 1964, pp. 161–62.

[62] Ward and Kassebaum, *Women's Prison*, p. 68.

[63] Ibid., p. 69.

women. These perspectives work together in providing them with frames of reference which influence their behavior in the prison setting.[64] There are variations within the female population with regard to these values. Greater emphasis appears to be placed on solidarity and loyalty by those women who have internalized criminal norms in the community or in previous prison experiences. "Those least likely to support group loyalty and the norms of the inmate code were those women serving time for the once-only offense—homicide—and for 'white collar' offenses, such as embezzlement, forgery, and bad checks."[65] In general Ward and Kassebaum found little evidence of the differentiated inmate types or of the degree of solidarity reported in the studies of prisons for men. They point out that in all interviews the "inmates responded that informing on other inmates was characteristic of almost the entire inmate population."[66]

Giallombardo suggests that both men and women develop inmate subcultures as a means of responding to the general deprivations of being in prison but that the nature of the response in the two communities is influenced by the differential participation of men and women in the external society. She found that the cultural definitions and content of *both* men's and women's roles are brought into the female prison setting and that they function to determine the direction and focus of the inmate cultural system. "These general features I have suggested are those concerned with the orientation of life goals for males and females; second, cultural definitions with respect to dimensions of passivity and aggression; third, acceptability of public expression of affection displayed toward a member of the same sex; and, finally, perception of the same sex with respect to what I have called the popular culture."[67]

The female prison inmate, like her male counterpart, quickly learns there are few escape routes because psychological and physical withdrawal are not usually effective means for easing the pain of imprisonment. Giallombardo says that women develop a subcultural structure to attempt to deal with the harmful effects of physical and social isolation. They attempt to develop a world in which they may preserve an identity that is relevant to life outside the prison. "In this structure, the inmates' orientation is quasi-collectivistic, depending upon where one stands in terms of homosexual or kin relationships; the degree of mutual aid and the expectation of solidarity decrease as one goes from nuclear members to proximal relationships to distal relationships."[68]

---

[64] Ibid., p. 58.

[65] Ibid., p. 48.

[66] Ward and Kassebaum, "Homosexuality," p. 163.

[67] Rose Giallombardo, "Social Roles in a Prison for Women," *Social Problems*, Winter 1966, p. 288.

[68] Giallombardo, *Society of Women*, pp. 103–4.

Another important difference between men's and women's prisons is that among the women there are far fewer leadership roles to be filled. As a result the female prison world is much less characterized by struggles for power. In fact leadership appears to be very diffuse in women's prisons. What gives the women's prisons their stability is the dynamic mechanism of "kinship" relationships. This means that relatively durable homosexual relationships are the basic unit of the social structure. Clearly defined social roles also develop as a form of adaptation to the prison setting. In fact the sharpness with which roles are defined and filled is a striking feature of the women's prisons. This sharpness does not occur with the same degree in male prison subcultures.

We will briefly define and describe some of the roles filled by female prisoners. "Square" is a derisive name given to the inmate who is believed to be an accidental criminal. This person is usually oriented to the prison administration and holds "anticriminal" attitudes. There are "hip squares" who tend to sympathize with the inmate code and follow some of its principles. But what makes a woman a "hip square" is that she does not engage in homosexual behavior, because any inmate who does not engage in homosexual activities is automatically labelled a square.[69] Another role is that of the "jive bitch," who is seen as a troublemaker because she usually creates unrest among the inmates and cannot be depended on. There is also the "snitcher," the female counterpart to the "rat" in the male prison. To accuse an inmate of snitching is the most serious accusation that one inmate can make about another. Yet, in women's prisons the inmates do not usually show any great surprise at another inmate's deviations from the restrictive norms. Actually many deviant acts are overlooked or are not strongly punished. "In contrast to the situation in the male prison, we find the violation of the 'no snitching' norm does not often result in violence."[70] Another role is that of the "pinner," who serves as a lookout. This is an inmate who can be trusted and who will stand up under pressure.

Some inmates become what are called "rap buddies," chosen because they are easy to talk with and because one can assume that what one says will be secret and mutually binding. The "homey" role is about the closest thing to a "blood" relationship that can be found and holds a special place in the thinking of inmates. The homey is an inmate from another inmate's home town or from a nearby community. Homeys develop patterns of mutual aid and are close to each other, but exclude all homosexuality. Giallombardo suggests that the occupants of the homey role are buying insurance for the future. After getting out of prison homeys will not speak negatively about each other's prison behavior to anyone in society.[71]

[69] Giallombardo, "Prison for Women," p. 277.

[70] Ibid., p. 275.

[71] Giallombardo, *Society of Women*, p. 119.

Homosexuality

The most striking finding in the two studies was the high degree of involvement in homosexuality and its great importance to the prison subculture. On the basis of the two studies it can be estimated that between 50 percent and 75 percent of the inmates were homosexually involved at least once during their prison terms. However, very few of the inmates practiced homosexuality before they entered prison. About 5 percent of the female inmates had had homosexual experience prior to entering prison. The female homosexual is in a favored position in prison because the competition of males has been removed. However, most women who enter into homosexual experiences while in prison end them when they leave and return to the heterosexual world. And it must also be stressed that, unlike the situation in the men's prisons, in the women's prisons inmates are rarely physically forced into homosexual activities.

In general the inmates make a distinction between a "penitentiary turnout" and a "lesbian." The lesbian is seen as a woman who prefers homosexual relations even in the free community. In this respect she is like the fag in the male prison. There is also some evidence that lesbian inmates are like male homosexual inmates in some other ways. For example, among those few inmates who can be classified as prison politicians and merchants are a large number who are true homosexuals.[72] The penitentiary or jailhouse turnout receives her introduction to homosexuality in prison and does not see it as basic to her personality.

The question arises as to why so many women prisoners turn to homosexual experiences. Ward and Kassebaum suggest that these women are faced with a lack of experience in serving time and the absence of conventional sources of emotional support, such as husbands, lovers, or families. This makes many of them receptive to homosexuality as a means of adjustment when it is offered to them upon their arrival at prison. "Our data clearly indicate that more inmates resort to homosexuality than to psychological withdrawal, rebellion, colonization or any other type of adaptation."[73] As discussed in Chapter 12, it seems clear that homosexuality is much less threatening to the female than to the male. And for women in prison it is seen as a temporary adaptation to prison life.

As suggested, female inmates are rarely forced into homosexual relationships. Yet, force and violence do sometimes develop around homosexuality in prison. The real violence that occurs tends to be around a homosexual triangle. When such fights occur the great fear is not

---

[72] Ward and Kassebaum, "Homosexuality," p. 168.

[73] Ibid., p. 175.

usually for one's life but rather about disfigurement—"the fear that an inmate 'out to get' another will use razor or scissors to disfigure one's face."[74] Often female inmates are less fearful about physical threats than about gossip. So the inmate often fears the vitriolic verbal attacks that may result from jealousy, and she suffers from insecurity in handling the frequent attacks through the "penitentiary darby"—"gossip which takes place at all times on all sides with the prison."[75]

Two major homosexual roles are filled in the women's prison. The first is that of the "butch," "stud broad," "drag butch," or "daddy," who is the aggressive, active sexual partner. Most lesbians fall into this role, but there are also many jailhouse turnouts. The butch wears her hair short, uses no makeup, leaves her legs unshaven, and often wears pedal pushers, or, if she wears a dress, wears the belt low on the hips. "Masculine gait, manner of smoking, and other gestures are adopted."[76] Usually this role is accorded prestige by the other inmates because there relatively few butches and they are in great demand.

The role complementary to that of the butch is that of the "femme" or "mommy." The femme maintains a female appearance and ideally plays a more submissive, passive role. She continues to act out many of the female functions performed in the outside society, and she emphasizes her role primarily through her behavior. She walks with her arms around the butch, embraces and kisses her in public, and allows the butch to speak in her behalf.[77]

Often the homosexual pair are cast in the context of a "marital" relationship in the prison. While this kind of relationship seems to be repugnant to most women when they are in the outside world, the uniqueness of the prison world forces them to redefine homosexual behavior. "For the vast majority of the inmates, adjustment to the prison world is made by establishing a homosexual alliance with a compatible partner as a marriage unit."[78] These marriages are generally monogamous and the inmate who "chippies from one bed to another"—that is, terminates affairs too quickly—is held in scorn by the others as her behavior is held to be promiscuous. "This behavior draws forth words of scorn from the inmates because the ideal cultural pattern in the prison is to establish a permanent relationship."[79]

While a sense of belongingness and affectional ties are important in a homosexual marriage, the couple is also usually involved in some kinds of sexual activities. In all cases the butch performs sex on the femme, but

---

[74] Giallombardo, "Prison for Women," p. 274.

[75] Ibid., p. 274.

[76] Ward and Kassebaum, "Homosexuality," pp. 168–69.

[77] Ibid., p. 284.

[78] Giallombardo, "Prison for Women," p. 282.

[79] Ibid., p. 284.

about one third of the butches refuse to let the femme reciprocate sexually. In some cases the butches remain clothed during sexual activity. In part this may be in order to maintain the illusion of masculinity. In the sex act the role of the femme is completely passive where the butch "*gives work,*" that is "engages in cunnilingus, manual manipulation of the clitoris, and breast fondling. While the butch gives work, the denial of sexual gratification for herself is called "*giving up the work.*" Such self-denial militates against becoming obligated to the femme and from developing emotional ties that would be painful to disturb or break."[80] This concern is often a result of the fact that many of the women in the butch role have been unsuccessful in having affectionate heterosexual relationships, and they fear being rejected again in a homosexual relationship.

This discussion indicates that women's prisons have developed around living patterns similar in many ways to those of the outside world. This is far truer in women's prisons than in men's prisons. It seems that prisons for men and women have been both successes and failures. They have succeeded in removing the threat of the individual criminal from the broader society, but they have failed to significantly reduce the future criminality of the inmates.

BIBLIOGRAPHY

Cressey, Donald R., and John Irwin, "Thieves, Convicts, and the Inmate Culture," *Social Problems*, Fall 1962, pp. 142–55.

Davis, Alan J., "Sexual Assaults in the Philadelphia Prison System and Sheriff's Vans," *Trans-Action*, December 1968, pp. 8–16.

Garabedian, Peter G., "Social Roles and Processes of Socialization in the Prison Community," *Social Problems*, Fall 1963, pp. 139–52.

Giallombardo, Rose, *Society of Women*. New York: Wiley, 1966.

Hazebrigg, Lawrence, ed., *Prisons within Society*. New York: Anchor Books, 1969.

Johnson, Norman, et al., eds., *The Sociology of Punishment and Correction*. New York: Wiley, 1962.

Kirkham, George, "Homosexuality in Prison," in James M. Henslin, *Studies in the Sociology of Sex* (New York: Appleton-Century-Crofts, 1971), pp. 325–49.

Thomas, Charles W., and Samuel C. Foster, "Prisonization in the Inmate Contraculture," *Social Problems*, Fall 1972, pp. 232–40.

Ward, David A., and Gene G. Kassebaum, *Women's Prison*. Chicago: Aldine, 1965.

---

[80] Ward and Kassebaum, "Homosexuality," pp. 171–72.

chapter fifteen

Militant women

The most basic factor related to the changing nature of the American family has been the changes in the roles filled by women. This has been true of their roles as wives, as mothers, and in occupations. There has also developed a new interest in the roles that women might fill both within and outside the family. Therefore, this chapter will explore the changing nature of women's roles in America today. To better understand the changes now taking place it is necessary to present a brief historical discussion of the roles of women in the United States over time. This chapter will also discuss the meaning and influence of the women's liberation movement.

In the late 1960s in the United States a new militancy seeking female equality or liberation emerged. The United States has had a long history of feminism that has brought about many significant social changes. But the new militancy has been much more aggressive and demanding than anything that has gone before. To a great extent this is because the women's liberation movement has developed out of such militant movements of the 1960s as the civil rights movement, student protests, and the politically radical left. There are many who see the militant women's movement as a temporary fad that will quickly fade away because women really are not discriminated against and have no basis for protest. However, it is suggested here that the movement will not fade away and that it may become one of the most important social movements of the 1970s. This suggestion is based on the contention that in many ways American women are still treated as second-class citizens and oftentimes as inferior to men. To better understand the roles of women today it is necessary to first look at how women have been defined and treated in the past.

HISTORICAL BACKGROUND

It has been pointed out that almost all past societies have been patriarchal, meaning in effect that women have had second-class status. If we go back to early Greek civilization it can be seen that the powers the Greek husband had over his wife were as great as those he had over his children. (If they had no children he could divorce her.) The dowry of the wife became the husband's property during his lifetime, and he had the right to any separate earnings she might acquire. She was under his jurisdiction almost entirely and could not even leave the house without his permission. By contrast the early Roman wife occupied a position of complete social equality with her husband and was seen as having dignity and honor within both the family and the state. She was both honored and subordinated: "she was highly respected, and yet she was given no tangible legal rights."[1]

Whatever status women gained during the Roman period they began to lose with the rise of Christianity. In that period a tendency developed to restrict women's legal and social rights. Women were given no special position or recognition in early Christian teaching. Jesus expressed no new ideas with respect to the position of women. The apostle Paul advocated that women take a position subordinate to men, and over time this became the dominant attitude among early Christian leaders. Therefore, the status accorded to women by Christianity was a step backward compared to their status in ancient Rome. Eventually women were excluded by Christians from any offices. Still less were they men's equals in private life. "In marriage wives were bidden to be subject to their husbands."[2]

Christianity developed an obsession with sexual matters which also placed a great strain on women. Treated by the Saxons as property, by the Middle Ages women were often seen as the source of all sexual evil. "It was argued that sexual guilt really pertained to women, since they tempted men, who would otherwise have remained pure."[3] The combined views of her as inferior to man and as a repository of sin placed her at a level of inferiority from which she has never completely recovered in the eyes of traditional Christian thought. In time, and due to Christian influence, she also came to be legally defined as inferior. In the English common law the husband's rights over the wife's personal property were almost unlimited. After the 13th century the common law put the absolute property in the wife's chattels with the husband. The wife was not even permitted to make a will without the husband's consent. In many

---

[1] Helen I. Clarke, *Social Legislation* (New York: Appleton-Century-Crofts, 1957), p. 35.

[2] Richard Lewinsohn, *A History of Sexual Customs* (New York: Harper, 1958), p. 92.

[3] G. Rattray Taylor, *Sex in History* (New York: Ballantine Books, 1954), p. 64.

respects, up until the 20th century a woman's status was not too different from that of a slave. This was the general state of affairs that existed at the time the American colonies were founded.

In many ways early American women were treated almost like slaves. Both women and slaves were expected to behave with deference and obedience toward their masters. Both had no official existence under the law and but few rights with regard to education. "Both found it difficult to run away; both worked for their masters without pay; both had to breed on command, and to nurse the results."[4] It is of interest that from the very start the woman and the black have been compared in terms of their second-class status and that this comparison is basically as appropriate today as it was during the colonial period.

The inferior status of American women comes in part from the feeling that they, like their prototype, Eve, are provokers of sin. As suggested, women were constantly condemned during the early history of the Catholic church and during the Puritan eras in England and America. Even the horrible practice of witch burning stemmed from the belief that women were "servants of Satan."[5]

The 18th century

During this century women continued to be treated in many respects as second-class persons. They received very little formal education because it was commonly believed that girls were unfit in brain and character to study seriously. It was argued that girls should be taught how to run a household, "and, if suitable how to display the graces of a lady." However, near the end of the 18th century there were voices that spoke out against the traditional definition of women. And if helplessness was one common adaptation of women to the world around them, for other women a new militancy was coming to be an alternative. For a few women there was the choice of either barricading themselves in the home with the myth of frailty or of struggling to get outside the home and find some new definitions of femininity.

In 1792 the first comprehensive attack on marriage as it then existed and on the way in which it subjugated women was made by Mary Wollstonecraft in a book called *A Vindication of the Rights of Women.* Mary Wollstonecraft did not want to do away with marriage but rather to correct some of the inequalities that existed. She argued that women should have increased social and economic rights as well as greater education so that they would be equal rather than submissive to their

---

[4] Andrew Sinclair, *The Emancipation of The American Woman* (New York: Harper, 1965), p. 4.

[5] Wainwright Churchill, *Homosexual Behavior among Males* (New York: Hawthorn Books, 1967), p. 24.

husbands. Women were also being heard in other areas of protest. In general, in the 18th and 19th centuries when voices of protest were heard they were from women. It was primarily women who fought against slavery, against child labor, and against slums. Women also fought for schools, libraries, playgrounds, and legislation to protect children. Women have historically been the social conscience of American society.

The 19th century

During this century great changes occurred in the United States. Industrialization meant a change in life patterns, as the productive unit shifted from the family to places of employment away from the home. For some women the chance to work in a factory appeared like freedom. Hard household work, for 12 hours a day or more, had been normal for most American women, and their tasks had been heavy, endless, and unpaid. For many of them the early factory system represented a semiskilled remunerative job which demanded little physical exertion.

As the 19th century unfolded, female rebels became more and more common. The first of these were basically rebels who happened to be women. That is, they were not champions of their sex but of themselves. They fought for the right to be treated as individuals, without distinction by sex. However, they did not consider themselves to be other than exceptions. "They never questioned that the general rule was the rule of women by men. Thus, they were not feminists so much as female rebels, made so by the accidents of birth and place and inspiration."[6] The early feminists also saw that the role of lady and enslaved American women because the very definition of a lady was based on inferior status and ability. Yet, many of the early feminists only felt free when they were playing that role. They never came to terms with this anomaly, and as a result feminism in the 19th century remained primarily a middle-class and ladylike business. "In fact, most American ladies—by their very social position—opposed anything other than safe and mild reforms of a religious or educational nature."[7]

In the decades prior to the Civil War in the United States a changing definition of women had developed on the part of men. The "animal" nature of women came to be stressed less, and women came to be seen as more spiritual than men. So the new explanation for their exclusion from politics came to be not their inferiority but rather their superiority. They were seen not as sinful but as too good for the world. Their moral value placed them above the nasty business of politics and money-making. The men turned over to them the spheres of "culture" and childrearing.

---

[6] Sinclair, *Emancipation*, p. 32.

[7] Ibid., p. 109.

Women were encouraged to believe that their sex gave them distinct functions that were different from and better than the mere getting of money. It is doubtful that very many men really believed that what women did was important. The really important world was the man's world of money-making and politics. So they could keep women out of their world and feel morally superior about it at the same time.

Despite all the forms of resistance the women's rights movement did develop and grow. The factor of industrialization continued to remove many women from the home and freed many of them from the functions they had performed in the past. There were a number of landmarks in the movement. For example, in 1833 Oberlin was the first men's college in the United States to admit women, and four years later Mount Holyoke, the first women's college, was opened. The first Woman's Rights Convention was held at Seneca Falls, New York, in 1848. The first to speak out in public for women's rights were Fanny Wright, the daughter of a Scotch nobleman, and Ernestine Rose, the daughter of a rabbi. There was great hostility toward those women; the former was referred to as "the red harlot of infidelity," the latter, as "a woman a thousand times below a prostitute."[8] The declaration that came out of Seneca Falls brought forth an outcry of revolution and insurrection, and the hostility to the declaration was so great that some women withdrew their signatures from it.

By the 1850s such respected intellectuals as the New England transcendentalists were aligning themselves with the women's rights movement. During that period in England the Unitarians and other liberal elements were also becoming involved. In 1869 John Stuart Mill wrote *The Subjection of Women*, a work which gave the mark of respectability to English feminism. By the 1860s women began to discard their crinolines and slowly slimmed down their skirts until only the bustle was left. "Once again they could and did begin to take exercise and play simple games of sport such as croquet and lawn tennis; and unchaperoned they could once again walk arm in arm with men."[9]

However, the major force in the growth of the feminist movement in the 1800s was the slavery issue. So the concern that turned many women into pioneer reformers was less an attack on sexual bondage than an assault on the slavery of the blacks. In seeking to free the slaves many radical women became more conscious of their own lack of freedom. "Through helping others, they learned to help themselves. The destiny of American women and American Negroes had been interacting, and still is."[10]

---

[8] Betty Friedan, *The Feminine Mystique* (New York: Norton, 1963), p. 86.
[9] Morton M. Hunt, *The Natural History of Love* (New York: Knopf, 1959), p. 332.
[10] Sinclair, *Emancipation*, p. 37.

As suggested, most men were strongly against the women's rights movement. The double-standard male saw his way of life as threatened and was fearful that some of his conveniences might be taken away from him. He had no desire to change his world but only to increase his rights as a male. On economic grounds he found his world ideal. A subjugated wife, even if cranky, was simpler and cheaper to deal with than an equal before the law who could leave with her property if she wished or could sue for redress if mistreated. From the business point of view women's low position made good sense to him. So such males often linked any plea for female education or reform in marriage with atheism, socialism, abolition, teetotaling, sexual immorality, and other despicable forces.

The male often assumed a pious posture in arguing against the women's rights movement. By supporting the image of the female as submissive, dependent, and inferior, he could argue that her basic being was under attack. So he could intone, as did one senator in 1866, that to give women equal rights would destroy that "milder, gentler nature, which not only makes them shrink from but disqualifies them for the turmoil and battle of public life."[11] Against this image he could then depict the feminists as violating their very nature as women, and it is indeed true that the picture they often presented was in sharp contrast to that of the traditional docile women. Some of the early feminists cut their hair short, wore bloomers, and tried to be like men. So the hostile image held of the feminists came to be one of inhuman. fiery man-eaters who had none of the traditional feminine qualities.

Near the end of the 19th century new forces for women's rights were developing. Over the long run one of the most important developments was higher education for women. In the late 19th century women's colleges were established. The new colleges created a demand for the services of academic women, and the demand, under the circumstances of the time, created the supply. Colleges were founded as a result of the great reform ferment that had started in the 1840s and, while slowed by the Civil War, reached a peak at the turn of the century. "Abolition, women's rights, temperance, prison reform, labor organization—these were only a few of the many causes which had been fostered in the great reform movement. The higher education of women had been one of the many."[12] In the first two decades after the turn of the century many of the elitist women's colleges were in conflict with themselves. "The academic women who staffed them were still for the most part women with causes, still reformers at heart, but action was becoming less attractive than contemplation within the ivy-covered walls. The feeling

---

[11] Friedan, *Feminine Mystique*, p. 86.

[12] Jessie Bernard, *Academic Women* (University Park: Pennsylvania State University Press, 1964), p. 31.

began to grow that the academic role was not an activist one."[13] But the colleges had provided the rallying point and the training ground for many of the women involved in the women's rights struggles that occurred around the turn of the century.

By the end of the 19th century some women began to believe in an option to the traditional roles of marriage and motherhood. This came about as customs changed and more women were able to work and support themselves without losing their self-respect. Also, during this period some women entered business and moved into the professions. Toward the end of the century essays appeared that argued that it was better for a woman to remain single and support herself than to become the wife of a dissipated man. The rights of lowly and genteel women to work provided the means of escape from unhappy or loveless marriages. So while the work pattern was not common for women, it existed and it provided the roots for rapid development in the 20th century. But at the same time the battle to keep women in the home continued. While anthropology and biology had destroyed the old belief that women were inferior, new arguments developed. Some men contended that immigration and eugenics provided reasons for keeping women in the home. They argued that old stock women were needed at home to bear children who would protect and preserve the nation. Such middle-class women were told to stay home and bear more superior beings like themselves to compensate for the "inferior" offspring of the immigrants. It is clear that whenever one argument against women lost its effectiveness new ones were invented.

The 20th century

As suggested, during the 19th century the battle for women's rights was closely related to battles for various social reforms. The feminist movement was linked with Jane Addams and Hull House, the rise of the union movement, and the great strikes against intolerable working conditions in the factories. And the final battle for the right of women to vote was fought primarily by the college-trained women. Social reform continued to be seen as something with which women could be concerned. These concerns were linked with the male stereotype of women as compassionate and impractical creatures. American men have always underestimated the influence of women as society's conscience. A reading of history indicates that man's inhumanity would have been much greater if women had not functioned to bring about a more compassionate view of the world and human beings.

---

[13] Ibid., 36.

[14] Carl N. Degler, "Revolution without Ideology: The Changing Place of Women in America," *Daedalus*, Fall 1964, p. 657.

The most dramatic change in the image of women came after World War I. This resulted from the upsurge in women's employment outside the home. The 1920s saw the emergence of the white-collar class in the United States, and women were a large part of it. For example, over twice as many women entered the labor force during that decade as during the previous one.[14] But the major event of the decade was the passage of the 19th Amendment to the federal Constitution, in 1920. It read that the "rights of citizens of the United States to vote shall not be denied or abridged by the United States or by any state on account of sex." This was an important landmark in the fight for women's rights. However, it did not bring about any great changes in the political life patterns of women.

The 1920s were the period of greatest change in the roles and rights of American women. The decade saw a revolution in morals that was most vividly reflected in the behavior of women. During the 1920s many taboos affecting women were thrown aside. For the first time women began to smoke and drink in public. As recently as 1918 it was considered daring for a New York hotel to permit women to sit at the bar. But during the '20s, despite prohibition, both sexes drank in public. As Degler points out, in the years since the '20s there have been few alterations in the position of women that were not first evident during that decade. "The changes have penetrated more deeply and spread more widely through the social structure, but their central tendency was then already spelled out."[15]

The 1920s were also a period of great change in the sexual behavior of women. Women then began to believe that they had the same rights to sexual satisfaction as did men. And during that decade there was an increase in the frequency of premarital coitus among women. The sexual superiority of the male was no longer an accepted belief for many men and women.

The legal right of women to vote did not lead to sex equality. This was because there could be no real sex equality until women actually participated on an equal basis with men in politics, occupations, and the family. "Law and administrative regulations must permit such participation, but women must want to participate and be able to participate."[16] Actually, in the 1920s the grip of the traditional political machines became even stronger. This was because the female relatives of every man connected with the political machines were registered to vote. For many of those machine politicians the vote of the women was merely a multiplication factor. In fact women refused to vote against an-

---

[15] Ibid., p. 659.
[16] Alice S. Rossi, "Equality between the Sexes: An Immodest Proposal," *Daedalus*, Spring 1964, p. 610.

tifeminists in Congress, and sent them back with increased majorities as their representatives. While women had the vote they generally continued to use it as their men told them to.

Since 1920 the number of women who have attained positions of power in the federal and state governments has been unbelievably small. Only three women have been elected as state governors. Two women have held cabinet rank in the federal government, and six have served as ambassadors or ministers. At the present time the United States has not one female senator out of one hundred. And while women hold about one fourth of all jobs in the federal civil service, they hold only 2 percent of the top positions. But a similar situation exists in many other countries. For example, even with the Soviet Union's wide base of professional women the number of women decreases disproportionately as one goes toward the top in the Soviet hierarchy.[17]

Western world today

The treatment of women has changed in most countries of the West. How women are treated in most countries appears to be related to the educational and social class level of men and women. Goode found in his cross-cultural studies that in the lower classes women had somewhat more authority. This was because the low standard of living gave the women a key position in the family. In the upper classes, where the men are better educated than in the middle classes, they are often more willing to concede rights and women are eager to demand them. "Men in the lower strata, by contrast, are much more traditional minded than their counterparts in the upper strata, and are less willing to concede the new rights being demanded; but they have to do so because of the increased bargaining power of their women."[18]

But when the countries of the Western world are examined, it can be seen that they are changing rapidly and that in some cases women have received greater rights than in the United States. The right to vote is now common to women in most countries. In 1968 women could vote and run for office in 117 countries. Only seven countries prohibited voting for women, and four others imposed some limitations. The number of women who go to college has increased. In the 1960s women in the United States and Great Britain made up a little over 30 percent of the college population, while in the USSR women made up well over 40 percent of the student population. While the proportion of women professionals remains small in most countries, the number of women in

---

[17] Women's Bureau, *1969 Handbook of Women Workers*, Bulletin 294, United States Department of Labor, Washington, D. C., 1969, p. 3.

[18] William J. Goode, "Industrialization and Family Structure," in Norman W. Bell and Ezra F. Vogel, *The Family*, rev. ed. (New York: Free Press, 1968), p. 118.

the professions in Sweden, Great Britain, the Soviet Union, and Israel has at least doubled during the past 20 years.

In Russia a woman would be expected to explain why she is *not* working while in the United States a woman is often expected to explain why she is working.[19] Russian women do not have the domestic help or the household appliances commonly taken for granted in the United States. Furthermore, Russian men, like other European men but unlike American men, typically do not, and are not expected to, help in the home.[20]

Sweden is probably the country most affected by feminist reform. In 1970, 14 percent of its parliamentary seats and two of its cabinet ministers were filled by women. Swedish women do such jobs as running cranes and driving cabs and buses. Fathers must support their children, although divorced women are expected to pay their own way. The schools have compulsory coeducational classes in metalwork, sewing, and child care. The new tax structure of Sweden is forcing many wives to go to work, and a start has been made on the development of day-care centers. A recent government-ordered revision of textbooks is expected to eliminate the stereotyped images of both sexes that have traditionally been presented.

The trend clearly has been one where societies have legislated reforms and altered the legal framework to provide economic opportunity for women. However, there is probably no modern society, with the possible exception of those of the Communist countries, "in which expectations of female-role behavior include a constellation keyed to women's participation in the productive and prestigious work of the economy."[21] In the United States the contribution of women to the economy is seen as secondary to that of men and as not equal in social worth to the contribution of men.

One expert on the family suggests that no family system granting full equality to women will emerge in the next generation, although the general position of women throughout the world will greatly improve. "The revolutionary philosophies which have accompanied the shifts in power in Communist countries or in the Israelic *kibbutzim* have asserted equality, and a significant stream of philosophic thought in the West has asserted the right to equality, but no society has yet granted it."[22] Goode goes on to argue that it is possible to create a society of full equality but that to do so would require radical reorganization of the social structure. A new socialization process would need to be developed because families continue to rear their daughters to take only a modest interest in careers

---

[19] Cynthia F. Epstein, *Woman's Place* (Berkeley: University of California Press, 1970), p. 43.

[20] Ibid., p. 103.

[21] Ibid., p. 46.

[22] Goode, "Family Structure," p. 119.

in which they would have equal responsibility with men.[23] Young girls continue to be reared in most societies to fill the secondary roles they have always filled.

AMERICAN WOMEN TODAY

An examination can now be made of the traditional roles of women as they are filled in the United States today. In this section our interest is in the traditional roles of wife, mother, and housekeeper. In the next section we will examine the work role of women and how that role is related to their traditional roles.

Wife role

The most modern and democratic view of the wife role is that of the colleague marriage. This type of marriage is not an association of complete equals but is based on the notion of the development of specializations within marriage. Both partners recognize that authority in various areas is vested in the role or in the interests and abilities of only one partner. This recognition allows each to defer to the other in different areas of competence, without loss of prestige. The division of labor in the colleague marriage is not based on a belief of complete differences between husband and wife roles, and often, if conditions demand, one partner can temporarily take over the other's role. But even in this setting various duties are sex assigned. While a husband might take over the washing of laundry if his wife were ill, in most cases she would reassume the duty as soon as she recovered. Even the most democratic marriage is generally one in which the husband has more privileges and does more of the things important and interesting to society.

An examination of power in marriage indicates differences for wives and husbands. It has been observed that women are often caught up in a vicious circle because their economic dependence on their husbands, their lack of contact with the work world, and their confinement to the home restrict to a great extent the kinds of decisions over which they can claim expertise and, ultimately, control. "Women, therefore, as a 'class' have not had the chance to obtain the 'resources,' skills and expertise that would allow them a share in most important types of family power."[24]

Mother role

Rossi has pointed out that in the United States for the first time in the history of any known society motherhood became a full-time occupation

---

[23] Ibid., p. 119.

[24] Constantina Safilios-Rothschild, *Toward a Sociology of Women* (Lexington, Mass.: Xerox College Publishing, 1972), p. 2.

for adult women.[25] In the past that was an impossibility because women then had far more things to do and more children to look after. Full-time motherhood came about as the result of technological development and economic affluence. Once full-time motherhood came about women were told how important it was, and the fact that mankind had previously functioned without it was generally forgotten. It seems clear that continuous mothering, even in the first few years of life, is not necessary for the healthy emotional development of the child. What is more important is the nature of the care rather than who provides it.

In fact there is strong evidence that not only is the full-time mother not necessary to the growth of the child but that she may create problems for her children. In a number of cases the etiology of mental illness is linked to inadequacies in the mother-child relationship. It is often the failure of the mother which perpetuates problems from one generation to the next that affect sons and daughters alike. Alice Rossi writes that full-time motherhood is neither sufficiently absorbing to the woman nor sufficiently beneficial to the child to justify the modern woman's devoting 15 or more years to it as her only occupation. "Sooner or later—and I think it should be sooner—women have to face the question of who they are besides their children's mother."[26]

Housekeeper role

Despite the development of inproved means for taking care of the home, many women have continued to spend as much time on household efforts as before. The American woman has often become subject to Parkinson's Law that "work expands to fill the time allotted for it." As cleaning aids have been improved, standards of cleanliness have been upgraded far beyond the thresholds of sanitation necessary for health.[27]

Regardless of the propaganda, housework is basically low-status work. This is reflected in a number of ways. Our society rewards occupational efforts with money, and yet housework is not within the money economy. In fact it is not always defined as real work. Many women who do not hold income-producing jobs will say that they don't work—they "only" take care of a house. Nancy Reeves has pointed out that a recent study of the mentally retarded reports that feeble-minded girls make exceptionally good housekeepers and nursemaids. "It should be added that they are also adequate sex partners and have the organic potential to reproduce themselves."[28]

---

[25] Rossi, "Equality between Sexes," p. 615.

[26] Ibid., p. 624.

[27] Epstein, *Woman's Place*, pp. 104–5.

[28] Nancy Reeves, *Womankind: Beyond the Stereotype* (Chicago: Aldine, 1971), p. 36.

Among women who work for money, domestic work is at the bottom of the occupational hierarchy. Young lower-class women prefer to work in offices and factories rather than to hire out and care for children and a house. Because they can't get domestic help, many middle-class women must do their housework themselves. So the low-prestige occupation of housework has become a major specialty of the educated woman.

Another reflection of how many women feel who take care of the house themselves is what they are willing to pay domestic workers. When the time comes to hire a woman they want to pay her the lowest salary possible. In fact many women who are quite liberal about increasing the pay of grape pickers are all for substandard wages for the domestics they hire. They often show their own low assessment of housework by saying that the women should be satisfied with the low pay because it is only housework.

There are persons of some respectability and influence who tell women how important housekeeping is. They change the name to homemaking because that sounds more creative. For example, one author writes that "homemaking during the early family years is a full-time job, and that the skills required are probably quite as exacting as those necessary in many of the professions."[29] What the professional skills of homemaking are she doesn't say. It appears that the efforts to sell women on housekeeping as a means of life fulfillment are failing in the middle class. Many women can understand housework as something that has to be done—but not as something that will give them any real personal satisfaction. Yet, the American system continues to socialize girls to want to grow up to fill the traditional roles. It is difficult to persuade high school girls to look beyond the goals of marriage and a family.

The value assigned to the housewife may vary with the different levels of the social class system. The upper-class system housewife may be much more highly valued in the overall social structure than is the lower-class housewife. Jean Acker suggests that it may be that the value of this position rises as its functions become more symbolic and less utilitarian. "Or, to put it another way, the value may rise as functions become centered more around consumption and less around productive activities."[30]

Traditional female roles in the family have been discussed for the middle class. However, there are some sharp differences between upper middle-class women and women in the lower middle and lower social classes. Most of the latter continue to live in a world that is patriar-

---

[29] Gladys E. Harbeson, *Choice and Challenge for the American Woman* (Cambridge, Mass.: Shenkman, 1967), p. 59.

[30] Joan Acker, "Women and Social Stratification: A Case of Intellectual Sexism," in Joan Huber, *Changing Women in a Changing Society* (Chicago: University of Chicago Press, 1973), p. 180.

chal—at least when the male is present. For many of them there is little in marriage that is shared between the husband and the wife. For example, Komarovsky found in her study of a working class group that the husband and wife shared little other than the immediate daily tasks. "The impoverishment of life and of personality curtails the development of shared interests."[31] In the sexual realm the great majority of the wives felt that men were more highly sexed than women. And less than a third of the women in her sample expressed high satisfaction with their sexual relations.[32]

Frequently in the lowest social class levels the husband participates very little, and the wife carries the responsibility for the home and the children largely by herself and seldom participates with her husband in outside activities. As Patricia Sexton writes, there is nothing "collective" about the working-class wife because she is basically unorganized. She is neither a joiner nor a participant. She may be quite religious but is much less likely to attend church regularly than her middle-class counterpart. She is virtually isolated from life outside the confines of her family and neighborhood.

Yet with all the restrictions on the life of lower-class women there does not appear to be a high degree of status frustration among them. They expect to be housewives—that is their reason for being and there is no real alternative. In her study of working-class housewives Komarovsky found hardly a trace of the low prestige that educated housewives attach to that role. Rarely did she find a woman saying, "I am just a housewife." The women were discontented, but this was not caused by a low evaluation placed on domesticity but rather by the frustrations of being a housewife.[33] Some of the women who expressed a dislike for housework felt guilty about their dislike of what they saw as the normal female responsibility. "Unlike some college-educated housewives who detest housework, our respondents never say that they are too good for it, that housework is unchallenging manual labor."[34]

MALE-FEMALE DIFFERENCES

Before we look at women in the work force and in occupational careers it is necessary to examine the basic differences between males and females. This is important because so much of the discrimination against the female has been and continues to be rationalized on the ground of unchangeable physical differences. It is argued here that almost all significant differences between the sexes can be explained on the basis of

---

[31] Mirra Komarovsky, *Blue-Collar Marriage* (New York: Random, 1962), p. 155.

[32] Ibid., p. 85.

[33] Komarovsky, *Blue-Collar Marriage*, p. 49.

[34] Ibid., p. 55.

differential socialization and that the effect of biological differences on the differential behavior patterns of the sexes has been greatly exaggerated.

It is obvious that men and women are somewhat different as sexual beings and often perform in complementary ways. However, there is no reason for believing that either sex is inherently dependent on the other for sexual satisfaction. Heterosexuality, homosexuality, and solitary sexuality are adaptations to sexual needs that are made by individuals. The vast majority of adults prefer heterosexuality as a means of sexual expression because they have been socialized to do so.

Probably the most important biological difference between men and women is the differential reproductive burden. The man is needed only to provide the sperm, and he doesn't even have to be present to do that, while in a normal pregnancy and birth the woman must carry the fetus for nine months. In the past many restrictions were placed on women during the pregnancy period. However, it seems clear that most women who have no pregnancy complications can work on most jobs with no more than a loss of a week or two for the birth of the child. Some flexibility could be set up to allow women to use vacation time to have children. So there is no reason why many women cannot pursue a career at the same time that they have children. It is common to argue that time off for pregnancy interferes with a career for women. Yet many men must also take time off for illnesses and other reasons, and this doesn't usually affect their careers. The point is that little that is inherent in the birth experience for women *necessarily* restricts them in the ways that have been used in the past.

Another common argument for differential treatment of women centers on the fact that the *average* woman is not as strong as the *average* man. That is, she has been excluded from certain jobs because it has been argued that she doesn't have the strength to do them. However, the range of physical strength among women is as wide as it is among men. This means that some women are stronger than some men. Strength, by sex, is not an absolute difference, but a relative one. Many times men are rejected from jobs because they are not strong enough. "Men only" becomes irrelevant; the job requirement should be simply the strength to qualify. In that way work would be available to individuals, regardless of sex, on the basis of abilities, skills, strengths, and motivation. Then a woman might be turned away from a job because she wasn't strong enough, but some men would also be turned away for the same reason.

It has also been argued that the physical differences of the sexes results in personality differences. A psychoanalytic view is that there are feminine personality types.[35] Yet, no personality traits found in women

---

[35] Clara Thompson, "Femininity," in Albert Ellis and Albert Abarbanel, *The Encyclopedia of Sexual Behavior* (New York: Hawthorn Books, 1961), p. 423.

are not also found in men. Once again it is a question of relative differences rather than absolute ones. And whatever being a woman means
is dependent on the socialization experience and what the individual
personality brings to bear. All of the so-called female personality traits are
found in some men and absent in many women.

In the United States male and female infants are immediately subjected to different socialization experiences. They are dressed differently
and are provided with toys seen as appropriate to their sex. As they grow
up, social values are often exerted on girls to be more gentle and
emotionally demonstrative than boys, but the differential socialization is
never total, and boys are sometimes reared like girls and vice-versa. The
impact of the socialization experience is clear. As boys and girls grow up,
they quickly learn that the male adult occupies the roles of greatest
prestige and influence. For example, seldom do even educated girls
develop a mental picture of a family basking in the glow of the mother's
achievement as a scientist or a judge unless she is also seen as a good
homemaker. No one asks whether a male Nobel prizewinner is also a good
father. But the headline in a recent article about a female Nobel
prizewinning scientist read "Grandmother Wins Award," as if having
grandchildren had some relevance to high professional achievement.[36]

It should also be pointed out that one of the most common arguments
against the equality of women is to ask why there are no great women in
the arts, science, and business. But as Linda Nochlin notes, "There have
been no great women artists, as far as we know—or any Lithuanian jazz
pianists, or Eskimo tennis players, no matter how much we might wish
there had been."[37] To condemn women for not having achieved what was
culturally impossible is erroneous and sexist.

An assumed difference between males and females has been an important part of the American historical heritage. Basically the difference
has been rationalized as not only inevitable but as desirable. The propaganda that women should marry early and breed often has prevailed.
The psychologists and psychiatrists have replaced clergymen as the
authorities. The most powerful intellectual influence has been that of
Freud. In this century the belief came to be that it was best for a woman
to become a mother, not because God said so but because Freud said so.[38]
Freud defined women as inferior human beings. The castration complex
and penis envy, two ideas basic to his thinking, were based on the belief
that women were inferior to men. Freud's view of women reflected the
times in which he lived. His middle-class world held highly conservative

[36] Epstein, *Woman's Place*, p. 66.

[37] Linda Nochlin, "Why Are There No Great Women Artists?" in Vivian Gornick and
Barbara K. Moran, *Women in Sexist Society* (New York: New American Library, 1971), p.
483.

[38] Sinclair, *Emancipation*, p. 359.

beliefs about the proper roles for men and women in marriage and society. Those beliefs have little validity for the kind of world that exists today. But the Freudian view continues to be perpetuated. For many years American women have been told through Freudian followers that there can be no greater destiny for women than through their traditional femininity. Women have been told to pity the neurotic, unfeminine, unhappy women who have wanted to be poets or physicians.[39]

Freud's followers generally have seen women in the same image as he did—as inferior and passive. They have argued that women will only find *real* self-fulfillment by affirming their natural inferiority. One of his followers writes that a woman must be willing to accept dependence on the male without fear or resentment and that she must not admit of wishes to control or master, to rival or dominate. "The woman who is to find true gratification must love and accept her own womanhood as she loves and accepts her husband's manhood. The woman's unconscious wish to possess the organ upon which she must thus depend militates greatly against her ability to accept its vast power to satisfy her when proffered to her in love."[40]

In recent years Freudian and other psychiatric interpretations have lumped the increased employment of women with many social and personal problems. Female employment has been linked with increased divorce, crime, and delinquency, and increased alcoholism and schizophrenia among women.[41] American society has also been inundated with the psychoanalytic viewpoint that any conflict in personal or family life must be treated on the individual level. "This goes with the general American value stress on individualism, and American women have increasingly resorted to psychotherapy, the most highly individualized solution of all, for the answers to the problems they have as women."[42] The psychiatric influence has been such that any problem is seen as individually based rather than socially determined. As a result many women who have felt miserable and unhappy as housewives have defined themselves as at fault or inadequate rather than recognizing that in many cases they are victims of social situations.

While the Freudian influence in the thinking about women has declined in recent years, there have been other "intellectual" spokesmen for the view that woman's place is in the home. Both Dr. Spock and Dr. Bettelheim in books and in their advice columns in popular women's

---

[39] Friedan, *Feminine Mystique*, pp. 15–16.

[40] Ferdinand Lundberg, and Marynia Farnham, "Woman: The Lost Sex," in Edwin Schur, *The Family and The Sexual Revolution* (Bloomington: Indiana University Press, 1964), p. 230.

[41] F. Ivan Nye, and Lois W. Hoffman, *The Employed Mother in America* (Chicago: Rand McNally, 1963), p. 7.

[42] Rossi, "Equality between Sexes," p. 613.

magazines have argued that women should not be employed during their children's early years. "Thus the mothers not only have difficulty finding good care for their children but they also feel guilty about it."[43] Only the literature of the women's liberation movement has presented women with information that counteracts the traditional views of woman's place.

Another area of difference across sex lines is the greater extent of problems related to mental health among women than among men. But this can be understood within the context of social values. There are several reasons to assume that the roles women usually fill are more likely to produce emotional problems. The most important reason is that many women are restricted to the single social role of housewife. If a woman finds that role unsatisfactory she usually has no alternative source of gratification. By contrast a man is more likely to have other role options if one of his roles is unsatisfactory.[44]

Women's greater role restrictions have several important consequences. For example, there is considerable evidence that women have more negative images of themselves than do men. There is also evidence that women are more likely than men to become depressed. The overall evidence on first admissions to mental hospitals, psychiatric treatment in general hospitals, psychiatric outpatient clinics, private outpatient care, and the practices of general physicians, as well as the evidence provided by community surveys all indicate that more women than men are mentally ill.[45] These findings reflect the consequences for women of living in a society of inequality in available roles.

WOMEN AND WORK

In one respect the general disregard of women's significance in the work force is seen in the fact that women are rarely, if ever, mentioned in the academic literature that deals with work and occupations. When they are considered it is almost always within the context of the family structure. That is, they are characterized as *still* single, as the secondary jobholder in an *organized* family, or as the major jobholder in a *disorganized* family.

It should also be recognized that female labor today is, as it has been for decades, a marginal section of the labor force. In this respect the current increase of women in the work force cannot be interpreted as progress because the provisional status of female labor has not been altered.[46] A sharp economic depression would probably eliminate most of the gains of working women.

---

[43] Epstein, *Woman's Place*, pp. 109–10.

[44] Walter R. Gove and Jeanette F. Tudor, "Adult Sex Roles and Mental Illness," in Huber, *Changing Women*, p. 52.

[45] Ibid., p. 69.

[46] Reeves, *Womankind*, p. 57.

About nine out of ten women work outside the home at some time during their lives. In general marriage and the presence of children tend to limit female employment, while widowhood, divorce, and decreased family responsibility tend to bring women back into the work force.[47] The percentage of women in the work force has steadily increased over the years. In 1900 only 18 percent of all workers were women; in 1940, 25 percent; and in 1968, 37 percent.[48] Furthermore, in 1968, 42 percent of all women of working age were in the work force, and of that group three out of five were married. Put another way, in 1972 40 percent of all married women were in the work force. The highest rates of participation in the work force among married women existed where the husband's income was in the lower range of middle-income levels. The rate then declined as the husband's income reached higher levels. About two fifths of all married women, and many single women as well, were both homemakers and workers. "During an average workweek in 1968, 50 percent of all women were keeping house full time, and about 42 percent were either full or part-time workers. Most of the remainder were girls 16 to 20 years of age who were in school."[49]

There have been changes in the life-cycle work patterns of women. In 1900, if a woman worked at all during her lifetime it was usually only before marriage and children, and the proportion employed declined steadily with age. By contrast, in 1970 between 49 and 54 percent of women in the 35–59 age group were in the labor force. Also, the number of years in the work force has increased greatly. The work expectancy for women born in 1900 was 6.3 years; for those born in 1940, 12.1 years; in 1950, 15.2 years, and in 1960, 20.1.[50]

Working mothers with children under 18 years of age represented 38 percent of all mothers in the population and 38 percent of all women workers. Of those mothers who worked (with at least one child under 14 years of age), 46 percent of the children were cared for in their own homes, with 15 percent looked after by their fathers, 21 percent by other relatives, and 9 percent by maids, housekeepers, or baby-sitters. Another 16 percent of the children were cared for outside their own homes, about half by relatives. Thirteen percent were looked after by their mothers while they worked, and 15 percent had mothers who worked only during school hours. Eight percent of the children were expected to care for themselves, while only 2 percent were in group-care units, such as day-care centers, nursery schools, and after-school centers.[51]

Of great importance with reference to women who work is their in-

---

[47] Women's Bureau, *1969 Handbook*, p. 7.

[48] Ibid., p. 9.

[49] Ibid., p. 12.

[50] Women's Bureau, "Facts About Women's Absenteeism and Labor Turnover," in Nona Glazer-Malbin and Helen Youngelson Wachrer, *Woman in a Man-Made World* (Chicago: Rand McNally, 1972), p. 267.

[51] Women's Bureau, *1969 Handbook*, p. 49.

come relative to that of men. In 1966 year-round, full-time woman workers had a median income or salary of $3,973, while men had a median income of $6,848. Not only is the income of women considerably less than that of men, but the gap has been widening in recent years. In 1956, among full-time, year-round workers, women earned 63 percent of what man earned; in 1966, only 58 percent.[52]

Not only does a woman earn less than a man for doing the same job, but she is also subjected to greater taxes and other working costs. The woman's income is slashed by the government's refusal to recognize household and child-care expenses as essential business deductions. In addition to paying between 20 and 50 percent of her income for domestic help, she must also pay income tax on the higher bracket into which her second salary places the family. It is estimated that if a husband earns $10,000 and a wife $5,000 the wife's contribution to the net family income would be only $2,175, and she couldn't afford full-time domestic help with that amount. Or if the husband earns $15,000 and the wife earns $10,000, the wife, after paying for nondeductible domestic help, will add only $650 to the yearly family income.[53]

More specific facts about the American work force and some variables related to women's participation are of interest here. Before the industrial revolution most men and women were co-workers on the land and in the home. But the industrial revolution removed work for most men from the home and separated them both psychologically and physically from the home. The same industrial processes that separated men's work from the home also provided the opportunities for women to work outside the home. In one sense the entrance of married women into the work force is a resumption of the part they played in the past as co-workers of their husbands. It should be recognized that the Victorian notion that a man's work alone should support his family continues to be accepted. Yet, when this notion emerged it was a new one in human history.

Education is also related to female employment. The more education women have the more likely they are to be in the work force. In March 1970, 34 percent of all wives who had 11 years or less of education were working. This compared with 44 percent of those who had completed high school and 47 percent of those with one year or more of college. The more education women bring to their jobs the higher their earnings.[54] But they earn less than men with the same education and type of job.

As mentioned previously, when women began to enter the work force in large numbers the belief developed that their husbands and children suffered as a result. Nye and Hoffman, in their extensive study of working

---

[52] Ibid., pp. 133–34.

[53] Julie Ellis, *The Revolt of the Second Sex* (New York: Lancer Books, 1970), p. 161.

[54] Elizabeth Waldman and Anne M. Young, "Marital and Family Characteristics of Workers, 1970," *Monthly Labor Review*, March 1971, p. 46.

women, found that some problems in the husband-wife relationship were associated with the woman's working. These may have been due to the husband's view that he should be the only family wage earner and to his feeling that having his wife work threatened his masculinity. But it may also be that some women entered employment because they were already dissatisfied with their marriage relationship.

Research indicates that the reasons wives work can have an impact on their marriages. One large study of four different communities found that marital happiness was lower for both partners when the wife worked only because she needed the money rather than by choice. When a wife works out of necessity, the husband has greater negative feelings in marriage and the wife sees a significant reduction in the positive side of marriage, especially in sociability with her husband.[55]

Nye and Hoffman found that none of the studies they examined showed any meaningful differences between the children of working mothers and the children of nonworking mothers.[56] Alice Rossi came to the same conclusion. She reports that children of working mothers are no more likely than children of nonworking mothers to become delinquent, to show neurotic symptoms, to feel deprived of maternal affection, to perform poorly in school, to lead narrower social lives, and so on.[57]

Another study found that adolescents' perceptions of parental interest, parental help with school and personal problems, and closeness to parents were largely unrelated to their mothers' employment status. This serves as evidence against the belief that parents are more likely to reject their children or to deny them emotional support because the mother is working. As Margaret Poloma points out, while there is no evidence from existing research that working mothers as a group are better mothers than those who do not work, the data do suggest that professionally employed women perceive their employment as making them better mothers than they would otherwise have been.[58]

Career women

We now look more directly at women who pursue occupations in the same way as most men, that is, as a potential lifework to which they will have a long-range commitment. In the past most American women have been interested in jobs, not careers. This is the primary reason why the United States, with one of the highest proportions of working women in

[55] Norman M. Bradburn and David Caplovitz, *Reports on Happiness* (Chicago: Aldine, 1965), p. 399.

[56] Nye and Hoffman, *Employed Mother*, p. 141.

[57] Rossi, "Equality between Sexes," p. 615.

[58] Margaret M. Poloma, "Role Conflict and the Married Professional Women," in Safilios-Rothschild, *Sociology of Women*, p. 191.

the world, has only a very small proportion of women in such professions as medicine, law, and the sciences. To argue, as many feminists have, that men have opposed and resisted the opening of career opportunities to women is only partly true. The complete truth is that American society in general, including women, has shunned like a disease any feminist ideology directed at high occupational commitment.[59]

An absolute requirement for entering most careers is that the individual have the formal education necessary for qualification. Therefore, it is important to look at how women in higher education fare as compared to men. In general, in most families there continues to be a somewhat greater stress on having the boy going to college. However, once girls enter college their chances of staying in are the same as those of boys. The college dropout ratio is the same, about four out of ten who enter. However, the reasons for dropping out are different. Boys are more apt to leave school because of academic problems or difficulties in their personal adjustment, while the most common reason girls drop out is to get married.

At the present time just about half of all high school graduates are girls, while in 1900 girls represented 60 percent of all high school graduates. The percentage of all bachelor's degrees going to women has been steadily increasing. In 1900, females received only 19 percent; in 1970, 41 percent.[60] As to higher degrees, there has been little change in the percentage of women receiving masters or doctorates since 1930.[61]

A disproportionate number of college women have sought their degrees in certain subject areas. Jessie Bernard points out that a field like political science, which emphasizes power, attracts relatively few women, whereas anthropology, "at least where it emphasizes kinship more than kingship, finds much more place for women."[62] Thus, although only 12 percent of doctorates are earned by women their share in certain fields has been considerably higher. Women received 20 percent of the doctorates conferred in 1967 in education, in the humanities, and the arts, and 19 percent of the doctorates in psychology. "On the other hand, although half of all doctoral degrees conferred in 1967 in the United States were in the basic and applied sciences, the women's share was only 6 percent."[63]

One consequence of achieving higher education is a greater interest in entering the work force. Not very many women who receive a higher education are going to be satisfied never to use it in any occupational

---

[59] Degler, "Revolution without Ideology," p. 665.

[60] Epstein, *Woman's Place*, p. 57.

[61] Women's Bureau, *1969 Handbook*, p. 191.

[62] Bernard, *Academic Women*, p. xx.

[63] Women's Bureau, *1969 Handbook*, p. 198.

way. So the more education a woman receives the more likely she is to seek employment, irrespective of her financial status. "The educated woman desires to contribute her skills and talents to the economy not only for the financial rewards, but even more to reap the psychic rewards that come from achievement and recognition and service to society."[64] In 1968, 71 percent of all women 18 years of age and over who had completed five years of college or more and 54 percent of those who had earned only a bachelor's degree were in the work force. The percentage dropped to 48 percent for women who had graduated high school and to 31 percent for women who had not gone beyond the eighth grade.[65] A study of 10,000 Vassar alumnae showed that in the mid-1950s most graduates wanted marriage, with or without a career, while in the mid-1960s graduates were strongly insisting on careers—with or without marriage.[66]

What kind of occupations do women enter? A large proportion of the women in the work force hold low-skilled clerical jobs. And the women who enter professional careers tend to go into teaching, nursing, social work, and related occupations. These are commonly seen by both men and women as occupations appropriate to the "special" qualities of women. However, what is defined as appropriate work for men or women changes over time. For example, during the colonial period elementary school teaching was seen as a male occupation, supposedly because women did not have the necessary stamina of mind to educate the young. Or, one rarely hears of an American woman dentist, yet 75 percent of the dentists of Denmark are women, and dentistry is considered to be a female occupation in some South American countries.[67]

Whatever the specific occupation it is clear that if women are given the chance to pursue satisfying careers they pursue them just as consistently as men. For example, the percentage of law degree and medical degree holders who are in practice is about the same for both women and men.[68]

The cultural definitions of the professions as linked to one sex or the other are often based on what are believed to be special sex-linked characteristics. In illustration, many times women are thought to be good elementary school teachers because as females they are believed to have compassion, sympathy, and a feeling for children that men do not have. Or, as Epstein points out, in the same way that blacks are said to be good jazz musicians because they "have rhythm" so women are encouraged to become social workers because they are said to have "intuition" and a gift

---

[64] Ibid., p. 9.

[65] Ibid., p. 205.

[66] Ellis, *Revolt of Second Sex*, p. 8.

[67] Epstein, *Woman's Place*, pp. 157–58.

[68] Elizabeth Waldman, "Changes in the Labor Force Activity of Women," in Glazer-Malbin and Waehrer, *Woman* p. 33.

for handling interpersonal relations. The image of women also includes some noncharacteristics: "lack of aggression, lack of personal involvement and egotism, lack of persistence (unless it be for the benefit of a family member), and lack of ambitious drive."[69] The career woman who is seen as having many of the above characteristics often has been viewed as the antithesis of the feminine woman.

How women perceive themselves and their careers is also important. One woman observer from the business world says that the difference between the women who have "made it" and those who have not makes it clear that the women who *have* behave as if they expected to be treated equal. "They know the myths about women, but they do not believe them."[70]

Randall Collins has argued that women constitute the subordinate class in a system of sexual stratification. What is meant is that the principle of the system is that women take orders from men but do not give orders to them. Hence only men can give orders to other men, and women can give orders only to other women. This is seen in the fact that professional women are concentrated in specialties in which they deal mainly with children or other women, rarely with men of high status. The highest ranking women's job is likely to be president of a women's college or mother superior of an order of nuns. Similarly, women can be given high status as actresses or singers, but not as movie directors or symphony conductors, because actresses and singers do not give orders to anyone.[71]

In some occupations with a large proportion of women, men have been replacing women in the positions of power and influence. For example, the decline in the percentage of female elementary school principals has been very great. In 1928, 55 percent of the principals were women; in 1948, 41 percent; in 1958, 38 percent; and in 1968 the figure was reported to have dropped to 22 percent.[72] The assumption seems to be that while a woman can be a teacher she is not qualified to administer a school. In many occupations women are employed as professional field workers, whether teachers, social workers, or nurses, but the administrative positions are filled by men. As Epstein points out, "No matter what sphere of work women are hired for or select, like sediment in a wine bottle they seem to settle to the bottom."[73]

One common myth is that women leave their jobs more often or take more time off than do men. But the evidence indicates that women

---

[69] Ibid., p. 22.

[70] Roslyn S. Willett, "Working in a Man's World: The Woman Executive," in Gornick and Moran, *Women*, p. 514.

[71] Randall Collins, "A Conflict Theory of Sexual Stratification," *Social Problems*, Summer 1971, p. 5.

[72] Epstein, *Woman's Place*, p. 10.

[73] Ibid., p. 2.

workers have favorable records of attendance and labor turnover as compared to men employed at the same job levels and under similar circumstances. A Public Health Service survey of time lost from work by persons 17 years of age and over because of illness or injury shows an average of 5.6 days lost by women and 5.3 days lost by men during a calendar year.[74]

Because the career woman, whether married or single, is filling a social role with a great amount of social confusion, she is defined by others in a variety of ways. For example, many housewives see the career woman as a threat to themselves. "The career woman is often seen as a competitor for their husbands (the working woman, though deprecated, also seems more glamorous—and often is, because she usually takes care of her appearance and is more interesting). The career also provides an alternative model to the domestic life and may cause the housewife to question her own choice of life style."[75] If the career woman is married and a mother and gives the appearance of being happy and satisfied with her life, she often becomes a severe threat to the woman who has rejected a career and is not very happy with her life.

Many men react to career women with confusion. If the woman is attractive, they can't quite cope with her as a nonsexual being. Because so many men are geared to seeing women primarily as sexual objects they find it very difficult to see them as something more. It is probably also true that many American men are uneasy in the presence of highly intelligent women in a way which they would not be with very intelligent men. But most men probably react to career women as potential threats to themselves, and in this sense their opposition is based not on ideology but on vested interest. "Because men typically have more power, they suspect and fear encroachment on that power. The situation is, of course, analogous to the fears of whites about retaining job priorities in the face of advancing opportunities for Negroes."[76]

Very often women who choose both marriage and career find their situation one in which the norms are confused and unclear. There are no clear guidelines that a woman can use to apportion her time and resources between her major role responsibilities. The ability to handle the roles of wife, mother, and career is still for the most part a matter of individual adaptation. So while fewer career women today are spinsters, among those who marry there is a high rate of divorce. "The proportion of divorced professional women is substantially higher than that of professional men."[77]

There have been some recent studies of families in which both partners

---

[74] Women's Bureau, "Women's Absenteeism," p. 266.

[75] Epstein, *Woman's Place*, p. 120.

[76] Ibid., pp. 17–18.

[77] Ibid., p. 48.

are involved in professional careers. There is some evidence that husbands
support the wives' careers. Generally the women choose a career for
personal rewards and expect their husbands to adjust. The husbands
frequently support the wives' independence. Husbands also show pride in
their wives' accomplishments and individuality. "Often the husbands
were more interested in getting their wives involved in careers than were
the women themselves."[78]

Another study found that some restrictions were seen by the woman in
a dual-career marriage. Garland found that in no instance did a wife
want to be more successful than her husband. When career women had
children guilt feelings did occur, but they were occasional and situational
rather than overriding. "Very few mothers revealed any signs of being
guilt-ridden and all such cases were employed on a full-time basis and
because of the family's economic need."[79] But, among the husbands, the
most commonly cited benefit of the dual-career marriage was that the
wife's professional involvement made her happier and a more interesting
marriage partner.[80]

Alice Rossi has argued that these role problems can be worked out by
what she calls socially androgynous roles for men and women. These
would be roles in which the husband and wife were equal and similar in
such spheres as intellectual, artistic, political, and occupational interests
and participation. The two would be complementary only in those
spheres required by physiological differences between the sexes. "An
androgynous conception of sex role means that each sex will cultivate
some of the characteristics usually associated with the other in traditional
sex role definitions."[81] Rossi goes on to point out that this is a point of
contrast with the early feminist goals. That is, rather than a one-sided
plea for women to adapt a masculine stance in the world, "this definition
of sex equality stresses the enlargement of the common ground on which
men and women have their lives together by changing the social
definition of approved characteristics and behavior of both sexes."[82] This
suggestion is based on the assumption that men and women can work out
a solution together and that there is no inherent incompatibility between
the male and the female that cannot be worked out. However, this assumption is not shared by some of the present-day feminists in the
women's liberation movement.

---

[78] Catherine C. Arnott, "Husbands' Attitudes and Wives' Commitment to Employment," *Journal of Marriage and the Family*, November 1972, p. 683.

[79] T. Neal Garland, "The Better Half? The Male in the Dual Professional Family," in
Safilios-Rothschild, *Sociology of Woman*, p. 714.

[80] Ibid., pp. 713–14.

[81] Rossi, "Equality between Sexes," p. 608.

[82] Ibid., p. 608.

THE WOMEN'S LIBERATION MOVEMENT

There is a risk about an emerging movement because what is happening at a given time can soon become obsolete. However, the women's liberation movement is so important that it should be looked at even though it is in a state of emergence. The movement has a long history, and one of the purposes of this chapter has been to provide a background for looking at the contemporary women's liberation movement. Basically the movement wants complete equality for women and it wants it fast. This makes its basic aims the same as those of the black militant movement. The new militant feminism has taken hold in territory that at first glance looks like an unlikely breeding ground for revolutionary ideas, "among urban, white, college educated, middle-class women generally considered to be a rather 'privileged lot.'"[83] As the movement developed in the late 1960s, it came out of two primary influences. The first was the influence of Betty Friedan's book *The Feminine Mystique*, published in 1963. The second was the influence on young women of the civil rights and radical left movements.

Friedan's influence

Through the 1950s and into the 1960s there was little in the way of a feminist movement in the United States. During those years no one argued about whether women were inferior or superior; they were simply seen as different. Women during that period were assumed to be happy being wives and mothers. Given the great influence of psychoanalytic thought, it was assumed that if a woman felt frustrated she had a personal problem and that if she could work her problem out she could once again be happy doing what women should do. During that period words like *emancipation* and *career* sounded strange and embarrassing; no one had used them for years.[84] It should be remembered that the 1950s were conservative years in American history. The period was characterized by the political conservatism of McCarthyism, student complacency, and the benevolent paternalism of the Eisenhower administration. When Betty Friedan's book appeared it sold in large numbers and brought forth great indignation from the traditional and conservative forces of society.

The major thesis if Friedan's book is that the core problem of women is not sexuality but the problem of personal identity. She wrote, "It is my thesis that as the Victorian culture did not permit women to accept or gratify their basic sexual needs, our culture does not permit women to

---

[83] Susan Brownmiller, "Sisterhood Is Powerful," *New York Times*, March 15, 1970, p. 27.

[84] Friedan, *Feminine Mystique*, p. 19.

accept or gratify their basic needs to grow and fulfill their potentialities as human beings, a need which is not solely defined by their sexual roles." She went on to say that there was growing evidence that woman's failure to develop to complete identity had hampered rather than enriched her sexual fulfillment and that this "virtually doomed her to be castrative to her husband and sons, and caused neuroses, or problems as yet unnamed as neuroses, equal to those caused by sexual repression."[85]

For Friedan work was the means by which women could achieve identity. She felt that work was the key to the problem because the identity crisis of American women had started a century before, as "more and more of the work that used their human abilities and through which they were able to find self-realization, was taken from them."[86] She said that one of the first things women must do was to reject the housewife image. "The first step in that plan is to see housework for what it is—not a career, but something that must be done as quickly and efficiently as possible."[87]

In the years following the publication of her book Betty Friedan was the most influential spokeswoman for what little female rebellion did exist. The passage of the Civil Rights Act of 1964 make it clear to a number of women that there was a need for a civil rights organization that would speak out for women. In June 1966 Betty Friedan and a number of other women founded NOW (National Organization for Women). Its purpose was to take action that would bring women into full participation in the mainstream of American society by giving them all the privileges and responsibilities necessary to make them completely equal to men. In August 1967 NOW organized its first picket line. The members dressed in old-fashioned costumes to protest the old-fashioned policies of the *New York Times* in its male and female help wanted ads. They handed out thousands of leaflets and were for the first time featured on television news and given wide mass media coverage.

The big issues for NOW came to be: (1) Passage of the Equal Rights Amendment, which had been kicking around Congress since 1923. The amendment states: "Equality of rights under the law shall not be denied or abridged by the United States or by any state on account of sex." (2) Abortion law repeal. (3) Day-care centers for everyone. (4) Equal employment opportunities and equal pay for equal work.[88] The NOW group includes men who are concerned about the civil rights of women. However, the more radical groups in the women's liberation movement do not accept men, whether or not they are sympathetic to the cause.

---

[85] Ibid., p. 77.

[86] Ibid., p. 334.

[87] Ibid., p. 342.

[88] Ellis, *Revolt of Second Sex*, pp. 47–48.

Civil rights and the radical left

The Betty Friedan influence on the women's liberation movement has had its greatest appeal among older and less radical women. By contrast many of the younger and more radical women have come out of the civil rights and radical left movements. And some of the terms they use are a reflection of their origin. For example, *sexist* is a women's liberation term for a male supremist, and its similarity to *racist* is clear. This was inevitable in a movement that drew much of its rhetoric and spirit from the civil rights revolution and that, like America's first feminist movement, evolved out of the effort to liberate blacks.

Jo Freeman says that 1967 was the crucial year. That was the year in which the blacks threw the whites out of the civil rights movement, student power was made suspect by Students for a Democratic Society, (SDS), and the organized New Left was fading out. Only the draft resistance movement was on the rise. "And this movement more than any other exemplified the social inequalities of the sexes. Men could resist the draft; women could only counsel resistance."[89]

Yet many young women left the other movements because they found that often the men in them were as chauvinistic as the men in more conservative groups. As "movement women" they were tired of doing the typing and fixing the food while "movement men" did the writing and leading. For example, during the student takeover at Columbia University a call went out for women volunteers to cook for the hungry strikers. One young female revolutionary protested that "women are not fighting the revolution to stay in the kitchen," and the call was amended to ask for *people* to staff the kitchen.[90] Many movement women were living with or married to movement men who, they believed, were treating them as convenient sex objects or as somewhat lesser beings. This is illustrated by an often quoted statement of Stokely Carmichael to the Student Nonviolent Coordinating Committee (SNCC) that "the position of women in our movement should be prone." Many young radical women therefore felt that the radical men were taking a condescending approach to women's problems and that it was up to the women to do something about those problems.

So the radical women's liberation groups are made up only of women, although many of their tactics have been borrowed from the radical left and from civil rights groups. It is common in the women's liberation literature to see analogies drawn between the problems of blacks and the problems of women and between the civil rights movement and the women's liberation movement. This, as has been suggested throughout this

---

[89] Jo Freeman, "The Origins of the Women's Liberation Movement," in Huber, *Changing Women*, p. 40.

[90] Epstein, *Woman's Place*, p. 34.

chapter, has been an historical characteristic of the feminist movement in the United States. Morton Hunt, in a *Playboy* article, has argued that this analogy is misleading. He says that whites and blacks do not have innate differences that commit them to different roles in education, politics, employment, and so forth. However, men and women can eliminate all role differences "only by ignoring and suppressing a vital part of their inherent natures and by accepting the frustration that results from unmet needs and unfulfilled desires."[91] However, there is no clear evidence of different "inherent natures," and Hunt's arguments in the *Playboy* piece are really those of a male chauvinist, sophisticated but nevertheless chauvinistic. No one would deny that there is a biological basis for blackness, but no one argues that blackness should be treated with a biological solution. In the same sense sex is also a biological fact but a social problem.

There are other ways in which the radical women's liberation groups are believed to resemble the militant black groups. Many liberation women feel that, like the blacks with their Uncle Toms, they are hampered by an enormous fifth column of women, referred to as "Aunt Tabbies" or "Doris Days." Also like the blacks, the militant women are asking that their "hidden history" be taught in schools and colleges. The intellectuals in the movement are challenging many of the psychiatrists, psychologists, sociologists, and anthropologists who have espoused the theory that for women their "anatomy is their destiny."[92]

In 1969 and 1970 a wide range of women's liberation groups developed. The most conservative was NOW, and the spectrum moved leftward to the highly radical and revolutionary groups. Groups now in existence besides NOW are FLF (Female Liberation Front), W.I.T.C.H. (Women's International Terrorist Conspiracy from Hell), the Redstockings, and so forth. The revolt is growing rapidly, and "instead of Lucy Stone in bloomers, we have Abby Rockefeller in bare feet, dungarees and workshirt."[93]

Barbara Polk describes the radical groups as independent, and typically they are composed of no more than 10 to 15 women who come together in "consciousness-raising" or "rap" groups for the purpose of developing their own understanding of the condition of women on the basis of their own experiences. These groups acquired from their radical antecedents the belief that structures are always conservative and confining.[94]

---

[91] Morton Hunt, "Up against the Wall, Male Chauvinistic Pig," *Playboy*, May 1970, p. 207.

[92] Ellis, *Revolt of Second Sex*, pp. 9–10.

[93] Ibid., p. 19.

[94] Barbara Bovee Polk, "Women's Liberation: Movement for Equality," in Safilios-Rothschild, *Sociology of Women*, p. 322.

The loosely defined rap groups have been very successful at changing individual attitudes. But they have not been very successful in dealing with social institutions. Individual rap groups often flounder when their members have used up the possibilities of consciousness-raising and decide that they want to do something more concrete. "The problem is that most groups are unwilling to change their structure when they change their tasks. They have accepted the ideology of 'structurelessness' without realizing its limitations."[95]

The ultimate goal of the radical groups is revolution. As one radical journal writes, revolution must occur because the condition of female oppression does not "depend on," is not "integrated to," the structure of society; it is the structure. "The oppression of women, though similar to that of blacks, differs from it in that it depends not on class division but rather on a division of labor premised on private property and resulting in the family as the primary unit for the function of the economy."[96]

Another radical liberation group, the FLM, through its journal, *No More Fun and Games*, urges women to leave their husbands and children and to avoid pregnancy. It also wants women to dress plainly and simply, to cut their hair very short, and to "reclaim themselves" by discarding their husbands' or fathers' names. The journal also urges women to live alone and to abstain from sexual relations. FLM women refrain from wearing makeup—though chapstick and hand lotion (for karate calluses) are allowed.[97]

All of the liberation groups see the present conjugal family structure with its traditional division of labor as destructive to full female identity. Much of the focus has been on alleviating the burdens of housework and on getting help through free collective child care. The more radical groups, such as the FLM, have contempt for the family. Roxanne Dunbar, a leader of that group, writes: "The family is what destroys people. Women take on a slave role in the family when they have children. People have awful relationships. It's a trap, because you can't support it without a lot of money."[98] Another spokeswoman writes that marriage, which is made to seem attractive and inevitable, is a trap for female children as well as mothers. "Most women do not grow up to see themselves as producers, as creators—instead they see their mothers, their sisters, their women teachers, and they pattern themselves after them. They do not see women making history."[99] Still another spokeswoman, Ti-Grace Atkinson, said at a women's liberation conference in New York

[95] Freeman, "Women's Liberation," p. 47.

[96] "I am Furious (Female)," *Radical Education Project*, Detroit, Michigan (no date).

[97] Ellis, *Revolt of Second Sex*, p. 54.

[98] Ibid., pp. 54–55.

[99] Laurel Limpus, *Sexual Repression and The Family* (Boston: New England Free Press, 1970), p. 65.

City that the prostitutes were the only honest women left in America because they charged for their services rather than submit to a marriage contract which would force them to work for life without pay.[100]

It seems clear that for most groups in the women's liberation movement marriage is a relationship which makes the woman subservient and secondary. The possible solutions range from ending marriage to modifying it. It also seems clear that many men also believe that a married woman is a second-class citizen. For example, in the recent article on the women's liberation movement in *Playboy*, Morton Hunt wrote that in the foreseeable future the most workable answer for the American woman—"the scheme of life that most nearly fits her own needs and those of the American man—is a combination of marriage and career in which she accepts a secondary part in the world of work and achievement in order to have a primary part in the world of love and home."[101] This statement is a good example of the kind of male thinking that women's liberations groups of all types are fighting against.

Another role activity which many feminists object to is that of motherhood. They rebel against the belief that childbearing and child rearing are the fulfillment of a woman's destiny. Limpus writes that this belief is by far the most damaging and destructive of the myths that imprison women. Having children is no substitute for creating one's own life, for producing. And since so many women in this culture devote themselves to nothing else, they end up becoming intolerable burdens upon their children, because in fact those children are their whole lives.[102] The women are objecting to the fact that not only is there a mystique about parenthood but that the mystique *really* equates motherhood with parenthood. People frequently say how important a father is to his children, but the empirical evidence shows that when the father is absent the children suffer no more psychological problems than when the father is present. However, no one has ever studied those families where no mother is present and the children are reared by the father. It may be that those children are not significantly different from children reared by a mother.

Most women's liberation groups are not opposed to women's having children if they so desire. What they object to is the woman's being required to fill the mother role and care for the children. The liberation women insist that society should take care of the children. They argue that child-care centers are needed not just for women at the poverty level but for all working women, and that they should be used in the same way as any other public facilities, such as museums, libraries, or parks. At the present time the United States is the only industrialized country which

---

[100] *Philadelphia Bulletin*, May 29, 1970, p. 2.

[101] Hunt, "Up against the Wall," p. 209.

[102] Limpus, *Sexual Repression*, p. 66.

does not provide child-care services. There are close to 4 million children in the United States who need supervision while their mothers work, and the present facilities can handle less than half a million.

Because most members of women's liberation groups see themselves as women who have been sexually exploited by men, there is a great deal of concern with sexual participation with men and what it means. Yet, in the areas of male-female interaction women have felt freer in recent years to speak of their rights in the sexual sphere than in the social sphere. And, as suggested earlier, sexual rights for women have been gained, and increasingly women have been obtaining the means of sexual equality. In fact the right of women to sexual equality is now established and even treated as acceptable in the mass media. For example, such conservative national women's publications as *Ladies' Home Journal* and *McCall's* carry articles almost every month dealing with some aspects of sex in detailed clarity.[103]

However, the objection that many liberation women have to sex is how it is used to manipulate both men and women by various agencies in society. Much of the resentment results from the fact that women feel that they are being treated as sexual objects by men. "Fashion, advertising, movies, *Playboy Magazine*, all betray the fact that women are culturally conceived of as objects and still worse, often accept this definition and try to make themselves into a more desirable commodity on the sexual market."[104] The objection is not that females or males make themselves sexually attractive but rather that the mass media focus on the sexual attractiveness of the woman and do not present her as a human being.

One writer for the women's liberation movement, a sociologist, sees the problem of sexuality as a dual one. When she speaks of women's liberation, she refers to liberation from the myths that have enslaved women in their own minds as well as in the minds of others. "Men and women are mutually oppressed by a culture and a heritage that mutilates the relationships possible between them."[105] She further suggests that the problem of sexuality illustrates that men and women are oppressed together. She argues that women shouldn't become obsessed with freeing themselves from sick male sexuality, but rather that it is more important for both males and females to free themselves from structures that make them sexually sick. "The male definition of virility which makes women an object of prey is just as much a mutilation of the human potential of the male for the true love relationship as it is the female's." Limpus goes on to say that even though it is women who experience the predatory attitude they also contribute to it. "We must both be liberated together, and we must understand the extent to which our fear and frigidity, which

---

[103] Epstein, *Women's Place*, p. 37.

[104] Limpus, *Sexual Repression*, p. 70.

[105] Ibid., p. 61.

had been inculcated in most of us from infancy onwards and against which most of us have had to struggle for our sexual liberation, has hurt and mutilated them."[106]

Limpus further points out that the socialization to female sexual repression is so strong that even highly liberated women cannot completely shake their earlier restrictive sexual training. She observes that even in supposedly radical circles girls can still be labeled "promiscuous." "There are tremendous residual moral condemnations of female sexuality in all of us, in spite of our radical rhetoric. A woman, even a relatively sexually liberated one, often finds it hard to approach a man sexually the way a man can approach her."[107]

Probably the most publicized and most important statement about sexual expression made in the women's liberation movement is Anne Koedt's "The Myth of the Vaginal Orgasm." Koedt points out that frigidity has usually been defined by men to mean that women have failed to have a vaginal orgasm. The myth of the vaginal orgasm has been perpetuated primarily by psychoanalysts. In actual fact the vagina is not a highly sensitive area and is not physiologically constructed to achieve orgasm. All physiologically based orgasms in the female come from the clitoris. Koedt points out that men have orgasms primarily through friction of the penis with the vagina, not with the clitoris. "Women have thus been defined sexually in terms of what pleases men; our own biology has not been properly analyzed. Instead we have been fed a myth of the liberated woman and her vaginal orgasm, an orgasm which in fact does not exist."[108] She goes on to say that women must redefine their sexuality and discard the "normal" concepts of sex and establish new guidelines. "We must begin to demand that if a certain sexual position or technique now defined as 'standard' is not mutually conducive to orgasm, then it should no longer be defined as standard."[109] It is also important that, from Freud on, it has been men who have defined the standards of sexual satisfaction and adjustment for women. Actually the "vaginal orgasm" has been a part of the overall Fruedian belief in the inferiority of women. The myth of the vaginal orgasm is recognized by most sexual authorities today.

Constantina Safilios-Rothschild argues that women's sexual liberation includes the right to refuse to make love with any man and for a variety of reasons other than just fear of pregnancy or belief in a double standard. "But it seems that few men are liberated enough to grant this right to a woman they desire. True sexual liberation means the woman can determine with whom, when, how often, and in which way to have

---

[106] Ibid., p. 67–68.

[107] Ibid., p. 69.

[108] Brownmiller, "Sisterhood," p. 130.

[109] Ibid., p. 130.

sexual relations in order to derive maximum gratification and, therefore, be able truly to satisfy her partner."[110]

The women's liberation movement, like the movements of the militant black, the militant college student, and the hippie, has been greatly influenced by television. If a group of women interested in the liberation movement meet and carry on their session without theatrics they are not covered by the mass media. As a result many people believe that the women's liberation movement is made up of nothing more than far-out, deviant types of women. Thus, a reaction may develop against a kind of caricature of the movement. A common reaction is not to take the movement seriously and to respond with ridicule—which has been the reaction to feminists for decades. However, some men have begun to react to the liberation movement with anger, and many members of the movement are expecting an increased backlash from both men and women.

Women have often reacted to the liberation movement with confusion and hostility. What they hear goes contrary to their socialization experiences as females. Women are often their own worst enemies and are willing to attack one another in ways that men will not. Women everywhere refer to female "cattiness" and disloyalty. "They claim to dislike other women, assert they prefer to work for men, and profess to find female gatherings repugnant. This set of attitudes constitutes a barrier to women's aiming high in the occupational world."[111] There are also many women who have established careers in male-dominated fields who are resentful of the liberation movement because their individual success gives them a sense of superiority over other women. Some of these women say that they encounter no discrimination. It may be that the men who work with them show respect to indicate that they are not prejudiced. Many organizations employ not only token blacks but also token women.

Probably the most hostile reaction to the women's liberation movement has come from the many women who have spent a good part of their adult years doing the things that the liberation women say are demeaning and valueless. To a great extent the hostility is a generational one. The middle-aged woman who has spent her adult years as a wife, mother, and housekeeper feels very threatened by the young woman who tells her that her life has been empty and that she has been a victim of male viciousness. For her to admit that the liberation women may be right is to admit that her life has been a charade. So one can predict increasing resistance and hostility from the majority of American women who are wives, mothers, and housewives.

---

[110] Safilios-Rothschild, *Sociology of Women*, p. 102.
[111] Epstein, *Woman's Place*, p. 125.

There is a great deal of disagreement on goals among the various factions of the women's liberation movement, but most of the factions want gender difference to become secondary to human equality; that is, they want all persons to be treated as human beings first and as male or female second. What is often overlooked is that full equality may mean equality in areas that are not always desirable. As women have achieved greater equality with men in the United States, their rates of alcoholism, drug addiction, and so on have increased. But many women are quite willing to accept these negative possibilities along with the more desirable ones.

It may also be that many women have an idealized image of the freedom of some men, because the only really independent people are those with no interpersonal relationships at all. Yet this is not something that very many persons want. And many of the women in the liberation movement who reject husbands and family turn to each other to meet their interpersonal needs. One writer suggests that few of the women she met in the liberation movement accepted the notion that life itself was unfair. "Most of them cherish an apocalyptic conviction that a society that assumed the drudgery of child-rearing would free women."[112] The question is, To free women for what? To fill the jobs that men now fill and often hate? Very few men could be described as creating their own histories by transcending themselves.[113] Many women believe that the fight for total sexual equality is the issue and that if equality is achieved and women find themselves along with men in undesirable life patterns, then the fight can be made for overall human betterment. It seems clear in any case that the women's liberation movement is going to have far-reaching effects on marriage and family roles in the United States.

BIBLIOGRAPHY

Acker, Joan, "Women and Sexual Stratification: A Case of Intellectual Sexism," in Joan Huber, *Changing Women in a Changing Society*, (Chicago: University of Chicago Press, 1973), pp. 174–83.

Bernard, Jessie, *Academic Women.* University Park: Pennsylvania State University Press, 1964.

Brownmiller, Susan, "Sisterhood Is Powerful," *New York Times*, March 15, 1970, pp. 27–28, 30, 132, 134, 136, 140.

Degler, Carl N., "Revolution without Ideology: The Changing Place of Women In America," *Daedalus*, Fall 1964, pp. 653–70.

Ellis, Julie, *Revolt of The Second Sex.* New York: Lancer Books, 1970.

Epstein, Cynthia F., *Women's Place.* Berkeley: University of California Press, 1970.

---

[112] *Newsweek*, March 15, 1970.
[113] Limpus, *Sexual Repression*, pp. 62–63.

Friedan, Betty, *The Feminine Mystique*. New York: Norton, 1963.

Glazer-Malbin, Nona, and Helen Youngelson Waehrer, *Woman in a Man-Made World*. Chicago: Rand McNally, 1972.

Gornick, Vivian, and Barbara K. Moran, *Women in Sexist Society*. New York: New American Library, 1971.

Huber, Joan, *Changing Women in a Changing Society*. Chicago: University of Chicago Press, 1973.

Reeves, Nancy, *Womankind: Beyond the Stereotype*. Chicago: Aldine, 1971.

Safilios-Rothschild, Constantina, *Toward a Sociology of Women*. Lexington, Mass.: Xerox College Publishing, 1972.

Sinclair, Andrew, *The Emancipation of the American Woman*, New York: Harper, 1965.

Women's Bureau, *1969 Handbook of Women Workers*, Bulletin 294, United States Department of Labor, Washington, D.C., 1969.

Author index

423

Subject index

429

*This book has been set in 10 and 9 point Cale-
donia, leaded 2 points. Chapter numbers and
titles are 18 point Caslon. The size of the type
page is 27 x 45½ picas.*